SAP PRESS e-books

Print or e-book, Kindle or iPad, workplace or airplane: Choose where and how to read your SAP PRESS books! You can now get all our titles as e-books, too:

- By download and online access
- For all popular devices
- And, of course, DRM-free

Convinced? Then go to www.sap-press.com and get your e-book today.

Central Finance and SAP S/4HANA®

SAP PRESS is a joint initiative of SAP and Rheinwerk Publishing. The know-how offered by SAP specialists combined with the expertise of Rheinwerk Publishing offers the reader expert books in the field. SAP PRESS features first-hand information and expert advice, and provides useful skills for professional decision-making.

SAP PRESS offers a variety of books on technical and business-related topics for the SAP user. For further information, please visit our website: *www.sap-press.com*.

Stefanos Pougkas
SAP S/4HANA Financial Accounting Certification Guide: Application Associate Exam
2017, 447 pages, paperback and e-book
www.sap-press.com/4414

Anup Maheshwari
Implementing SAP S/4HANA Finance (2nd Edition)
2018, 570 pages, hardcover and e-book
www.sap-press.com/4525

Kathrin Schmalzing
CO-PA in SAP S/4HANA Finance: Business Processes, Functionality, and Configuration
2018, 337 pages, hardcover and e-book
www.sap-press.com/4383

Dirk Neumann, Lawrence Liang
Cash Management with SAP S/4HANA: Functionality and Implementation
2018, 477 pages, hardcover and e-book
www.sap-press.com/4479

Carsten Hilker, Javaid Awan, Julien Delvat

Central Finance and SAP S/4HANA®

Editor Meagan White

Acquisitions Editor Emily Nicholls

Copyeditor Yvette Chin

Cover Design Graham Geary

Photo Credit iStockphoto.com/143921504/© jimkruger

Layout Design Vera Brauner

Production Hannah Lane

Typesetting III-satz, Husby (Germany)

Printed and bound in the United States of America, on paper from sustainable sources

ISBN 978-1-4932-1719-9

© 2018 by Rheinwerk Publishing, Inc., Boston (MA)

1ˢᵗ edition 2018

Library of Congress Cataloging-in-Publication Control Number: 2018027101

Contents at a Glance

PART I   Getting Started with Central Finance

1   The Basics: What Is Central Finance? 31

2   The Mechanics: How Does Central Finance Work? 57

3   The Motivation: Why Central Finance and Why Now? 73

4   Reporting: What Can I Learn About My Data? 93

5   Finance Processes: What Can Central Finance Improve? 115

6   Deployment Options: How Do I Implement Central Finance? 149

PART II   Deploying Central Finance

7   System Architecture 177

8   Implementing Central Finance 203

9   Central Finance Operations 299

10   Master Data Management 315

PART III   Next Steps with Central Finance

11   Mergers and Integrations 343

12   Central Finance as a Stepping Stone to SAP S/4HANA 361

13   Finance Transformation 379

14   Platform Transformation 411

15   Central Finance Business Case Development 429

Dear Reader,

Moving is stressful.

First there's the sorting and disposing of belongings that you aren't taking with you, the careful packing and labeling, and then the hauling of your belongings from one site to another in one grueling day. It can be interruptive, frantic, and risky; somehow it feels like something always gets broken.

A recent overlap in leases revolutionized my moving experience by enabling a staged process: Transport the living room furniture, then my books (at least two trips for those!), and then the kitchen and bathroom. I could begin to enjoy my new place while fitting the project into a work week.

For SAP S/4HANA customers, Central Finance has similarly transformed the implementation experience. You can move your financial processes first (or even just your financial reporting), immediately embrace the perks of your new SAP S/4HANA system, and transition your logistics or CRM processes when you're able. Like my lease overlap, Central Finance allows you to choose your pace and set your priorities—and between these pages, our expert authors and contributors will how you how.

What did you think about *Central Finance and SAP S/4HANA*? Your comments and suggestions are the most useful tools to help us make our books the best they can be. Please feel free to contact me and share any praise or criticism you may have.

Thank you for purchasing a book from SAP PRESS!

Meagan White
Editor, SAP PRESS

meaganw@rheinwerk-publishing.com
www.sap-press.com
Rheinwerk Publishing · Boston, MA

Contents

Foreword on Enterprise Management 19

Foreword on Technology Simplification 21

Foreword on Finance Transformation 23

Acknowledgments 25

Preface 27

PART I   Getting Started with Central Finance

1   The Basics: What Is Central Finance?   31

1.1	**A Centralized Finance System**	31
	1.1.1	Evolution of Central Finance	32
	1.1.2	Central Process Execution Model	34
	1.1.3	Standard SAP Solution	36
	1.1.4	Technical Foundation	38
	1.1.5	SAP S/4HANA Deployment Option	39
	1.1.6	System Consolidation Path	40
1.2	**Central Finance Building Blocks**	41
	1.2.1	Source System	42
	1.2.2	Data Replication	45
	1.2.3	Central System	48
	1.2.4	Cloud Integration	50
	1.2.5	Backposting	50
1.3	**Central Finance Results**	52
1.4	**Boundaries and Restrictions**	53
1.5	**Summary**	56

2   The Mechanics: How Does Central Finance Work?   57

2.1	**Functional Foundation**	57
	2.1.1 Finance Value Map	57
	2.1.2 Key Process Candidates	58
2.2	**Central Finance Capabilities**	59
	2.2.1 Data Logging	60
	2.2.2 Data Replication	62
	2.2.3 Business Mapping	64
	2.2.4 Data Digitization and Inbound Posting	66
	2.2.5 Error Handling	67
	2.2.6 Drilldown/Audit Trail	69
	2.2.7 Data Reconciliation	69
2.3	**Summary**	71

3   The Motivation: Why Central Finance and Why Now?   73

3.1	**Central Finance as a Silver Bullet**	74
3.2	**Innovation Acceleration**	78
	3.2.1 Pressure to Innovate	79
	3.2.2 Earlier Innovation	80
	3.2.3 Faster Cycles, Faster Adoption	82
3.3	**Process Transformation**	82
3.4	**Business Model Evolution**	84
	3.4.1 Enterprise Optimization	85
	3.4.2 Business Model Changes	85
	3.4.3 Mergers and Acquisitions	86
	3.4.4 Divestitures	86
3.5	**Technology Transformation**	87
	3.5.1 Rationalization	87
	3.5.2 Consolidation	88
	3.5.3 Cloud Transition	89

3.6		**SAP S/4HANA Adoption**	90
	3.6.1	Continued Evolution	90
	3.6.2	Side Car Adoption	90
3.7		**Summary**	92

4   Reporting: What Can I Learn About My Data?   93

4.1		**Advanced Reporting**	93
	4.1.1	Line Item Access	94
	4.1.2	Universal Reporting	95
	4.1.3	Multidimensional Reporting	97
	4.1.4	Microsoft Excel Analysis	97
	4.1.5	Root Cause Analysis and Storytelling	98
	4.1.6	Embedded	99
	4.1.7	Real-Time KPIs	100
	4.1.8	Predictive Reporting	101
	4.1.9	Problem Solving Solutions	102
4.2		**Extended Dimensional Reporting**	104
	4.2.1	Microsegment Profitability	104
	4.2.2	Cross-Organizational Functional Reporting	106
	4.2.3	Business Continuity Reporting	107
4.3		**Entity Reporting**	108
	4.3.1	Local Processes	109
	4.3.2	System of Record	109
	4.3.3	Company Code Alignments	110
	4.3.4	Tax Optimization	111
4.4		**Group Reporting**	111
	4.4.1	Multi-Entity Reporting	112
	4.4.2	Harmonized/Standardized	112
	4.4.3	Benchmarking	113
	4.4.4	Consolidated Reporting	113
4.5		**Summary**	114

5 Finance Processes: What Can Central Finance Improve? 115

5.1	**Processes and Process Orchestration**	115
5.2	**Payables and Receivables**	119
	5.2.1 Accounts Payable	119
	5.2.2 Payables with Direct and Indirect Procurement	121
	5.2.3 Three-Way Matching	122
	5.2.4 Accounts Receivable	123
	5.2.5 Receivables with Central Credit Management	125
5.3	**Accounting and Financial Close**	127
	5.3.1 General Ledger	128
	5.3.2 Entity Close	129
	5.3.3 Corporate Close	130
	5.3.4 Financial Reporting and Disclosure	130
	5.3.5 Financial Close Governance	130
5.4	**Banking and Treasury**	131
	5.4.1 Adoption of Treasury Best Practices in Central Finance	131
	5.4.2 Bank Account Management	132
	5.4.3 Cash Operations and Liquidity Management	136
	5.4.4 Payment Factories	138
	5.4.5 Collection Factories	138
5.5	**Controlling Processes**	139
	5.5.1 Operational Expenses (OpEx)	140
	5.5.2 Capital Expenditure (CapEx)	141
	5.5.3 Profitability Analysis	142
5.6	**Beyond Core Finance**	143
	5.6.1 SAP Cash Application	144
	5.6.2 SAP S/4HANA Cloud for Customer Payments	145
	5.6.3 SAP S/4HANA Cloud for Credit Integration	146
5.7	**Summary**	147

6   Deployment Options: How Do I Implement Central Finance?   149

6.1	Getting Started	150
6.2	On-Premise	152
	6.2.1 Required Deployments	153
	6.2.2 Optional Deployments	154
	6.2.3 SAP Business Warehouse	158
	6.2.4 SAP Business Planning and Consolidation	160
6.3	Cloud	161
	6.3.1 Private Cloud	163
	6.3.2 Public Cloud	164
	6.3.3 Managed Cloud	167
	6.3.4 Project Cloud	169
6.4	Hybrid	171
6.5	Two-Tier Strategy	173
6.6	Summary	174

PART II   Deploying Central Finance

7   System Architecture   177

7.1	Technical Architecture	177
	7.1.1 SAP HANA Database	179
	7.1.2 SAP S/4HANA Core Application	179
	7.1.3 Source System	180
	7.1.4 The Data Bus	180
	7.1.5 Third-Party Data Integration	181
7.2	Central Finance Landscape	182

7.3	**SAP Landscape Transformation Replication Server**		188
	7.3.1	Deployment Options for the SAP LT Replication Server	189
	7.3.2	Data Migration Server	191
7.4	**SAP Application Interface Framework**		191
	7.4.1	SAP Application Integration Framework Message Processing	193
	7.4.2	BC Sets for SAP Application Integration Framework	194
	7.4.3	Configuring the SAP Application Integration Framework	194
	7.4.4	Monitoring SAP Application Integration Framework for Central Finance	195
7.5	**SAP Master Data Governance**		195
7.6	**Frontend Tools and Central Finance**		196
	7.6.1	SAP GUI	197
	7.6.2	SAP Fiori	197
	7.6.3	SAP Analysis for Microsoft Office	199
	7.6.4	SAP Analytics Cloud	199
	7.6.5	SAP Business Client	201
7.7	**Summary**		201

8 Implementing Central Finance

203

8.1	**Rollout**		203
	8.1.1	Iterative Rollout versus Big Bang	203
	8.1.2	Milestone-Based Rollout	205
	8.1.3	Process Selection	205
8.2	**Roadmap**		206
	8.2.1	First Wave	207
	8.2.2	Subsequent Waves	207
	8.2.3	End State	208
8.3	**System Setup**		208
	8.3.1	Landscape	209
	8.3.2	Central Finance Instance	211
	8.3.3	SAP Landscape Transformation Replication Server	224

8.3.4	SAP Source Systems	227
8.3.5	Non-SAP Source Systems	228
8.3.6	SAP Master Data Governance System	229
8.4	**Data Integration Framework**	230
8.4.1	Master Data	230
8.4.2	Transactional Data	240
8.4.3	SAP Source Data	244
8.4.4	Non-SAP Source Data	247
8.4.5	Third-Party Interface	249
8.5	**Replication Setup**	251
8.5.1	SAP Source Systems	252
8.5.2	Non-SAP Source Systems	253
8.5.3	Pre-Implementation Assessment	254
8.5.4	Test Data Load	255
8.5.5	Initial Data Load	259
8.5.6	Online Replication	260
8.6	**Process Design**	261
8.6.1	Process Settings	261
8.6.2	Configuration	267
8.7	**Master Data**	270
8.7.1	Master Data Objects	270
8.7.2	Harmonization (Golden Record Creation)	272
8.7.3	Hierarchies	273
8.8	**Business Mapping**	276
8.8.1	Master Data Objects	276
8.8.2	Strategies	277
8.9	**Initial Data Load**	280
8.9.1	Prerequisites	281
8.9.2	Configuration in Source System	282
8.9.3	Initial Load of CO Postings	283
8.9.4	Initial Load for Financial Accounting	286
8.9.5	Final Steps	294
8.10	**Summary**	296

9 Central Finance Operations

299

9.1	**Centers of Excellence**	299
9.2	**Ongoing Replication**	301
	9.2.1 Transaction Replication	302
	9.2.2 Error Correction	303
	9.2.3 Data Reconciliation	304
9.3	**Master Data**	305
	9.3.1 Maintenance	306
	9.3.2 Governance	307
9.4	**System Onboarding**	307
9.5	**Process Onboarding**	310
9.6	**Mergers and Acquisitions**	311
9.7	**Divestitures**	312
9.8	**Summary**	313

10 Master Data Management

315

10.1	**Data Loads**	315
	10.1.1 Initial Data Loads	315
	10.1.2 Delta Loads	318
	10.1.3 Golden Record Creation	318
10.2	**Master Data Processes**	320
	10.2.1 Request for Change	322
	10.2.2 Approval of the Request	323
	10.2.3 Execution of the Change Request	324
10.3	**Master Data Objects**	325
	10.3.1 Chart of Accounts	326
	10.3.2 General Ledger Account	328
	10.3.3 Business Partners	329
	10.3.4 Material Numbers	331

10.3.5 Profit Centers 331

10.3.6 Cost Centers 332

10.3.7 Activity Types 333

10.3.8 Statistical Key Figures 333

10.4 Governance 334

10.4.1 Master Data and Master Data Objects 334

10.4.2 Dynamic Cost Object Creation 335

10.4.3 Extraction 337

10.4.4 Harmonization 337

10.4.5 Rationalization 338

10.4.6 Dissemination 339

10.4.7 Maintenance 339

10.5 Summary 340

PART III   Next Steps with Central Finance

11   Mergers and Integrations

343

11.1 Integration Catalyst 343

11.1.1 Merger and Integration Platform 344

11.1.2 Merger and Integration Playbook 345

11.2 Mergers and Acquisitions 345

11.2.1 Central Finance as an M&A Platform 346

11.2.2 Building Blocks 347

11.2.3 Capabilities 352

11.3 Post-Merger Integration 355

11.3.1 Process Execution Considerations 356

11.3.2 Platform Considerations 356

11.3.3 System Continuity 357

11.3.4 Interim versus End State 357

11.4 Summary 360

12 Central Finance as a Stepping Stone to SAP S/4HANA 361

12.1	Charting Your Journey	362
	12.1.1 First Step: Central Finance	363
	12.1.2 End State	366
12.2	Choosing Your Route	367
	12.2.1 Brownfield versus Greenfield	368
	12.2.2 SAP S/4HANA Cloud Code Line	368
12.3	Planning the Process	370
	12.3.1 Transition Planning	370
	12.3.2 Adoption Patterns	374
	12.3.3 Moving a Single ERP to SAP S/4HANA Using Central Finance	375
	12.3.4 Moving Multiple ERP Systems to SAP S/4HANA Using Central Finance	377
12.4	Summary	378

13 Finance Transformation 379

13.1	Strategy Management	380
13.2	Value Management	386
13.3	Risk Management	388
	13.3.1 Technical Risk Factors	389
	13.3.2 Business Change and Organizational Risk Factors	391
	13.3.3 Financial Risk Factors	394
13.4	Business Process Management	395
13.5	Organizational Change Management	398
13.6	Summary	408

14 Platform Transformation 411

14.1 Platform Transformation Strategy 412

14.2 System and Application Consolidation 415

14.2.1 Corporate SAP HANA Reporting Platform 416

14.2.2 Corporate Finance Service Platform 417

14.2.3 Stepping Stone to Consolidated SAP S/4HANA Platform 418

14.2.4 Corporate MA&D Platform 418

14.2.5 Orchestration of Source Systems of Record with Central Finance 419

14.3 Digitization 421

14.4 Readiness for Services Consumption in the Cloud 424

14.5 Summary 427

15 Central Finance Business Case Development 429

15.1 Identifying Stakeholders 429

15.1.1 Finance Organization and the Impact to Resources 430

15.1.2 IT Organization 431

15.2 Evaluating the Status Quo 432

15.2.1 Current Landscape 432

15.2.2 Anticipated Challenges 434

15.3 Determining Key Value Drivers 434

15.3.1 Flexibility 435

15.3.2 Efficiency 436

15.3.3 Service Level 436

15.3.4 Cost Reduction 436

15.3.5 Working Capital Improvement 437

15.3.6 Profit and Margin Management 437

15.3.7 Simplification 437

15.3.8 Business Continuity 438

15.3.9 Risk Mitigation 438

15.4   **Assessing the Cost** 439

    15.4.1   Initial Implementation 439

    15.4.2   Maintenance 440

    15.4.3   End State 440

15.5   **Return on Investment** 441

15.6   **Summary** 443

The Authors 445

Index 449

Foreword on Enterprise Management

Until recently, most companies were only able to provide high-quality financial information based on a resource-intensive reporting process. Did they have fully integrated systems which were able to provide harmonized and quality-assured KPIs and charts just with one click for the top management? Not a chance!

The daily business in companies is shockingly inadequate and sobering. Tons of workers are continually working to collect, validate, and transform data, in order to prepare reports; that is, if the reports are any good at all. Ad-hoc requests by the board end up requiring considerable amounts of additional time and capacity. Such work is less reminiscent of the digital age than of the Stone Age.

SAP, even shortly after it was founded in 1972, basically pursued the idea of fully integrating the quantities and value flows of a company in order to provide information in real time. Since then, the software has become more and more effective; the current software, SAP S/4HANA, is in a totally different league compared to the first versions of SAP R/1 and SAP R/2.

It is surprising that marketing messages have barely changed over time. The description has ever been: "Using high-quality and fully harmonized data to provide the information needed for upper management decision-making in real time with one click."

Although every software release and every new update technically provides better support, this seems not to make a practical difference in companies. The last excuse for many CFOs to not integrate the ERP systems to a single finance system is that the processes and systems of a large corporation are too complex and constantly subject of change due to their highly dynamic nature.

SAP, however, has responded to this issue and found a solution. Central Finance, which has now been on the market for a few years, offers a great opportunity, especially for large companies, to create a unified operating database which can be based even on heterogeneous process and system landscapes.

With Central Finance, data is harmonized and made available in real time. The high granularity of data (posting level!) combined with the high performance of the SAP HANA allows for information to be retrieved and made available to management in any view and at any aggregation level on demand.

However, that's still not enough. With complete integration starting with shop floor data derived, for example, via SAP Leonardo, up to the interactive presentation of information with SAP Digital Boardroom, upper management has the chance to access company insights digitally in real time. This not only allows for the past to be intensively analyzed and understood, it also integrates simulations, trends, and forecasts of the future, and is therefore the basis for automated decision support.

Welcome to the digital age! Now everything is technically possible, up to the complete automation of nearly all financial activities. Reporting no longer requires scores of employees. The quality of the basic data now can be so high that expensive quality assurance measures may be something of the past. Information is now available ad-hoc for every type of situation and can be used at the press of a button.

However, software is just one side of the coin. Such a system must of course be set up well, otherwise it will not live up to its full potential. During our years of consulting experience, we saw two key mistakes. The first is going ahead with the system installation before developing a sound business blueprint. This results in an ERP system that, despite being technically very capable, unfortunately does not fit the requirements of day-by-day management and is therefore hardly useful. The second is the development of a very sophisticated business blueprint without paying sufficient attention to the functionalities of the software. This results in systems that are highly modified and therefore very inflexible and expensive to maintain.

The intention of this book is to bridge that gap. Practical information from highly experienced authors should help to create a clear understanding and establish discussions and sound decision-making to set up a perfect and well-designed Central Finance system.

The age of digitalization has begun. You, dear reader, now have the opportunity to shape it. Let's get started!

René Linsner
Partner, Horváth & Partners

Foreword on Technology Simplification

We live in an ever expanding digital universe, with corporate IT being at the center of many changing trends. Organizations are keen to embrace new and valuable technology as rapidly as they can; however, the technical reality on the ground is often not as clear-cut, simple, and glossy as many high-level strategies on corporate digital transformation might suggest. In fact, many global corporations operate complex processes and systems landscape, and numerous CIOs are constrained by a level of intricacy which is holding back crucial innovation and increasing the risk of transformation initiatives.

The reasons for this trend are manifold. The fact that many transformations, mergers, and acquisitions are conducted on an incremental IT strategy surely contributes to a complex end-state landscape, but adding new capabilities to the IT portfolio (e.g. cloud apps, analytics) without a consistent integration platform can also be named as a root cause.

The conclusion we are drawing from these finding is that "more of the same" will definitely not solve the issue at hand. There will never be "the one" big bang implementation that addresses all the various needs and requirements without putting crucial core processes at risk along the way. Instead, we need to rethink how process and applications can effectively work together while IT and business are tackling the long-term simplification of the landscape. This transformation process can take years, and business needs a clear path to safely run the backend processes while also reaping benefits from new technology such as in-memory computing, machine learning, and enhanced user experience. New business models and disruptive technologies will emerge every day; our challenge is to redefine enabling processes and systems to achieve efficiency, agility, and value at the same speed as the changes and disruption we are experiencing.

In 2015, Central Finance was introduced as a key architecture element to help solve systems and application complexity. Central Finance allows customers to consolidate detailed financial reporting data in an SAP S/4HANA environment while maintaining the integrity of the legacy environment, thereby allowing the ability to adopt new technology, capabilities, and business models without business disruption and implementation risk of past ERP transformation projects.

One main insight from applying Central Finance at our customers is the tremendous risk reduction we gained from the fact that the legacy ERP processes are not disrupted, while a fully transactional SAP S/4HANA data set is being built in Central Finance. A Central Finance implementation is low risk, as the implementation approach allows for a period of dual reporting to enable full reconciliation and operational adoption. Previously, ERP implementations created timing and reconciliation challenges with transformation of data and organization structure changes. Central Finance breaks this cycle, and allows ability to iterate and re-model the finance implementation during the project without any impact on the current ERP data along the way.

Central Finance consolidates full data records from various ERP systems without a classic data warehouse staging process, which oftentimes produced overly aggregated and untimely results. Finance teams can leverage real-time and rapid insights into totals and drill-down on all source document data in a centralized and unified reporting structure, an extremely valuable feature in an ERP landscape marred by slow performance, complex mapping steps and other data handling complexities. This also supports accelerated M&A scenarios where fast data integration is key to success.

Finally, Central Finance allows business end users to practice and adopt new reporting instruments such as run-time data, predictive analytics, and machine learning enriched reporting. These technologies take time to take root in the internal Finance community, and Central Finance gives business enough time to explore the new process paradigm of 'insight into action' before the larger ERP transformation into S/4HANA and SAP's Cloud Platform, which usually runs in parallel while Central Finance is already live. This reporting strategy can be a stepping stone to a long-term SAP platform strategy: our Infosys author Bahram Maghsoudi details this context in Chapter 14.

Infosys has collaborated with SAP from the beginning in 2015, and implemented various scenarios and add-ons together with SAP and our customers. We are happy to share our best practices and project insights in this book and hope that it helps clarify the possibilities and capabilities that customers gain from including Central Finance in their SAP S/4HANA journey.

John Brizzi
Vice President and Partner, Infosys

Foreword on Finance Transformation

Central Finance is a very attractive path to innovate and establish a modern finance application landscape. The choice to implement Central Finance is driving a significant finance transformation for many organizations and will impact their short and long-term strategy. Experience has shown that Central Finance helps organizations realize business objectives like innovation, greater efficiency, better insights, and faster processes, all while reemphasizing the classical transformational change methodologies: strategy management, value management, risk management, business process management, and organizational change management.

At first, a consideration of the company's strategic imperatives should precede any decision to establish Central Finance as a component of the future application and system landscape. The main group-wide strategic objectives should be established, along with the expectations for the future finance organization and the role of the CFO. Often, this is done implicitly during the identification of Central Finance use cases, but it is recommended to identify, discuss, and define the finance transformation strategic direction upfront, in order to assess the strategic fit of Central Finance.

The decision to implement Central Finance has numerous implications for the application landscape and for finance, including other areas in the organization like master data and the general IT landscape strategy. It can also lead to a stronger centralization of processes, governance, and data usage. Unaligned strategic direction will harm the success of any finance transformation—especially with Central Finance as long-term platform for financial processes.

The second key activity is the definition of the Central Finance value proposition. The opportunities provided by Central Finance are numerous and should be thoroughly investigated and assessed. Every company needs to identify their individual use cases for Central Finance and ensure the strategic fit with the organization's objectives. Documentation is critical at the point of assessment, as only then is a measurement of benefit realization possible. Additionally, use case descriptions are an essential input for the design and build phase.

Any transformation has an intrinsic risk profile, and it is essential to establish risk management strategies, which ensure assessment, mitigation, and continuous monitoring of project risks. It is important to consider that the nature and architecture of Central Finance brings a specific risk profile, which is different from a typical global SAP template implementation project.

Process reengineering is not necessarily the key to Central Finance. A reporting scenario can be introduced with little or no impact on the entry point and processing of data. However, as soon as Central Finance becomes the platform for centralized financial processes, the existing business processes need a careful redesign and validation, as the replication interface creates new system boarders with related restrictions. As soon as processes like central payment, central planning, central month end closing, etc. are part of the Central Finance use case, a careful assessment of process management must be included.

The involvement of all key stakeholder and assessment of their interests and concerns are part of an organizational change management. As Central Finance is usually a collector of all financial data across the company, there are many relevant stakeholders. Different measures of organizational change management tailored for Central Finance should be the fundamentals of each finance transformation and Central Finance project.

Tobias Nyholm
Principal Business Consultant, SAP Deutschland

Acknowledgments

This book, much like Central Finance itself, is not a book written and done. It will live on and will need to reflect the learnings and journeys of those customers engaging in such an undertaking.

Only four years into the Central Finance journey, it seemed like the right time to put down what we've learned and what we know. In doing so, we wanted to provide the opportunity to hear different perspectives and read about similar (and sometimes identical) aspects of Central Finance expressed in a different ways to provide the best understanding possible.

Thanks to Berker Kilinc (EY) on his thoughts on how Central Finance works; Julien Delvat (TruQua) for his chapter contributions on implementing Central Finance, Central Finance operations, and master data management; Rakesh Mehta (PWC) for the mergers and integrations chapter; Tobias Nyholm (SAP BTS) for his thoughts on finance transformation; Bahram Maghsoudi (Infosys) for the chapter on platform transformation; and Randy Garrison (SAP) for the chapter on the Central Finance business case. To all, we owe a great amount of gratitude for the time they took to share with you what they learned. These contributors were some of the most involved, and we truly appreciated their contributions.

For the forewords, thanks to Rene Linsner (Horvath & Partners) for the many discussions here in the US, as well as back in Germany, on the cultural and situational differences and priorities Central Finance customers are facing; John Brizzi (Infosys) for being one of our first implementation partners and continuously helping our customer go live successfully; and Tobias Nyholm for the many, many conversations from day 1 in many places in the world, yet never home.

The content of this book also would not have been possible without the many shared conversations, discussion, presentations, and workshops with our colleagues from SAP Central Finance Development—most of all Bastian Distler and Stefan Fischer as well as SAP AGS Lars Buescher and Andreas Planck—without them we would not have had an SAP product to write about to begin with—*thank you*. And of course our super important system integrator network—especially with those involved in our annual Central Finance Thought Leadership summits including, but not limited to, Eric Bramley, Rakesh Metha, Paul Gierstorf, Art Kalemba, Phuong Nguyen, Mitch Paull, Rene Linsner, Scott Cairncross, and Howard La Kier.

Last but not least some key individuals like Ian Ward (BP), Laurence Uzureau and Kim Burke (Cargill), Thierry Langer and Bertrand Janvier (Engie), Jean-Christophe Ringot and Philippe Desfontaine (Electricite De France), Dave Drever (Exxon), Paul Gallini (Flowserve), Harlan Monk (General Mills), Jared Alamat (General Motors), John Zimmermann (Hershey's), Katrina Druery (Lockheed Martin), Joachim Hannapel (Lufthansa), Joachim Mette (SAP), Lori Groth, Jenn Snyder, and Leighton Haywood (Stanley Black & Decker), Anish Kantawala (Sony Pictures Entertainment), Doug Beebe, Jason Ballard, and John Kennelly (Toyota)—you inspired us, you challenged us, and made us and the Central Finance product better and more valuable for all our customers—thank you very much as well.

Preface

Welcome to the first book on Central Finance. Due to the popularity of Central Finance in the market, SAP customers, partners, and consultants have been demanding more resources to understand fully the depth and breadth of Central Finance. Whether you're looking into Central Finance as an end in-and-of itself, or using it as a stepping stone to SAP S/4HANA, this book will answer your questions.

We've organized this book into three main parts:

- **Part I: Getting Started with Central Finance**
  The first part of the book is designed to help someone evaluate the Central Finance deployment option for SAP S/4HANA and to make a decision about implementing it. This part contains the following chapters:
  - Chapter 1: This chapter explains the basic idea behind Central Finance: a centralized finance system that create a single source of truth among disparate financials applications, and a means to tap into the benefits of SAP S/4HANA without a full-blown data migration.
  - Chapter 2: This chapter explains how a Central Finance system works and the underlying capabilities that make it work.
  - Chapter 3: This chapter explains what makes Central Finance the silver bullet for a variety of IT/business concerns, and why organizations are choosing to implement it now.
  - Chapter 4: This chapter explains how a Central Finance implementation provides improved reporting and analytics information.
  - Chapter 5: This chapter explains how Central Finance impacts organizations' financials processes.
  - Chapter 6: This chapter explains the on-premise, cloud, and hybrid deployment options for Central Finance.
- **Part II: Deploying Central Finance**
  Part II gives step-by-step instructions for implementing and operating Central Finance as well as information regarding the system architecture and landscape in which Central Finance lives. This part contains the following chapters:
  - Chapter 7: This chapter explains the Central Finance reference architecture, including the required SAP components and third-party technologies.

- Chapter 8: This chapter gives step-by-step instructions for a Central Finance implementation project. The focus here is on the technical steps for system setup, data integration, replication, and master data.

- Chapter 9: This chapter teaches you how to operate an active Central Finance implementation once it has gone live.

- Chapter 10: This chapter explains how Central Finance customers can change their master data management practices in their new landscape. It also looks at some changes to master data in Central Finance.

- **Part III: Next Steps with Central Finance**
  Part III explains how Central Finance customers can use the system as a stepping stone for broader organizational projects (e.g., full migration to SAP S/4HANA or finance transformation). This part contains the following chapters:

  - Chapter 11: The focus of this chapter is on mergers and integrations: after a merger, how to handle legacy software in an IT landscape of a Central Finance implementation, and before a merger, how to leverage Central Finance as a mechanism for integrating third-party systems.

  - Chapter 12: SAP customers looking to adopt SAP S/4HANA can take a number of paths to get there. Many customers use Central Finance as a first step, and implement full finance and logistics functionality at a later date. This chapter elaborates on options, circumstances, and recommendations for this move.

  - Chapter 13: This chapter outlines how the Central Finance model introduces new financials possibilities and as means to trigger broader changes in your financials processes and in your organization.

  - Chapter 14: This chapter outlines how Central Finance can be the first step toward platform transformation.

  - Chapter 15: This chapter creates a template that organizations can use to organize their Central Finance business case.

Let's now jump into our first part and get started with Central Finance.

PART I

Getting Started with Central Finance

Chapter 1

The Basics: What Is Central Finance?

Central Systems for finance have been around for ages and in different styles. SAP's Central Finance represents yet another step in the evolution of central systems for finance, based on next-generation technologies and innovations in process execution that are substantially different from the traditional, central ERP systems for finance of the past.

In this chapter, we'll explain the basic idea behind Central Finance: a central finance system that creates a single financial source of truth for executing reporting and finance processes among disparate financial applications and a way to reap the benefits of SAP S/4HANA without a full-blown data migration. In this chapter, we'll describe the building blocks of Central Finance and also elaborate on its natural limits.

1.1   A Centralized Finance System

The idea of a central ERP system to use for financial processes has been around for as long as multi-ERP system landscapes have existed. Mostly as a consequence of mergers and acquisitions (M&A) and post-merger integration (PMI) or business consolidation (organic growth initiatives and business model optimizations), many companies find themselves needing to bring together different and diverse ERP systems for centralized financial reporting and process execution.

In the following sections, we'll begin by describing the evolution of Central Finance, starting with how traditional approaches to finance created the need for a new system. We'll then move on to discuss more specific information about Central Finance itself, as follows:

- Central process execution model
- Standard SAP solution
- Technical foundation of Central Finance

- Deployment option for SAP S/4HANA
- System consolidation path

These topics are all equally important factors that you'll need to consider when deciding whether to replace/upgrade an existing traditional system or to introduce a new central system for finance.

1.1.1   Evolution of Central Finance

In traditional approaches deployed over the last 10 to 15 years, a central ERP system was deployed and custom integrated with source systems; integration used ETL (extract, transform, and load) tools and was batch-oriented; the coding block was limited. Reporting may have been performed in separate data warehouses, and planning and consolidation performed in separate, parallel applications outside the central ERP.

Traditional central ERP systems for finance are limited by the technologies available at the time they were developed. Everything was about duplicating and moving data to where the data needed to be; thus, all the interfaces had to be updated every time an organizational or business model changed. Perhaps, additional interfaces to yet another system have been introduced, causing master data to get out of hand. Finally, due to timing and latency issues and on-the-fly personal macros in Excel spreadsheet-based reporting, finance information was rarely consistent, true, or trusted.

Today's centralized finance system should be different with technological innovations like in-memory databases, predictive analytics, machine learning, cloud-based applications and services, and virtualized reporting and analysis.

With today's technologies, a central finance system can—in one system, regardless of number of records or size of the coding block—be the digital twin of all the financial records in your entire organization, enterprise-wide, across systems, and agnostic with regard to business models—in other words, harmonized.

With finance processes built into the central system, moving data to separate applications for finance processes like reporting, planning, and consolidation is no longer required.

Everyone, for reporting and for process execution, can work on the same dataset, the single source of truth, with one process execution layer and one SAP S/4HANA user interface, with the first layer facing the organization internally and the second layer facing the customer. Additionally, if desired, central process execution can be performed via scalable shared services.

A central finance system today is no longer a barrier holding back finance departments but rather an enabler of business growth (M&A, business optimization, business model changes) and business optimization.

SAP's Central Finance is different from traditional central systems for finance in that Central Finance is based on a next-generation, intelligent ERP system called SAP S/4HANA, shown in Figure 1.1. SAP S/4HANA leverages many in-memory, business network, predictive, cloud, machine learning, and UX technology innovations that have become mainstream since traditional ERP systems were developed. Next-generation ERP systems like SAP S/4HANA only come around every 15 to 20 years, and now is the time.

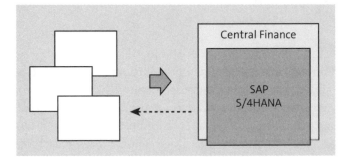

Figure 1.1 SAP S/4HANA at the Core of Central Finance

What also makes SAP S/4HANA different is that the business environment and the state of information technology are different, with various disruptive technologies, like Central Finance, now mainstream.

Today's digital economy requires functional and technical integration beyond the company's own boundaries, with other organizations as part of business networks. Finance capabilities traditionally not core to an ERP system will need to be integrated, as will capabilities outside the core ERP system (procurement, travel management, contingency workforce planning), often delivered by vehicles not native to a traditional ERP stack or technology, like a cloud deployment.

Today's business environment requires companies adapt and adopt with speed. The complexity created by past approaches, involving nonintegrated systems, redundant applications, and decentralized data storage, alongside older technical approaches to integration that involved batch dates, manual work, and ongoing support, have been a barrier for many—sometimes, you can't digitize complexity.

Previously, traditional central systems focused on the integration of ERP systems together, with separate external finance applications for financial planning and consolidation and for reporting.

Companies must find a way to operate across the enterprise and across systems by leveraging the technologies of today, adopting them quickly and without disruption, in a way that reduces complexity.

Central Finance not only addresses the traditional, central process execution aspect of a central ERP system for finance but also helps SAP and non-SAP ERP customers adapt quickly to SAP S/4HANA's new and innovative capabilities. Central Finance provides an expedited path to adopting SAP S/4HANA via a standard SAP solution bundle, all while helping to simplify and consolidate your IT landscape.

1.1.2   Central Process Execution Model

Central Finance enables a central business execution operations model. In this mode, financial data from decentralized systems is brought together in a central system for financial reporting and process execution executed in the central system rather than locally, in the source system(s). Specifically, Central Finance provides advanced segment, entity, and group reporting as well as scalable local and central process execution.

At the core of a Central Finance system is SAP S/4HANA. SAP S/4HANA provides the execution layer (business processes) in Central Finance.

Three different scenarios for local and central process execution in the context of Central Finance are available: executing local processes in a central system, executing central processes in a central system, and executing processes in a shared services model.

Executing Local Processes in a Central System

Central Finance allows organizations to execute local finance processes like reporting and executing financial transactions in the central system.

For local processes, like running a balance sheet report for a single company code, as shown in Figure 1.2, Central Finance allows you to take advantage of newer technologies available in the SAP S/4HANA-based central system to increase productivity.

Local processes, like cash application in accounts receivable or Excel reporting, can leverage SAP S/4HANA-based innovations like robotic process automation (RPA), machine learning, and direct access to financial data without needing data download and extraction steps or, at least, substantially reduced human involvement.

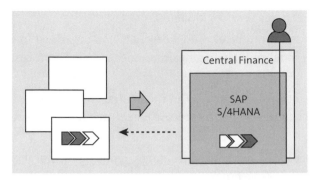

Figure 1.2 Execution of Local Processes in the Central System

Executing Central Processes in a Central System

Central Finance allows for the execution of corporate/central processes like reporting and financial transaction execution in the central system, as shown in Figure 1.3. Processes that are effectively the same but run in parallel (with different parameters in different source systems) can be executed once in the central system. An example of this is a payment run for all entities within the organization.

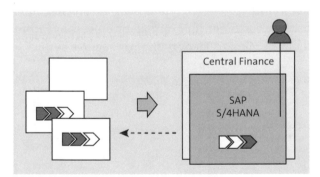

Figure 1.3 Execution of Central Processes in the Central System

Processes split across different systems, like intercompany reconciliation between seller and buyer company codes in different systems, can be executed together in the same system, rather than separately in different systems.

Processes executed in applications separate from the core ERP (like management accounting allocations in separate SAP Business Warehouse [SAP BW] systems or corporate enterprise-wide reporting) can be executed in the ERP system itself, rather than in a separate system or business application.

Executing Central Processes in a Shares Services Model

In Central Finance, finance processes can be executed centrally and organized in a shared services-based business model, thus leveraging economies of scale for process execution.

Process execution can be moved to a single process (in the Central Finance system) independent of which part of the organization the process is executed for (standardization).

Processes can be executed by dedicated, centralized resources, reducing the number of people required for the execution of the process. This centralization can happen in a loose fashion, with or without supporting local sources in the underlying entities, or in a shared service model where dedicated resources within the organization provide process execution services for the underlying entities (with corresponding service level agreements), and process execution is entirely removed from local systems.

Processes can be executed centrally in one system only. Whether following a shared service model, as shown in Figure 1.4, or not, the processes are not only executable in one way, by a dedicated pool of people across the organization, but also only in one system (and not across different source systems). Using only one system is key to optimizing the overall cost of financial operations, to establishing and further building best practices, and to best serve the customer, for example, by processing incoming invoices or complaints without needing to identify the right source system in which to process them first.

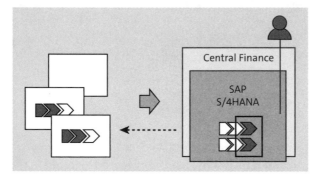

Figure 1.4 Process Execution in a Shared Services Scenario

1.1.3   Standard SAP Solution

Central Finance is a standard SAP solution delivered for easier, faster, better, and cheaper adoption and subsequent operation of a central system for finance, reducing the effort and risk of a customized project implementation. Traditional one-off implementation project integration and operational aspects are replaced by standard SAP product capabilities, content, and usage rights.

The Central Finance solution is comprised of two layers, the enabling layer and the execution layer, as shown in Figure 1.5.

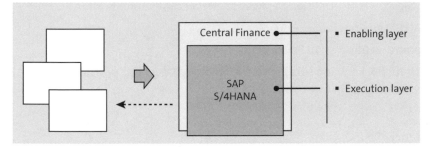

Figure 1.5 Central Finance: Integrated Standard SAP Solution

The execution layer is represented by the process capabilities of SAP S/4HANA and related finance products.

The enabling layer consists of Central Finance-specific SAP products, content, and best practices to make finance processes in a central SAP S/4HANA system work. This layer allows for the execution of finance processes in the central system and supports the integration of (but also the operations of running) a Central Finance system.

The enabling layer provides a set of capabilities required to make a Central Finance system work in a standard deployment, rather than a custom one-off implementation. The standard deployment includes the following activities:

- Initial data load
- Data logging
- Real-time replication
- Business mapping
- Data digitization
- Inbound posting
- Error correction
- Data reconciliation
- Backposting

The enabling layer is based on purpose-built standard SAP products for Central Finance, predefined content for those products, and use rights (access to additional SAP products for use with Central Finance).

Key SAP products in the enabling layer are:

- SAP S/4HANA for central finance foundation
- SAP Landscape Transformation Replication Server (SAP LT Replication Server)
- SAP Master Data Governance (SAP MDG)
- SAP Application Integration Framework
- Application Link Enabling (ALE), intermediate documents (IDocs), and other SAP or non-SAP integration mechanisms

1.1.4   Technical Foundation

Central Finance is based on a number of technical core components, each contributing to and providing key capabilities that drive the overall set of functions and features in Central Finance:

- **SAP HANA**
  The in-memory database that stores and provides instant access to datasets of any size on any system with unabbreviated dimensionality across the entire enterprise

- **SAP S/4HANA**
  The application layer providing the functions and features available in a Central Finance system

- **SAP Landscape Transformation Replication Server (SAP LT Replication Server)**
  The replication mechanism, the way to get financial transactions created in source systems into Central Finance

- **SAP Application Integration Framework**
  The error correction and accounting suspension mechanism to postprocess postings that cannot be posted initially

- **SAP MDG**
  A user interface to maintain business mappings between source and target systems for key finance master data objects

- **Business intelligence and analytics**
  Embedded, adjacent, or complementary capabilities to leverage the single source of truth for financial data from end-user- to boardroom-level reporting

- **Cloud components**
  Dedicated functional capabilities enhancing the functional scope of Central Finance outside the core Central Finance system, usually software as a service (SaaS) or platform as a service (PaaS)

1.1.5   SAP S/4HANA Deployment Option

Central Finance is also a deployment option for SAP S/4HANA. Since the business processes execution in Central Finance is based on the capabilities found in an SAP S/4HANA system, SAP S/4HANA must be deployed as part of Central Finance. SAP S/4HANA and Central Finance are co-deployments in three different ways:

- Central Finance is the deployment of an SAP S/4HANA system in an organization. This central system for finance works in conjunction with source systems, both SAP and non-SAP, that feed into the central system.

- Central Finance is the deployment of the finance innovations found in SAP S/4HANA. These innovations become available to the finance user community across the enterprise, no matter what source system the users interacted with before Central Finance was deployed.

- Central Finance is the deployment of SAP S/4HANA in a nondisruptive fashion, providing business continuity. This case is especially true when the central SAP S/4HANA system is deployed as a side car implementation in addition to, and not as a replacement for, existing ERP source systems.

Central Finance is not a special version of SAP S/4HANA or an alternative to SAP S/4HANA. The Central Finance approach is based on a standard SAP S/4HANA system at its core delivering finance reporting and process execution capabilities. If you deploy Central Finance, you don't necessarily need to move to SAP S/4HANA later on—you're already using SAP S/4HANA!

Central Finance can be the starting point of your organization's journey towards adopting SAP S/4HANA because Central Finance can be used as a stepping stone to SAP S/4HANA by enabling onboarding onto the Central Finance platform and the decommissioning of SAP and non-SAP ERP source systems.

With a multi-ERP footprint as the target end state—albeit likely with a substantially reduced (consolidated) number of ERP source systems—Central Finance will still be the integration layer even in the end state. Even if the goal is that Central Finance will be the only SAP S/4HANA system eventually, until then, Central Finance can still serve as the integration layer for current and future M&A ERP system integrations.

In a single-system scenario enabled by Central Finance, Central Finance functionalities and capabilities can remain idle and don't have to be uninstalled because these capabilities do not impact the production system.

1.1.6 System Consolidation Path

Central Finance is also a possible path for reducing or consolidating existing SAP and non-SAP ERP systems, as shown in Figure 1.6. An SAP S/4HANA-based Central Finance system can be used as a platform to onboard and decommission existing SAP and non-SAP ERP source systems, thus moving logistics and finance processes into the Central Finance system.

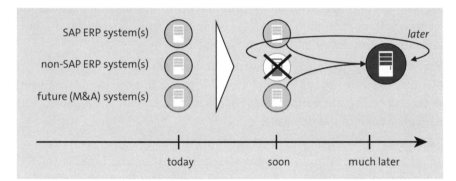

Figure 1.6 Consolidation Platform

From a technology perspective, system consolidation is not only possible with Central Finance, from a use case perspective, it makes absolute sense. Central Finance is based on a standard SAP S/4HANA system with complete finance and logistics abilities. Just because you may only use finance capabilities initially does not mean logistics cannot be later moved and executed in that instance.

Once established, the Central Finance instance has SAP S/4HANA's technology foundation to onboard logistics and finance processes from other SAP and non-SAP ERP systems.

Which systems and how many you consolidate are entirely up to you. Some general guidelines include the following:

- Some systems will never consolidate, and you'll always keep Central Finance as a dedicated, central system for finance.

- Some systems will move smaller entities, perhaps region based, like a Latin America business, or based on business size, like business units with smaller/older ERP systems due for reconsideration anyway.
- Many systems will move, and the number of systems should be reduced at least somewhat.
- All systems will move, which really depends on company culture more than anything.

Some organizations, even more so in the digital economy, are breaking up their single ERP systems into several, parallel ERP systems. This change might be permanent, allowing the organization to gain more operational flexibility, for example, to adopt innovations at a higher rate, or may be temporary, for example, to prepare for a forthcoming divestiture.

Central Finance can bring carved-out businesses and their corresponding ERPs together for centralized financial reporting and process execution.

1.2   Central Finance Building Blocks

The conceptual building blocks of SAP's Central Finance system, as shown in Figure 1.7, shape its opportunities, as follows (as well as its limits):

❶ Source system

❷ Data replication

❸ Central system

❹ Cloud integration

❺ Backposting (optional)

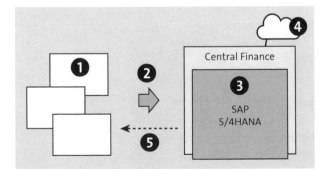

Figure 1.7 Central Finance: Building Blocks

1.2.1   Source System

As in traditional central Finance systems, Central Finance can consume financial transactions from your underlying ERP source systems. In these ERP source systems, the original logistics business transactions are executed and their corresponding finance transactions created, or finance transactions are entered as part of regular finance activities.

Central Finance can consume finance transactions from the following:

- Multisystem ERP landscapes
- Single-instance ERP systems
- Divestitures
- Future M&A systems

Multi-ERP System Landscapes

Most enterprises have at some point engaged in M&A activities. Additional business capabilities and entities are added, and with this change, additional ERP source systems. Few organizations, typically only serial acquirers, develop a core competency to bring in new systems into an existing, single ERP system.

For most organizations, multi-ERP system landscapes are a matter of ongoing, or not yet completed, post-merger integration, both from a system perspective as well as from a process execution perspective.

Most multi-ERP system landscapes feature a mix of ERP vendors (SAP and non-SAP, like Oracle, PeopleSoft, JD Edwards, or Microsoft) with a few landscapes having up to several hundred source systems in place.

From a Central Finance perspective, as shown in Figure 1.8, which ERP vendors you use or how many, does not really matter.

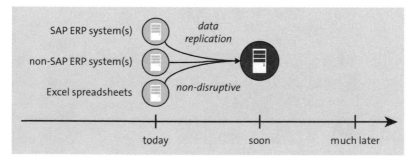

Figure 1.8 Multi-ERP System Landscape Scenario

While overall complexity increases with the number of source systems involved, the key driver of effort is mostly about the number of unique source system vendor/ release level combinations in play. Once a technical mapping for such unique combinations exists, this mapping can be reused or at least used as starting point for additional mappings and rollouts.

Single-Instance ERP Systems

A single-instance ERP system is not a typical scenario—as Central Finance's multisystem reporting and transaction processing capabilities aren't involved, but even single-system ERP organizations can take advantage of Central Finance as a stepping stone to SAP S/4HANA, as shown in Figure 1.9, which is an iterative way towards full SAP S/4HANA adoption (see Chapter 12).

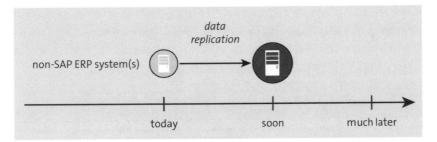

Figure 1.9 Single-Instance ERP System Scenario

Divestitures

With global, geographical expansion sufficiently explored and growth predominantly about business model changes and M&A scenarios in the age of the digital economy, more companies have also chosen to split up existing, consolidated systems (carve-out).

This split could be temporary—for a transitional time to prepare for moving from actual ownership to the eventual sale of a part of the business—or more permanent to give different parts of the business more flexibility to optimize their own business models without being tethered to a single core ERP system, as shown in Figure 1.10.

ERP source systems derived from divestiture activities can brought back together via Central Finance for finance reporting and process execution purposes.

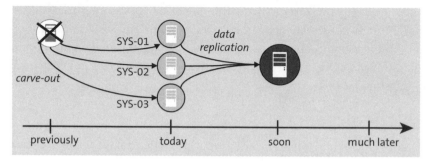

Figure 1.10 Divestiture/Carve-Out System Consolidation

Future Systems from Mergers and Acquisitions

A key capability of Central Finance is to, at any time, incorporate additional ERP source systems. In this scenario, the focus shifts from dealing with an as-is (post-merger) integration to a more forward-looking (M&A adoption) perspective focused on execution of a future state vision. Prevalent in the digital economy, M&A scenarios are an everyday reality for the foreseeable future, as shown in Figure 1.11.

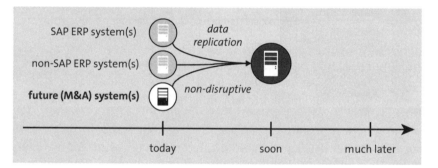

Figure 1.11 Future M&A System Integration

Central Finance provides the flexibility to bring in financial transactions from additional EPR systems and to accommodate consolidated reporting within 90 days.

Data formats between a new source system and the central system can be exchanged (and tested) immediately after the announcement of the intent to merge. Also, values can be exchanged starting with the day the merger is announced. No longer do you need to wait until the end of the quarter to see how the numbers add up. Instead, a continuously updated stream of postings from additional source systems can create a combined, real-time financial picture.

For serial acquirers, a Central Finance instance can become an acquisition platform, so that the process of connecting an additional source ERP system can follow a repeatable playbook.

1.2.2   Data Replication

From a Central Finance perspective, several key aspects of data replication include the following:

- Real-time replication
- Business mapping
- Line item detail
- Transactional posting
- Error correction

Data replication is the key to Central Finance and makes the central system work. Without data replication, no reports can be run nor transactions be processed.

Real-Time Replication

Replication is the reposting of financial transactions created in the source systems into the Central Finance system. Data replication in Central Finance happens in real time, unlike traditional central ERP systems for finance, which usually feature regularly scheduled, batch-based data integration.

Financial transactions are replicated (identified, extracted, mapped, and loaded) into Central Finance as soon as these transactions are posted in the source system. These transactions are available in real time for SAP source systems and near real-time for non-SAP ERP source systems.

Reporting in Central Finance is always based on the most current data (in the source system)—no longer based on datasets with older time stamps. At period end, no delay in data availability exists; adjustment postings made in the source systems are available in the central system right away with no delay.

Since replication happens in real time, the performance of the ERP source systems is not impacted, unlike in traditional, batch-based data integration scenarios. It is not unusual for Central Finance customers to replicate millions of postings per day without any issues.

Business Mapping

The key to replication into Central Finance is the business mapping layer, allowing the mapping of a current source value for, for example, a general ledger (G/L) account, profit center, or customer to a harmonized, standardized value in Central Finance (for example, a new corporate value) or to address overlapping values.

If you can easily change values in the source systems rather than mapping them in Central Finance, for example, by changing manual posting procedures or changing inbound interfaces, we recommend changing the data in the source system. However, this approach is not always pragmatic or economically viable.

With Central Finance, desired or required changes can be mapped, thus negating any changes to the source systems; in this way, the business mapping layer makes Central Finance nondisruptive.

Changes in source systems over time and different business models, whether in the same system or between different source systems, can be also brought together via the business mapping layer. With Central Finance, the central system is business model-agnostic both at the time of implementation and going forward as the business model of the organization evolves further.

Line Item-Level Detail

Financial transactions are replicated in Central Finance on a line item level. As a result, you can avoid aggregations or the loss of dimensional detail unlike with traditional central ERP systems for finance. Central Finance has the processing power of SAP HANA's in-memory database, and thus, the limitations of past technologies, which limited how many records or the level of detail could be processed, no longer exist. In other words, you no longer need to "save" your ERP from large data volumes.

With Central Finance, data will be brought in on the lowest available level. If the source data exists on the line item level, then that level of data is replicated. If the data in the source system is already aggregated or not posted in real time, you can go back and change that. You can go live with Central Finance with what the source system has and change timing and level of detail of those aggregated financial postings later.

With data replicated on the line item level, you'll have full auditability and drilldown access to the line items making up an account balance. These capabilities add a level of reliability to your aggregated data previously not available.

Transactional Posting

In traditional central data warehousing scenarios, transactions are posted as table updates on the database level. In contrast, financial transactions from source ERP systems are posted as standard SAP financial transactions in Central Finance. As a result, from a reporting perspective, you'll always have the full scope of the underlying financial transactions (line item level and full, unabbreviated dimensionality).

From a process execution perspective, you can be confident that the standard SAP transactions updated all relevant fields in all the required SAP S/4HANA tables in accordance to the customizing, completely and consistently, for subsequent processing in the central system.

Posting a standard SAP finance transaction means that standard data validations and substitutions are executed, and a complete audit trail (who, what, when) of the transaction, once processed in Central Finance, is available. Every transaction posted in Central Finance can be traced back to the underlying financial or logistics transactions in the source system, depending on the following scenarios:

- **SAP ERP source systems**
  Via the standard SAP ERP document relationship browser, the standard menu options in the document display allow you to drill down into the financial or logistics source document in the source SAP system, based on the source system ID and document number saved when posted in Central Finance.

- **Non-SAP ERP source systems**
  Via custom API build-outs or via partner products (like Magnitude's SourceConnect), line item details from non-SAP ERP source systems can be stored in an SAP HANA table for reporting purposes.

Error Correction

Since replication happens via standard transaction posting in Central Finance and not via direct table updates in the database, you won't need to scramble through logs or parse and reprocess files when postings don't make it through right away.

An inbound posting that cannot be processed (i.e., the posting period might not be open or the cost center might be blocked) will automatically be moved into the standard suspense accounting area in SAP Application Integration Framework. SAP Application Integration Framework generally allows you to explore erroneous interface postings and postprocess them. The underlying error can be fixed (i.e., posting period can be opened or the cost center can be unblocked), and the records can be postprocessed individually or in bulk.

Replication postings in Central Finance never get lost: $500,000 and 500 postings in the source system will always be $500,000 and 500 postings in Central Finance.

1.2.3 Central System

Traditional central systems for finance are mostly based on last-generation ERP systems. The technologies available at the time have been surpassed. Key attributes of such legacy systems include the following:

- **Database**
  Relational database models and a high degree of data normalization, which breaks up transactional and master data into a series of tables to reduce redundancy and increase throughput. In other words, data is all over the place.

- **Reporting**
  Financial reporting is limited to transactional finance reporting. OLAP/business analytics require a separate business warehouse or business intelligence system.

- **Application**
  Financial planning and consolidation capabilities are separate from the central, core ERP system. Thus, data needs to be moved and maintained in multiple systems.

- **Technology**
  Intelligent ERP capabilities like predictive analytics, robotic process automation (RPA), and machine learning are basically absent, unless you have a mainframe and data scientists.

- **User interface**
  GUI-based end-user frontends are focused on capturing business transaction data without addressing process execution.

SAP's Central Finance, based on SAP S/4HANA, is a central system for finance and is based on a technologically and functionally advanced version of ERP. With these technologies, additional capabilities available in the central system also mean a far higher value potential.

The key components of the central system, as shown in Figure 1.12, include the following:

- **SAP HANA**
  - The SAP HANA database is optimized for data storage and data processing based on today's technologies. Its columnar data storage principles negate the need for data fragmentation and duplication, which was introduced by relational database designs and normalization principles.
  - Using in-memory technology, SAP HANA allows you to execute transactions on the same platform as advanced analytics—same, single-system reporting—and removes the need for data duplication between operational and decision support systems.
- **SAP S/4HANA**
  - SAP Fiori serves as a personalized and simplified UI for SAP S/4HANA applications. Based on modern UX design principles, SAP Fiori delivers a role-based (process execution focused and streamlined for higher productivity), consumer-grade user experience across finance tasks and across devices.
  - SAP S/4HANA's digital core, the ability of SAP S/4HANA to natively connect to and synchronize with people, devices, and networks beyond what your core ERP allows. You'll be able to run integrated business processes in real time, avoiding latent custom data integration and management scenarios.

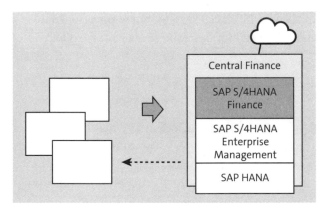

Figure 1.12 Central Finance Core Technical Components

- **SAP S/4HANA Finance**
  - Embedded, natively connected financial planning and consolidation capabilities negate the need for data duplication and master data maintenance and governance in multiple, separate applications.

- Embedded predictive analytics capabilities for forward-looking projections and simulations, as well as complementary machine learning capabilities for finance process automation, negate the need for special hardware or specialist resources that can be hard to find and expensive.

1.2.4 Cloud Integration

Traditional central ERP systems for finance are built on older, less advanced technologies. The functions and features found in such ERP systems are usually limited to the functions and features coded within that system.

Traditional ERP systems for finance are not *cloud ready*. Lacking a digital core, these ERPs lack the ability to seamlessly and natively connect to and adopt complementary cloud-based finance capabilities. These systems cannot, or only in a limited way, be integrated with today's vast offerings of new and extended cloud-based finance processes.

The SAP S/4HANA system at the center of Central Finance is cloud-ready and allows you to extend the traditional scope and value of a central system for finance beyond a traditional ERP's boundaries.

The SAP S/4HANA system at the core of Central Finance not only provides the current finance functionality found in a Central Finance system, but is also the enabler of future cloud-based innovations in finance. Cloud-readiness is a key aspect and differentiator of Central Finance.

1.2.5 Backposting

In a reporting-only scenario (a typical initial wave in a Central Finance implementation), no transactions are posted in the central system. The source system and the central system are exact mirrors of one another; every financial transaction posted in the source system also exists in the central system. At this point, backposting is not necessary because no postings need to be backposted.

Backposting comes into play when transactions, business processes that create financial transactions, or business processes that change data relevant for financial transaction execution are executed in the central system. In this case, the information only exists in the central system and not in the relevant source system(s).

Backposting is not a pertinent requirement in a Central Finance scenario. The basic premise of Central Finance is to execute processes in the central system. If the report or process is executed in the central system, you no longer execute the activity in the source system. If you no longer need to execute the activity in the source system, why do you still need the data there?

In general, this mindset shift doesn't have to be a large change management hurdle. Change management simply moves the data to where the process is executed. The question of backposting or not is usually based on preference. Naturally, you may want both systems to be in sync—being in sync is good but isn't required for Central Finance. However, some special circumstances should be mentioned:

- **Timing**
  Source systems today may provide data feeds or reports or enable other processes that may require the entire set of financial data in the source system. With processes moving to Central Finance, this situation should become the exception rather the rule; optimally, these processes are eliminated entirely or switched to Central Finance. Where the rollout roadmap cannot accommodate an elimination from a timing perspective, a backposting might in fact be required, if only temporarily.

- **Conglomerates**
  If your company is part of a conglomerate, you might just want to use backposting. You want all data in your own, local ERP systems that exist centrally for your division. That situation is fine, and in such a case, backposting would in fact be required.

If you chose to backpost, you must reverse-map data objects for which a business mapping was applied, and if changed over time, you'll have to take these changes into account as well. Based on the mapping table, you'll have to reverse-derive the source system value from the central value. In case of N:1 business mappings, you'll need to identify unique attributes that you can use to determine which source value to select.

If you backpost transactions, you must avoid "double postings," i.e., avoid transactions backposted to the source system that already exist in the central system being not replicated again to the central system.

If you chose to backpost, you must also accommodate the target data model, which may differ across source systems and require several interfaces. Further, for each system, you must put proper interface processing procedures (error processing) in place.

1.3   Central Finance Results

Deploying Central Finance provides puts organizations with multi-ERP system landscapes, whether SAP or non-SAP ERP source systems, in a position to execute finance processes in a central SAP S/4HANA system—enterprise-wide and cross-system. Using Central Finance provides for the following capabilities:

- **Central reporting**
  Key aspects of central reporting in Central Finance are:

  - Advanced reporting: Reporting in Central Finance is in real time (all posted transactions are available right away and without dimensional omissions) and directly accessible via various frontends including Microsoft Excel (without any need for data extraction, data transformation, or further data loads).

  - Segment-level reporting: Reporting in Central Finance can be on a microsegment level. Due to the customizable coding block in the underlying SAP S/4HANA system, custom dimensions (like the color of a product, the age of a customer, or the time and temperature at the moment of a sale) can be added and used for microsegment financial reporting.

  - Entity reporting: Just because Central Finance contains enterprise-wide financial information does not mean only corporate headquarters can run aggregated financial reports. Central Finance can also provide advanced segment-level reporting where desired, as well as entity-level reporting.

  - Group reporting: Central Finance can provide financial reporting across the financial transactions of the entire enterprise, no matter what source system originally captured the transaction.

- **Central process execution**
  Key aspects of central process execution in Central Finance are:

  - Local process execution: Processes traditionally running in the source system can be executed in the central system instead.

  - Central process execution: Processes executed in separate source systems (in parallel or split across systems), or in systems outside the source system can be executed once only, together within the same (ERP) central system.

  - Scalable process execution: Central Finance allows for the central execution of finance processes as well as execution in a shared services business model.

- **Finance transformation platform**
  Key aspects of Central Finance as a finance transformation platform include:
  - Common data foundation: Central Finance provides for a harmonized single source of truth in a central financial repository available across the enterprise.
  - Common information model: Central Finance provides for a standardized single source of truth in a central financial repository available across the enterprise, including added microsegment dimensionality (custom coding block enhancements).
  - Common application stack: Transaction processing, reporting, planning, and consolidation operate out of the same technology stack without the need for data replication and/or duplicate (master) data maintenance.
  - Same-system, single-system transaction recording and reporting: In Central Finance, financial data is stored in the central financial repository (SAP S/4HANA's Universal Journal) and can be accessed directly without extraction, transformation, and data load into external reporting and analytics frontends.
  - Digital core: Central Finance is based on the SAP S/4HANA system, which has native integration/connectivity (digital core) for business networks and cloud solution beyond the core ERP.

1.4   Boundaries and Restrictions

Central Finance is the central provisioning/enabler of one or more finance processes in a central, standard SAP S/4HANA system. Central Finance does not have its own set of finance processes or additional finance transactions that are not already part of the underlying SAP S/4HANA system. As such, the boundary conditions are as much about the concept behind Central Finance and the implementation path chosen and not the underlying products (SAP S/4HANA and SAP S/4HANA and Central Finance foundation), as follows:

- **Conceptual restrictions**
  Central Finance takes financial documents created in the underlying ERP source systems (both SAP ERP or non-SAP ERP) and replicates them into the Central Finance instance. Whether those finance documents were created directly as finance documents or were created to record the financial aspect of an underlying logistics transaction does not matter.
  - Central Finance does not replicate logistics documents (like purchase orders or sales orders).

- Central Finance does not allow for a "de-coupled finance" system—that is, a system where the source system only has logistics transactions (and no finance transactions at all) while Central Finance has only finance transactions.

- **Technology limitations**
Central Finance can be deployed on-premise or in the cloud (hosted or private). However, selected complementary components might only be available in the cloud only and not on-premise.

  - Organizations that are not ready for the cloud will still be able to use the majority, but not necessarily all, the enabled Central Finance-based finance processes.

  - Customers with "off-grid" systems—that is, systems that are not connected to the Internet or to an Intranet at all or at offshore locations (batch uplinks)—won't be able to take advantage of Central Finance's direct real-time replication capabilities. These customers can, however, still replicate data via batch or manual file transfers.

- **Setup prerequisites**
Central Finance is not a data warehouse where data records are added to tables via inserts or updates. Central Finance reposts financial documents received from the underlying ERP source systems as proper financial transactions. Thus, Central Finance requires:

  - Process configuration

  - Master data provision

  - Load of historical data

  Without these prerequisites, data cannot be replicated, and reporting and finance processes cannot be executed. While these prerequisites might seem burdensome, the advanced reporting and central process execution capabilities that Central Finance enables are well worth the effort.

- **Replication limits**
Central Finance allows for the replication of various finance transaction types from SAP and non-SAP ERP systems. Out-of-scope items are:

  - Replication of logistics documents (sales orders, purchase orders)

  - Replication of statistical documents (parked items, notes)

  - Replication of costing-based Profitability Analysis (CO-PA) records into Central Finance

  - Replication of plan data from source systems

- **Data constraints**

  Reporting and process execution in Central Finance is based on the data replicated/posted into the Central Finance system. Simply put, if you don't provide the data you need during the initial data load and/or during later replication into Central Finance, the data won't be available later for reporting or transaction execution.

  The universe of possibilities in Central Finance is largely based on what data has been replicated, which needs to be considered when planning the rollout—ensure that what data is needed, even if only later, is provided or at least considered. Of course, additional data elements as well as transaction types can always be added later (and are available at any time after go-live).

Process Boundaries

Finance processes from a customer perspective and finance processes from a Central Finance perspective are often two different things. You must differentiate between SAP finance processes enabled by Central Finance and finance processes outside the standard Central Finance scope. These latter processes may or may not be achievable with Central Finance or with related SAP HANA and SAP cloud capabilities. Consult your SAP or SAP SI consulting partner for feasibility and implementation options.

Selected (mainly plant-level) entity finance processes related to closings need to remain in the underlying ERP source systems because of their inherent integration with logistics processes in those source systems. Examples include:

- Performing inventory and posting inventory differences
- Reclassifying clearing accounts for goods receipts/invoice receipts
- Material (re)valuation
- Closing operations in subsidiary ledgers
- Analyzing GR/IR clearing accounts
- Automatic clearing of GR/IR accounts
- Foreign trade regulation reports

A few finance processes are not supported by Central Finance at this time:

- Product costing and the material ledger
- Fully integrated (bidirectional) asset accounting
- Investment management
- Funds management

Always check for the most recent Central Finance product roadmap to learn what planned and future features are in the development pipeline.

1.5   Summary

In this chapter, we provided information about the basic concepts behind Central Finance, the evolution of central systems for finance and process execution, the relevant options, the building blocks of the source system, data replication in the central system, and functional and process boundaries. We also discussed key value pillars—central reporting, central process execution, and a central platform for transformation to a digital enterprise.

The next chapter will provide additional information on the mechanics—the functional and technical foundation for Central Finance and the set of enabling capabilities.

Chapter 2

The Mechanics: How Does Central Finance Work?

Key to a good understanding of Central Finance is not only under-standing what a Central Finance system is, but also how a Central Finance systems works, its key components, its functional foundation, and the "glue" that ties it all together.

In this chapter, we'll provide an introduction into the origin of Central Finance and review some options for Central Finance's functional deployment and use. We'll also discuss the underlying capabilities that make it all work.

2.1 Functional Foundation

The functional foundation of a Central Finance system is driven by the functions and features available in the underlying central SAP S/4HANA system. This system includes components that are now part of SAP S/4HANA (reporting, planning, con-solidation, shared services, etc.), which were previously not part of a core SAP ERP system or were separate products or applications integrated with a core system. Not all standard capabilities are a good fit for an organization, and not all need to be implemented at once or ever. Which capabilities you chose is up to you.

2.1.1 Finance Value Map

The functional foundation for Central Finance is provided directly by the underlying SAP S/4HANA system, its functions, its features, and its standard capabilities, which are enhanced every release cycle.

Central Finance does not provide that any finance processes that are not already part of SAP S/4HANA. What's available in SAP S/4HANA is theoretically available for use in Central Finance.

However, just because a given process is available in SAP S/4HANA (see the finance value map shown in Figure 2.1) and thus in Central Finance, running the process centrally may not automatically make sense nor will that process automatically provide additional value.

However, many, if not most, standard finance processes are feasible and worth executing in the Central Finance system.

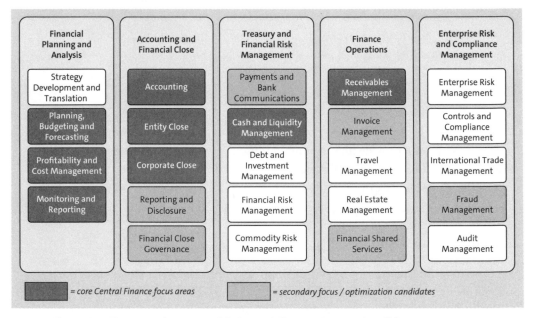

Figure 2.1 Finance Value Map with Central Finance Process Candidates

Which process is suitable for a Central Finance implementation is different from organization to organization. The order in which processes might be implemented will also differ from company to company.

2.1.2   Key Process Candidates

On the finance process level, three process groups are available as candidates for reporting and process execution in Central Finance, as follows:

- **Reporting and analysis-related processes**
  Once financial transactions are replicated from your ERP source systems into Central Finance, these transactions can be used in Central Finance for advanced segment, entity, and group reporting.

- **Finance operations processes**
  Based on the replicated finance transactions, selected finance processes can now be executed within Central Finance, as a complement to or a replacement of executing that process in the source system.

- **Additional finance processes**
  Finance process capabilities, available in the SAP S/4HANA stack and thus embedded in the same system, can be leveraged to further use the replicated finance transactions (i.e., consolidation); can complement such datasets (i.e., by adding plan and budgeting data); or can aid finance transaction execution within Central Finance (i.e., the shared services framework).

Again, which processes you select for execution and in which order they are implemented depend on your requirements. Besides the key processes around financial and management reporting and business analytics, Table 2.1 lists key process candidates for Central Finance.

Finance Operations Processes	Additional Finance Processes
- Financial accounting - Management accounting - Intercompany reconciliation - Accounts payable - Accounts receivable - Credit management - Collections management - Dispute management - Group/cash management - Cash position/liquidity forecast	- Closing - Planning and budgeting - Consolidation/group reporting - Disclosure management - Master data governance - Financial shared services - Exception/fraud management

Table 2.1 Key Central Finance Process Candidates

Of course, a number of additional, adjacent finance capabilities—cloud-based or not—can be leveraged in conjunction with a Central Finance system, and more information on these capabilities is provided in subsequent chapters.

2.2   Central Finance Capabilities

Unlike traditional central ERP systems for finance, which often require custom integration, Central Finance comes with a standard set of enabling capabilities, as listed in Table 2.2, thus reducing the need for such custom integration.

Process	Capabilities
Data logging	■ Preservation of transaction information in SAP source systems for replicating/posting into Central Finance
Replication	■ Real-time replication from SAP source systems: SAP-provided technical SAP Landscape Transformation Replication Server (SAP LT Replication Server) data mapping template ■ Nearly real-time integration with non-SAP ERP source systems: SAP-provided "standard data flow architecture"
Business mapping	■ Mapping via SAP Master Data Governance (SAP MDG) user interface and mapping tables; business rule-based mapping via SAP BRFplus
Data digitization and inbound posting	■ User exit extension to augment transaction posting for "digital enterprise" reporting and process execution ■ Central Finance interfaces, optimized for posting into Universal Journal; support of general ledger (G/L), accounts payable (AP)/accounts receivable (AR) open items and clearing documents, and CO postings
Error handling	■ Functional interface monitoring and error handling (post-processing, mass error handling)
Drilldown and audit trail	■ Functionality to relate new documents in the Central Finance system to underlying source documents
Reconciliation	■ Auditable source-target reconciliation reporting
Backposting	■ Custom option through standard SAP integration capabilities like IDocs (ALE) or SAP Process Integration (PI)

Table 2.2 Enabling Capabilities in Central Finance

In the following sections, we'll discuss each these capabilities in more detail.

2.2.1   Data Logging

Simply put, Central Finance's data logging capability in an SAP source system is the preservation of the original transaction information for replication/posting to the Central Finance system.

You may ask, "Isn't the original transaction information already captured and logged in the accounting tables of the source system? What then is this new data logging capability?" Fundamentally, the "original transaction information" is actually more than what eventually appears in the final accounting document in the source system.

Think of accounting as the recording of real-life events that have a monetary impact to the organization, based on certain rules. When such a real-life event occurs (we made a purchase, we made a sale, we paid someone, etc.), the event should be recorded in the finance modules found in the source system. All information related to this event is captured temporarily in a data structure. These pieces of information can be related to logistics or other aspects of the event that are not strictly financial information. Therefore, even if this information will be used in "constructing" the financial document, the final accounting document will not display this information as fields.

In other words, the information needed to construct an accounting document includes more attributes about the underlying event than what normally ends up displayed in an accounting document.

An example of this extra information could be the **Sales condition** field in SAP. When a billing document is created, certain sales conditions are captured in the billing document to facilitate the calculation of the sale's financial impact. The sales condition field does not appear in the final accounting document but contributes to building the document. This information is used, for example, to derive the appropriate revenue G/L account based on the configuration in the system.

In this example, in the source system, if we captured/logged the finalized and saved accounting document only, we would be capturing the derived G/L account, not the underlying sales condition (a nonfinancial attribute of the underlying event). In other words, we would be replicating (in fact, copying and pasting) the final accounting document, just as we would in a SAP Business Warehouse (SAP BW) extraction scenario. In other words, we wouldn't be fully capturing the underlying event with all its relevant attributes, which can potentially construct a different accounting document when we post to Central Finance, depending on how Central Finance is configured.

One major advantage of a Central Finance deployment over a normal financial data collection scenario (i.e., using SAP BW) is an important distinction: We're not copying and pasting the final accounting document; we're reposting the event in the Central Finance system.

This difference can create a richer, and in some cases simpler, accounting document that aligns an enterprise-wide, global understanding and mindset. In other words, when a local event triggers an accounting posting, we'll post the same event into our global finance system, with a potentially different, more broad, accounting or reporting philosophy.

The data logging functionality, in short, is designed to capture all the information that will be used to post the same event in the Central Finance system, based on the configuration and rules in the Central finance system.

All this information is captured and logged in Central Finance tables in the source system for replication into Central Finance. We'll discuss the replication approach in the next section.

2.2.2   Data Replication

The main tool for the replication of financial postings from SAP as well as from non-SAP systems is the SAP LT Replication Server, used for these two fundamental tasks, which we'll discuss in the following sections:

- Initial load
- Ongoing replication (after Central Finance go-live)

Initial Data Load

The initial load is the transferring of existing accounting documents or balances into the Central Finance system.

In most cutover strategies to a new accounting system, loading existing historical financial data into Central Finance is the desired goal. After all, in most cases, we're changing our financial system of record to Central Finance, and historical data is necessary for comparison reporting and analysis.

Let's look at some best practices and recommendations regarding how much detail should be replicated and how deep into the history you should go. For example, in some cases, replicating balances or using aggregated results, rather than each historical line item, would make sense. In fact, we recommend keeping the historical time period for determining which individual documents will be transferred quite short, for example, from the beginning of current fiscal year because transferring individual documents is a performance-heavy task. When individual transactions are transferred, the initial load will try to select documents from different tables and convert these documents into the new data model in SAP S/4HANA Finance.

Still, typically, you'll make case-by-case decisions, driven by specific organizational needs, for each implementation project.

The initial load is a required technical step to start live replication in a Central Finance scenario, even for an *empty load*, where nothing is replicated or posted to Central Finance. Another important aspect of the initial load is that the technical methodologies for replicating posted transactions from history and ongoing replication of real-time transactions after go-live are two very different things.

Many technical and functional steps will need to be executed to perform and confirm the initial load in a Central Finance scenario. You should follow the recommendations found in the relevant SAP Notes and implementation guides, which can help improve performance or facilitate a successful load in general.

The initial load for non-SAP finance systems is something that can be performed differently depending on the systems and must be handled by project teams on a case-by-case basis.

Production Replication Post-Go-Live

The SAP LT Replication Server collects the data that has been written into databases in the source systems and feeds this data into the corresponding accounting interface in Central Finance. The collection of these relevant sets of data is triggered in real time, based on the database changes made to these systems. Put simply, the SAP LT Replication Server listens to certain tables in the source systems, and when a relevant change is made to these tables, it knows what data to capture and hand over to the Central Finance accounting interface.

This data, after going through the business mapping and error handling processes, is posted to Central Finance and recorded in the Universal Journal. In Section 2.2.3 and Section 2.2.5, respectively, we'll discuss the business mapping and error handling functionalities in Central Finance, as well as its capabilities for manipulating the raw source data on its way to Central Finance.

The following replication scenarios are supported:

- Replication of Finance (FI) and Controlling (CO) postings
- Replication of profit center accounting postings
- Replication of CO internal postings
- Replication of commitment postings
- Replication of cost objects

The replication of cost objects is achieved by the cost object replication framework. This functionality allows the automated creation of short-lived objects, such as orders from source systems to Central Finance. The cost object replication framework can map the following scenarios:

- Production order to product cost collector (N:1)
- Product cost collector to product cost collector (1:1)
- Internal order to internal order
- Service order to service order
- Quality management (QM) order to QM order
- Production order to internal order
- Service order to internal order
- QM order to internal order
- Process order to internal order

2.2.3   Business Mapping

Financial postings replicated to Central Finance include master data elements that can be mapped to target values in Central Finance.

Master data must be in place before you start triggering postings for transactional data because the postings will be validated against this master data. In other words, the relationship between a master data ID or code used in the source system and the corresponding ID or code used in the Central Finance system must be defined for each object.

Central Finance provides for business mapping based on standard SAP MDG foundation capabilities. However, SAP MDG's master data governance processes don't need to be set up, nor is an extra SAP MDG license required for this standard mapping.

Whether you use full SAP MDG functionality for master data consolidation or governance or not, several different kinds of mapping include the following:

- Mapping for business object identifiers, such as customer IDs, vendor IDs, or material IDs using SAP MDG's key mapping functions
- Mapping for codes, such as company codes, business areas, etc. using SAP MDG's value mapping functions
- Mapping for short-lived objects, for example, a maintenance order or an internal order

Identifiers or codes differ between the source system and the Central Finance system, thus making updating the value through mapping necessary. For example, a vendor might have the ID 1234 in the source system but ID 5678 in the Central Finance system. While replicating an invoice for this vendor, the ID will need to be changed, through mapping, to 5678.

For some specific cases of cost object replication, you might also need to change the object type. For example, a replicated finance document may have a reference to a production order, but the system is set up so that it does not require capturing individual production orders in Central Finance. In this case, multiple production orders can be mapped to a single cost collector, and the Central Finance document can reference this single cost collector instead of the original production order(s).

In addition, we can also define, for each object, the desired mapping action when replicating documents. The following standard mapping actions are available in the system:

- **Keep the data**
  The field value coming from the source system is retained. This option is the default if no configuration is changed for an object and a source system combination.

- **Mapping obligatory**
  The field values must be mapped; if there is no mapping for a particular field value, an error is raised.

- **Clear the data**
  Clear the field value coming from the source system.

- **Map, if possible**
  If a mapping has been maintained for an incoming field value, the system will use the mapped value in Central Finance. If no mapping exists, Central Finance will retain the incoming value from the source.

In some cases, you may need to define different mapping actions for the same object from different source systems. For example, for vendor IDs coming in from source system A, let's say we want to retain the data, but for vendor IDs coming from system B, let's say we want to make mapping mandatory. In this case, we would populate the "business system" field in the configuration for the mapping action. If this field is left blank, the mapping action applies to all source systems.

If we have complex mapping requirements that the standard mapping functionality cannot meet, we can implement our own mapping logic via a Business Add-In (BAdI). Still, many customers find some of these complex requirements can also be met using standard substitutions or validations in the Central Finance system: For example, consider the following requirement: map vendor 1234 to vendor 5678 only if the business area is ABCD; otherwise, keep the vendor ID as 1234. This requirement cannot be met by simple mapping using the standard functionality, but the Central Finance system can meet this requirement using a simple substitution, rather than employing a BAdI.

You should understand how Central Finance approaches the determination of cost object-dependent objects: Imagine an expense posting being replicated from the source system, which includes a cost center and a profit center. The profit center in the source system was either derived from the cost center master data or through some custom method, like a substitution. When this document is replicated, the profit center will not be replicated with it; rather, the system will first try to derive profit center from the (mapped) cost center's master data in Central Finance. If the cost center has not been assigned in the Central Finance, the posting will try to use a dummy profit center. If a dummy profit center has not been defined in the controlling area, only then will Central Finance keep the profit center coming in from the source system. If that profit center does not exist, then the document is sent to error handling.

Let's say, in a document, the profit center is not derived by the system from other objects but is manually entered (like some balance sheet postings). In this case, the system will know to keep the profit center in the incoming source document while posting to Central Finance.

This general behavior is inspired by the philosophy of getting a second chance to post the same event in Central Finance. The master data, data model, and the configuration in Central Finance may be (and in most cases should be) different, resulting in a different accounting document. How account determination and account assignment is performed throughout the Central Finance system follows a simple principle: If possible, derive the field from the Central Finance environment; if not, try to retain the original source information.

Finally, you can also map customer-defined fields in the accounting interface. You can define business objects to be used for key mapping using the customer namespace. Please refer to the latest Central Finance administrator's guide for details on the configuration required for this functionality.

2.2.4   Data Digitization and Inbound Posting

Data digitization is concerned with augmenting and enriching raw data before posting into Central Finance for digital enterprise reporting and process execution.

One possible way to enrich an accounting document on its way from the source system to Central Finance is through user exits before the posting in Central Finance occurs. For example, nonfinancial information might be required for more robust recording and reporting capabilities in the Central Finance system than is available or that can be captured through some logic applied to the incoming dataset.

An example could be a field that is derived for specific needs in the source system (for example, a special purpose ledger), which will not be captured in the accounting document but is still needed in Central Finance for reporting. The derivation logic for this field can be replicated in the user extension, and this field can be added as an extension to the Universal Journal. This field can facilitate the enrichment of the document for more robust management reporting in the Central Finance system.

Similarly, master data attributes that are not captured by default in the accounting document (for example, the person responsible field in the master data of an internal order) can also be captured and used to enhance a document.

In addition to enriching the raw data coming in from the source system using these functionalities, you can also manipulate, enrich, and (in some cases) simplify Central Finance documents. Since the document will be posted into Central Finance again, all derivations and checks will be reexecuted, based on the configuration and master data settings maintained in Central Finance. For example, a cost center that rolls up to profit center A in the source system can roll up to profit center B in the Central Finance system, based on its master data, if required.

Similarly, while posting in Central Finance, you can apply validations and substitutions that are not in the source system, which enables you to define rules and policies that are not necessarily applicable in the source systems for whatever reason.

Financial records brought into Central Finance are then, enhanced or not, posted by dedicated Central Finance programs supporting the posting into the Universal Journal.

2.2.5   Error Handling

In Central Finance, the governance around the accuracy of initial loads as well as the ongoing replication of finance documents is of the utmost importance.

Documents may fail to be posted in Central Finance for a number of reasons. For example, the posting period could be closed in the Central Finance system, a cost center may not exist/may be locked, or a mapping may be incorrect.

Initially, error correction and suspense accounting was used to handle errors in replication; with introduction of SAP S/4HANA, however, the SAP Application Integration Framework has become the new standard. The SAP Application Integration Framework is a robust tool for error handling that allows the use of alerts, the distribution of messages to different users, and actionable reports.

Two different ways for error handling are available in the initial load process:

- **Initial load of FI documents**
  If the errors relate to the initial load of FI documents, the Customizing activity **Monitor Postings** can be used in the Central Finance system.

- **Initial load of internal CO documents**
  Handled in the Central Finance system using the SAP Application Integration Framework.

The SAP Application Integration Framework handles errors that arise during ongoing replication in all FI postings, internal CO postings, and cost object replication, etc.

From the Interface Monitor in the SAP Application Integration Framework transaction, a hierarchical representation of the interfaces relevant to Central Finance can be reviewed. You can also see the number of errors and warning messages for each of these interfaces. The monitoring and error handling transaction can show you details about these errors.

In practice, assuming that thorough testing before go-live has been performed around the design and logic for replication, most errors captured in the SAP Application Integration Framework will be related to master data. Sometimes a mapping is missing, or a master data item has not been created for whatever reason. In rarer cases, some configuration might be missing in the Central Finance. No matter the root cause, the error will be well reported and explained in the error message, and corrective actions can be taken.

The right way to clear the list of failed documents is to remove the root cause (create the right master data, correct mapping, or correct configuration) and then to repost the document using the **Restart** button. The system will try to repost the document, and if the root problem has been successfully resolved, the document will be posted.

Another way to correct a document is called the *emergency corrections mode*. The system allows certain users (users with a certain authorization object) to change field values directly in the SAP Application Integration Framework system. Thus, a manually changed document can be reposted using the **Repost with user changes** button. (If the **Restart** button is clicked after making manual changes, these user changes will be discarded.) The emergency corrections mode should be used carefully because the manual changes made to the document in the SAP Application Integration Framework can lead to serious inconsistencies between source and Central Finance systems. The preferred method should always be to remove the root cause and restart the replication to keep systems consistent. The emergency corrections mode should be used as the exception and not the norm.

2.2.6   Drilldown/Audit Trail

As documents are successfully posted to Central Finance, functionality is needed to relate the new document in the Central Finance to the underlying source document in the source system. Central Finance keeps references to the source system and to the underlying source system document for every document that is replicated.

In a normal SAP environment, the reference document is the preceding document that triggered the financial posting. If we have a billing document in SAP, the revenue versus accounts receivable posting in Central Finance can show the sales billing document as its reference document in the document header of the finance document.

Similarly, an accounting document that has been replicated into Central Finance will show the source system accounting document in its header. In fact, in the header of the Central Finance document created, the sender (source) logical system, the sender (source) document number, sender company code, and the sender fiscal year will all be captured.

The SAP relationship browser functionality is the standard for drilling down to the source document since it is the initial document used in creating the Central Finance document. Source system information will also be displayed in the relationship browser.

For non-SAP ERP source systems, line item detail can be preserved and accessed through Magnitude's SourceConnect accelerator.

2.2.7   Data Reconciliation

Moving to a Central Finance scenario, and especially making a Central Finance system your new system of record, comes with a certain degree of anxiety around ensuring that the replication logic is healthy and that all relevant documents are successfully replicated. Auditable and robust source target comparison reporting is available to alleviate risk and facilitate reconciliation across systems.

A number of reports come standard with the system that will facilitate reconciliation across source systems and the central system, as listed in Table 2.3.

Report	Use and Features
Central Finance: Comparison of FI Document Headers	This report selects accounting documents that need to be replicated to the Central Finance system, compares the document headers of the journal entries, and identifies any journal entries that are missing in the Central Finance system. The report counts the number of journal entries in both the source system and the Central Finance system.
Central Finance: Comparison of FI Balances	This report shows the debit balance, the credit balance, the balances total, and the currencies of your G/L accounts in both the source systems and the Central Finance system, for a specified fiscal year or posting period. You'll execute this report in the Central Finance system to check whether G/L account balances in the source system match the corresponding balances in the Central Finance system. You can choose whether to compare balances in company code currency or in transaction currency. Both currencies and their relevant amounts will be displayed in the results screen, and the currency that you chose will be highlighted.
Central Finance: Comparison of FI Line Items	You'll execute this report in the Central Finance system to check whether the line items in the Central Finance system correspond to all line items for the selected G/L accounts in the source system and whether these line items have the same amounts. The report displays details about the line items in both the source systems and the Central Finance system, such as the document number, fiscal year, G/L account, currency, and reference key.
Central Finance: Comparison of CO Document Headers	This report selects CO documents that need be transferred to Central Finance, compares the document headers of the CO documents (table COBK), and identifies any CO documents that are missing in the Central Finance system. The report counts the CO documents in the source system and in the Central Finance system.

Table 2.3 Standard Reconciliation Reporting in Central Finance

Report	Use and Features
Central Finance: Comparison of CO Balances	This report shows the debit balance, the credit balance, and the total balance for selected cost elements in both a source system and the Central Finance system, for a specified fiscal year or posting period. You'll execute this report in the Central Finance system to check whether the debit or credit totals for cost elements used in secondary postings are identical in both the source systems and the Central Finance system.
Central Finance: Comparison of CO Line Items	You'll use this report to compare CO line items for the selected cost elements in a source system against those in the Central Finance system. You'll execute this report in the Central Finance system to check whether the line items in the Central Finance system correspond to all the CO line items for the selected cost elements in the source systems. The report displays details of the line items in both the source systems and the Central Finance system, such as the document number, fiscal year, cost element, currency, and reference key.

Table 2.3 Standard Reconciliation Reporting in Central Finance (Cont.)

Since the more recent use cases of Central Finance involve central process execution possibilities, such as central payments, central allocations, reclassifications etc., be aware that some documents, line items, and balances may exist in the Central Finance system but not in the source systems. You'll need to design a reconciliation approach to take into consideration these natural and expected differences.

2.3   Summary

A stack of innovative technical SAP components, together with SAP S/4HANA's core functional finance capabilities, are the foundation for Central Finance as modern central system for finance. Central Finance comes with a set of enabling capabilities that negate the need for custom integration, which is typical necessary for central systems for finance based on legacy system technology.

Chapter 3

The Motivation: Why Central Finance and Why Now?

When considering Central Finance, some key questions everyone should ask include "Why should I consider Central Finance?", "What's different in or with Central Finance?", and "Why should I act now?" In this chapter, we'll answer these questions and uncover the many advantages of adopting Central Finance.

In this chapter, we'll explain what makes Central Finance the silver bullet for a variety of IT/business concerns and why many organizations are choosing to implement it now. Today's multi-ERP system landscapes are complex and may involve several different ERP source systems, several (often parallel) installations of applications for business planning and consolidation, and numerous business intelligence (BI) and business warehousing (BW) systems and tools for analytics and reporting. A multitude of interfaces and transformations may be necessary to ensure the data is duplicated to all the places required.

Every time a business transaction is posted in your organization, copies of this transaction are moved and stored all over the place—that's how a traditional legacy system operated. With the cost of hardware and its throughput limitations, this duplication of data was the only way to do it.

Adding a new entity or a system, changing your business model (even just a standard annual reorganization), divestitures, or joint ventures can be nightmares to accommodate, requiring a lot of effort and time and bringing in a great deal of risk every time you touch the system landscape.

3.1   Central Finance as a Silver Bullet

Central Finance represents a new approach to finance and is based on a new set of technologies in a central ERP system. Expensive custom integration and traditional legacy system technologies create barriers that prevent the provision of central reporting and transaction processing.

Central Finance is a more easily deployable central system for finance, enabling consolidated transaction execution, business planning, group consolidation, and reporting and analytics—all out of a single system without the need for further data duplication.

Central Finance provides a path to simplifying your system landscape; Figure 3.1 shows a representation of a traditional legacy system and the complicated, often messy, movement of data and integrations necessary. Figure 3.2, on the other hand, shows a representation of a Central Finance system, with a much smoother flow of information.

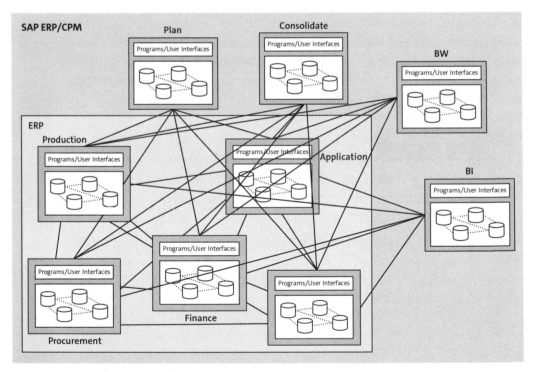

Figure 3.1 Complexity in Traditional Legacy System Environments

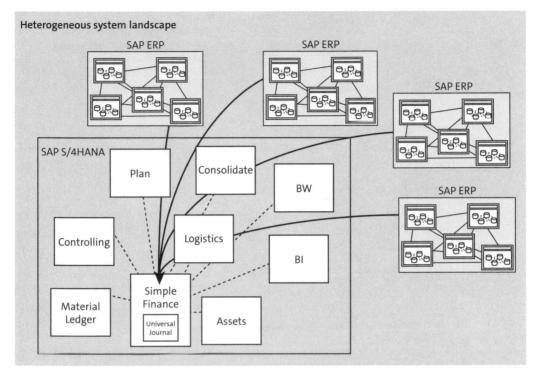

Figure 3.2 Simplicity with Central Finance

Adding a new entity or system, changing your business model, including reorganizations, are much easier to deal with when you only have a single Central Finance system. With traditional legacy systems that have been used for years, organizations know what to do and what can be done but may require expensive investments, and IT and financial resources could be locked in for extended times.

However, this "more of the same" approach generally does not remove complexity but instead increases it. Every additional application or system requires even more interfaces and even more redundant transformations. A new report added requires another data extract, perhaps another data model, and still may not provide information across the entire enterprise or may not use all the dimensions captured in the financial transaction.

By definition, a silver bullet refers to something that cuts through complexity and provides an immediate solution to a problem. Central Finance is a silver bullet for many finance issues, as shown in Figure 3.3.

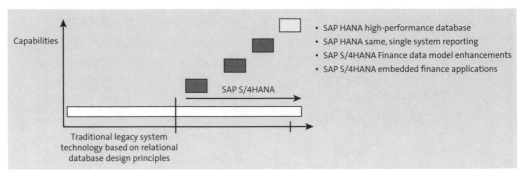

Figure 3.3 Central Finance as a Silver Bullet

Key innovations that make Central Finance a silver-bullet solution include the following:

- **SAP HANA as a high-performance database**
  The arrival of the SAP HANA database, a high-performance database, has removed the barriers stemming from relational database design principles. Data no longer needs to be parsed and moved around to applications in redundant pieces and portions.

- **SAP HANA for single system reporting**
  End users can consume financial data directly via their frontend applications using the Universal Journal of Central Finance, rather than having to extract and transform datasets as prerequisites to consuming the data.

- **SAP S/4HANA Finance data model**
  The SAP HANA database has resulted in a new architecture for the SAP S/4HANA Finance data model and has introduced the Universal Journal, a single table that captures all financial data, rather than the data being spread out to different tables for the general ledger (G/L), subledgers, or management accounting. The customizable Universal Journal can capture additional dimensionality like the color of a product, the age of a customer, the time of the day, and even the temperature at the time of a posting for microsegment profitability analysis.

- **SAP S/4HANA Finance embedded applications**
  With SAP S/4HANA Finance, you can post financial transactions in the same system as you would your business planning, group consolidation, and shared services. Your users will share the same set of transaction data and master data and benefit from real-time reporting without further data duplication.

Central Finance also provides central reporting and process execution capabilities enterprise-wide, as follows:

- **Coverage across all legal entities and lines of business in an organization**
  Financial transactions from any ERP source system in the organization, no matter the ERP source system the data resides in or how many ERP source systems or ERP vendors are involved—or how old they are—can be brought together into one central system. Because transactions are reposted as standard SAP financial transactions into Central Finance, a complete audit trail, with drilldown capability to source transactions, is available.

- **Business model-agnostic data harmonization**
  Financial transactions replicated into Central Finance can be mapped from the local customizing and design choices for master data and past business processes—intended to accommodate the business model at the time—to a common, central information model. No changes are required to the ERP source systems, and the data is immediately ready for analysis in Central Finance from the new business model perspective.

- **A single source of truth for financial data**
  All the financial transactions of the organization are stored in one and only one table, the Universal Journal, which is updated in real time every time a new transaction is added anywhere in the organizations. This information is easily consumable for all users directly from the various SAP and non-SAP frontends, including Microsoft Excel. No additional ETL (extract, transform, and load) tools, data provisioning, or data extraction is required; information is directly accessible by same-stack SAP S/4HANA applications like SAP Business Planning and Consolidation (SAP BPC).

- **Central and scalable process execution**
  Unlike past data warehouse approaches, financial transactions can be used for enterprise-wide reporting, including integrated group reporting, in Central Finance. If desired, shared services can execute processes in the same system, increasing quality and performance and leveraging economies of scale across the organization.

Central Finance provides cross-system reporting and centralized process execution capabilities. Central Finance accommodates replication from the following:

- **SAP source systems**
  Integration of SAP ERP source systems today is supported by standard technical mapping content, which allows financial transactions from ERP systems to be

brought in no matter the release of the source system. In a worst-case scenario, where the source system is too old to integrate through the standard capabilities, use the Central Finance third-party staging area.

- **Non-SAP source systems**
  The integration of non-SAP ERP source systems can be accommodated through the standard Central Finance third-party staging area. Data provisioning to that staging area can be custom-built or can use predefined templates (see Chapter 8) like Magnitude's SourceConnect accelerator, which has predefined technical mapping templates and years of quality improvements built in for fast, cheap, high-quality integration. Using predefined templates accelerates your non-SAP ERP integration, allowing the technical mapping of a source system in as little as 15 to 20 days. Mapping financial data from non-SAP ERP systems is not a big deal!

- **Subsidiary instances (like SAP S/4HANA Cloud in a public cloud)**
  Integration of SAP S/4HANA Cloud instances, used to move selected businesses or regional systems into the cloud, is supported today by the standard technical mapping content in Central Finance.

- **Financial data on spreadsheets**
  Smaller businesses or entities in selected regions, and sometimes systems with offline, batch submissions, can be integrated today with the standard Central Finance third-party staging area. To increase adoption, even in this case, we recommend using predefined templates as accelerators.

- **Future ERP systems (mergers and acquisitions)**
  Integration of future ERP systems follows the routes mentioned earlier in this list, whether for an SAP source system or a non-SAP ERP source system. The advantage of Central Finance is that it serves as a platform, with the underlying replication and error correction infrastructure, built-out central process execution, and a playbook of project plans from previous ERP system integration activities that can be reused and scaled for the onboarding of additional entities and systems.

3.2   Innovation Acceleration

Traditional multi-ERP systems landscapes, with or without a central system for finance attached, are built on legacy system technology.

As discussed in the previous section, innovation today is realized largely using a "more of the same" approach, involving introducing limited changes to the ERP source system in question or adding data replication to additional, nonintegrated applications, thus making the overall system landscape even more complex. In multi-ERP system landscapes, this process occurs for each SAP source system as well as for each non-SAP ERP source system.

Central Finance, in contrast, replicates financial transactions into a separate SAP S/4HANA-based central system for finance reporting and transaction execution and creates an abstraction layer, as shown in Figure 3.4, which is a layer between the central system and the source systems running on legacy technologies.

Where the original financial transactions are created and where they are used for reporting and further process execution is now separate; the legacy system is no longer preventing innovation.

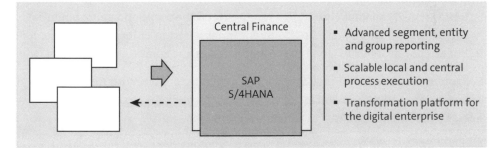

Figure 3.4 Central Finance as Side Car/Abstraction Layer

Innovation acceleration in the context of Central Finance generally includes pursuing innovation, hastening innovation, and the speed and frequency for delivering innovations, as we'll discuss in the following sections.

3.2.1   Pressure to Innovate

Choosing SAP S/4HANA-based Central Finance allows you to bring its innovations into your organizations, without disruption, without dependencies, and without impacting your ERP source system landscape. The pressure to innovate in the context of Central Finance can be influenced by several factors, as follows:

- **Shift of processes**
  Users of local finance processes in source systems can now execute these processes in a streamlined, centralized, automated manner in the Central Finance system, no matter the source system technology (SAP ERP or non-SAP ERP) in which the finance process was originally executed.

- **Nondisruptive**
  No changes to the source systems are required; financial transactions can continue to be created in the source systems as usual and are replicated into the Central Finance system automatically.

- **Business model-agnostic**
  Financial transactions can be mapped but are mapped in the target system once and only once, rather than in various interfaces, to accommodate the different business models of the underlying source systems in Central Finance.

- **Iterative and milestone-based**
  Central Finance can be rolled out in milestone-based, typically quarterly, intervals, sequenced by priority, providing value with each release.

- **Cloud-connected**
  SAP S/4HANA's digital core allows you to extend the scope and value potential of the Central Finance system, not only for innovations in enterprise management but also innovations in cloud-based technologies and solutions.

Economic pressure in the digital economy mandates action. With Central Finance, organizations can take advantage of various new technologies to improve their businesses in a standardized way, as shown in Figure 3.5.

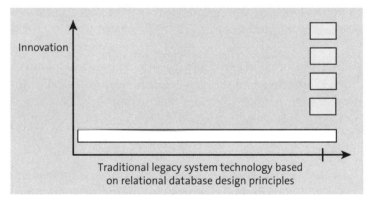

Figure 3.5 Innovation in a Central Finance Scenario

3.2.2   Earlier Innovation

Choosing SAP S/4HANA-based Central Finance allows you to bring innovations into your organizations earlier than with other approaches.

With Central Finance, you can introduce innovation independent of changes to the underlying SAP and non-SAP ERP source systems. You don't have to wait because you're not dependent on the ability to introduce changes into the source systems to bring them into your organization. You can hasten innovation adoption at these points:

- Earlier than provisioning an existing ERP source system, even more if non-SAP ERP source systems might require reimplementation
- Earlier than a migration to SAP S/4HANA, especially if many ERP source systems are involved and the last system upgrade was years ago
- Earlier than the provision of a central system for finance by traditional means, that is, using custom project integration of system today in a typical buy-versus-build decision

Local processes executed in source ERP systems can be moved to Central Finance without any changes to or migrations of the ERP source systems—as soon as Central Finance instance is up and running. Central processes can be implemented, potentially optimized by shared services, and possibly automated immediately in Central Finance.

Benefits can be realized more quickly, as shown in Figure 3.6, and are more valuable in a modern SAP S/4HANA-based Central Finance system rather than an outdated legacy system with its functional and technical limitations.

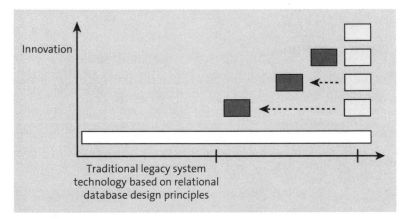

Figure 3.6 Accelerating ROI with Central Finance

From an opportunity cost perspective, the option to realize benefits for finance earlier will reduce the overall cash outlay and increase profits.

3.2.3   Faster Cycles, Faster Adoption

Choosing SAP S/4HANA-based Central Finance allows you to benefit from the more frequent innovations releases in the overall SAP S/4HANA portfolio. Barriers today preventing the faster adoption of innovation include the following:

- Delivery cycles on the software provider's part
- Amount of customizing in an ERP system (brownfield)
- Upgrade readiness, such as availability/capacity of resources
- System and organizational readiness, including time windows for upgrades
- Scope, including the amount of testing/validation effort required

Central Finance inherits new innovations from its underlying SAP S/4HANA portfolio, which is updated frequently, especially with the connected SAP S/4HANA Cloud portfolio.

With Central Finance, the scope of retesting is limited to finance and, when implemented properly, requires little or no customization that would otherwise add to validation efforts. Installed as separate system, the dependencies typically found in legacy source systems, like nonfinancial resources, evaluation and testing of new nonfinancial scope items, or nonfinancial time window restrictions, no longer exist.

New innovations can leveraged faster and increase the overall business value of Central Finance.

3.3   Process Transformation

Central Finance allows for enterprise-wide process transformation by accommodating the redesign and optimization of process flows and execution.

> **Note**
> For more information on transforming your organization using Central Finance as the catalyst, see Chapter 13 and Chapter 14.

Process transformation in the context of Central Finance includes aspects of standardization, rationalization, centralization, and automation, as follows:

- **Standardization**

  Reporting and process execution can be standardized in Central Finance, as follows:

  - Unified reporting, data, measures: Performance management is easier and more meaningful because it is based on the single source of truth, the trusted set of harmonized enterprise-wide and cross-system financial data found in the single Universal Journal. In other words, everyone looks at the same number, the same way.

  - Same-way, single-way processes: Process execution is consistent, involving one way to process and one system to process in, across the organization.

  - Transparency and quality: Process execution is consistent and comparable via key performance indicators (KPIs) and benchmarking across the organization to determine the single best way to run and execute the process.

- **Rationalization**

  Reporting and process execution can be rationalized in Central Finance, as follows:

  - Better, redesigned processes: The option to rethink process execution based on new business models including centralization and on new technologies, including automation, allows you to streamline future process execution.

  - Faster processes: With many process steps now executable in SAP Fiori, process execution time will be reduced because of the optimized-for-productivity design principles behind SAP Fiori apps.

- **Centralization**

  Reporting and process execution can be centralized in Central Finance, that is, processed once for everyone like in a central payment run or a management allocation, thus negating the need for redundant activities in the different ERP source systems across the organization.

  A special aspect of central process execution are shared services, the execution of finance processes by a dedicated group of people (subject to a service level agreement) for the organization at large or selected regions or business area.

  While organizational and location-specific arrangements (where people physically work and what organization pays them) are entirely separate from Central Finance. How and where these processes are executed is very much relevant to Central Finance.

  Central Finance provides for shared service-based process execution in the process transaction/execution layer. Central Finance also allows for process orchestration, task initiation, task checklists, task documentation, and status/completion updates via its embedded shared services capabilities, allowing economies of scale principles drive the new finance process design and execution.

- **Automation**
  Reporting and process execution can be automated in Central Finance, and the system can take over selected tasks via robotic process automation (RPA) and machine learning.

  Process execution can be turned over to the system where activities are repeatable based on specified business rules (RPA) or where algorithms allow the system to propose or even execute selected processes (machine learning), thus eliminating non-value-adding human interaction.

  Reporting and process execution can also be automated in Central Finance so the system can better identify exceptions.

  Central Finance provides capabilities for defining business queries, scheduling them to run at intervals or continuously, and letting the machine prompt for human interaction based on predefined thresholds rather than requiring continuous manual monitoring and screening.

  Central Finance allows you to move decentralized and distributed finance process execution from traditional legacy system-based multi-ERP landscapes to centralized process execution—with or without shared services—and potentially even automate these processes outright in Central Finance.

3.4   Business Model Evolution

Central Finance allows an organization to continuously evolve its business model, including these considerations:

- Enterprise optimization
- Business model changes
- Mergers and acquisitions (M&A)
- Divestitures

Central Finance provides a consistent and coherent framework to support your organization with various initiatives and growth over time.

> **Note**
>
> For more information on mergers and acquisitions with Central Finance, see Chapter 11.

3.4.1   Enterprise Optimization

Central Finance supports enterprise optimization initiatives by providing the following capabilities enterprise-wide and cross-system:

- **Benchmarking information**
  This information is provided via standardized real-time KPIs and harmonized functional and financial reporting—based on a set of harmonized financial data that serves as a single source of truth.

- **Modeling and simulation capabilities**
  These capabilities are available in the embedded business planning applications, for example, SAP BPC, SAP Predictive Analytics, or SAP Financial Statement Insights, a cloud-based SAP app focused on modeling and simulation of organizational changes.

- **Central process execution capabilities**
  These capabilities allow you to leverage economies of scale and scope as well as automation across the organizations.

3.4.2   Business Model Changes

Central Finance supports business model changes by simplifying the ERP system landscape and providing access points to make finance-related changes.

With opportunities for growth exhausted from a global and market (customer) perspective, the current growth focus is on innovation acquisition—products, services, and capabilities that the organization does not yet possess but the digital economy offers or demands.

Being able to integrate such capabilities is more complex than adding new countries to an already existing regional footprint or adding new customers to an existing customer base. Adding these capabilities requires a simplified system landscape so you can swiftly set up and integrate new processes that work.

With the introduction of Central Finance as an abstraction layer, a layer between the source ERP system and the Central Finance system, business model changes can be introduced earlier and easier.

3.4.3   Mergers and Acquisitions

Easily the most important aspect of Central Finance, Central Finance allows you to bring together financial data from different ERP source systems for advanced reporting and central process execution.

Without preceding M&A activities, a larger number of source ERP systems would not exist within the organization to begin with. And the fact that they are still around means mergers and acquisitions were executed from a people, location, and sales perspective integration—yet system, application and process integration is yet outstanding.

Central Finance helps with the last mile of post-merger integration—the integration and optimization of data, systems, application, and process execution.

Central Finance supports (new) mergers and acquisitions by providing a platform and a playbook for onboarding new entities and systems—a fast tracked available at any time.

New entities and systems for Central Finance are no different than any other ERP source systems. New entities can be treated just like any other source system added to the already existing platform with advanced reporting and central process execution capabilities.

Where companies are repeat or serial acquirers, the onboarding project plan and work activity list can be developed into a repeatable playbook. This playbook allows you to improve quality by applying lessons learned and improvements after every revision. You can also use the playbook to move execution work from external consultants to in-house resources and potentially even outsource the process—make it faster, better, cheaper.

3.4.4   Divestitures

Central Finance enables both enterprise optimization initiatives like the permanent physical separation of source systems to provide increased local agility as well as business portfolio initiatives like a temporary separation in preparation for divestiture.

Central Finance can also support bringing back together physically separated ERP source systems (system splits or carve-outs) for advanced reporting and scalable process execution in the central system.

3.5 Technology Transformation

Central Finance provides a natural path to technology rationalization, consolidation, and modernization in your organization in the following ways:

- **Information aggregation**
  Bringing data and information together cross-system and storing it once in Central Finance, which can be exposed to and consumed directly by end users without further replication.

- **System rationalization**
  Consolidating source ERP systems and finance applications and running them in one system only or at least reducing the overall number of ERP systems and applications involved.

- **Application consolidation**
  Consolidating complementary finance application capabilities and running them as integrated solution in one system only.

- **Platform transition**
  Supporting the move from on-premise only to hybrid or cloud scenarios.

Technology transformation in the context of Central Finance includes aspects of rationalization, consolidation, and cloud transition, as we'll see in the following sections.

> **Note**
> For more information on transforming your organization using Central Finance as the catalyst, see Chapter 13 and Chapter 14.

3.5.1 Rationalization

Central Finance can help reduce the number of ERP systems and finance applications installed in the organization, as shown in Figure 3.7. Most important, Central Finance can help reduce the number of ERP source systems, which can be brought into/migrated to the Central Finance instance (see Chapter 12).

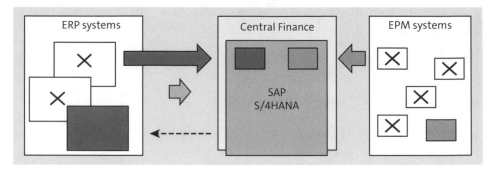

Figure 3.7 ERP System and Finance Application Rationalization

Central Finance can also help reduce the number of redundant finance applications installed. While typically only one application for group consolidation has been installed, numerous separate, nonintegrated applications for business planning and analytics may be present.

3.5.2   Consolidation

Central Finance can help consolidate complementary finance capabilities and run them as an integrated solution in a single system.

In Central Finance, the following capabilities can be installed and run in the same technical stack as Central Finance:

- Business planning (using embedded SAP BPC)
- Consolidation/group reporting (using embedded SAP BPC or SAP S/4HANA Finance for group reporting)
- Business analytics (using SAP Fiori or Microsoft Excel as the frontend)
- Shared services (no longer requiring a separate SAP Customer Relationship Management [CRM] installation)

These capabilities are now embedded or connected to the core SAP S/4HANA stack underlying Central Finance and no longer require interfaces for data integrations between the Central Finance system and the respective application.

For business planning and group reporting, as a result, shared master data, direct access to real-time actual data, the recording of calculated or manually entered consolidation or plan data back into data into the SAP HANA database financial transactions are recorded in Central Finance. Thus, real-time reporting is available without the need for any additional data extraction and replication. Rather than having separate technical installations of the different capabilities, in Central Finance, they can all run on the same stack.

3.5.3   Cloud Transition

The trend to move platforms and applications to the cloud, with initial concerns about data reliability, service level, and data security cannot be reversed. For most organizations, running systems and applications is simply not their core business, and besides, these processes might be already outsourced.

Where free to choose, that is, with country, industry, or regulatory limitations aside, the economic advantage, from a cost perspective, of transitioning to the cloud is substantial and growing each day. Additionally, the shift to the cloud, especially with subscription billing for cloud-based products, changes from a capital expenditure (CapEx) to an operating expense (OpEx).

But what's important is not only costs—it's also organizational agility and scalability. Buying and selling entities and capabilities are common activities today, and changing business models might mean a substantially different service level required now (i.e., in terms of database size, data volume, transaction throughput, regional availability, etc.) than in the future.

Transitioning to the cloud in the context of Central Finance includes aspects like running Central Finance in the cloud, related components running in the cloud, complementary finance functions running in the cloud, and/or ERP systems (already running or migrating to the cloud):

- Central Finance can run in the cloud: For those open to or driven by economic factors, Central Finance can run in either a private or hosted cloud.
- Core functional components can run in the cloud: Business planning, group consolidation and analytics, and several finance operations have specific SAP cloud apps available.
- Complementary finance functions can run in the cloud: Cloud-based business network capabilities, such as SAP Ariba for indirect procurement, Concur for expense management, or SAP Hybris for omnichannel and product content management, can be adopted and natively integrated through standard cloud connectors with Central Finance.
- ERP source systems can run in the cloud: SAP S/4HANA Cloud systems running parts of your business in the cloud can be integrated with Central Finance (on-premise or in a private or hosted cloud) through standard integration mechanisms.

3.6   SAP S/4HANA Adoption

Central Finance allows you to bring SAP S/4HANA into your organization no matter what your existing, perhaps heterogeneous, SAP ERP and non-SAP ERP system landscape looks like. Once you understand the benefits and value potential of SAP S/4HANA in the ERP marketplace, Central Finance can answer how and when to adopt and roll out SAP S/4HANA. For more details regarding using Central Finance as a stepping stone to SAP S/4HANA, see Chapter 12. In this section, we'll specifically look at motivation to adopt Central Finance on your way to SAP S/4HANA but not technical steps in this process.

Considerations of SAP S/4HANA adoption in the context of Central Finance include the continued evolution of such SAP S/4HANA system over time, the growing value of it compared to the (more static) ERP source systems, and its deployment option as lower-risk adoption scenario.

3.6.1   Continued Evolution

Choosing SAP S/4HANA-based Central Finance allows you to benefit from the continued provision of innovations in the overall SAP S/4HANA portfolio. Central Finance is based on SAP S/4HANA, and new innovations are no longer constraint by traditional ERP technologies. While some innovations are downported to the traditional ERP level, many are not because the underlying legacy system technology just does not allow for that.

The longer you wait with SAP S/4HANA adoption for finance, the larger the gap will be the between capabilities offered by and business value achievable with Central Finance and the capabilities and business value implemented and available to the users in your organization.

A decision for Central Finance is not only a point-in-time decision based on the functions, features, and value propositions available at the time of the decision. You should also consider planned and future roadmap items that will become available but are not accessible without a Central Finance approach.

3.6.2   Side Car Adoption

Central Finance is the best way to bring SAP S/4HANA's finance innovations holistically into your organization in an accelerated and nondisruptive way. Central Finance allows for SAP S/4HANA adoption via the "side car" concept, as shown in

Figure 3.8. In this approach, a central SAP S/4HANA system is established and integrated with ERP source systems via real-time data replication.

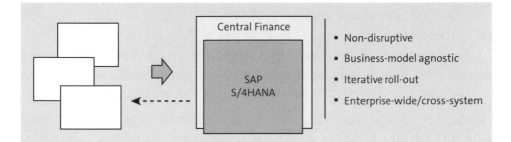

Figure 3.8 Central Finance as a Side Car

Using Central Finance as a side car implementation for your future adoption of SAP S/4HANA provides the following benefits:

- **Nondisruptive**
  Changes are not required to the ERP source systems, and Central Finance does not impact source system, whether SAP or non-SAP.

- **Separated from logistics**
  You can adopt SAP S/4HANA for finance without concern for your organization's logistics readiness (or lack thereof).

- **Business model-agnostic**
  Source ERP systems can be either brownfield or greenfield systems from a customizing and master data perspective; if the source system is a brownfield system, it can be mapped to a greenfield system.

- **Iterative**
  Source systems to be integrated (and their business processes) can be rolled out iteratively, that is, prioritized and sequenced based on your organization's business priorities. In contrast, a typical ERP rollout following a big bag approach requires large teams for several quarters, and value won't be realized until the overall project is released.

- **Time-to-value**
  The iterative rollout option allows for milestone-based (usually quarterly) releases of new functionalities to new users, thus providing a consistent stream of realized value to your organization.

- **Transformation**
  Deploying Central Finance allows you to redefine the system setup, the master data, and the process execution for finance in the central system, a "finance first" step in your overall business transformation.

- **Enterprise-wide**
  You'll get improved local finance capabilities (where the process shifts from local to central system) and enterprise-wide cross-system reporting and transaction processing for finance.

Rolling out SAP S/4HANA via the Central Finance approach allows you to limit exposure and risk while providing value to the organization. You'll also be able to adopt the underlying technologies like SAP HANA, SAP Fiori, and the SAP Cloud Platform in a parallel system first rather than immediately jumping to using a productive logistics and finance system of record. Thus, you'll develop the in-house skills required to run those later in SAP S/4HANA as well.

Unlike all-encompassing reimplementation or migration efforts, in terms of scope, only finance is involved and not logistics. As a result, the project will be smaller and less complex, and the project team will be smaller too because rollout is iterative with smaller teams in a more agile fashion.

Implementing Central Finance in a side car scenario can be a catalyst for a larger finance and business transformation. Finance can be at the forefront, the beachhead that helps develop the organizational mindset and readiness necessary for discussing process transformation at large. Many deliverables created or lessons learned from implementing Central Finance, like the mechanisms, development, and rollout of virtual reporting, can be applied and leveraged beyond finance and into logistics in source systems.

3.7 Summary

In this chapter, we provided information about the motivations behind adopting Central Finance, the why of Central Finance. We discussed how Central Finance accelerates the nondisruptive adoption of innovations and supports business model evolution and technology transformation. We also explored how the technology Central Finance uses removes many barriers that once applied to traditional legacy systems.

In the next chapter, we'll provide information about the advanced reporting and analytics capabilities available in Central Finance.

Chapter 4

Reporting: What Can I Learn About My Data?

With Central Finance, data resides in one central, accessible place and is standardized, harmonized, and enriched, without further steps needing to be taken for embedded capabilities for segment, entity, or group reporting.

Reporting is a key value driver of Central Finance. Unlike in traditional ERP systems, with Central Finance, you are no longer tied to old legacy system technologies and outdated database design principles. What was formerly the only way you could do something is no longer is the best way to do it.

With modern SAP S/4HANA technologies, you can provide enterprise-wide, cross-system reporting and analytics based on a single source of truth for financial data on the transaction level—without further data movements and in real time, without any delay in access. You can do things differently (and better) and do things previously not possible.

In this chapter, we'll explain the how implementing Central Finance enables improved reporting and analytics information. You'll learn about how new SAP S/4HANA technologies provide for far more advanced reporting and analytics capabilities, how data model innovations allow for more enriched reporting, and how enterprise-wide and cross-system entity and group reporting is improved, all within the same technology stack.

4.1 Advanced Reporting

Reporting in Central Finance might seem advanced when compared to reporting in a traditional central ERP system for finance, in a single traditional SAP system, or in a non-SAP ERP system. For example, Central Finance performs the following functions:

- Allows you to use the latest innovative reporting and analytics capabilities, regardless of the source system technologies in place
- Goes beyond reporting, providing SAP Fiori apps with integrated process execution capabilities
- Leverages database and application architecture innovations like the Universal Journal to allow for unified, end-to-end reporting out of the box without the need for manual data unification by IT

Reporting in Central Finance is oriented towards the business user and provides real-time insights, advanced analytics, and contextual information, when possible, visually. Examples of advanced reporting in Central Finance include the following:

- Line item access
- Unified reporting
- Multidimensional reporting
- Microsoft Excel analysis
- Root cause analysis
- Embedded reporting
- Key performance indicator (KPI) reporting
- Predictive reporting
- Problem solving reporting

4.1.1   Line Item Access

Reporting in Central Finance allows access to line item-level financial information. With performance no longer an issue, selections can be wide. You'll no longer need restrictions in data selection to avoid runtime errors.

Data exploration can be a bottom-up process, starting with the maximum dataset, rather than parsing out various datasets to accommodate resource limits and avoid runtime errors. Results can include all fields/dimensions in the Central Finance coding block (Universal Journal), including business mapping values, which are stored and served in advance, like old account, profit center, or vendor numbers.

The Line Item Browser, shown in Figure 4.1, can now display this lowest level of transactional information no matter the selection criteria, how many records are involved, or how many fields will be displayed.

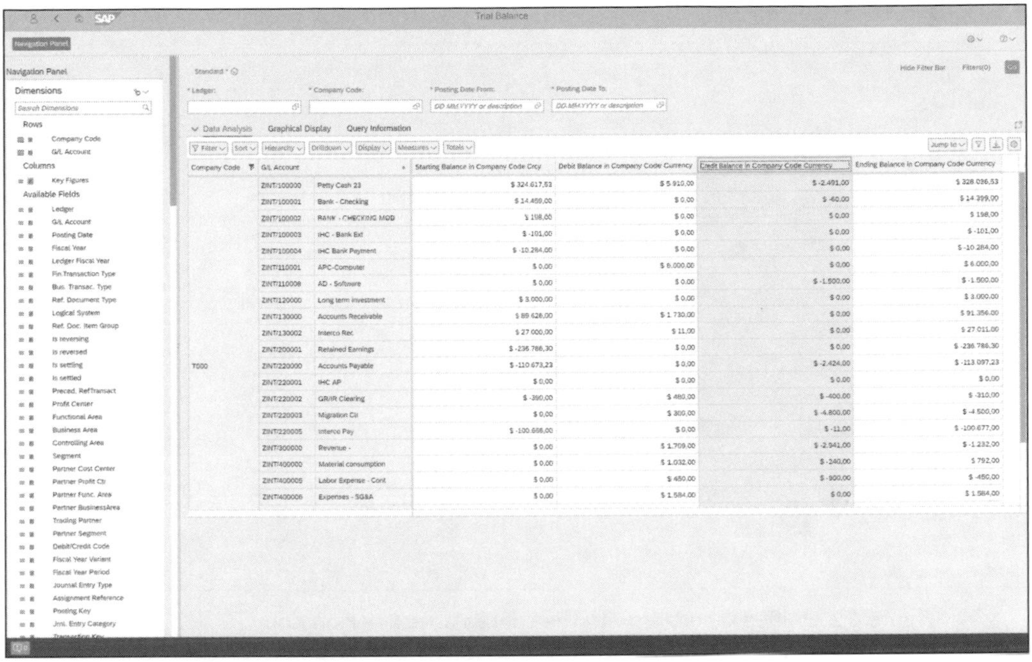

Figure 4.1 SAP Customer Line Item Browser SAP Fiori App

4.1.2   Universal Reporting

Reporting in Central Finance allows access to all dimensions within the Central Finance coding block, including the following:

- All standard financial dimensions across the main ledger and subledgers
- Custom dimensions, like the color of a product or the age of a customer
- Pertinent source system information, such as system IDs and document numbers

Basically, all 355+ dimensions of the financial coding block in Central Finance can be accessed (for filtering, sorting, etc.). For example, using the Trial Balance SAP Fiori app, as shown in Figure 4.2, you can select from dimensions in the coding block and add them to the data analysis section as needed.

Of course, standard SAP security capabilities govern access to this information.

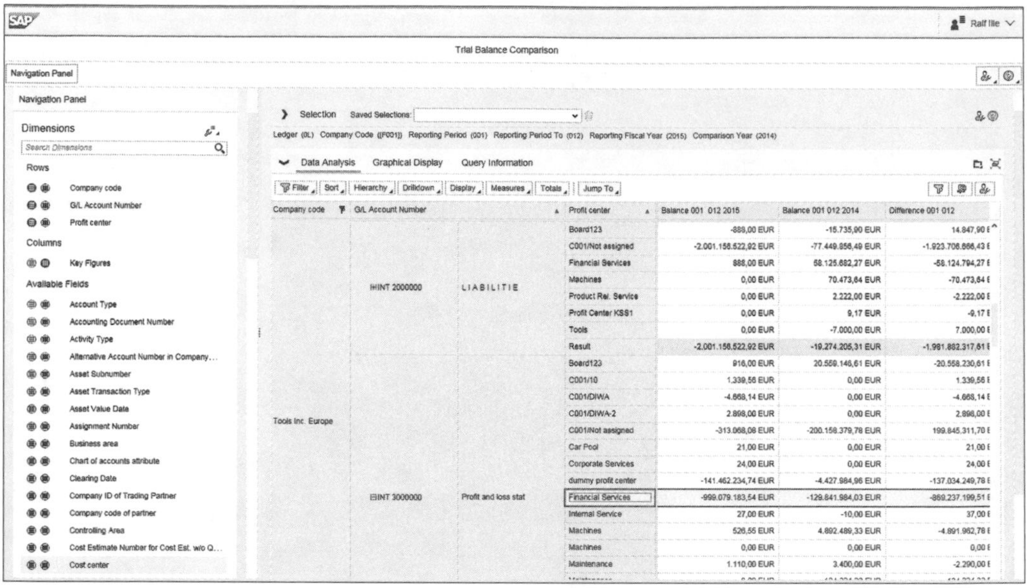

Figure 4.2 Unified Reporting with the Trial Balance SAP Fiori App

Reporting in Central Finance allows access to financial information, no matter what subledger might have previously stored that information. With the unified coding block in Central Finance (Universal Journal), all financial transactions are stored in the same table. It is no longer required to jump from report to report or reenter selection criteria so that the balance in the general ledger (G/L) report matches the balance for the selection in a subledger report. Especially when reporting is used for validating reconciliation accounts—e.g., for vendor details behind an accounts payable (AP) balance, for customer details behind an accounts receivable (AR) balance, for inventory details behind an materials management balance—the need to use different reports in different subledgers, which was inefficient, is no longer required.

Reporting in Central Finance allows you access to financial data from a top-level overview down to the line item level, the transaction. Account balances can be easily traced via drilldown capabilities to view the transactions and line items making up that balance.

Especially when using reporting to explore exceptions, the need to run different reports for data residing in different applications or tables, which was inefficient, no longer exists.

4.1.3   Multidimensional Reporting

Reporting in Central Finance allows you to explore transactional financial information in Central Finance in an analytical fashion.

As shown in Figure 4.3, you can navigate and explore the entire financial dataset of your organization (or just specific portions) using the concept of facets instead of a transactional or line item view.

Figure 4.3 Multidimensional Reporting with SAP BusinessObjects Explorer

Facets are dynamic dimensional filters that allow users to select and group the overall dataset by the dimensions desired (like company code, product, customer, channel), thus finding more specific information within a potentially quite large dataset.

The option to navigate, explore, and search real-time transactional data by (all its) captured key financial dimensions (standard coding block dimensions, added custom dimensions, source and target system business values) allows you to drill down into the details (microsegments) and understand the real reasons and drivers of financial performance.

4.1.4   Microsoft Excel Analysis

Reporting in Central Finance allows you to use Microsoft Excel as the analytical tool to create financial analyses.

Almost every financial analyst uses Excel. However, often a series of data preparation steps is required before the data can be analyzed. Usually, data must be extracted from somewhere, often from multiple sources; merged with customizing data (period 3 = "March") and master data (customer 1789 = "Mike Miller"); and then use VLOOKUPs and custom macros to prepare the data.

This whole process likely is repeated as new transactions come in as part of period-end closings or within reporting timeframes.

With SAP Analysis for Microsoft Office as part of Central Finance, the data preparation phase is basically eliminated, and you can jump right into data analysis:

- Financial data can be accessed directly via Excel and already incorporates key customizing and master data elements.
- Financial data in Central Finance is already harmonized, standardized, and enriched, negating the need for additional transformations.
- New transaction postings can be included anytime.

Instead of opening a file on a network drive, with the corresponding SAP login and access validation, users will now access views of the Universal Journal.

You can select from all 355+ dimensions defined in the coding block, including standard dimensions, added custom dimensions, and old/transitional source system values. You also determine which dimensions to use as filters in row or columns, and you can have your financial data presented as a pivot table.

If new transactions are available, as part of month-end closing, for example, you can refresh the view in Excel, and the latest dataset will be loaded instantaneously—no need to wait for a data warehouse replication run that may only happen every 4 hours.

4.1.5   Root Cause Analysis and Storytelling

Reporting in Central Finance allows for ad-hoc root cause analysis from a top-level overview, i.e., for upper management or team leaders, down to the underlying business transactions that make up the financial performance. Management discussions, say, to determine an action or a change in course, can be based on facts—that is, based on a financial dataset that serves as a harmonized, real-time single source of truth—and include contextual information from the underlying business transactions.

Leadership teams across the organization—including team leaders, middle management, senior managers, executives, and senior executives, all the way up to the board, can, all with their own views of the "same" financial data—can use visual exploration capabilities, based on predetermined tiles with drilldown capabilities, to more fully understand the company's financial performance and its root causes.

Different aspects of a performance review can be combined into sets of tiles on, for example, the SAP Digital Boardroom or SAP Analytics Cloud, as shown in Figure 4.4, leading to a more visual and connected storytelling analysis rather than a traditional presentation that requires jumping from spreadsheet to spreadsheet.

Figure 4.4 Storytelling with SAP Analytics Cloud

4.1.6   Embedded

Reporting in Central Finance also allows you to use SAP S/4HANA's embedded analytics.

Embedded analytics in SAP S/4HANA allows you to switch between complex, visual, and facet filters and facilitates navigation to specific SAP Fiori apps that are semantically linked to the data.

The Product Profitability SAP Fiori app, for example, allows you to analyze product-related KPIs in a contribution margin structure with multiple dimensions. From the Product Profitability SAP Fiori app, as shown in Figure 4.5, you can navigate to the Actual/Plan P/L SAP Fiori app.

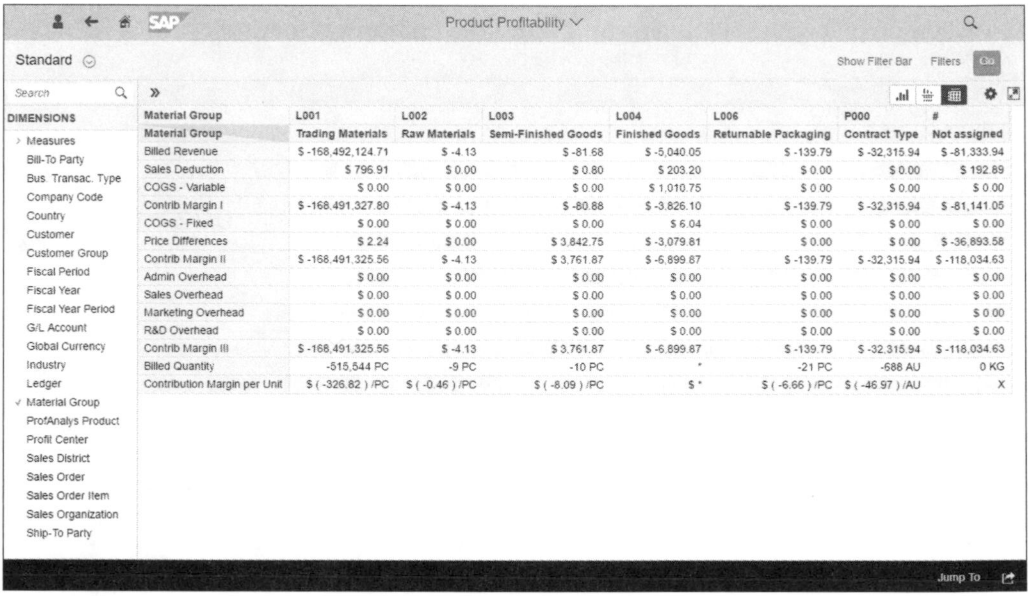

Material Group	L001	L002	L003	L004	L006	P000	#
Material Group	Trading Materials	Raw Materials	Semi-Finished Goods	Finished Goods	Returnable Packaging	Contract Type	Not assigned
Billed Revenue	$ -168,492,124.71	$ -4.13	$ -81.68	$ -5,040.05	$ -139.79	$ -32,315.94	$ -81,333.94
Sales Deduction	$ 796.91	$ 0.00	$ 0.80	$ 203.20	$ 0.00	$ 0.00	$ 192.89
COGS - Variable	$ 0.00	$ 0.00	$ 0.00	$ 1,010.75	$ 0.00	$ 0.00	$ 0.00
Contrib Margin I	$ -168,491,327.80	$ -4.13	$ -80.88	$ -3,826.10	$ -139.79	$ -32,315.94	$ -81,141.05
COGS - Fixed	$ 0.00	$ 0.00	$ 0.00	$ 6.04	$ 0.00	$ 0.00	$ 0.00
Price Differences	$ 2.24	$ 0.00	$ 3,842.75	$ -3,079.81	$ 0.00	$ 0.00	$ -36,893.58
Contrib Margin II	$ -168,491,325.56	$ -4.13	$ 3,761.87	$ -6,899.87	$ -139.79	$ -32,315.94	$ -118,034.63
Admin Overhead	$ 0.00	$ 0.00	$ 0.00	$ 0.00	$ 0.00	$ 0.00	$ 0.00
Sales Overhead	$ 0.00	$ 0.00	$ 0.00	$ 0.00	$ 0.00	$ 0.00	$ 0.00
Marketing Overhead	$ 0.00	$ 0.00	$ 0.00	$ 0.00	$ 0.00	$ 0.00	$ 0.00
R&D Overhead	$ 0.00	$ 0.00	$ 0.00	$ 0.00	$ 0.00	$ 0.00	$ 0.00
Contrib Margin III	$ -168,491,325.56	$ -4.13	$ 3,761.87	$ -6,899.87	$ -139.79	$ -32,315.94	$ -118,034.63
Billed Quantity	-515,544 PC	-9 PC	-10 PC	*	-21 PC	-688 AU	0 KG
Contribution Margin per Unit	$ (-326.82) /PC	$ (-0.46) /PC	$ (-8.09) /PC	$ *	$ (-6.66) /PC	$ (-46.97) /AU	X

Figure 4.5 Product Profitability SAP Fiori App

The Supervise Collections Worklist app allows you to monitor the status of groups, teams, and collection specialists; allocate and reassign worklist items; assign groups to collection segments; and assign collection specialists and temporary substitutes. From the Supervise Collections Worklist app, as, you can also navigate to the Process Receivables app.

4.1.7 Real-Time KPIs

Reporting in Central Finance provides real-time KPI reporting. The financial status of your organization and its entities, business units, market segments, and departments can be monitored in Central Finance much like a stock ticker tracks publicly traded companies. Predefined, customizable KPI tiles can be included in the SAP Fiori launchpad, as shown in Figure 4.6.

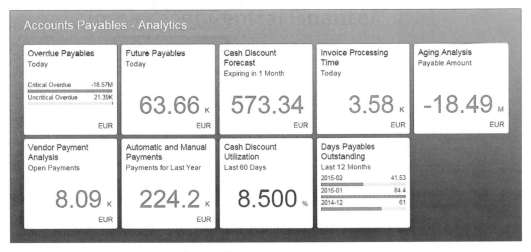

Figure 4.6 Real-Time KPI Tiles in the SAP Fiori Launchpad

These tiles provide real-time financial status information—quantitative and qualitative—with drilldown capabilities to view the underlying source data. These tiles can be personalized, that is, thresholds can be maintained, and selection criteria saved, to only show the KPI relevant to a particular business area.

KPI tiles can be modified to adjust the drilldown and appearance. Appearance is important because not every financial status translates perfectly into information that is just a number.

4.1.8   Predictive Reporting

Reporting in Central Finance allows you to use forward-looking, predictive data calculated by business users rather than data scientists.

You can use predictive algorithms and machine learning to calculate and visualize trends and forecasts or predict the likelihood of future outcomes, as shown in Figure 4.7.

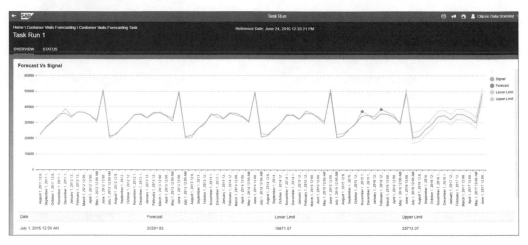

Figure 4.7 SAP Predictive Analytics

You can quickly build and visualize predictive models, such as the one shown later in Figure 4.9, and also access a wide variety of machine learning algorithms—no coding required. You can join internal and external data like demographics; you can score data and apply predictive models as soon as events occur and even embed predictive results into business processes.

4.1.9   Problem Solving Solutions

Reporting can also include purpose-built solutions available in the cloud on the software as a service (SaaS) model. In many cases, these solutions simply require you enable the standard SAP Cloud Connector for data provision. Two solutions that may be useful to you include the following:

- **SAP RealSpend**
  With SAP RealSpend, shown in Figure 4.8, you can gain better insights into budget and spending information via ad-hoc analysis of real-time spending information, combined with flexible tagging, to enable new reporting dimensions on the fly, to add future expenses to the dataset, and to use dynamic replanning capabilities.

- **SAP Financial Statement Insights**
  With SAP Financial Statement Insights, shown in Figure 4.9, you can discover hidden trends and make strategic decisions through real-time analysis of your profit and loss (P&L) statement. The solution includes the ability to simulate organizational changes to compare potential business performance across different divisions, products, and organizational units and drivers over time.

Figure 4.8 SAP RealSpend

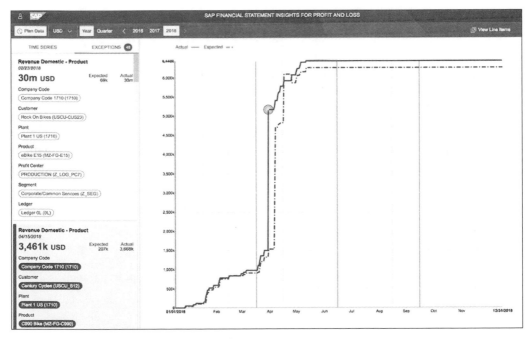

Figure 4.9 SAP Financial Statements Insights

4.2   Extended Dimensional Reporting

A key differentiator of Central Finance is its ability to provide enhanced dimensionality in reporting and analysis. Traditional central systems for finance, often with a static coding block focused on external financial accounting, may provide rudimentary business segment reporting to accommodate external financial and internal management reporting (i.e., balance sheets and P&L statements).

Analysis (depth, dimensionality, line item detail) can be limited in these traditional systems. Analysis may take place in upstream systems, for example, billing systems, and then be parsed for specific uses, like revenue analysis, or in specific systems (business intelligence/business warehouse systems for profitability reporting, for example), and this analysis may accommodate multidimensional reporting and larger data volumes without impacting reporting performance or the performance of the underlying (transaction-processing) system.

Reporting in Central Finance is based on the speed and performance of the underlying SAP HANA in-memory database. Workarounds like data parsing, abbreviation, normalizing, and spreading data across different reporting systems is no longer required to avoid the performance and throughput issues of the past.

Central Finance, for example, leverages the ability to add additional fields to the coding block and stores the <source system ID> and the <source document number> to provide an audit trial (drilldown) to the finance and logistics business transactions in the underlying SAP source systems. The dimensions you add will likely be based on the reporting or incentive systems already in place elsewhere in the organization.

The number of additional fields needed varies by company. While no real technical limitation of additional fields exists on the database level, pragmatically, you might consider a limit somewhere between 10 and 15 fields because you'll also need to fill them in, create reports with them, and spend time analyzing them.

Examples of extended dimensional reporting in Central Finance include:

- Microsegment profitability
- Cross-organizational attribute reporting (functional reporting)
- Business continuity reporting (new and old dimensions kept in parallel)

4.2.1   Microsegment Profitability

The ability to provide microsegment profitability reporting is a key innovation in Central Finance.

Many organizations have fairly detailed profitability reporting in place already. For those using SAP ERP systems, profitability reporting is generally provided by Profitability Analysis (CO-PA); in selected cases, additional SAP solutions might exist, for example, for the financial services or retail industries. Others companies might simply use custom data warehouse solutions.

In any case, profitability reporting is an integral part of financial analysis, but the core financial data may reside in separate datasets or applications. This scenario can be costly due to the additional data duplication effort required and runs the risk that the data is not detailed enough, lacking line item or dimensional detail.

Looking at financial performance only on an entity or business segment level, without the right level of business transaction detail and dimensionality, may prevent a full understanding of the drivers of profitability, which are necessary for proper business management, because aggregates and averages dilute profitability information.

Microsegment profitability, based on entity, line of business, product, customer, region, channel, etc., can help you run your business today. Along these reporting dimensions, you'll see organizational responsibilities defined and incentive systems in place.

The level of detail in your microsegments (combinations of dimensionality) varies. More and more, in the digital economy, additional attributes in a business transaction seem necessary to capture, such as the weather at the time of a transaction, the relation between a product sold and a customer's rating of your website, or a customer's payment history. These attributes may be not directly needed for profitability calculations on an attribute level (for example, associating the IT cost of collecting customer ratings for products) but could still serve as additional, contextual information to identify trends, strengths, and weaknesses, which are vital in sentiment analysis.

In Central Finance, profitability can be reported and analyzed on a detailed microsegment and attribute level for every dimension you decide to include in the Universal Journal-based coding block.

Revenue can be captured on any level you need, and costs can be brought in with additional detail as well. Through allocations and various other mechanisms in SAP S/4HANA, costs—captured on a much more detailed level—can be associated with revenue for extended microsegment and attribute profitability.

With Central Finance, you can analyze profitability information, an integral part of your financial analysis, without requiring data duplication and without compromising on dimensional or line item detail, latency, or performance.

So, how deep should you go, in terms of level of detail, and how broad, in terms of dimensionality?

You can't really control the number of records/line items replicated because the feeds come from the source systems. If those source systems capture financial transaction at a very low level, for example, a point of sale (POS) transaction in retail, then that's what you'll have to replicate. At this point, you might evaluate how you use the G/L (in the ERP source systems) and the level of information posted there and rethink how much is captured in the G/L versus enabled subsequently through reporting scenarios.

On the dimensional level, we recommend going further than you have been in two ways: First, you can and should bring in more dimensionality than previously, some of which you may use for information purposes only while others could be useful in real profitability calculations.

Second, we generally recommend using one level of detail lower than your organization has been using. To go to the lowest level of detail right away, for instance, the transaction level, is not advised. Don't forget that, with increased depth of detail and breadth of dimensionality, you'll need to establish organizational responsibilities and incentives; if not, you'll be providing information that no one looks at.

Whether including additional dimensions in the coding block is the right decision depends on several factors, including performance or the need to use these dimensions in derivations or allocations or in standard SAP Fiori reporting. An alternative to inclusion in the coding block would to use advanced reporting capabilities (i.e., joins or unions on a database or reporting level) or virtual consumption via SAP Data Hub or SAP Vora.

Some reasons for including addition dimensions via reporting include:

- Dimensions can be dynamic, like customer credit ratings
- Dimensions are subject to change over time, like when regional responsibilities are rolled up for internal management accounting, which may be better served with a reporting scenario. Bringing these dimensions into the reporting layer might also improve alignments after an organizational change.

4.2.2   Cross-Organizational Functional Reporting

Similar to the addition of dimensionality (for more detailed) microsegment profitability, additional dimensionality can also provide information on enterprise-wide, cross-organizational perspectives like functional reporting, as shown in Figure 4.10.

Instead of going deeper, down to the microsegment level, this kind of reporting focuses more on going wider, providing additional or alternative views of the enterprise. This reporting could involve any number of attributes, for example, including energy compliance, gender equality, or cybersecurity.

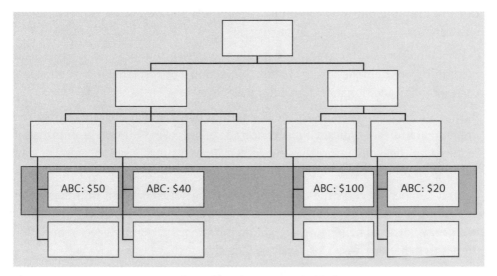

Figure 4.10 Cross-Organizational Functional Reporting (Wider)

Based on additional attributes, cross-organizational reporting is more about the organizational (structural) elements of an enterprise, which are tagged with certain attributes, rather than about reporting and analysis of underlying business transactions.

With underlying business transactions often executed in different ERP systems, additional cross-organizational reporting based on common attributes provides the additional benefit of allowing for harmonized, standardized perspectives, possibly to be used in benchmarking (Section 4.4.3).

4.2.3   Business Continuity Reporting

Just as you can add dimensionality to accommodate additional microsegment or cross-enterprise attribute reporting, additional dimensionality can be added to accommodate business transformations or change management, for example, in a Central Finance implementation project.

In traditional migrations, business users of the old systems usually loose information due to data harmonization and standardization. With Central Finance, the old dimensions can be preserved, recorded in the Universal Journal in Central Finance.

The old, local information can be kept in addition to (in parallel) to the new information, for example, old and new company codes, old and new profit centers, old and new vendors.

Central Finance uses, for example, data like <source system ID> and <source document number> from the source system/transaction and posts that information into corresponding additional fields in Central Finance.

Business users concerned about the disruptions of a planned migration or system implementation are typically most concerned about losing important information required for their jobs, rather than concerned about the data harmonization or standardization process per se.

Central Finance provides the option of preserving source system information, an important negotiating token from a change management perspective. Business users may not mind helping with the harmonization and standardization once they are assured that they won't lose what they need.

Note that additional dimensionality is not always automatically pulled into SAP Fiori apps or into business transactions, which is perfectly fine, because you ultimately want new transactions use new values anyway. From a reporting perspective, the inclusion of the old and new values by adjusting core data services (CDS) views is entirely feasible.

4.3   Entity Reporting

Entity reporting (i.e., balance sheet reporting, P&L statements, or cash flow statements for company codes or major business segments) or management accounting reporting (for cost centers, orders, projects, etc.) are important capabilities in Central Finance. Just because Central Finance typically contains financial information for more than one entity does not mean financial reporting can only be done on an aggregated, corporate level.

You can use Central Finance for both local entity reporting (through Central Finance instead of through the original source system) as well as on an aggregated level. Entity reporting with Central Finance is not just for corporate finance!

The value and benefit of entity reporting in Central Finance is directly linked to the business transactions replicated or recorded in Central Finance (Section 4.3.1) and also the state of the system of record, the Central Finance system (Section 4.3.2).

Entity reporting in Central Finance can also help align company codes by splitting or combining them in the central system rather than in the source systems (Section 4.3.3) or can help your organization pursue tax optimization scenarios, for example, setting foreign principal company codes in tax-friendly countries (Section 4.3.4).

4.3.1   Local Processes

All financial transactions posted in the source systems are replicated onto the central system, including regular business transactions that occur during the month, as well as period-end postings. Period-end postings can also be made in the central system itself.

In either case, with regular and period-end postings available in the central system now, local finance teams can run entity reporting processes in the central system instead of in the source system(s).

The advanced reporting capabilities available in Central Finance bring many benefits, such as advanced reporting capabilities (Section 4.1) and extended dimensionality (Section 4.2), features not available in the traditional SAP and non-SAP ERP source systems.

Furthermore, financial performance information can be harmonized using Central Finance's business mapping layer. Information can still be reviewed in terms of the old, local nomenclature in addition to in the new, enterprise-wide and cross-system standard.

4.3.2   System of Record

When no additional financial transactions are posted in Central Finance, the source system and the central system contain exactly the same transactions. From an entity reporting perspective, which system is the system of record does not matter. Even if you consider the source system the system of record, you can still use entity reporting in Central Finance.

Once financial transactions are posted in Central Finance, the tipping point typically is the use of central AP/AR processing. The central system now has more postings than the source systems and has basically become your system of record. Entity reporting through Central Finance uses the full set of transactions, whether locally posted in a source system, replicated to the central system, or centrally posted in the Central Finance system itself.

If you still want entity reporting enabled in the source systems, you'll need to ensure transactions created in the central system are propagated back to the source system(s).

In sum, regardless of which system is the system of record, you can use Central Finance for entity reporting.

4.3.3   Company Code Alignments

For most companies, entity reporting in Central Finance will be based, in a one-to-one relationship, on already existing entities set up in the source system. In some cases, these alignments might vary to accommodate the following:

- Appearance
- Company code merges
- Company code splits

In Central Finance, you can use a business mapping layer for purely cosmetic reasons; for example, perhaps you always wanted to use company code 1000, but source system used company code 47.

In Central Finance, you can merge multiple entities that exist in source systems into a single entity in the Central Finance system. Sometimes, different parts of various business entities are spread out over different ERP source systems (perhaps using different entity identifiers); in Central Finance, these entities can now be brought together.

In Central Finance, you can also use an enhanced business mapping layer to split an entity in the source system into different entities in the central system.

Both scenarios are rather exceptional. Where already accommodated in reporting or consolidation applications, they might as well be incorporated into the Central Finance design and rollout as well.

Both scenarios require proper diligence, especially when splitting company codes. Be sure to take into account the proper tagging of business transactions for intercompany processing and year-over-year balance sheet reporting needs as well as any potential backpropagation requirements.

4.3.4   Tax Optimization

Entity reporting in Central Finance can provide the opportunity for your organization to realize a tax optimization-oriented business model.

An entity set up as a foreign principal in a tax-friendly country can act as the contractual partner for a customer, carrying economic risk but also earning profit. Local entities set up as subsidiaries are reimbursed for their contributions based on concepts like cost-plus pricing or fixed markup fees or margins in accordance to local tax provisions.

Central Finance can easily set up and manage foreign principal companies, which will only need be created from a finance, not a logistics, perspective. In other words, organizational structures won't need to be customized; master data won't need to be provisioned because Central Finance is separated from the underlying source systems. Subsidiaries can execute business transactions in source systems, while aggregated reporting on the principal level can take place in Central Finance.

Neither Central Finance nor this book should be seen as encouraging or endorsing tax-optimization practices—any such action is entirely at the discretion of your business and should be subject to careful consideration, coordination with professional tax service providers, and alignment with the relevant tax and regulatory authorities.

However, for organizations pursuing this approach, Central Finance might be a good option.

4.4   Group Reporting

Central Finance provides group reporting capabilities using both preconsolidated and consolidated data, for example:

- Reporting for all entities making up the enterprise, no matter what source system captures their data (multientity reporting)
- Provision of financial information in a uniform, homogenous way (harmonized/standardized reporting)
- The ability to compare and evaluate performance across the organization (benchmarking)
- The ability to combine and financial data from several subsidiaries or business entities within an organization, for example, to a parent company, for reporting purposes (consolidated reporting)

4.4.1   Multi-Entity Reporting

Central Finance allows you to bring together cross-system financial data for enterprise-wide reporting and analysis, as shown in Figure 4.11. Reporting on multiple entities at the same time—whether all entities or a selected group of entities within Central Finance—is a key value proposition of Central Finance.

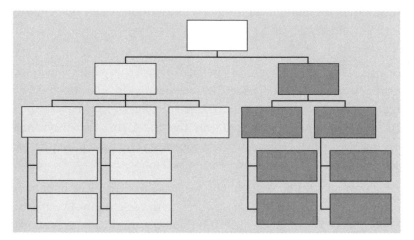

Figure 4.11 Enterprise-Wide Aggregated Reporting

Financial information is stored in Central Finance on a transactional, line item level with full, unabbreviated dimensionality. In any financial report, you'll be able to drill down from any higher level to the transaction level, or vice versa, at any time. This capability is an important distinction from traditional data warehouses, although the results of the report may be the same.

Traditional data warehouses are typically built on separate datasets, with dimensionalities parsed or with the use of precalculated aggregates that only work for the levels calculated, and these values are not updated in real time when a new posting is made.

4.4.2   Harmonized/Standardized

Reporting, especially legal and group reporting, in Central Finance can involve whatever level of harmonization and standardization you need.

Diverse or overlapping master data object values, as shown in Figure 4.12, can, through the business mapping layer, be brought together into a coherent set of values consistent across the entire organization. Apples are now apples, and oranges are now oranges.

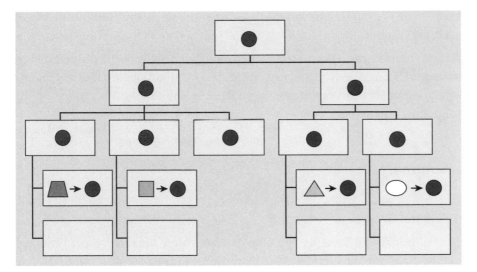

Figure 4.12 Harmonized Enterprise-Wide Reporting

4.4.3   Benchmarking

Having access to harmonized and standardized financial data enterprise-wide brings transparency into the organization and allows for internal comparisons and benchmarking—across the organization, comparing apples to apples and oranges to oranges.

4.4.4   Consolidated Reporting

Group reporting in Central Finance is not limited to period-end closings. Based on preconsolidated information, Central Finance allows you to execute consolidation/group closing steps in Central Finance to derive fully consolidated statements, including intercompany eliminations.

Consolidation can take place in Central Finance within or natively connected to the central system. Using the embedded path via SAP Business Planning and Consolidation (SAP BPC) or SAP S/4HANA Finance for group reporting, the real-time consolidation features are within Central Finance, part of the same underlying SAP S/4HANA system.

Data duplication to the consolidation application, traditionally a standard approach, is no longer necessary; the data already exists in the central system. If a separate consolidation application is in place, whether temporary or permanent, only one interface, from Central Finance, is required, rather than needing multiple interfaces for multiple systems.

This single interface can use real-time, unabbreviated data from the Universal Journal in Central Finance, so data updates or additional dimensionality for the separate consolidation application can be accommodated at any time—thus improving the consolidation system too.

4.5   Summary

In this chapter, we discussed the advanced reporting and analytics capabilities available in Central Finance.

While traditional ERP systems for finance have been limited by performance, throughput, and the data model design principles of the past, the SAP S/4HANA-based Central Finance exposes advanced capabilities by leveraging a single source of truth in the form of a financial repository with an advanced financial data model and dynamic dimensional coding block setup. These capabilities enable standardized and harmonized enterprise-wide and cross-system financial and management reporting.

In the next chapter, we'll discuss what Central Finance can improve from a financial process perspective.

Chapter 5

Finance Processes: What Can Central Finance Improve?

Many patterns for deploying Central Finance are potentially possible, but often, the chance to leverage a single version of the truth is a missed opportunity in process enablement. While Central Finance is part of SAP S/4HANA, some attention must be directed to understanding the relevant finance processes.

The top benefits identified by the users of Central Finance range from transparency across systems (a single version of the truth) to business continuity. How are these benefits realized through process management using Central Finance?

The role of Central Finance in the SAP ecosystem is often misunderstood, mainly due to a lack of understanding about the relevant processes and what can and cannot be done, exacerbated by the fast development and rapid adoption of the solution. In this chapter, we'll help you understand process orchestration using Central Finance. In addition, we'll illustrate some common process use cases with diagrams to understand process flows. These process flows cover the line of business (LOB) finance features found in the SAP S/4HANA core.

5.1 Processes and Process Orchestration

To understand how to use Central Finance, you must be aware of the difference between using a process in Central Finance and the orchestration of a process with Central Finance. The two uses are quite distinct and require different tools, skills, scoping, and phasing when deploying Central Finance.

Using a process means that the end user will log on to Central Finance and execute a process. The process's steps require that data be set up in Central Finance, and this data in turn is used to complete an activity. The activity can be as simple as looking at the status of a line item or as sophisticated as carrying out a closing valuation with reversals. Using a process in Central Finance, you could read, write, update, and mark for deletion master data or transactions that have not yet posted.

For process orchestration, the end user will log on to Central Finance and remotely execute an activity in a source system. This situation removes the need for the user to understand process in the source system, an understanding that may be unnecessary from the user's day-to-day perspective.

Combining processes and process orchestration allows you and your organization to achieve more than is usually perceived as possible using tools accessible in Central Finance. Three basic patterns of process orchestration form the basis for many other patterns. Figure 5.1 shows the general technical pattern that is mandatory for all three basic scenarios.

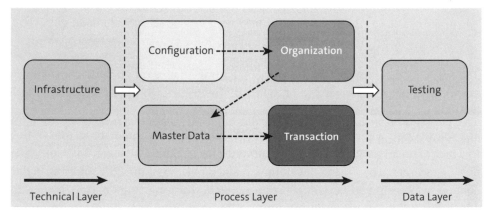

Figure 5.1 Project Process Orchestration

The first process orchestration pattern occurs during a project that can be replicated after go-live as part of supporting a transition. The process layer is the middle layer, which can only start properly once the infrastructure has been delivered. The data layer is an outcome of the process layer to be used for integration testing and user acceptance testing.

In this scenario, process orchestration starts with the configuration management of the various processes in scope at the client level. These processes would serve as the common layer for all users, such as SAP Application Integration Framework. For each process in scope for the finance function, different finance modules are configured around three major groups. Organizational settings such as company codes, controlling areas, etc. must be set up with the future finance process scope in mind and not only account for work packages initially in consideration.

Next, master data must be designed as a process during the project for a successful outcome after go-live. Changing data that is already live is a problem of poor planning and short-term decision-making. Master data processes consider quality of data as a priority above and beyond process diagrams and ownership. Transaction process management is the last step to be completed once the organization and the master data have been set up to ensure correct process outcomes. Most errors in transactions are driven by master data issues. Transactions are often processes, either manual steps, parts of another process, or an interface. Figure 5.1 shows process orchestration at the project level.

Three levels of processes must be orchestrated in Central Finance, as follows:

- Organizational structures, such as company codes, and how they are used in Central Finance
- Master data to enable integration across processes and systems
- Transaction settings driven by organizational structures, master data, and specific process step attributes

The second process orchestration pattern occurs when closing is carried out in the source system, as shown in Figure 5.2, and the value flow must be understood.

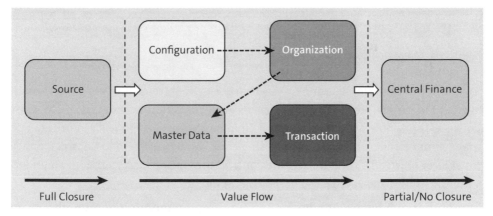

Figure 5.2 Closing Process in Source and Central Systems

In this scenario, the project is live with Central Finance, and the source system is used for full or partial closing. This capability adds a level of sophistication previously unavailable for finance processes: The source system can now have different structures in terms of organization, master data, and transaction data when compared to the data in Central Finance.

What gets done fully in the source system and what gets done partially in the Central Finance system requires the user understand the process as well as close master data coordination, including avoiding transaction delinquency. Values will always flow from the source to Central Finance with no posts back to the source system from the Central Finance system. The nature of the closing must be aligned with the business, and processes must be managed to ensure no duplication of values.

The third process orchestration pattern, as shown in Figure 5.3, occurs when an organization wants to avoid using source systems for closing and wants instead to use Central Finance for closing the books.

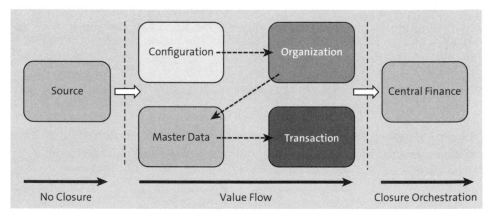

Figure 5.3 Managing Processes from Central Finance

In this scenario, master data and transaction design requires a different process management than the first two scenarios because transition accounting must exist between the source system and Central Finance. Process design will require change management and planning to shift closing from a source system to Central Finance for at least master data and will require controls on transaction access with an understanding of how and when data should be entered.

Master data management requires a tool, or at least a process, to ensure that mapping errors for raw transactions are not impacted on a real-time basis. Without this process, mapping errors will increase in all scenarios, but this problem is particularly amplified in closings due to the classic organizational needs for specific closing tasks at month end, quarter end, and year end.

Compliance also require process orchestration from Central Finance aligned to the values generated by the source system and closing actions that are centralized.

5.2   Payables and Receivables

All processes and systems are built on the two logical parts of an organization: finance and logistics. Finance includes all tasks related to accounting, controlling, treasury, risk, compliance, audit, consolidation, and disclosure (to both external and internal stakeholders). Logistics includes sales, manufacturing, warehousing, procurement, maintenance, and other tasks. In other words, if a task is not in finance, it is in logistics. Logistics tends to be process oriented, while finance tends to be function oriented, around which finance departments build daily, monthly, quarterly, and annual schedules.

In general, any customer and vendor activity up until an accounting entry is created can be classified as a logistics activity. Once an accounting entry is made, this activity becomes part of the finance world with full traceability back to logistics. Logistics generates the bulk of accounting documents with enough information for an audit trail. Once the data is in the finance domain of source systems, this data is ready to be replicated into Central Finance. At this point, a multitude of possibilities to consume data from processes become operational in Central Finance. For example, receivables and payables are composed of subprocesses in Central Finance, and each process must be considered in its own context. Each process provides different options and provides outcomes based on scope and target end state. We'll outline each of these processes in the following sections.

5.2.1   Accounts Payable

First, let's look at accounts payable (AP) without central payments before showing you what the process looks like when Central Finance is used.

Accounts Payable without Central Payments

The Central Finance engine needs master data for suppliers to be set up correctly according to the master data processes in SAP S/4HANA. For accounts payable, our main object is the vendor in SAP ERP, but in SAP S/4HANA, our main object is a business partner. In a basic procure-to-pay process, integration with Central Finance can really matter.

The accounts payable process starts with a purchase order, as shown in Figure 5.4. Let's say that our organization has decided to use Central Finance for the reporting of payables with offsetting general ledger (G/L) accounts. As a result, open items will be managed in the source system.

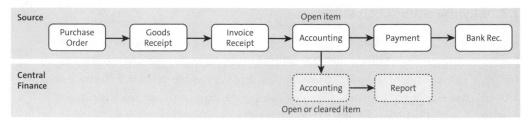

Figure 5.4 Central Finance with Source System Payments

Although the open item will be managed in the source system, Central Finance can consider item as an open item with a clearing document to follow or can use the open item as a reporting item without a clearing document. In this scenario, we're not interested on the status of the open item but rather on its value for analytical reasons.

The payment will be made in the source system with the clearing document replicated only if configured to do so based on customer requirements. Because the payment is managed in the source system, bank reconciliation will also be carried out in the source system.

Based on experience, taking only open items as technically cleared does not make sense because reporting capabilities would be limited. For example, overdue payables with aging would not show the actual correct balance. Taking open items and their clearing documents will give you fuller reporting capabilities with the correct item statuses and balances, including offsetting bank postings.

Accounts Payable with Central Payments

One feature often requested by customers of Central Finance is the ability to make payments centrally for all vendor activity that exists in underlying ERP systems, both SAP and non-SAP. This feature was released with SAP S/4HANA 1709.

In this instance, an invoice is created using a three-way match carried out in the source system. An accounting document is thus generated that would make a posting to the GR/IR account and create a payable in the finance ledgers.

Both the GR/IR side and the payable side are automatically reflected in Central Finance. However, unlike the previous scenario where the source system made the payments, the delta open item is automatically marked as **Technically Cleared**, and the actual open item is replicated in Central Finance. As a result, the technically cleared item cannot be accidently paid in the source system.

The actual open item in Central Finance behaves like a normal item and can be cleared in Central Finance with a payment or by offsetting entries, as shown in Figure 5.5. The standard payment engine in SAP S/4HANA will clear the open item only in Central Finance with an offset to a bank clearing account. Since the payment is made in Central Finance, two events will also occur in Central Finance. First, payment instructions to the bank will be generated in Central Finance, and second, as a result, bank reconciliation will also be carried out in the same Central Finance instance, which helps ensure process completion and integrity.

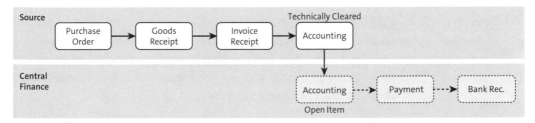

Figure 5.5 Central Finance Making Payments

Open item balances, line item analysis, and the aging analysis will only be available in Central Finance in this scenario. In addition, any correspondence with the vendor, such as account statements or payment advices, will be generated in Central Finance too.

5.2.2 Payables with Direct and Indirect Procurement

So far, we've addressed a simple scenario where every step of the process is either in the source system or in Central Finance. With the advent of cloud solutions integrating with Central Finance, you can now also separate direct and indirect procurement. Indirect procurement is generally not necessary in on-premise environments, which don't deal with high volumes of high-value inventory, and therefore don't need heuristics.

We recommend separating the process of creating procurement orders based on procurement categories. Procurements will still be generated, whether directly or indirectly, in each buyer's system, using each buyer's purchase orders. However, in most organizations, the management of payables is usually separated between direct and indirect procurement. Indeed, the concept of shared resources is a long-standing virtue in finance processes, unlike in logistics processes. This virtue requires the follow conditions be met:

- All payables are managed centrally at least for the company code in question, if not across all company codes.
- Invoices must be sent to a single place for verification and approvals.
- Payments to the same supplier, independent of spending, are made together to reduce bank fees and the need for reconciliation.
- A single statement and payment advice are delivered to the supplier from finance, independent of the point of origin of the purchase order.

These outcomes demand a payables handling function for all spending independent of source, including travel and expenses, as shown in Figure 5.6. In this case, assuming that SAP Ariba is handling the indirect procurement and that SAP procurement is creating automatic purchase orders from demand planning, the central payments feature of Central Finance can handle and group payments across different categories of procurement and across different systems.

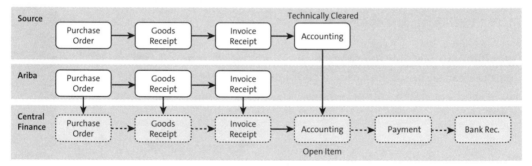

Figure 5.6 Central Finance Making Payments for All Procurement

5.2.3   Three-Way Matching

A frequently asked question about SAP and Central Finance relates to the process of three-way matching. Three-way matching is usually triggered by an invoice linked to a purchase order. A goods receipt is not needed because the purchase order is usually sufficient. Three-way matching involves two distinct process scenarios but is not available out of the box—you'll need to implement a Central Finance instance using a partner solution, OpenText Vendor Invoice Management for SAP Solutions (VIM), that would operate within Central Finance. Figure 5.7 shows the functional process that would be implemented.

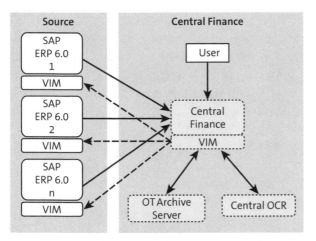

Figure 5.7 Central Finance and Three-Way Matching

Using VIM, you can carry out three-way matching using a Central Finance instance. A paper invoice and an electronic invoice will be sent to a physical location, and the user will log on to a single Central Finance instance. The VIM would search for the purchase order linked to the invoice in the source system and carry out a virtual three-way match. Once a match is made, VIM will make a posting in the source system for the three-way match on a physical basis, which in turn will generate the payable postings to be replicated in Central Finance.

Then, VIM analytics will update automatically to create an audit trail for the postings. At this point, the three-way matching is completed. This process works for both direct and indirect spending in the SAP portfolio as project activities. This process provides a consistent shared services model for accounts payable functions for any procurement category by leveraging the common data model in SAP.

For non-SAP systems, the same process could be carried out as part of project deployment on an instance-by-instance basis depending on the data model.

5.2.4 Accounts Receivable

In this following section, we'll first look at accounts receivable (AR) without central payments before turning to what the process looks like when Central Finance is used.

Receivables without Central Payments

The opposite of payables can also be managed using Central Finance for reporting. In this instance, the customer resides in the local system and carries out the order fulfillment process as usual without disruption. Account-relevant events trigger accounting entries into Finance (FI) and Controlling (CO), depending on how the local system has been configured, as shown in Figure 5.8.

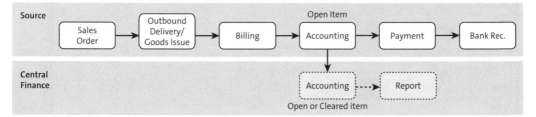

Figure 5.8 Central Finance and Local AR

Once the accounting document is posted to the source system, an automatic copy copied is replicated to Central Finance as a new accounting document with a full audit trail. Assuming the mapping and configuration are correct, the reporting of the customer, as an open item or cleared item, can be viewed in Central Finance with native drilldown functions to the source system.

Payments would be carried out in the source system as would bank reconciliation and customer-related processes. However, Central Finance would hold the harmonized single version of the truth.

Receivables with Central Payments

Your organization can move the handling of payments to customers into Central Finance as part of the project scope. The process would, however, be set up differently from a design and build scenario, including how users access customer activities. In this scenario, accounting-relevant movements from order fulfillment are the same as receivables without central payment. The difference is that the open item is cleared technically in the source system according to this configuration to ensure the item cannot be paid accidently.

Because the open item is no longer available for payment in the source system, it can only be paid using the Central Finance instance, as shown in Figure 5.9.

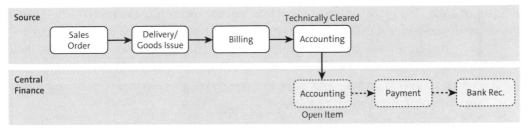

Figure 5.9 Central Finance and Central AR

This scenario forces payments to be made on the Central Finance system along with follow-on bank reconciliation activities. As a result, bank statements from third-party banks would be connected to the system that is making the payment. In this instance, the Central Finance system has been operationalized and has moved away from being a reporting system only.

5.2.5   Receivables with Central Credit Management

Naturally, you may question whether credit management for customers is impacted by the movement of payments from customers into Central Finance. The reason would be obvious to any finance person as the movement in receivables and, consequent, payments drives the basic net exposure from a business perspective. The second part of the formula is how is this managed given the logistics transaction still resides in the source system.

This scenario is not complicated with Central Finance. The receivables management functionality resides in the same instance of SAP S/4HANA as the Central Finance instance, as shown in Figure 5.10. As open items and their clearing documents are already available in Central Finance, credit management can also be used in Central Finance with configuration that supports integration with logistics transactions in the source system.

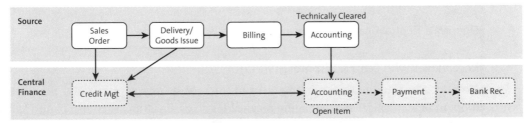

Figure 5.10 Central Finance and Central AR and Credit

An organization that wants to adopt this central process must activate the new credit management in SAP S/4HANA and then use the service-oriented architecture to provide real-time credit limit and exposure information to the source system to allow management of the sales order fulfilment process in sales and distribution. Sales order, delivery, invoice, and payment (or clearing) movements will continually update credit management process.

To use central credit management in Central Finance, your technical team must activate web services and set up the consumer proxy. The SAP Basis team would need to configure the technical architecture correctly as part of the project set up.

Receivables with Central Collections

Let's say we have receivables in Central Finance and credit management activated. This scenario gives us partial operational management for the customer. Better management would require that the receivables process be extended to actively manage activities linked to collecting funds from customers.

The collections process in Central Finance allows you to automatically generate daily worklists based on collection strategies, which can be used as the basis for receivable collection by your collection specialists. How collections fit into Central Finance and receivables management is shown in Figure 5.11. Items, such as collection strategies, must set up in Central Finance.

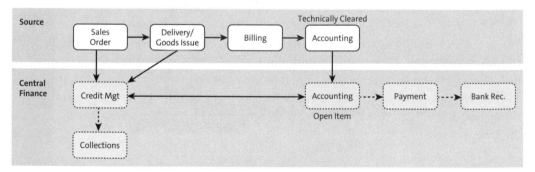

Figure 5.11 Central Finance and Central AR and Collections

Receivables with Central Disputes

Now, let's turn to the final missing piece in the process jigsaw puzzle and close the loop on best practices for managing receivables across multiple systems. Figure 5.12 shows how disputes will need to be integrated into the overall process of managing customers.

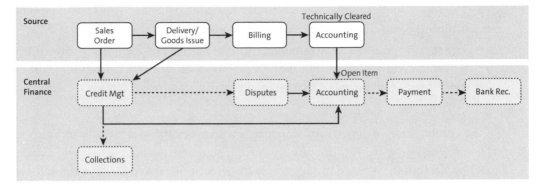

Figure 5.12 Central Finance and Central AR and Disputes

With Central Finance, your organization could benefit from using a centralized repository for managing the processing of receivables-related disputes and for handling short payments or non-payments of outstanding invoices. Disputes can be raised directly in Central Finance because open items are automatically replicated from the source system.

5.3   Accounting and Financial Close

One negative reaction may be concern that Central Finance does not allow books to be closed by a new user or one that is not experienced with SAP S/4HANA or the available tools. The best way to understand the closing cycle using Central Finance is to remember that Central Finance is a full SAP S/4HANA system. In other words, the capabilities and tools available in SAP S/4HANA for closing books are also available in Central Finance, perhaps in a different way. The second step to understanding the closure of books is to understand the processes and modules in the scope of a Central Finance project and the source systems. In this way, mapping the closing cycle to Central Finance and the source systems is easier.

In essence, the determination of the closing steps would move from only the execution of tasks, a traditional approach, to the orchestration of the closing cycle with Central Finance. Orchestration is dependent on at least three business dimensions, as follows:

- Processes that require closing that are not specifically accounting related, for example, a final billing run in a source system

- The industry sector that the customer operates in when using SAP systems, including Central Finance, for example, services, trading, or manufacturing
- Any specific legal and fiscal requirements that require nonaccounting data, which is never available in an accounting process but which relies exclusively on logistics movements, for example, Intrastat reporting that declares receipts and dispatches information

The combination of these three dimensions will determine what actions can be performed using Central Finance directly or can be orchestrated using Central Finance. By orchestration here, we include the management of closing tasks or the remote execution of closing tasks using the Central Finance instance, as shown in Figure 5.13, which includes some typical tasks that may be relevant in a closing scenario.

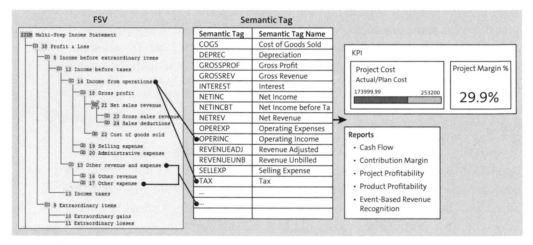

Figure 5.13 Central Finance and Closing Orchestration

Closing differences that exist between entities and groups, whether central or local, can be resolved using frameworks available in SAP S/4HANA or in partner solutions that can orchestrate and/or execute these tasks. In the following sections, we'll discuss main areas of closing with Central Finance in general.

5.3.1   General Ledger

The G/L's capabilities for closing will directly depend on the deployment of Central Finance. In the reporting scenario, you may limit these capabilities to the source systems deliberately to allow real-time reporting. However, once the deployment of

Central Finance moves to the operational scenario, the system of record will also shift, and closing activities can be initiated for the G/L using standard financial closing tasks based on the Universal Journal. As the system of record has shifted, users will stop carrying out G/L closing in the source system, and access to these controls will be adjusted accordingly.

5.3.2   Entity Close

Closing in the G/L is part of an overall entity close. An entity in the Central Finance system might be different than its equivalent in the source system. For example, an entity in Central Finance could have been the result of a merged or split company code or could have been derived from custom rules.

Closing subledgers for AR/AP can also be carried out in Central Finance assuming that operational finance processes have also been shifted to Central Finance. As a result, payment, valuation, and regrouping tasks can be performed directly, assuming the relevant SAP S/4HANA release and notes are available.

When banking is directly managed for internal partners (in-house cash) or external partners, bank statements can be imported and reconciled directly in the Central Finance instance based on the entities that live in the system. Any valuations for foreign currency accounts would use the valuation approaches available in the SAP S/4HANA instance.

In terms of management accounting, a cost allocation run could also be performed and reported using Central Finance for operational expenses (OpEx) and capital expenditure (CapEx) purposes. For CapEx, the work breakdown structure (WBS) elements must be real and not statistical. As long as the mapping has been carried out with real WBS elements in Central Finance, settlement rules could be used to allocate costs to other cost objects for CapEx purposes.

However, where the CapEx must be settled to an asset under construction, fixed assets must only be run in Central Finance and must be configured to allow settlements from WBS elements. Ultimately, final settlements that allow depreciations will be calculated only in Central Finance. This scenario will require a process change in the organization, which we'll discuss later in Section 5.5.2 as part of a CapEx scenario. Without these process changes in the source system and the asset register in Central Finance, settlement would need to be orchestrated using Central Finance using a closing governance tool.

5.3.3   Corporate Close

Central Finance can provide different levels of corporate close depending on the consolidation tools in place. Corporate close will only involve two scenarios. In the first scenario, a consolidation tool may not be embedded in the SAP S/4HANA instance where Central Finance resides (called a *side car implementation*). In the second scenario, an embedded consolidation tool, such as SAP S/4HANA-optimized SAP Business Planning and Consolidation (SAP BPC) or SAP S/4HANA Finance for group reporting, is available in the same Central Finance instance.

For the first scenario, let's say a harmonized and standardized trial balance should be extracted from Central Finance and passed to the side cart for direct consumption from the SAP HANA database or via the application layer. The side car implementation would then be responsible for validation and would determine the level of granularity available. Drilldown capabilities back to Central Finance from the side cart would not be available. Corporate closing steps would be specific to the side cart and be corporate in nature with all data impacts only available once the extraction has occurred.

Under the embedded scenario, data from a single entity or cross-entity data is always available to the corporate close team using the lowest level of granularity of the system. This scenario enables corporate close to move closer to the entity close, eventually resulting in reduced differentiation between entity and corporate closure since real-time data is harmonized and standardized and can be reported immediately as part of preconsolidation activities based on access controls.

5.3.4   Financial Reporting and Disclosure

Assuming G/L, subledger, entity, and corporate close are under the umbrella of Central Finance orchestration, reporting can be made available in real time across the enterprise daily rather than monthly or quarterly. Events could be triggered immediately to an entity based on corporate or entity reports. An organization can build SAP Fiori apps to enhance the look and feel of reports to match the reporting and disclosure needs for senior management and external stakeholders.

5.3.5   Financial Close Governance

Closing may require governance at the entity and/or corporate level depending on your organization's needs and its internal control processes. Central Finance leverages the SAP Financial Closing cockpit to ensure governance is in place to provide transparency and visibility to relevant stakeholders independent of the physical location where a task is being executed, for example, in a shared service center or in a specific country. SAP Financial Closing cockpit can be hosted in the Central Finance instance to allow the management of tasks, including their execution, monitoring, and eventual reporting. Governance can cover an entity, a group of entities, corporate closings, or a slice of events between responsibility areas.

5.4   Banking and Treasury

Once the tipping point to move to Central Finance is reached for operational activities, shifting your banking, cash, and treasury management processes into Central Finance may make sense. As a rule, treasury is not a process but an outcome of other transactions that generate cash flows. Cash flows are handled in treasury processes with the exception of actual third-party deals and settlements in the forex market, money market, capital markets, etc.

Because the definition of "treasury" varies across organizations (from just banking to payables to full hedge fund management), we'll only discuss the main building blocks of treasury management in the following sections.

5.4.1   Adoption of Treasury Best Practices in Central Finance

The basic starting point for all treasury processes and system components is cash flow. Cash flows effectively represent the lowest movement or an aggregated movement from spending, selling, borrowing, and investing decisions. Management of these cash flows ranges from bank accounts, receivables, payables, and any funding or hedging transactions that may or may not be related to exposure. Central Finance is the foundation for delivering, not only banking and treasury harmonization, but also best practices that allow your organization to evolve around an implementation roadmap as part of the overall finance transformation.

Figure 5.14 shows the path to adopting best practices in treasury management in Central Finance, starting with setting up a shared service, moving to a payables factory for receiving and scanning invoices, fine-tuning collections from customers, and finally creating an in-house bank that allows for intracompany and third-party payments/receipts. Creating and adopting an organizational model that reflects the target operating model for finance has always been easy, but now, using shared resources to implement a "more with less" concept can lead to savings for your organization.

The challenge has always been getting the information into a single place at the transactional debit and credit level to allow cross-system, enterprise-level reporting and actions. This challenge can be met by Central Finance processes, which can help you establish processes that will be relevant in the future.

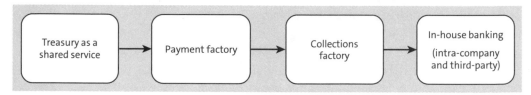

Figure 5.14 Best Practices for Treasury with Central Finance

Banking and treasury may take different forms in each organization, and processes should be established to reflect the desired phasing of the project. In general, a five-point process should help to establish scope of these processes, as shown in Figure 5.15.

Figure 5.15 Central Finance: Five Steps for Banking and Treasury

With Central Finance, the entire suite of treasury-related activity can be utilized once cash flows are captured as part of the replication process from accounting documents. Once the cash flows are known and payments are entered into Central Finance, any exotic treasury activity (such as hedging, funding needs for borrowing, excess funds investments, and debt management) can be carried out within the Central Finance instance. These activities will also be reflected in cash operations, liquidity management, and bank reconciliation movements alongside the full accounting for period end, which can also be automated by the SAP Financial Closing cockpit.

5.4.2   Bank Account Management

Before SAP S/4HANA, a core issue was the relatively simple nature of the bank master record. This master record did not contain fields for tracking compliance and control because the bank master record object was built for SAP Business Suite on SAP HANA and required IT to control and manage.

With the arrival of SAP S/4HANA, Central Finance can fully leverage the redesign of the banks that belong to your organization. These banks can be managed centrally all at once or on a remote basis. Managing remotely only makes sense when not using Central Finance. When Central Finance is in use, your organization can move to the new Bank Account Management (BAM) framework. Central Finance represents an opportunity for your treasury department to realign their processes across multiple systems and gain control. Consolidating bank accounts, not only in terms of banking relationships but also systemically, is considered a best practice.

BAM can be quite useful for Central Finance processes as the end-point for process closure. Almost all buying and selling accounting movements end with a payment or a netting effect. Therefore, if the starting points (the receivables) and the payables are both operationally managed in Central Finance, then moving house banks and their related accounts to Central Finance makes sense. This change would allow any authorized user, regardless of location, to access this process in a single place.

As organizations increase their footprint in international markets, processes for managing bank accounts often become localized without any central control. This situation creates risk for an organization in terms of the movement of funds in existing accounts and the opening of accounts. Using Central Finance, an organization can gain global visibility of and control over both local and global bank accounts as well as their opening, operating, and closure processes, as shown in Figure 5.16.

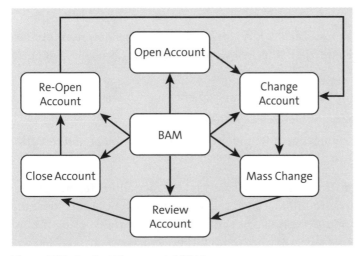

Figure 5.16 Central Finance and BAM

BAM represents master data in Central Finance and comes with its own workflow templates to manage various events in the lifecycle of a bank account. These workflow templates can be used out of the box within the Central Finance instance or can be copied and tailored to specific customers. Using standard SAP S/4HANA workflows as a starting point for BAM can act as a solid foundation to assess any changes after operational experience has been gained to reduce time cycles and cost. Examples of workflow templates for BAM include WS7430047 (account opening), WS7430047 (account changes), WS7430049 (mass changes), WS7430050 (bank closing), WS7430065 (review account), and WS02800011 (reopen account). A company's organizational model can be embedded into these workflows where required as a BAM implementation activity.

Once the workflows are activated as per process design for BAM, the signatories of the accounts, their locations, etc. can also be added for reporting purposes. To utilize these workflows, you'll need to activate an additional component (FIN_FSCM_CLM) in the Central Finance instance of SAP S/4HANA using Transaction SFW5. Once BAM is available and the workflow templates to use are determined, the classic user interface for BAM will no longer be available as per SAP S/4HANA for Central Finance.

Note

Once activated, the FIN_FSCM_CLM component remains installed. Make a backup or carry out this action in a sandbox.

For example, the old Transaction FI12 is no longer available. The new user interface consists of SAP Fiori-based tiles. The following features are available in Central Finance:

- Carrying out workflow-based account management
- Managing bank accounts as hierarchies with the banks
- Cataloguing bank accounts into different groups for management and reporting purposes

The centralization of process and control in Central Finance allows further process steps with external parties on BAM. Each time an account event occurs (opening, closing, etc.), an electronic message can be sent, as a project activity, using the SAP S/4HANA platform where Central Finance resides. These messages can take the form of XML messages that support eBAM file transfers. The eBAM protocol provides standard, Common Global Implementation XML formats for any organization that utilizes SwiftNet messaging services with their partner banks.

Using eBAM with generated, centralized, and harmonized bank data not only leads to increased savings and increased control but also can help establish a company culture that encourages standardized processes. Without this standardization, complexity and compliance issues may remain, as shown in Figure 5.17.

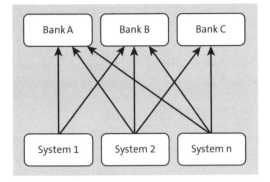

Figure 5.17 BAM without Standardization

In addition, this simplification agenda, as shown in Figure 5.18 from an IT perspective, can be pursued by reducing multiple connections to a single banking connection for all banks across the enterprise with access controls at the local and/or global levels. With a standardized model for BAM, local systems that feed into Central Finance no longer need to maintain their own BAM processes but instead can use a shared service model.

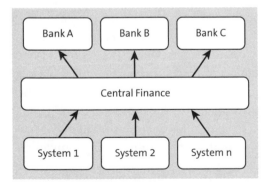

Figure 5.18 BAM with Standardization Using Central Finance

5.4.3   Cash Operations and Liquidity Management

We've separated the topic of cash operations and liquidity management from BAM, even though these topics are all technically part of any full Cash Management solution in SAP S/4HANA used by Central Finance. This separation can introduce clarity to the process, which is often lacking during early discussions.

While BAM is all about the process of managing bank accounts and their attributes for compliance and control across the enterprise, cash operation and liquidity management are transactional reporting tools that encompass movements generated by these bank accounts.

In addition to these bank movements, cash operations and liquidity management also captures movements relevant for reporting cash flows, as shown in Figure 5.19.

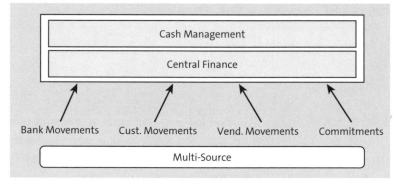

Figure 5.19 Data Feeds into Central Finance for Cash Management

Central Finance takes the transactional accounting documents generated by the underlying systems and provides enterprise-level data in a single place, which can be used by Cash Management. Once the data from underlying systems has reached into SAP S/4HANA using Central Finance, the use of the new One Exposure from Operations hub table is triggered. This single table replaces a substantial number of classical cash management and liquidity forecast tables that existed in SAP ERP. The new table for the generated transactions posted by Central Finance is table FQM_FLOW. In addition, memo table FDES is maintained to allow manual entries for items not covered by standard processes, for example, income tax provisions for the company.

Cash Management offers two categories of cash analysis using the data generated by Central Finance. The first category, based on the planning level of the group, looks at future cash flows in terms of cash position as defined during the design process for working capital movements on the balance sheet. The second category looks at the historical analysis of cash in the form of liquidity items.

The One Exposure from Operations hub table keeps track of the cash and liquidity forecast on a real-time basis using data from multiple source systems and centralized or decentralized bank account management, depending on the implementation of Central Finance.

To use cash operations and liquidity forecast, as shown in Figure 5.20, Central Finance must be set up in SAP S/4HANA with the correct master data and process definitions. Technical integration between the source system and Central Finance must be correctly undertaken by your SAP Basis teams. Once the technical integration is completed, the business integration for this process can be carried out by a functional consultant.

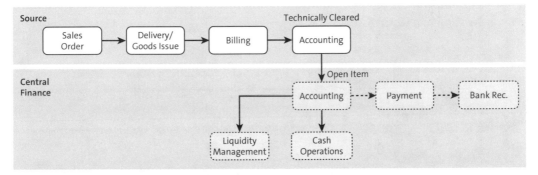

Figure 5.20 Central Finance with Cash Operations and Liquidity Forecast

> **Note**
>
> Think of cash operations as a more sophisticated version of classic cash management across multiple systems using Central Finance and compare the old liquidity forecast in SAP ERP to liquidity management in Central Finance with cash flows from SAP and non-SAP systems. Both provide real-time visibility and analysis, thus enabling action for funding, for the treasurer, or for any user with access to these apps.

We now have payables, receivables, and bank movements in Central Finance. The next step is to make payable and receivable processes operate in real time with enterprise-level data from multiple source systems. To achieve this, we'll look at two concepts next: payment factories and collection factories.

5.4.4   Payment Factories

The definition of a payment factory varies between organizations, from scanning invoices to running full-service in-house banking for all suppliers. From a Central Finance perspective, each definition is valid, can be accommodated with different implementation process patterns, and can include both direct and indirect procurement activities. A basic prerequisite is that Central Finance must act as the owner of open items and payments.

Enabling payment factories requires the use of all the master data and transaction data linked to a supplier, now business partner, to allow payments to be processed in Central Finance and for following up on the payment file sent to the bank. This scenario requires the use of central payments and represents a shift away from the source system to the Central Finance system. The use of *payment on behalf of* (POBO) for one of more companies and, therefore, one of more systems, would be activated, as shown in Figure 5.21.

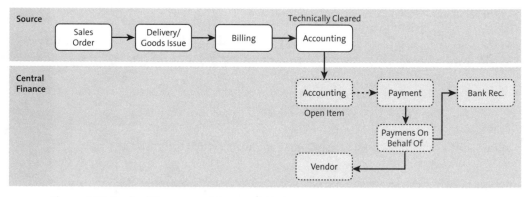

Figure 5.21 Central Finance and Payment Factory

5.4.5   Collection Factories

Before outlining the process for collection factories, let's first define a collection factory in terms of banking and treasury. First, a collection factory does not chase down debt or organize resources for teams that interact with customers for late payments. Collection factories are processes whereby all receivables from across the enterprise (and hence, across systems) are fed into Central Finance. This process enables a total picture of payments due in an analysis that has been designed for Central Finance, at a useful level of granularity.

Once these receivables are in Central Finance, including the follow-on processes that interact with the customer receivables, the process for a collection factory for customer payment could be implemented, as shown in Figure 5.22.

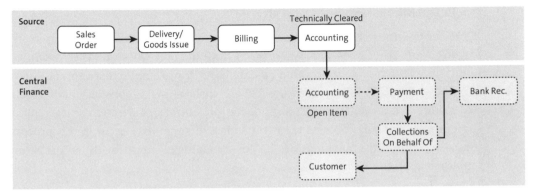

Figure 5.22 Central Finance and Collections Factory

The customer would engage with the shared resources or shared services center. In turn, the shared services center would generate the files to collect cash from customer banks automatically or to receive cash from customers directly through other forms of payment and/or channels. This process requires the use of *collections on behalf of* (COBO) and must be within the scope for the Central Finance project. COBO cannot be implemented without central payments.

5.5   Controlling Processes

So far, we've addressed financial processes that relate to accounting events that eventually become the treasury cash flows that define cash operations to payables factories. Now, let's turn our attention to management accounts, part of Central Finance processes. Management accounts can be categorized as managing costs for overhead (OpEx), managing costs for investment-related activity (CapEx), or managing profitability for business units based on a range of attributes using Profitability Analysis (CO-PA).

Each of these three categories looks at the profit and loss side of the accounts and utilizes cost elements created in the operational chart of accounts. These cost elements must be set up and mapped appropriately, and the relevant cost objects must not be missing from the line items being replicated from the source systems. In particular, non-SAP line items must be analyzed, like any other accounting line, to allow the correct mapping to find the right account and object in Central Finance.

5.5.1   Operational Expenses (OpEx)

OpEx represents overhead and is part of responsible management accounting in any organization. These costs maybe managed in SAP and non-SAP systems across different nomenclatures for objects that capture costs, for example, cost centers. Figure 5.23 shows the main points of capture for such costs: either a goods receipt or a manual invoice. These events are system agnostic for Central Finance because the replication process not only captures the debit and credits that may occur in this process, but also captures the mappings needed for standardized reporting (thus comparing apples to apples).

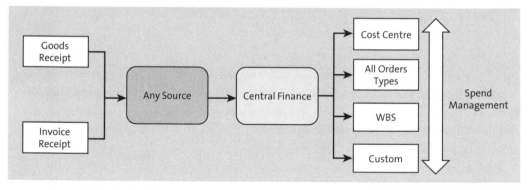

Figure 5.23 Central Finance and OpEx

Central Finance supports the mapping of the standard SAP cost objects during the replication process. Because the destination is an SAP S/4HANA system, the mapping for non-SAP systems must be made according to the naming conventions found in SAP S/4HANA. As a result, non-SAP line items must contain a separate attribute per cost object.

Assuming all systems that generate OpEx are connected to Central Finance, you can now use standard SAP Fiori apps for spend management for OpEx purposes across the enterprise. With the power of flexible hierarchies for cost centers and profit centers, real-time analysis becomes more powerful as well. Where an organization may have used custom attributes to analyze costs, for example, corporate initiatives for cost efficiency, these attributes can also be analyzed by adding custom mappings to

Central Finance and updating the linked SAP Fiori apps for these nonstandard attributes. OpEx, however, represents just one part of the overall cost management process.

5.5.2   Capital Expenditure (CapEx)

Three main methods exist for moving capital expenditure into asset management for SAP S/4HANA, as shown in Figure 5.24. First, with manual capitalization, a manual journal entry is made in asset accounting or in the G/L with the correct transaction type. This method tends to ignore logistics movements and is not used often because this method is not considered a best practice.

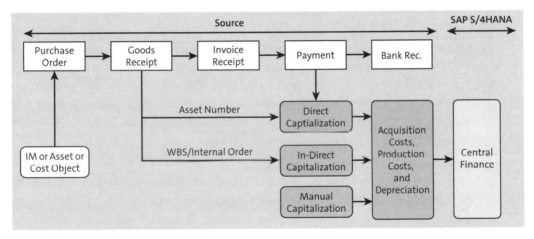

Figure 5.24 Central Finance and CapEx

In the second method, the direct capitalization of an asset can use a purchase order assignment in procurement that is used in the good receipts. This method will involve movement between balance sheets only, but the value will be instantly reflected into the real asset. Again, this method is not common for organizations using SAP because it does not consider profit and loss analysis requirements for cost management.

Therefore, a best practice is to use a logistics process for all asset purchases but use a cost object. The two most common cost objects in this context are internal orders or WBS elements. Both objects will hold values in the profit and loss (P&L) account to allow any user to use complete spend management across OpEx and CapEx in Central

Finance for data from all SAP and non-SAP systems. The same would apply to assets under construction.

Central Finance, however, does not replicate the asset register because only one depreciation run can be carried out at the business level. In a reporting scenario, only G/L-level data is held in Central Finance. For an operational scenario, both G/L- and asset-level data can be held in Central Finance, but asset management must be activated in the Central Finance instance of SAP S/4HANA. Using best practices for asset capitalization, costs would be posted to WBS elements, for example, and replicated in Central Finance. These costs would then be settled appropriately to the asset register within Central Finance. Depreciation would then only occur within Central Finance.

5.5.3   Profitability Analysis

Account-based CO-PA is the recommended way forward for SAP S/4HANA. In this scenario, Central Finance will by default use account-based CO-PA during the replication process from the source system. However, the sources of data for working out CO-PA could be from either account-based or costing-based instances. For non-SAP systems, this difference is not an issue because the incoming line item would be reconstructed using the account-based approach.

In SAP S/4HANA, the account-based model represents a thick ledger, that is, a ledger completely integrated into the financial accounting line item but that contains the attributes needed for CO-PA. No reconciliation issues between the G/L and account-based CO-PA should occur for primary postings. Secondary postings can be determined easily using record types and excluded from reconciliations, which will reduce month-end effort and reduce the amount of IT support needed.

Generally, most lines of CO-PA can be re-created by reconfiguring the source system or by copying line items as-is from primary postings. For example, almost all lines, unless summarized, contain the relevant attributes to populate account-based CO-PA from revenue, to OpEx to advertising and promotion (A&P), as shown in Figure 5.25. The cost of sales can also be replicated with the relevant cost depending on how the material master has been set up. One exception is the customer attribute in a goods issue during the order fulfillment process, which must currently be populated as part of the project activity. This scenario assumes that you require gross margin analysis in Central Finance CO-PA. For OpEx and A&P, these values can be held in cost objects as usual and can be settled in Central Finance depending on the scenario being implemented by the project.

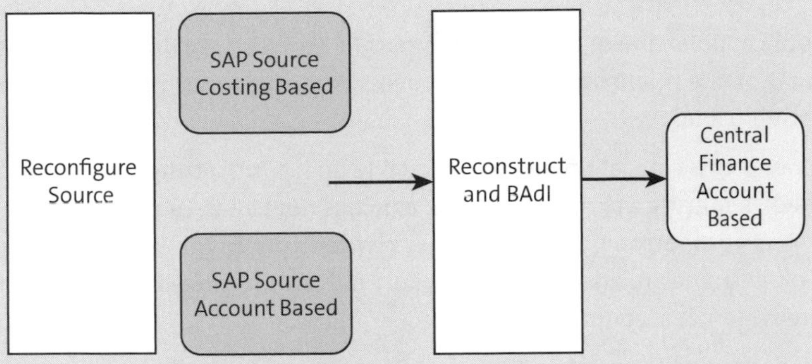

Which line are you talking about?

	Co. Code	Customer	CG	MG	SKU
Revenue	100.00	30.00	70.00	100.00	80.00
Net Revenue	95.00	25.00	65.00	95.00	60.00
COGS	**25.00**	**20.00**	**25.00**	**25.00**	**30.00**
GM	70.00	5.00	40.000	70.00	30.00
A & P	20.00		10.00		
OPEX	10.00				
Net Profit	40.00		30.00	70.00	30.00

Figure 5.25 Central Finance and CO-PA

Note that CO-PA requires reconstruction, rather than replication, and that each project may have specific requirements in the current system setup; you may need a project-based activity to fill any gaps.

Often, a source of contention lies in the cost of sales line for manufacturing entities using cost component splits. These postings can, however, be posted into Central Finance as a project activity that is part of a month-end activity due to its rare occurrence at period end only.

5.6   Beyond Core Finance

In this section, we'll discuss applications delivered as standalone SAP Fiori apps that integrate with each other but are small enough to not materially disrupt core SAP S/4HANA processes.

5.6.1   SAP Cash Application

SAP Cash Application is one of the first examples of how SAP S/4HANA and Central Finance can automate manually intensive processes through machine learning and SaaS in the public cloud.

In general, open items can get unwieldy if they pile up (i.e., offsetting postings aren't being matched), requiring a cleanup exercise, which is not trivial. In particular, inefficiency and lags in properly applying customer payments to invoices can be an awkward strain on customer relationships, especially if customers need to be contacted to help resolve internal accounting messes.

For Central Finance and the roadmap to central operations, centralized cash application is a natural place to start and is highly complementary with central cash, treasury, credit, collections, and disputes as part of an integrated payment factory strategy with Central Finance.

The use of additional add-on software supporting open item matching and clearing is not a new concept to the industry (being a problem that has been around a long time). For example, BlackLine has a transaction matching product to facilitate the matching and clearing of accounts, not only for receivables and cash, but all open items and clearings. However, the transaction matching rules must be provided to the software by a person who understands how to reliably automate matching and clearing. When the rules are obvious and self-evident, providing them to the transaction matching engine is straightforward.

In contrast, SAP Cash Application can take the history of bank statements and invoices and determine how they were matched and thus learn from the data to create implicit rules. These machine-generated rules can then be applied to future matching and clearing. The rules don't have to be given to the application. Instead, the machine figures out implied rules leveraging SAP's machine learning platform known as SAP Leonardo Machine Learning Foundation. SAP Cash Application is integrated with SAP Leonardo Machine Learning Foundation. At the time of this writing, SAP Cash Application can also intelligently apply payment advices and lockbox items against receivable invoices but only for SAP S/4HANA public cloud scenarios.

Some common processes managed in SAP S/4HANA transactions and SAP Fiori apps include the following:

- Importing bank statements (the Manage Bank Statements SAP Fiori app or Transaction FF_5).

- Executing standard clearing rules (the Clear Incoming Payments SAP Fiori app or Transaction F-28).

- Scheduling jobs for receivables line item matching (the Schedule Accounts Receivable Jobs SAP Fiori app or Transaction FEB_AUTO_REPRO). During this process, the SAP machine learning engine makes proposals, and based on preconfigured matching confidence thresholds, clearings are made based on these proposals.

- Remaining uncleared items must be handled manually on an exception basis (the Reprocess Bank Statement Items app or Transactions FEB_BSPROC, FEBA, or FEBAN).

5.6.2   SAP S/4HANA Cloud for Customer Payments

Consumers and businesses expect easier and more electronic ways to review their customer profile information, check on account balances, analyze billing statement details, resolve payment disputes, and make secure payments against outstanding amounts.

Historically, many SAP organizations had to build custom customer portals to support these functions and features. Today, these customer self-service capabilities can be quickly delivered in a plug-and-play way via SAP S/4HANA Cloud for customer payments. The solution is delivered as a series of SAP Fiori applications as follows:

- **Match Payments with Invoices app**
  The customer selects any payments and invoices that need to be cleared against each other, which generates a payment advice that in turn is forwarded to the responsible accounts receivable (AR) clerk for processing.

- **Pay My Bills app**
  The customer picks any open bills that need to be cleared with a payment or by applying a credit balance. In turn, payments are forwarded to the responsible A/R clerk for processing. Memos can be left for any underpayments.

- **Display My Account Statement app**
  The customer can look at monthly account balances with transactional details. If transactions are in the same currency, an annual account balance can be viewed as well.

- **Display My Account Master Data app**
  The customer can review their customer profile and information for accuracy.

The solution also integrates with SAP S/4HANA accounts receivable (AR) and Cash Management including the SAP Cash Application for automated payment matching against bank statements.

In the Central Finance context, central payment processing must be implemented to take advantage of SAP S/4HANA Cloud for customer payments to make those clearings centrally.

5.6.3   SAP S/4HANA Cloud for Credit Integration

Aside from central payments, central credit is another use case for Central Finance. Before creation, sales orders in local source systems can benefit from a centralized credit check. Many external credit-scoring agencies can be integrated into a credit check. By using Central Finance and SAP S/4HANA Cloud for credit integration, the system can act as centralized system for credit management against which local systems can perform credit checks.

In the past, implementing this type of functionality would have required a custom point-to-point development for each credit agency and would have required constant upkeep. Alternatively, SAP Credit Management would have to be updated manually and painstakingly with a review of each credit report received.

One advantage of SAP building a solution like this is that SAP S/4HANA Cloud for credit integration can serve as a hub to all of the integrated credit agencies. Instead of having to integrate each relevant credit agency, SAP can handle the integration with each agency once and make it instantly available for all users of the application. This solution enables companies to stay up to date with the latest changes.

SAP S/4HANA Cloud for credit integration is designed to help the credit controller manage the process of reviewing and updating SAP credit management with the latest information from credit reports, as shown in Figure 5.26.

The solution is delivered as a series of SAP Fiori applications for the credit controller role as follows:

- **Manage Credit Reports for Business Partner app**
  Allows for importing, updating, displaying, and marking for deletion credit reports from external agencies (business partners).
- **Find Business Partner app**
  Used for searching external agencies and assigning business partner IDs to them.
- **Manage Credit Reports app**
  Provides a list of credit reports across all business partners, thus allowing for the side-by-side comparison of two reports.

- **Display Inbox app**
Used for tracking monitoring updates where new credit reports can be compared with older ones. The inbox is automatically updated for any reports that are subscribed to.

- **Request Investigation app**
Manages which credit agencies and companies you want to raise an investigation for.

- **Manage Investigation app**
Used for reviewing all investigations requested and their status, including communications with the credit agencies.

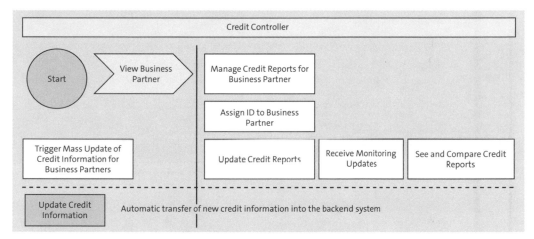

Figure 5.26 Process for SAP S/4HANA Cloud for Credit Integration

5.7   Summary

Process orchestration is the key to managing Central Finance under any scenario. In this chapter, we covered the most common problems with master data and reviewed the most common processes. However, other processes also exist in Central Finance or are not valid for Central Finance. For example, consolidation, intercompany operations, cloud solutions, FP&A, closing operations, industry-specific topics, and machine learning are beyond the scope of this book.

Chapter 6

Deployment Options: How Do I Implement Central Finance?

The public cloud, hybrid clouds, and private clouds now dot the land-scape of IT-based solutions. Because of that, the basic issues have moved from 'what is the cloud' to 'how will cloud projects evolve'.
—Chris Howard, Research Vice President at Gartner

The purpose of this chapter is to explain various Central Finance deployment options, discuss how Central Finance fits in your overall landscape, and explore how using cloud-based technologies changes the topology of your system landscape. Complementary on-premise software applications (both mandatory and optional) each have their own deployment considerations, such as the SAP Landscape Transformation Replication Server (SAP LT Replication Server), SAP Master Data Governance (SAP MDG), SAP Business Warehouse (SAP BW), and SAP Business Planning and Consolidation (SAP BPC). In the first part of the chapter, we'll focus on on-premise deployment considerations before explaining how the cloud fits in.

The cloud can be used for various Central Finance use cases, including the following:

- A project accelerator for use with the SAP Activate methodology or for ongoing production operations

- Extension and enhancement of capabilities via cloud-based solutions

- Incorporation of SAP cloud-based financial systems as part of a two-tier strategy

In this chapter, we'll begin by providing you with some high-level concepts to help you better understand cloud landscapes. Afterwards, we'll discuss the mandatory and optional *on-premise* software that comes along with Central Finance. Next, we'll discuss various cloud deployment options, before moving on to discuss a hybrid landscape. Finally, we'll end by briefly looking at Central Finance as part of a two-tier strategy.

6.1   Getting Started

Before we get started, let's introduce some key concepts and terms. For instance, the use of the word *cloud* can have multiple meanings, sometimes conflicting, depending on the vendor or analyst. Our use of terms is mapped to the SAP lexicon and is defined as follows:

- **Traditional versus cloud hosting**
  Two types of traditional hosting exist:
  - Dedicated (hardware is only used by a single organization)
  - Shared (hardware is shared by more than one organization)

  The fundamental difference between traditional and cloud hosting is the use of virtualization (as opposed to the management of physical hardware). Virtual space and resources can be provisioned on-demand, following a concept called *utility computing*, which shifts software pricing to follow specific usage rather than levy fixed fees.

  In the industry, dedicated cloud hosting models are called *private clouds*, and shared cloud hosting models are called *public clouds*.

- **Cloud-based service models**
  Cloud offerings have expanded from delivering on-demand, as-needed infrastructure to enabling software development and packaged applications. The terms infrastructure as a service (IaaS), platform as a service (PaaS), and software as a service (SaaS) are based on the notion of renting assets rather than buying them.

  Examples of SAP's IaaS, PaaS, and SaaS offerings include, respectively, SAP HANA Enterprise Cloud, SAP Cloud Platform, and SAP S/4HANA Cloud. Note that on-premise SAP S/4HANA, and even SAP HANA Enterprise Cloud, can run on IaaS platforms such as Amazon Web Services (AWS) and Microsoft Azure. Furthermore, SaaS solutions like SAP S/4HANA Cloud are based on PaaS (SAP Cloud Platform) and IaaS (SAP HANA Enterprise Cloud).

- **SAP S/4HANA and the cloud**
  SAP S/4HANA is written as one code line but with different levels of scope depending on the deployment option, either on-premise or on a public cloud (SaaS). On-premise SAP S/4HANA is also available in the cloud as an IaaS either in a dedicated private cloud or in a public cloud such as AWS, Google Cloud Platform, or Microsoft Azure.

  The application management services of these options can be either owned by the customer or by a vendor, who could be SAP.

SAP S/4HANA Cloud is a public cloud solution that runs on the SAP IaaS and PaaS platforms. SAP S/4HANA Cloud, single tenant edition, is based on the SAP S/4HANA on-premise scope and code but hosted and managed in a cloud. The primary difference between using SAP S/4HANA Cloud, single tenant edition, and running SAP S/4HANA on a private managed cloud is pricing. The former follows the same packaged subscription licensing model for SAP S/4HANA Cloud (public cloud version) while the latter is based on the customized pricing model for SAP HANA Enterprise Cloud IaaS and managed services (which may involve a perpetual bring your own license [BYOL] model). In addition, many SAP service providers offer similar options, as shown in Figure 6.1.

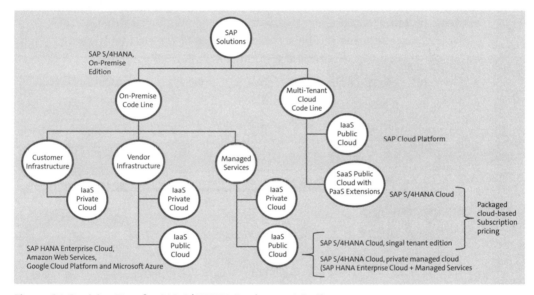

Figure 6.1 Decision Tree for SAP S/4HANA Deployment Options

- **Central Finance and the cloud**
  Central Finance is only available within the scope of on-premise SAP S/4HANA's code line. As a result, the only way Central Finance can be hosted in the cloud is via an IaaS provider either managed by you, the customer, or by an outside vendor. Because SAP S/4HANA Cloud, single tenant edition, and SAP S/4HANA on a private managed cloud use the on-premise version of the software, Central Finance is available in the private cloud or public cloud as an IaaS.

Note that SAP Activate is predicated on the use of the cloud to follow agile principles and to accelerate projects. Furthermore, Central Finance can integrate with the SAP S/4HANA Cloud either as part of the two-tier landscape or via extensions.

These various cloud-related deployment scenarios with be covered in more detail later in Section 6.3, after a deeper treatment of the key considerations for an on-premise deployment of Central Finance.

6.2   On-Premise

In this section, we'll cover both the mandatory and optional software that comes along with Central Finance many of which can be co-deployed with Central Finance. However, some will need to be separately deployed (or we highly recommended doing so). The scope of on-premise applications we'll cover include:

- SAP Landscape Transformation Replication Server (SAP LT Replication Server)
- SAP Solution Manager
- SAP Master Data Governance (SAP MDG)
- SAP Data Services
- SAP Business Warehouse (SAP BW)
- SAP Business Planning and Consolidation (SAP BPC) and SAP S/4HANA Finance for group reporting

Note

For more information about the system architecture and the landscape for Central Finance, please check out Chapter 7.

As mentioned earlier in Section 6.1, Central Finance only comes with the scope of on-premise SAP S/4HANA's code line. As a result, a separate installation of SAP S/4HANA is not needed for Central Finance. However, additional software installations will be needed for integration, such as the SAP LT Replication Server and the Data Migration Server (DMIS) add-on in your source systems. A preexisting SAP ERP system can be converted to SAP S/4HANA and used as a Central Finance instance (brownfield implementation). This option was popular in earlier implementations when the scope of SAP S/4HANA was limited to finance applications. However, SAP S/4HANA now spans most enterprise management processes, so new greenfield installations of SAP

S/4HANA have become the most pragmatic option, whether Central Finance is a stepping stone to SAP S/4HANA or will serve as a hub.

SAP is strategically interested in making Central Finance available as a multitenant public cloud solution, but the product development is not yet on the immediate-term SAP roadmap. SAP S/4HANA Cloud, single tenant edition is the current solution.

When putting Central Finance in the cloud via an IaaS platform, other on-premise solution components related to Central Finance (both mandatory and optional) must be considered. In addition, how you centralize or distribute additional applications (physically or in the cloud) is a key consideration that extends into the next section on other cloud deployment considerations.

6.2.1   Required Deployments

In addition to the SAP S/4HANA installation, Central Finance requires the SAP LT Replication Server to connect and replicate data from various source systems (whether SAP or non-SAP). Meanwhile, the SAP Solution Manager is required for the maintenance and support of any SAP solution. Several paths to SAP S/4HANA include the following:

- New greenfield implementation of SAP S/4HANA
- Brownfield system conversion of SAP ERP to SAP S/4HANA
- Central Finance as the first phase in the roadmap to SAP S/4HANA

In turn, the Central Finance system can be established as either as a greenfield implementation (a new implementation) or as a brownfield implementation (a system conversion of an entire SAP ERP).

SAP LT Replication Server

The SAP LT Replication Server can be installed either on the Central Finance system, one of the source SAP ERP systems, or separately as a standalone system (the last option being SAP recommended). The SAP LT Replication Server can either be installed on-premise or hosted in the cloud.

For integrating non-SAP data, the SAP LT Replication Server has a staging area known as the third-party interface (see SAP Note 2610660: SAP LT Replication Server for Central Finance - Third-Party System Integration 1709, FPS 2 for more details). Data integration tools like SAP Data Services or custom programs can be designed and implemented to update the third-party interface's staging tables, which then, in turn, update Central Finance.

SAP Solution Manager

SAP Solution Manager is an application to manage all your other applications. The solution can help optimize and gain control of complex and distributed IT landscapes. SAP Solution Manager manages both SAP and non-SAP enterprise solutions whether those solutions are running on-premise, in the cloud, or in a hybrid scenario. SAP Solution Manager contains integrated modules that cover all aspects of application lifecycle management including implementation, maintenance, monitoring, operations, and adapting for future innovations. SAP Solution Manager runs on its own server and can be used for other central technical services, such as the System Landscape Directory (SLD).

For Central Finance deployments, SAP Solution Manager can manage the promote-to-production landscape for transports as well as for performance monitoring and fineOtuning the production system.

The SAP Activate methodology for SAP S/4HANA also includes SAP Solution Manager components for project management functionality and predelivered methodology content.

Because SAP requires that SAP Solution Manager be deployed with SAP solutions to receive support from SAP, most customers have at least the minimum installed. Your organization will need to define to what degree SAP Solution Manager will be used to manage Central Finance and all of its associated solutions.

6.2.2   Optional Deployments

In addition to the mandatory use of the SAP LT Replication Server and SAP Solution Manager, other on-premise SAP software that may be used with the Central Finance system include:

- SAP MDG, which may also need SLD set up
- SAP Data Services
- SAP BW as a separate instance, which has its own SAP HANA sizing and deployment considerations
- SAP BPC as a standalone instance either on its own or in a shared SAP BW instance

SAP Master Data Governance

SAP MDG is designed to address a specific business need: achieving standardization and quality control of master data across a heterogeneous system landscape. For more information about SAP MDG, see Chapter 7, Section 7.5, and Chapter 10.

SAP MDG has many different deployment options for Central Finance. Your first fundamental decision will be to pick one of these options:

- Deploy SAP MDG on its own dedicated server as a master data hub
- Co-deploy SAP MDG with Central Finance on the same SAP HANA server
- Deploy Central Finance using a preexisting SAP MDG deployment

In general, not just when considering SAP MDG, separating applications onto their own servers has some advantages and disadvantages, such as:

- Technical upgrades and functional improvements can be performed with less impact to other applications and processes in the same environment, but changes will have to be redundantly and separately managed.
- Cleaner governance from a control and autonomy perspective instead of managing business and operational conflicts in a shared environment, which would translate to redundancies in data and processes.

For example, a standalone master data governance system used for central governance will need to replicate master data to Central Finance and all of its source systems. If SAP MDG is co-deployed with Central Finance, you would need to manage one less system to which to replicate data including its connectivity over a network.

If SAP MDG has already been deployed, but without SAP HANA, then a key question is whether the solution should be migrated. For example, if SAP MDG was co-deployed on an SAP ERP source system, then a natural question to ask is whether the solution will be left alone or moved to Central Finance. The use of SAP HANA for searching and matching shouldn't be the overriding reason to migrate SAP MDG; SAP HANA can be deployed as a secondary database connection and side car implementation to SAP MDG nondisruptively. The larger question is concerned with overall governance: Shouldn't SAP MDG be moved to Central Finance with all the other centralized data and processes? You'll need to weigh pragmatic approaches against ideal states, and tradeoffs may be needed.

Note that, if SAP MDG is separated from Central Finance, as opposed to being co-deployed, how the SAP HANA database system can be shared will be restricted, as described in SAP Note 1661202: Support multiple applications one SAP HANA database/tenant DB. The key takeaways are:

- You'll need to review a white list of applications that can run together on the same SAP HANA database as separate deployments.

- At the time of this writing, SAP MDG and SAP S/4HANA are not on that white list.

- However, as of SAP HANA SPS 09, multitenant database containers (MDCs) were introduced that allow separate SAP MDG and SAP S/4HANA deployments to reside in the same SAP HANA system by having their own tenants.

- As of SAP HANA 2.0 SPS 01, MDCs are the only database operation mode allowed. As a result, the natural recommendation is to keep each deployment in their own tenant, if possible.

SAP MDG Foundation

Using SAP MDG with Central Finance is optional. The only SAP MDG component that comes with Central Finance is SAP MDG Foundation primarily as a mapping engine and application enveloping the Unified Key Mapping Service (UKMS). SAP MDG Foundation functionality is also optional.

System Landscape Directory)

The System Landscape Directory (SLD) is a central directory of all installed software components and a repository of what can be installed. This directory helps manage the landscape and the software lifecycle. SLD runs as its own server. Similar to UKMS, this functionality is part of SAP NetWeaver.

If SAP MDG Foundation mapping is used, SLD is required unless a Business Add-In (BAdI) is used, as documented in SAP Note 2225086: Enabling Central Finance Business Mapping without the need to setup Systems Landscape Directory (SLD). Otherwise, SAP MDG key mappings need SLD to populate the **Business Systems** dropdown menu where you'll select the configuration by source system. Business systems are in turn mapped to logical system names that represent source systems.

Where to put the SLD server in the landscape and how to connect it to Central Finance (if at all) are infrastructure decisions that you'll need to make.

SAP Data Services

As an alternative or as an additional integration, SAP Data Services, Application Link Enabling (ALE) master data distribution, or custom interfaces can be used to replicate and consolidate master data from source systems into Central Finance. Also note that Central Finance BAdIs can be used instead of SAP MDG Foundation to map master data during transactional updates. Central Finance BAdIs are often used for complex multidimensional and rule-driven mappings that UKMS in the Central Finance context cannot address without enhancements.

SAP Data Services is a data transformation and management tool. Prior to the SAP's acquisition of BusinessObjects, the solution was an ETL (extract, transform, and load) tool known as the Data Integrator. After the acquisition, other data management functionality was merged into the Data Integrator such as de-duplication, address validation, and data quality management, and the expanded tool was rebranded as SAP Data Services.

SAP Data Services offers two groups of predefined content for SAP S/4HANA:

- **SAP Best Practices**

  As part of SAP's Activate methodology, SAP delivers project accelerators known as SAP Best Practices, which consist of installable content and documentation. In terms of master data, SAP S/4HANA and SAP Data Services, SAP offers rapid data migration to the SAP S/4HANA Best Practices package.

  SAP Best Practices is designed for one-time data migration cutovers from SAP and non-SAP systems as opposed to Central Finance operations. Thus, the scope of data supported goes beyond master data relevant to Central Finance. Also, the content is designed for one-time loading instead of ongoing replication.

  However, because the content is based on SAP Data Services, you can easily modify and enhance the content for ongoing Central Finance operational needs.

- **Magnitude SourceConnect Harmonization**

  Magnitude is an SAP software partner with solutions specifically designed for Central Finance. Magnitude's SourceConnect Harmonization solution for master data replication is also built using SAP Data Services. As opposed to SAP Best Practices for rapid data migration to SAP S/4HANA, Magnitude SourceConnect Harmonization has been purpose-built for ongoing replication in Central Finance.

  While Magnitude SourceConnect Transaction handles the replication of non-SAP data into Central Finance, Magnitude SourceConnect Harmonization is designed for the replication and consolidation of master data (from both SAP and non-SAP systems) into Central Finance.

  Magnitude SourceConnect Harmonization integrates with the UKMS of SAP MDG Foundation and updates the mappings after the master data has been consolidated and loaded. The solution is not designed to replace the SAP MDG central governance option but is an alternative to or enhancement of the SAP MDG consolidation and mass processing options.

SAP Data Services has its own server and metadata repositories separate from SAP NetWeaver. As a result, SAP Data Services cannot be installed on SAP S/4HANA like the SAP LT Replication Server, SAP MDG, or SLD but must be a separate installation. Note that the rapid data migration to SAP Best Practices package for SAP S/4HANA is based on a Windows-based architecture in terms of the database the transformations expect as sources as well as for the server and repositories in SAP Data Services.

SAP Data Services configurations, known as *datastores*, support connectivity to a wide variety of data sources such as:

- Databases and mainframe file systems
- Applications via adapters
- Web services
- Remote servers using FTP, SFTP, and SAP Cloud Platform file transfer protocols

Each datastore must be evaluated vis-à-vis the network and where the data source resides, whether in a data center or in the cloud.

6.2.3   SAP Business Warehouse

Since 2004, SAP BW has been an embedded part of SAP ERP, but the functionality was rarely adopted due to sizing and performance issues. With the introduction of SAP Business Suite on SAP HANA and SAP S/4HANA, many of these performance issues have been addressed. The use of the embedded SAP BW in SAP S/4HANA should be considered as part of every Central Finance deployment. Central Finance has many benefits and use cases, but one of the most popular, standardized financial reporting and analysis, is considered a low-hanging fruit.

As a result, the need (or lack thereof) for a separate SAP BW system (or the SAP HANA-optimized version known as SAP BW/4HANA) also must be evaluated, particularly for real-time financial analytics. However, governance, sizing, and performance reasons to keep SAP BW (or SAP BW/4HANA) and SAP S/4HANA separate may still exist, especially depending on how SAP HANA is sized and distributed.

When deploying SAP BW and SAP HANA vis-à-vis Central Finance, you'll also need to evaluate some key data warehousing design factors.

If you decide a separate SAP BW system (or SAP BW/4HANA) is still needed, then you'll next evaluate sizing and determine how the database and applications should be distributed (i.e., within a single data center or across several data centers; on-premise or in the cloud).

In this section, we'll cover the same topics we covered in Section 6.2.2 for SAP MDG and related SAP HANA white list applications and for the use of SAP HANA database tenants, but from a data warehousing perspective.

Figure 6.2 shows several application and database deployment scenarios related to sizing.

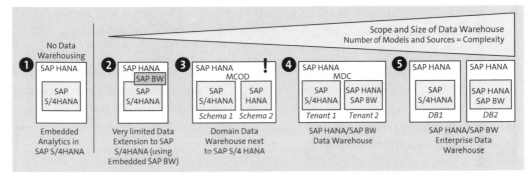

Figure 6.2 Data Warehousing Options and Complexity

Let's look at each scenario as follows:

❶ Central Finance without SAP BW: Because Central Finance is a fully functional SAP S/4HANA system, embedded analytics, such as SAP Fiori applications, are included without the need to use SAP BW.

❷ Central Finance with embedded SAP BW: Central Finance is a more powerful financial analytics tool when used in combination with SAP BW for real-time insights. However, Central Finance is not an enterprise data warehouse (EDW) solution. For certain scenarios, such as historical trending and machine learning, the lines can be blurred, thus putting a strain on the sizing of the system needed to support both transactions and analytics.

❸ Central Finance with SAP HANA analytics as a side car: Central Finance and SAP BW (or SAP BW/4HANA) are not white-listed applications for use together within the same SAP HANA database or tenant. Multiple components in one database (MCOD) are supported for side car SAP HANA scenarios and analytics, but cross-schema integration techniques will be needed to bring the data together with Central Finance. Hybrid scenarios are possible where side car implementations of SAP HANA, SAP BW (as well as SAP BPC), and Central Finance are all combined together. For example, sales and logistics data can be replicated via the SAP LT Replication Server into a separate SAP HANA database schema that joins with data in the Central Finance database schema for use in integrated and real-time SAP BW reporting.

❹ Central Finance with a separate SAP BW (or SAP BW/4HANA) sharing SAP HANA: Central Finance can share the same SAP HANA system with SAP BW (or SAP BW/4HANA) if they are installed in different database tenants. The SAP HANA system must be appropriately sized, appropriately distributed, and fine-tuned to ensure that the database system can support both transactional and analytic loads from Central Finance processing, operational analytics, and enterprise data warehousing—all combined.

❺ Central Finance with a separate SAP BW (or SAP BW/4HANA) not sharing SAP HANA: If the resource demands of using Central Finance both for enterprise data warehousing and for finance processes become more than one SAP HANA system can effectively manage, then you should use separate SAP HANA databases to ease the competition over resources.

6.2.4   SAP Business Planning and Consolidation

SAP BPC is currently an embedded part of SAP BW. As a result, as of SAP S/4HANA 1610, SAP BPC is included with SAP BW and, thus, in turn, is embedded within SAP S/4HANA. (For more information, refer to SAP Note 2103585: Product Component Matrix for SAP Business Planning & Consolidation 10.1, version for Net Weaver 7.40/7.50, SAP S/4HANA 1610, and SAP S/4HANA 1709 and Business Planning & Consolidation 11.0, version for BW/4 HANA 1.0.)

As a result, many of the considerations for deploying SAP BW also apply to SAP BPC, at least for the SAP NetWeaver version of SAP BPC. However, the additional resource load for planning and consolidation can be quite different than for reporting, analysis, and enterprise data warehousing. For example, planning tends to be demanding in terms of memory (e.g., many user planning sessions) and computationally intensive (e.g., allocations). Financial consolidation is typically less intensive, since as a corporate function, summarized financial data is used at period-end intervals.

What is unique to SAP BPC are its various applications, each with its own deployment considerations, such as:

- SAP BPC optimized for SAP S/4HANA
- Consolidation/group reporting for SAP S/4HANA
- Embedded SAP BPC for standalone SAP BW or SAP BW/4HANA deployments
- Standard SAP BPC for SAP S/4HANA, SAP BW, or SAP BW/4HANA
- Standard SAP BPC for the Microsoft platform

The first two options are included in SAP S/4HANA and should not be deployed separately as you would for the other options. Similar to Central Finance, SAP BPC is not available in the SAP S/4HANA Cloud but can be hosted on an IaaS provider. SAP BPC is not offered as a SaaS solution, but rather other SAP offering feature planning and consolidation as SaaS solutions. SAP S/4HANA Cloud utilizes SAP Analytics Cloud planning for FP&A and group reporting for financial consolidations. The Group Reporting solution is available with Central Finance as of SAP S/4HANA 1809.

Standard SAP BPC came into the SAP portfolio via the acquisition of Outlooksoft in 2007. Due to its architecture (first on the Microsoft platform and then ported to the SAP NetWeaver technical platform), Standard SAP BPC has always been designed as a standalone solution even when made available in SAP S/4HANA. Therefore, in most customer environments, SAP BPC was a separate deployment that has been either retired and reimplemented as SAP BPC optimized for SAP S/4HANA or has been kept in the landscape as a separate system. In many cases, SAP BPC is also kept separately from the rest of SAP BW, although in some cases, they are co-deployed.

The current recommendation for consolidation in SAP S/4HANA is the recently-released SAP S/4HANA Finance for group reporting solution. SAP now suggests that you use this new solution for consolidation/group reporting and continue to use SAP BPC for business planing.

6.3   Cloud

Through the virtualization and the sharing of computing resources, the cloud enables organizations to readily access infrastructure, development platforms, or software services either on-demand or as a subscription. Flexible payment options for cloud solutions are a stark contrast to the traditional way of paying for perpetual licenses upfront. Such purchases run the risk of underutilized or obsolete assets, especially in, but not limited to, hardware.

From an IaaS perspective, the deployment considerations for on-premise software is no different for on-premise data centers as for the cloud data centers except for more specialized networking and the additional security needed for connectivity.

Figure 6.3 shows the impact that IaaS cloud hosting can have on the landscape.

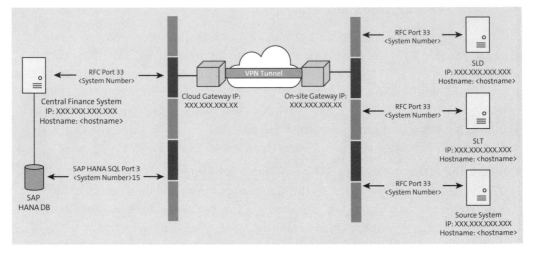

Figure 6.3 Impact of Cloud Hosting on Hardware Landscape

Let's discuss Figure 6.3 from left to right: To far left are all the software applications hosted in the cloud. Central Finance is represented on the SAP HANA database where it resides. Both servers need to connect with themselves in the cloud as well as other systems that reside inside the on-premise network. To communicate in the cloud, message traffic must go through a firewall (to restrict traffic to only from trusted sources) and then a cloud gateway (to route the traffic). In some organizations, routing to another gateway and passing through another firewall is redundant and unneeded. In other organizations, this case represents another layer of security, as shown in Figure 6.3. In either case, data is routed to communication endpoints known as *ports* that have been opened to receive messages. SAP systems use TCP/IP for communication and the application server uses Remote Function Call (RFC) ports while the SAP HANA database uses SQL ports.

On the far right, SLD, the SAP LT Replication Server, and SAP source systems are represented as on-premise deployments. Those applications could have just as easily been put on the far left (in the cloud) once the networking and security protocols are established (e.g., VPN). Messaging traffic is bidirectional, and different ports are used for different scenarios, for example:

- Central Finance document-level drilldown back to the source
- The initial extraction of financial history into Central Finance (In this case, Central Finance directly connects to the source SAP system rather than through the SAP LT Replication Server.)
- The replication of real-time financial transactions via the SAP LT Replication Server

The Internet Protocol (IP) address and hostname are technical labels to identify and locate systems on the network and in the cloud for the gateway and firewall to use.

What follows is a deeper explanation of terms and concepts that describe who controls the cloud and the activities that come with ownership, namely: private cloud, public cloud, managed cloud, and project cloud. Let's look at each next.

6.3.1 Private Cloud

As shown earlier in Figure 6.1, the term *private cloud* means different things from infrastructure (IaaS), platform (PaaS), and application (SaaS) perspectives. Across all perspectives, the word "private" represents a dedicated environment that is not shared with others.

IaaS

From an IaaS frame of reference, a private cloud represents virtualized infrastructure either managed internally or externally by a vendor that is exclusively dedicated to the customer. If managed internally, the private cloud is also referred to as an *internal cloud*. If managed externally, the hosting provider ensures privacy.

Contrast these private clouds to public cloud offerings like AWS, GCP, and Microsoft Azure, where customers share resources and computing power. Many SAP customers leverage SAP-certified public clouds for internal use but can also use external vendors who provide "managed services" or a "managed cloud".

A *managed cloud* consists of vendor-managed services performed within a private or public cloud environment. Those vendor activities are described in more detail later.

The SAP HANA Enterprise Cloud IaaS offering covers the range of private, public, and managed cloud deployment options for Central Finance. In the private cloud option, two different pricing options are available: one following the SAP S/4HANA Cloud (SaaS) subscription model and the other based on a more traditional pricing model for IaaS private cloud and managed services.

In any case, the benefits of using the cloud for a Central Finance implementation are all essentially the same whether private or public cloud or whether internally or externally managed. What differs are the dynamics of each option, but these dynamics can be overridden by the quality of delivery. For example, an internal cloud is typically difficult to scale and grow like a large public cloud but offers much more control and visibility around the infrastructure setup, operations, and security. However, such dynamics doesn't necessarily mean that a public cloud will scale more reliably or that the private cloud will be more secure; those concerns depend on the quality of the people and process behind each.

PaaS

From a PaaS frame of reference, a private cloud is similar to an IaaS private cloud in that the environment needs to be dedicated and exclusive.

In fact, by some definitions, a private PaaS environment must be predicated on a private IaaS environment (i.e., software installed and managed within private data centers). Another, more flexible definition defines PaaS as private, even in a public IaaS cloud, as long as it meets the following criteria:

- Data, storage, and network isolation
- Dedicated environment for a specific customer
- Data security, privacy, and protection protocols and measures

The SAP Cloud Platform, private edition, meets these criteria. You'll need to choose between private and public PaaS versions. In either case, SAP Cloud Platform (or a non-SAP PaaS provider) can be used to extend the functionality of Central Finance. For example, SAP Analytics Cloud runs in the SAP Cloud Platform and can be used to build analytics in the cloud that query the Universal Journal in real time as a direct and live connection.

SaaS

A custom application built with SAP Cloud Platform, private edition, would qualify as a private SaaS solution. Otherwise, virtually all of SAP's SaaS solutions are based on a public cloud such as SAP Ariba, SAP C/4HANA, SAP Cloud for Customer, SAP Concur, SAP Fieldglass, and SAP S/4HANA Cloud.

6.3.2   Public Cloud

Before moving onto a deeper treatment of public cloud options for Central Finance, let's look at Table 6.1, which lists the key similarities and differences between on-premise solutions, private clouds, and public clouds.

On-Premise (Complete Coverage for the Enterprise)	Private Cloud (Complete Coverage for with Accelerated Deployment)	Public Cloud (Focused Coverage for Accelerated Deployment)
Full scope, all industries	Full scope, all industries	Standardized processes
Configure, extend, modify	Configure, extend	Configure, extend within boundaries
Customer infrastructure or IaaS	SAP infrastructure	SAP infrastructure
Yearly innovation cycle	Yearly innovation cycle	Quarterly innovation cycle
Traditional perpetual licensing	Subscription or perpetual	Subscription licensing

Table 6.1 Deployment Options

The on-premise deployment option includes a full-featured set of SAP S/4HANA functionality, including Central Finance and complementary solutions like SAP MDG and SAP BPC. The SAP S/4HANA release cycle is annual. The predecessors to SAP S/4HANA 1809 (September 2019) were SAP S/4HANA 1709 (September 2017), SAP S/4HANA 1610 (October 2016), and SAP S/4HANA 1511 (November 2015). Since the on-premise version inherited its extensibility framework from SAP ERP, the on-premise version is highly customizable and even modifiable (though not recommended). The pricing for on-premise SAP S/4HANA has historically been based on a perpetual license model.

The same SAP S/4HANA on-premise solution can be priced as a private cloud option with subscription pricing. SAP S/4HANA Cloud, single tenant edition shares the same code line as the SAP S/4HANA on-premise edition. As a result, SAP S/4HANA Cloud follows the same annual release schedule. However, private clouds have some restrictions. For example, for modules included in the standard packages, modifications to the code is restricted, and only new greenfield installations are supported (i.e., no system copies for brownfield system conversions are allowed).

An à la carte private cloud option is available with SAP HANA Enterprise Cloud that can be based on a perpetual license—available as under a bring your own license (BYOL) model—or based on subscription licensing that is priced for each customer. The level of managed services is also customizable and optional.

The code behind SAP S/4HANA Cloud was written to support multitenancy as part of a public cloud solution. As a result, the functionality is more focused and streamlined than the on-premise version but with more frequent updates and versioning (every quarter). The extensibility of the solution is handled via SAP Cloud Platform with more limitations and controls than the on-premise version. And, of course, being a public cloud solution, the pricing is based on subscription fees.

IaaS

The full power of virtualization is achieved through economies of scale in a shared public environment driving down costs and accessibility through efficiencies. As a result, the market for IaaS is ruled by large public cloud providers like Amazon, Google, and Microsoft.

A full list of IaaS certified providers can be found at *https://www.sap.com/dmc/exp/ 2014-09-02-hana-hardware/enEN/iaas.html*.

Also, SAP HANA Enterprise Cloud provides IaaS in both public and private clouds. Setting up a public cloud account and starting to rent space is an easy and quick thing to do and can help speed up innovation and implementations.

PaaS

Many IaaS public cloud providers, such as Amazon, Google, and Microsoft, also offer PaaS platforms. In fact, the lines are blurring between IaaS and PaaS platforms. For example, on top of its Google Compute Engine (IaaS), Google offers its Google App Engine (PaaS), which can be used to build applications that integrate with SAP HANA.

SAP Cloud Platform is a PaaS platform available in both public and private clouds. SAP Cloud Platform can act as the main bridge between SAP on-premise and public cloud solutions. Because SAP Cloud Platform is a development platform with many connectivity options, it can integrate with other cloud platforms and can enhance SAP with innovative capabilities like machine learning.

SaaS

While on-premise software can be made available as a service via a private cloud, purpose-built SaaS solutions are designed for the public cloud and can handle multitenancy (i.e., many customers sharing the service but keeping data private and protected). For that reason, the scope of functionality available in the SAP public cloud solutions differs from their on-premise and private cloud counterpart solutions. The primary example is SAP S/4HANA Cloud versus on-premise SAP S/4HANA. While the scope of each solution is different, many overlapping and similar functionalities exist because both products share the same originating code line.

Meanwhile, solutions like SAP Analytics Cloud are available only in the public cloud. The closest on-premise equivalent for planning is SAP BPC, which is a completely different solution. Meanwhile, SAP BPC is only available as an on-premise solution that, at best, can be hosted in a private cloud.

While Central Finance must be on the on-premise code line of the software, it can source data from SAP (and non-SAP) public cloud solutions, such as SAP S/4HANA Cloud and SAP Business ByDesign.

Central Finance can also be integrated with cloud-based SAP solutions, which we discussed in more detail in Chapter 5.

6.3.3 Managed Cloud

Whether the infrastructure for Central Finance is hosted on a private or public cloud, someone needs to manage and maintain the solution. That person can be the customer, SAP (i.e., SAP HANA Enterprise Cloud), or a third-party provider.

The roles and responsibilities of a third-party provider will vary. Many managed service offerings are customizable. For example, SAP application management services can be added to SAP HANA Enterprise Cloud cloud costing. Some managed services come prepackaged or even bundled (such as SAP S/4HANA Cloud, single tenant edition).

Managed services typically encompass traditional SAP Basis and overall infrastructure activities. Some examples of services taken care of in a managed cloud may include:

- Installing and provisioning any software (and their prerequisites)
- Making backups on a schedule and upon request
- Ensuring restoration and disaster recovery infrastructure policy and procedures are in place
- Applying SAP Notes and raising SAP incident reports
- Applying patches and updates (to the operating system, the database, and to SAP applications)
- Doing upgrades (to the operating system, the database, and to SAP applications)
- Reviewing database growth in comparison with initial sizing to ensure space doesn't run out
- Setting up system monitoring and alerting especially for when resources start to become low
- Reviewing system logs for anomalies

- Troubleshooting issues as they arise
- Designing, configuring, and reviewing security models and protocols

Some of the activities that benefit from Central Finance and the SAP LT Replication Server expertise include the following:

- The SAP LT Replication Server cockpit has an application log that should be monitored. Because of all the communication between systems, looking at the gateway logs (i.e., Transaction SMGW) can be useful for finding communication issues. While the SAP Application Integration Framework has an application log, this log is typically the domain of the operations team and not the managed services team because this log primarily consists of application and data mapping errors.

- Throughput is often overlooked in sizing and fine-tuning for Central Finance initial loads. An analysis of the number of work processes or parallel threads needed in the source system, in the SAP LT Replication Server, and in SAP S/4HANA must be assessed and monitored (e.g., Transactions SM50 and SM51). Dialogue work processes may need to be converted temporarily to background work processes and then switched back on. Optimization includes having a few idle work processes (but not too many), ready for any on-demand spikes needed for running reconciliation, analysis, or another central transaction while loads are running. Other measures of CPU load also include workload analysis (Transaction ST03).

- In some cases, Central Finance and SAP LT Replication Server configuration can control the packaging and processing of large datasets into smaller datasets and chunks of work. During performance optimization and fine-tuning, these settings will need to be reviewed and possibly changed.

- Some Central Finance processes can have spikes in the amount of memory needed, and application operators may kick off programs without the knowledge of the other work processes, thus leading to resource competition issues that may even reach into the source production system. The managed services team needs tight communication with the operations team to avoid running out of resources across the landscape.

Another set of SAP Basis and infrastructure activities need to be performed on the source systems. In fact, in some cases, the work effort can be much greater, particularly during initial loads. Typically, source production systems already have management structures in place before a Central Finance implementation (either in-house or outsourced). If Central Finance is not in the same managed cloud as the source systems, the governance model needs to be reviewed for a clear delineation of roles and responsibilities. What follows are some example scenarios of how Central Finance can impact on source systems:

- The initial extraction of financial documents into Central Finance can be resource intensive on the source system database, requiring expertise not only to find bottlenecks but to help resolve the issues. SQL traces may need to be run on tables used by Central Finance to assess if adding indices (to be deleted afterwards) or hints or rebuilding database statistics will help.

- Very large extractions and loads of data are also memory intensive and can lead to ABAP dumps and program terminations if not properly managed. Both application server and the database server memory must be monitored proactively as with any SAP application, but in Central Finance deployments, special attention is needed during initial loads.

- When memory dumps occur, dump and system logs must be reviewed (e.g., Transactions ST22 and SM21, respectively) to troubleshoot and resolve the issue.

Some managed service offerings are more comprehensive, with responsibilities encompassing both infrastructure and application operations. For example, SAP HANA Enterprise Cloud provides the infrastructure as well as the deployment and management of the applications. Just as varied are the cloud technology options, deployment models, and managed services pricing and scope options. Because of the number of options and the rate of change in the industry, choosing the right model for managing an extended overall Central Finance landscape is a critical strategic decision.

6.3.4   Project Cloud

One variation to a managed cloud is to limit the scope of services to a project or a phase in the project. The notion of a *project cloud* is to utilize the managed cloud to support in-the-system iterative design and build-out including scenarios such as:

- A software purchase evaluation of Central Finance and/or a proof-of-concept to gain funding and approval for an implementation

- Support of rapid proof-of-concept designs early in blueprinting to identify gaps and risks

- Demonstrations and prototypes during blueprinting for training, education and more comprehensive functional and technical specifications

- Supporting early sizing efforts before procuring hardware

Some vendors, including SAP and TruQua, are specially licensed to support a "try-and-decide" exercise as part of the SAP sales process. The template's virtual image acts as an accelerator by having additional and relevant software already preinstalled such as SAP HANA, the SAP LT Replication Server, SAP Application Integration Framework, SAP MDG, SAP BPC, and SAP Fiori as well as having the key setup steps and configuration already performed. Central Finance and the SAP LT Replication Server are then connected to one or more representative source systems (either SAP or non-SAP) to either evaluate the technical mechanics or evaluate certain SAP S/4HANA functionalities with customer data. The challenge with such a "try-and-decide" exercise is finding useful demo scenarios with limited data in a short timeframe.

Alternatively, a project cloud can be used for the design phase (and possibly build phase) of a project prior to cutting a system copy over into an on-premise landscape, a private cloud, a public cloud, or another managed cloud provider. This approach fits well into the SAP Activate methodology designed for SAP S/4HANA implementations, as shown in Figure 6.4.

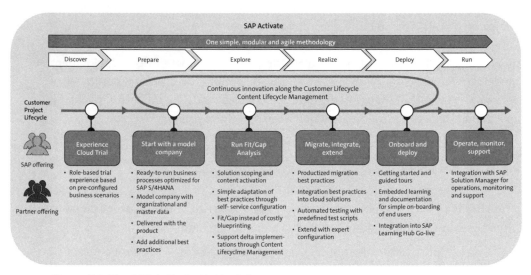

Figure 6.4 The SAP Activate Methodology

During the "explore" phase of SAP Activate, the methodology assumes the use of a cloud-based baseline solution with which to perform a fit-gap analysis. The baseline can either come from what is known as SAP Best Practices or the SAP Model Company. The SAP Model Company (separately sold and licensed) is an extension of SAP Best Practices packages (available with an SAP license). Both are similar in that they represent a set of application content, preconfiguration, tools, project documentation templates, and accelerators. However, SAP Best Practices does not have content designed specifically for Central Finance while the SAP Model Company does. In fact, the SAP Model Company for Central Finance is different than most SAP Model Company offerings and is focused on Central Finance-specific methodology and tools like source system data profiling and the identification of relevant conflicts in configuration and data across multiple source SAP systems and Central Finance. As opposed to using a public cloud trial license for software evaluation as part of the "discover" phase, these prepackaged solutions and systems are designed for downstream phases of the project.

In either case, prepackaged cloud-based virtual images integrated into a project methodology like SAP Activate can help jumpstart Central Finance initiatives in early phases.

6.4   Hybrid

On-premise SAP S/4HANA can be integrated into SAP's cloud-based solutions via the SAP Cloud Platform. As PaaS solutions go, one differentiator of the SAP Cloud Platform is its easy connectivity and integration with SAP applications both in the cloud and on-premise. The technology to handle connectivity in SAP Cloud Platform is known as the SAP Cloud Connector.

The SAP Cloud Connector has specific features for on-premise SAP solution integration. First, easy to install as an on-premise agent on an operating system, the SAP Cloud Connector is colocated with the on-premise SAP solution being connected. Due to the security protocol SAP Cloud Connector utilizes (called a *reverse invoke proxy*), you won't need to open any ports in the firewall for the reverse proxy servers to handle inbound calls nor are any firewall modifications needed for outbound calls. Furthermore, the SAP-native RFC protocol is supported so that native calls in ABAP (SAP's proprietary programming language) can be made without having to generate and accept HTTP requests and responses (although HTTP configuration and access control is popularly supported). Applications like SAP Analytics Cloud do use the HTTP protocol to communicate with SAP S/4HANA.

Another advantage of the SAP Cloud Connector is that it passes the identity of the user to the on-premise systems in a secure way.

For the SAP Cloud Platform developer, these features make integration easier and can benefit all SAP cloud applications built in the SAP Cloud Platform.

Central Finance can benefit from all the satellite cloud applications being developed for SAP S/4HANA as extensions.

We've selected three analytical applications and three transactional applications as representative examples to show you how the cloud can enhance and extend on-premise financial capabilities with distinct technological advantages.

The following are example SaaS solutions that operate with Central Finance:

- Analytical:
  - SAP RealSpend
  - SAP Financial Statement Insights
  - SAP Analytics Cloud
- Transactional:
  - Customer payments
  - Credit integration
  - Cash application

SAP RealSpend and SAP Financial Statement Insights are covered in more detail in Chapter 4, while SAP Analytics Cloud is covered in more detail in Chapter 7. In this section, we'll discuss transactional applications in the context of Central Finance.

All of these SaaS applications were built natively on SAP's PaaS platform, SAP Cloud Platform. These examples are part of a growing number of applications leveraging the latest innovations in technology. Some are relatively small applications designed to solve a specific need (like SAP RealSpend) while others can be much broader, representing a platform or a suite (like SAP Analytics Cloud). In either case, new capabilities can be rapidly deployed without disrupting the core solution. In addition, because these applications share a common customizable SAP Fiori user experience and standard SAP Cloud Platform connectivity standards, the integration is seamless and, many cases, in real time without the need for replication. Real-time access to on-premise data keeps the granular details securely within central storage in the back-end (e.g., Universal Journal).

Cloud-based extensions will be continuously improved and updated at a rate faster than the on-premise solution. For example, SAP S/4HANA Cloud has a quarterly release schedule while the on-premise version has an annual one. A notable benefit of SaaS is that dealing with complexity and keeping systems up-to-date has shifted to the provider. For these solutions, SAP will need to update solutions with continuous innovation while at the same time minimizing the impact to the core solution. Furthermore, public cloud-based solutions will dynamically scale with growth in usage.

The side-by-side architecture of these solutions makes them easy to plug in and rapidly implement without much integration impact while, at the same time, still being customizable.

6.5   Two-Tier Strategy

Central Finance is designed for deployment in at least two tiers, in which the central system and the source systems use different ERPs to support different requirements. For instance, a large consumer products manufacturing company might own smaller distribution entities in developing markets. Merging the systems and processes of these subsidiaries into the main ERP might be impractical (expensive in terms of hardware, software, and change management) when compared to integrating a smaller software package that better fits their business model. Similarly, a company may decide, after a series of acquisitions, to gain greater visibility into its subsidiaries' financials by standardizing with SAP but also allow for autonomy and innovation with SAP S/4HANA Cloud.

In this context, some benefits of SAP S/4HANA Cloud in particular to evaluate include the following:

- **Out of the box integration**
  Integration is usually the most complex and expensive part of such a project. Fortunately, SAP invested in this integration scenario, and prepackaged SAP Best Practices content is available for this scenario. Scope item 1W4 (Subsidiary Integration of SAP S/4HANA Cloud to Central Finance), available at *https://rapid.sap.com/bp/#/browse/scopeitems/1W4*, explains the configuration steps needed for SAP Cloud Platform and the SAP LT Replication Server.

- **Reusable testing**
  The financial processes in on-premise SAP S/4HANA and SAP S/4HANA Cloud are quite similar when executed through the SAP Fiori user interface. This similarity accelerates and streamlines testing because test automation and test scripts can be reused across systems.

- **Reduced change management**
  Since your headquarters and your subsidiaries will both be operating on SAP S/4HANA, all your users will use the same language and processes and interact with the same SAP Fiori user experience, which facilitates communication and user adoption. In addition, users trained in one system can easily migrate to the other systems, which supports employee mobility and efficiency.

If SAP S/4HANA Cloud becomes a favored solution for both small subsidiaries and corporate headquarters, an all public cloud Central Finance deployment is not supported at the time of this writing, as explained earlier. However, some Central Finance private cloud options can also leverage the financial consolidation capabilities available in SAP S/4HANA. This deployment model is needed when a financial holding company must have consolidated group reporting and requires automated eliminations along different levels of a reporting hierarchy.

SAP S/4HANA Cloud, single tenant edition; SAP S/4HANA on a private managed cloud; SAP S/4HANA on a dedicated vendor-managed cloud; or SAP S/4HANA on an internal cloud are all Central Finance private cloud options.

6.6   Summary

As we described in this chapter, many on-premise and cloud deployment options for Central Finance exist. The cloud has many dimensions:

- The part of the technology stack that is being virtualized and offered as a service, be it the infrastructure (IaaS), platform (PaaS), or software (SaaS).
- The level of customer exclusivity in the environment, whether dedicated (private cloud) or shared (public cloud).
- The level of management and support that comes with the cloud, whether unmanaged or a managed cloud. A limited-use managed cloud for use as a project accelerator or a project cloud is an integral part of the SAP Activate methodology.

The on-premise and cloud deployment options are not mutually exclusive and can be combined in tandem as hybrid integrations whether as part of a two-tier strategy or as a way to expand capabilities via SAP Cloud Platform.

The criteria for adopting one deployment option over the other will depend on your organization, but your evaluation should take into account the following:

- Organizational readiness to adopt the cloud
- Environment readiness, since some local countries, regulations, or technology constraints may not allow a cloud deployment
- Software readiness, since some features and functions might not be fully available in the cloud or on-premise

PART II

Deploying Central Finance

Chapter 7
System Architecture

One challenge in a Central Finance implementation project is fully understanding the architecture of Central Finance, mistakenly believing this solution is from the SAP S/4HANA core. In this core chapter, let's look at the Central Finance system's architecture to understand how this solution works.

In this chapter, we'll walk you through the concepts behind the architecture of Central Finance, focusing on two main elements: First, we'll discuss the differences between two concepts, a solution and a product, which will help you understand what components make up Central Finance. Second, we'll explain the technical architecture behind Central Finance and discuss the architectural options you could use when deploying Central Finance and its various components.

7.1   Technical Architecture

Before we discuss technical and functional architecture behind Central Finance, let's carefully distinguish between the Central Finance *product* and the Central Finance *solution*. Think of the product as the smallest software building block that can be a solution on its own or be bundled with other complementary products to form a working business model for an organization. The solution for Central Finance consists of the Central Finance product, other components of SAP S/4HANA core, cloud-based products, and any accredited third-party products that are meant to be used for business operations based on a business and IT architecture.

Thus, the *solution* is what interests customers, and the market, because a solution takes a more holistic look at business requirements. For example, although Central Finance as a product cannot replicate fixed asset (or asset accounting) master records or replicate the movements on this subledger, Central Finance can work with Asset Accounting. While the Central Finance product may not seem to deliver a specific functionality, the broader solution may deliver that functionality using other components, which we'll discuss throughout this chapter. With experience, you'll be able to answer complex business problems using the broader solution.

Let's highlight a key point: The *product* has been developed individually and is licensed, either individually or collectively with other products, but the solution combines different SAP products and is ultimately what drives a customer's SAP architecture. The *solution* is driven by business use cases, processes that are needed by the use cases, the choice of user interface, and a number of other requirements.

The Central Finance product receives information from source systems as a core part of SAP S/4HANA. The Central Finance solution includes capabilities and processes that are delivered with this product and other components of SAP S/4HANA and other SAP or third-party products. In terms of implementation, a basic technical architecture for the solution is shown in Figure 7.1.

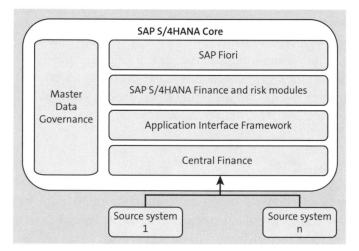

Figure 7.1 Central Finance Solution

Understanding of the product and solution perspectives will allow you to understand the technical architecture for Central Finance. You'll need to answer two basic questions to determine the technical architecture: First, what are the minimum components for Central Finance? Second, how do these different components interact to result in a working solution?

As shown in Figure 7.2, the technical architecture of Central Finance can be divided into five core parts that replicate SAP and non-SAP data, including transactional data. Other product components may be included in these parts or be optional.

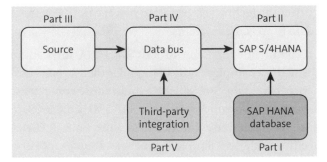

Figure 7.2 Five Architectural Parts of Central Finance

In this section, we'll discuss the core building blocks of the technical architecture of the Central Finance solution, including any subparts that make up a customer's solution architecture.

7.1.1   SAP HANA Database

In the SAP world, the SAP HANA database has probably been the most documented database in the last few years. As more than a database, the SAP platform delivers capabilities unmatched by rival databases, thus enabling functional process delivery in the form of SAP S/4HANA. SAP S/4HANA is a mandatory component of the technical architecture, and the latest version should always be adopted.

Not only does Central Finance use SAP S/4HANA as the database for fast transaction processing, but it can also be used in the solution architecture as a reporting and advanced analytics tool. Once the data has reached the SAP S/4HANA core application, the power of the Universal Journal becomes available to SAP S/4HANA for both SAP and non-SAP data sources.

7.1.2   SAP S/4HANA Core Application

The second part of Central Finance's technical architecture is the SAP S/4HANA core system. This core system is built on SAP HANA as a database.

SAP S/4HANA comes with a modern user interface and full suite of finance process functionality across line of business finance, such as financial accounting, controlling, cash management, treasury management, enterprise risk and compliance management, business integrity screening, financial planning and analysis, finance operations such as receivables management, and advance compliance reporting

(ACR) for taxes. Central Finance uses the technical integration power of SAP S/4HANA to provide real-time financial data from across systems.

The currently available and recommended version of SAP S/4HANA for Central Finance is SAP S/4HANA 1709, which is a complete suite of modules that support best practice processes. Central Finance follows the SAP S/4HANA on-premise core release cycle; at the time of this writing, the next planned version is SAP S/4HANA 1809. In older releases of Central Finance, you could use SAP Business Suite on SAP HANA with the SAP S/4HANA Finance (formerly SAP Simple Finance) as an add-on. However, with SAP S/4HANA 1610, SAP merged several different versions of SAP S/4HANA Finance into a single code line, and this architecture is no longer recommended. The advantages of using a single code page include increased functionality, ease of use, and upgradeability.

The key point to take away for now is that Central Finance cannot be deployed without SAP S/4HANA. Central Finance is delivered as part of SAP S/4HANA but has a separate IMG node and must be activated separately.

7.1.3   Source System

The third part of Central Finance is a *source system*. This source system can be an SAP source system, such as SAP ERP, or a non-SAP source system from a third-party provider.

> **Note**
>
> In this section, and for simplicity, our discussion will only consider SAP source systems. Later in this chapter we'll cover non-SAP systems as part of the technical and functional architecture.

The SAP source system must be SAP ERP 6.0, but you can set up earlier versions, such as SAP R/3 4.7 or 4.6, to act as a source system by using SAP Notes or contacting SAP for advice. The mainframe-based SAP R/2 is not supported.

7.1.4   The Data Bus

The next part of Central Finance's technical architecture is what can be referred to as the *data bus*. Just as a city bus carries people from point A to point B, a data bus's only job in Central Finance is to ensure that transactional line items are moving from the source system to the SAP S/4HANA core system where Central Finance is activated.

This "traffic" is managed by a specific SAP product: the SAP Landscape Transformation Replication Server (SAP LT Replication Server). SAP Note 1605140 provides detailed guidance on how to install the SAP LT Replication Server. For now, note that the SAP LT Replication Server is used by Central Finance as a data provisioning manager on a real-time basis.

Using the SAP LT Replication Server in the technical architecture of Central Finance offers the following benefits:

- Allows data replication in real time for use in Central Finance
- Uses trigger-based replication to enable transformational capabilities when needed by Central Finance
- Handles standard, cluster and pool tables
- Supports Unicode and non-Unicode encoding during replication
- Allows either the functional or technical user to monitor and manage data loads for Central Finance
- Allows the use of macros to enable data manipulation at the moment when data is pushed out of the SAP LT Replication Server into Central Finance
- Allows the project roadmap to onboard different companies using a phased approach, which is quite common in Central Finance
- Uses the SAP LT Replication Server for tertiary functionality for Central Finance processes and other benefits

Taken together, the SAP LT Replication Server makes Central Finance a powerful workhorse that can "bus" items from one source to multiple targets (called *1:N data provisioning*) or alternatively from many sources to a single target (called *N:1 data provisioning*). In our experience, 1:N data provisioning is the most common, but Central Finance's functional architecture, implementation methodology, and cost of ownership does enable the use of N:1 data provisioning to be used.

7.1.5   Third-Party Data Integration

The business benefits of moving data from point A to point B with Central Finance are not limited to transactions held in SAP ERP or SAP S/4HANA but also in non-SAP systems. For SAP-to-SAP transactional data replication, Central Finance leverages the SAP LT Replication Server—but this option won't work for third-party sources. Considering that transactional data could be held in a wide range of non-SAP technologies, from Oracle to Microsoft Dynamics, you may face challenges in standardizing the extraction, cleansing, and conversion of data into the Central Finance format. SAP offers SAP Data Services for extracting data from a non-SAP system and moving the data into Central Finance.

In addition, transactional data replication from non-SAP sources, SAP released an application programming interface (API) for pushing data into Central Finance beginning with SAP S/4HANA 1709. However, even with the API, the extraction and field formatting, including field lengths, is needed for converting transactional data into a format that the API can consume. At this point, an accelerator might be needed to allow customers implementing Central Finance to leverage prefabricated content based on SAP Data Services.

The SourceConnect accelerator was developed by SAP partner Magnitude. The technical foundation of SourceConnect is SAP Data Services with connectivity to the SAP LT Replication Server to deliver transactional data into Central Finance via a staging table delivered by SAP in the SAP LT Replication Server. This part is just one portion of the connectivity. The second, and more important, part of Magnitude's Source-Connect accelerator is using drivers for integration with non-SAP instances, pulling data into SAP Data Services based on prebuilt data structures, and applying transformation rules such as date formatting. Of course, the SAP Data Services repository must be established for SourceConnect to allow this processing to take place in the SAP Data Services instance.

Magnitude's SourceConnect accelerator is an important element in reducing time to value and increasing know-how about common non-SAP systems often integrated with Central Finance, particularly about their architecture, versions, data models and table structures, drivers, and field definitions and field content as well as their management, before this information reaches Central Finance.

7.2   Central Finance Landscape

Before you can begin a new Central Finance implementation, we recommend that your project team consider the following questions about the current IT infrastructure to avoid delays:

- How will Central Finance be hosted with SAP S/4HANA?
- What is the minimum number of tiers in the landscape required?
- How will each tier in the landscape connect to the SAP LT Replication Server?
- How will each tier be used as the project moves towards go live?

- How will phasing of the Central Finance project impact the landscape?
- Which source systems will connect to Central Finance?

To deliver a properly functioning infrastructure, the team responsible for installing SAP S/4HANA and the SAP LT Replication Server and applying the relevant SAP Notes should answer these questions 6 to 8 weeks in advance. The average lead time to acquire the necessary hardware, install the relevant software, and make various connections will require a minimum of 6 weeks for most customers, depending on procurement logistics and IT processes.

Let's look at the key elements in the Central Finance software landscape, as follows:

- **Sandbox**
  Most customers have a Central Finance sandbox for testing configuration and business models that may be impacted by the scope of the project. This sandbox can be used to build prototypes that are easily disposable if not needed. Whether project and support teams are operating on a single or a dual track, both can use this tier, which minimizes costs and facilitates the sharing of ideas between the two teams.

- **Development environment**
  The development (DEV) system is always required to hold the master configuration in at least one client for Central Finance. The DEV system is configured with transport management to capture and govern changes to the Central Finance configuration. Note that the DEV system can also be used for configuration unit tests and to test manual transactions. A second unit test client must be created for this purpose, but configuration issues would be fixed prior to the transports being released to the next tier. Any unit testing can be carried out using Transaction SCC1.

  When executing your project, we recommend setting up a third client in the DEV system to carry out unit testing on source transactions where a greater volume and breadth of data would enhance design consistency and agility.

- **Transport layer**
  The transport layer must be created between the development tier and the quality assurance (QA) tier to allow transports to be released and imported into QA. To minimize QA errors, we recommend that each configuration that is successfully unit tested in the development unit test client be released only when the transaction and master data has been tested as well. The QA environment can be an optional environment if tier costs are an issue as the pre-production environment could be used as a QA tier and later re-purposed to its original use.

- **Pre-production**

  The pre-production tier is not normally needed during the first phase of the go-live; whether to use one is primarily the decision of the customer in terms of its architectural and testing policies. Having a pre-production tier necessitates importing of all transports into this tier to maintain consistency. This tier can be used for simulation testing of go-live for Central Finance as well as operational acceptance testing.

- **Production**

  The final and most important tier is the production environment. The production environment is where all the configuration, master data, and initial loads for Central Finance are carried out. To ensure consistency, we recommend that you release all transports from development for the final build and carry out a configuration and master data freeze to prevent any issues arising in the Central Finance production tier. We also recommend that the full technical installation plan and simulation testing, sometimes called dress rehearsal, that was carried in pre-production tier be repeated as a run book.

Note that at least one landscape for Central Finance is needed for the project, as shown in Figure 7.3.

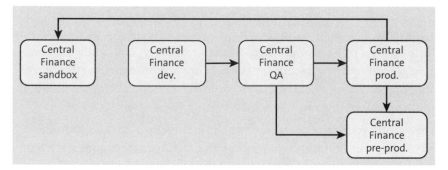

Figure 7.3 Single Central Finance Landscape

Some larger organizations, however, maintain a dual track for Central Finance as the project transitions into multiple markets, as shown in Figure 7.4. Dual tracks allow an IT organization to more flexibly respond to the business for fix breaks and resolve defects—but they do add to infrastructure cost and require more manpower to maintain technically. For example, software patches from operating system to application level have to be maintained in both tracks. In addition, maintaining configuration and master data consistency between two landscapes requires additional overhead.

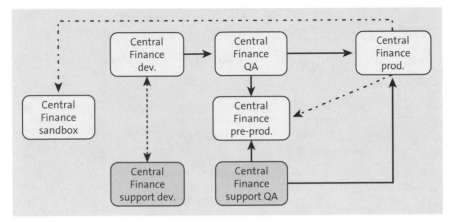

Figure 7.4 Dual Track Central Finance Landscape

So far we have just looked at a simple landscape that has Central Finance tiers. In real life, though, this is incomplete without the other core parts that are required as a minimum. There are three possible permutations that are driven by scope of the project.

First, the landscape only considers SAP product set in an organization and/or project scope. In other words, the source systems are exclusively SAP, as shown in Figure 7.5.

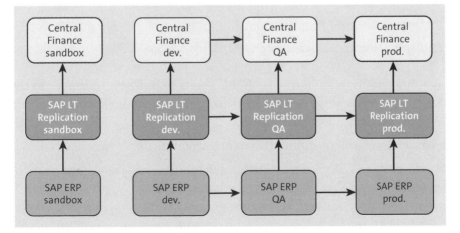

Figure 7.5 Central Finance with Only SAP Sources

Second, the landscape deploys both SAP technologies and non-SAP technologies in the organization and/or project scope. Figure 7.6 shows the source systems with a combination of SAP and non-SAP applications.

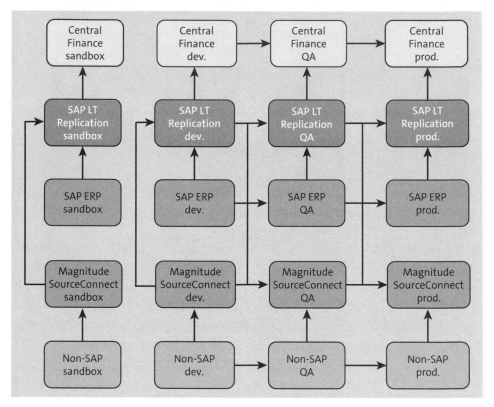

Figure 7.6 Central Finance Landscape with SAP and Non-SAP Sources

Third, a common scenario arises when *only* third-party technology is deployed by the organization or project scope—meaning that the source systems are exclusively non-SAP applications, as shown in Figure 7.7.

This scenario is increasingly common based on current customer trends:

- Firstly, the customer only is a non-SAP house and wished to leverage the power of SAP S/4HANA using Central Finance. The current non-SAP applications do not deliver the flexibility, features or real time process that SAP S/4HANA has to offer with Central Finance.

- Secondly, the customer may have SAP and non-SAP applications but the project scope is limited to non-SAP as a source system—perhaps due to a merger or an acquisition or the retirement of a non-SAP application due to cost or end of life scenario.

- Thirdly, it could be to evaluate as a quick POC to prove the speed of deploying Central Finance for a non-SAP application and showcase benefits to be gained for a real project at a later stage.

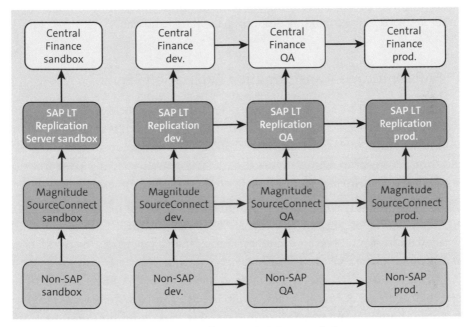

Figure 7.7 Central Finance Landscape for Non-SAP Sources Only

Of course, each landscape is organization-specific, and other permutations are also possible in terms of connectivity and tiers. These diagrams are meant to illustrate these landscapes for purposes of architecture rather than the full possibilities that may exist physically in a project.

Whatever the number of tiers, number of tracks, or the differences in applications that are acting as a source system, it is possible to connect using SAP product portfolio. In addition, we have only considered the on-premise landscape in terms of Central Finance, the SAP LT Replication Server, and source systems. If the project or the customer has SAP cloud solutions such as SAP Ariba, SAP Concur, or SAP Analytics Cloud, then these would also must be considered as part of the landscape.

One final note on the Central Finance landscape: Each tier in the landscape must be built on the same compatible software and hardware. It does not matter whether the software is installed on an SAP HANA appliance, manually installed on-premise or on cloud providers such as SAP HANA Enterprise Cloud, Amazon Web Services (AWS), or Microsoft Azure, for example. We strongly recommend that you prepare a technical installation plan with complete screenshots of the installation process to ensure consistency across resources building different tiers of the landscape.

7.3   SAP Landscape Transformation Replication Server

Replicating on a real-time basis for Central Finance makes the SAP LT Replication Server an essential pillar of technical architecture. Therefore, it is essential that the SAP Basis resource, sometimes called a technical architect, understand the SAP LT Replication Server component and how it needs to integrate with an SAP source system and the SAP S/4HANA system where Central Finance will be deployed.

The SAP LT Replication Server has the advantage that it works off database logging rather than application logging. This method allows the SAP LT Replication Server to replicate data from A to B on an event basis rather than a pull basis. The result, however, is a pull into the SAP LT Replication Server staging tables as a midway point to SAP S/4HANA. Figure 7.8 shows the basic architecture of the SAP LT Replication Server in the context of Central Finance with SAP as a source system. Notice that it's required for both SAP and non-SAP source systems, though for the latter, SAP Data Services is also a crucial intermediary tool.

Though you could install the SAP LT Replication Server either on the Central Finance Instance or the SAP source system, we recommend installing the SAP LT Replication Server into to its own server that is appropriately sized to ensure performance. This technical architecture also removes any dependency on patch or enhancement pack management on the Central Finance instance or the source SAP system. Consult the central SAP Note 2154420 for SLT and 2148893 for Central Finance before, during, and after your project.

The SAP LT Replication Server is a mature technology that can be used flexibly with Central Finance according to the landscape and organizational context, as you'll see in the following sections.

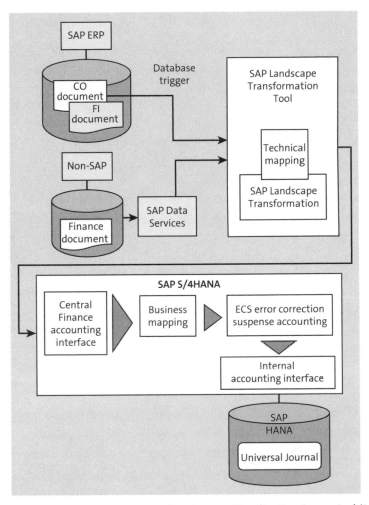

Figure 7.8 Central Finance and Basic SAP LT Replication Server Architecture

7.3.1   Deployment Options for the SAP LT Replication Server

The architectural patterns that drive the SAP LT Replication Server's integration with Central Finance are quite flexible. Central Finance connects to the SAP LT Replication Server using out of the box integration for SAP and non-SAP systems. The SAP LT Replication Server offers both a one-to-many or a many-to-one deployment option from the source or target perspective.

The most common scenario involves connecting multiple source systems to a single the SAP LT Replication Server, which then connects to a single Central Finance, as shown in Figure 7.9. If the source system is an SAP system, an RFC (Remote Function Call) destination is used by the SAP LT Replication Server. If the source system is a non-SAP system, a database connection is used directly.

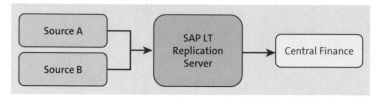

Figure 7.9 Central Finance and the SAP LT Replication Server Deployment: Many-to-One

In some cases, you may want to split multiple Central Finance instances with multiple sources, as shown in Figure 7.10. This scenario may seem unusual but is relevant when, for example, you need to segregate divisions within large companies. Often, large companies are split into strategic business units (SBUs) that run autonomously but in connection with a small central business hub, while a division may have multiple systems that need to provide a single version of the truth at the SBU level.

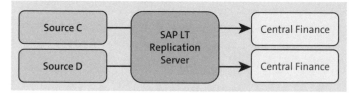

Figure 7.10 Central Finance and the SAP LT Replication Server Deployment: Many-to-Many

In scenarios where a divesture is planned or you're party to a joint venture that requires segregation of data and due diligence isolation, then you can consider a one-to-many deployment option, the architecture of which is shown in Figure 7.11.

Figure 7.11 Central Finance and the SAP LT Replication Server Deployment: One-to-Many

Under a one-to-many scenario, two instances of Central Finance interact with one instance of a source system. The SAP LT Replication Server and Central Finance either divert a full or partial set of company codes into either instance. One instance of Central Finance potentially has all the data, and the other only has a subset of data. In this scenario, the subset of data can be investigated for due diligence isolation during a divesture or can be carved out as its own an instance at the hardware level.

For non-SAP data with direct database connections, you'll need to consider license requirements when designing the technical architecture.

7.3.2   Data Migration Server

With SAP LT Replication Server, as the core element for building Central Finance, you'll need to use a Data Migration Server (DMIS) as part of the technical architecture. This software is an add-on that you'll need to download and installed with any support packs.

The DMIS makes the replication of tables available needed to perform certain tasks to the users and roles. These roles will become available after installing the DMIS (for example, role SAP_IUUC_REPL_REMOTE). Read and write operations are runtime objects that are generated after replication jobs are triggered.

To start the replication, the SAP LT Replication Server must be configured after installing DMIS in the relevant servers.

7.4   SAP Application Interface Framework

In Section 7.1, five parts of the architecture were outlined. The SAP S/4HANA core system contains the error handling component of the Central Finance architecture. As the data comes in to Central Finance, configuration and data checks are carried out. One of two outcomes will occur:

1. If these checks are passed by Central Finance, then the Universal Journal will post the document into SAP S/4HANA Finance.

2. If these checks fail, the SAP Application Interface Framework will be activated to handle how errors are queued, monitored, alerted, and reprocessed. Figure 7.12 shows the conceptual architecture of SAP Application Integration Framework in more detail.

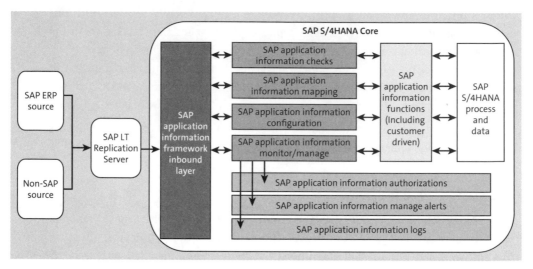

Figure 7.12 Central Finance and SAP Application Integration Framework Architecture Detail

SAP Application Integration Framework is complex: As an application, SAP Application Integration Framework is a single point for managing replication, successful and failed, from the SAP LT Replication Server into SAP S/4HANA core. SAP Application Integration Framework is also an interface, since any type of communication method can be handled by SAP Application Integration Framework. For example, intermediate document (IDoc) status can also be pushed into SAP Application Integration Framework for error management. Finally, SAP Application Integration Framework is a framework: Some features are provided out of the box, while additional features can be configured or developed using the standard integrated development environment of the SAP S/4HANA core.

To use SAP Application Integration Framework for Central Finance, you'll need to do two things: configure the SAP Application Integration Framework in each client where Central Finance is being used and import Central Finance-specific content into SAP Application Integration Framework as Business Configuration sets (BC sets). Without configuration and BC sets, SAP Application Integration Framework for Central Finance will not work.

Note

SAP S/4HANA and Central Finance cannot be separated architecturally. Therefore, because SAP Application Integration Framework is part of SAP S/4HANA, Central Finance can leverage all the advantages of a single point of connectivity for message processing.

Using SAP Application Integration Framework with Central Finance offers the following the operational benefits in terms of management, compliance, business, and IT:

- Faster implementation using BC sets for message monitoring
- Transparency, for both business and IT, in errors and their successful resolution
- Ability to reprocess errors without having to reload data from the source system
- Ability for the business to process errors with lower effort in a single place with standard or customized error messages
- Potential use of robotics process automation (RPA) for frequently recurring errors, which has the potential of substantially reducing business effort
- Simplified landscape management for all finance errors, which improves governance and allows you to focus on real data points
- Automation of testing using a test tool
- Alert management for both business and IT users
- Mass or individual processing for groups of errors (In Central Finance projects common errors that reappear can often be fixed together.)
- Access controls using authorizations to prevent undesired changes to accounting documents
- Ability to generate compliance reports for any document changes

With this architecture, you can create metrics in the form of KPIs that track and analyze root causes over time. You can even track down to field and value level, which allows you to proactively reduce the user or IT actions that lead to error messages.

7.4.1   SAP Application Integration Framework Message Processing

Typical errors that block replication into the SAP S/4HANA core from the SAP LT Replication Server are configuration and master data mapping issues or missing data. The SAP Application Integration Framework uses XML (extensible markup language) language to write the processing status of any message from the SAP LT Replication Server. This processing status is recorded regardless of whether Central Finance issues an error or success message to SAP S/4HANA. Once the SAP Application Integration Framework stores the XML message, the message can be viewed in the standard SAP S/4HANA table /AIF/PERS_XML.

Typically, the source system sends the accounting document to the SAP LT Replication Server, and then, the SAP LT Replication Server pushes the same accounting document to SAP S/4HANA using the Central Finance engine. Since a source system can have a large number of documents that could eventually become SAP Application Integration Framework messages (regardless of processing status), the size of table /AIF/PERS_XML could become too large even in a test system. Therefore, we recommend that you implement an archiving methodology as part of the first go-live to make future phases easier and to manage the in-memory size of this table. You should only archive successful messages and any messages that are in warning after review. Any messages in error in table /AIF/PERS_XML should be left in the SAP Application Integration Framework to allow for resolution and reprocessing. You can use Transaction SARA to access the archiving features. For the SAP Application Integration Framework, the archiving object is /AIF/PERSX. Note that an archive server must be added to the technical architecture of a Central Finance project to optimize the amount of hot data that sits in-memory of the SAP HANA database.

7.4.2   BC Sets for SAP Application Integration Framework

BC sets provide SAP Application Integration Framework-specific content for Central Finance. Open Transaction SCPR20 to import BC sets into a development client where data is being used and then ensure that the import is repeated for each tier/client as needed. The following BC sets are the most commonly deployed, though your choice will be based on your organization's requirements:

- ZFINS_CFIN_AIF_CO
- ZFINS_CFIN_AIF_CO_SIM_SAP_FIN730
- ZFINS_CFIN_AIF_DOC_CHG
- ZFINS_CFIN_AIF_DOC_POST
- ZFINS_CFIN_AIF_GEN
- FINS_CFIN_AIF_SEPA

Once imported, a transport may be generated depending on the client level settings for the relevant tier and whether change requests are active. The SEPA interface content is only needed if SEPA mandates are part of the scope of the project.

7.4.3   Configuring the SAP Application Integration Framework

We'll briefly discuss configuring the SAP Application Integration Framework in this section. Although often carried out by a technical person on a project, this step is simple enough that a good functional consultant could also easily fulfill this task.

The SAP Application Integration Framework monitor requires you import the latest BC sets into the system where the SAP Application Integration Framework is needed for each tier within the landscape strategy of the customer. The detailed configuration for SAP Application Integration Framework is beyond the scope of this book, but the main steps are all contained within the IMG of the SAP S/4HANA system where Central Finance has been activated and configured. The configuration must be carried out in the correct namespace, and you must be careful when taking copies of production data into non-production instances to avoid losing any settings.

7.4.4   Monitoring SAP Application Integration Framework for Central Finance

Assuming the content is installed correctly on the correct SAP S/4HANA server and the configuration has been complete, the monitoring for Central Finance will start once the replication from the source system to SAP S/4HANA is enabled. The same principle is applied to non-SAP data being loaded to the staging area within the SAP LT Replication Server.

Monitoring capabilities for the technical architecture can be tested with the assistance of the functional consultants who can trigger the initial data loads using Central Finance or triggering the replication scenario configured within the SAP LT Replication Server. To access the error monitor, open Transaction /AIF/ERR. Any installation and configuration errors can be resolved using data loads that span a variety of data. Once these are resolved, the SAP Application Integration Framework setup is complete.

7.5   SAP Master Data Governance

A primary requirement for Central Finance is the correct mapping of data values from the source system. You can manage the mapping manually, using Central Finance programs or partner tools such as from Magnitude, that can load master data and carry out quality checks before loading transactional data. If you're using SAP Master Data Governance (SAP MDG), only two choices of technical architecture, as shown in Figure 7.13, will be available.

Technical considerations regarding the architecture will be driven directly by use cases and the configuration of the landscape where Central Finance resides along the SAP source systems where configuration values are important for managing change requests within SAP MDG. The concept of golden record configuration may require deploying a separate landscape for SAP MDG and ensuring connectivity. Another major benefit is the ability to upgrade the SAP MDG instance independently from the Central Finance instance. However, you can't continue this independence indefinitely because eventually items, such as kernels, patches, and enhancement packs, will drive their convergence via upgrades.

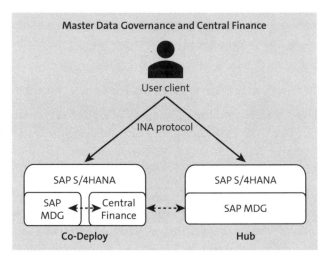

Figure 7.13 Central Finance and SAP MDG Options

Sizing needs for SAP S/4HANA must be added to the equation for the technical architecture because the two systems require incrementally more memory than their combined memory, especially with retention management implemented in a co-deployment scenario.

Note that a key requirement for Central Finance is that mapping be managed accurately and in a timely manner to avoid errors during the replication process, which would appear in the SAP Application Integration Framework monitor. To ensure consistency, make sure you consider transport management.

7.6   Frontend Tools and Central Finance

So far in this chapter, we've focused on the backend of the Central Finance solution. However, the solution needs to be accessible to many project stakeholders, from the SAP Basis teams to the end users who will eventually use Central Finance for day-to-day operations and reporting.

Central Finance uses an ABAP stack across the backend (that is, the SAP source systems and the SAP LT Replication Server) and the main application host, SAP S/4HANA. In addition, SAP S/4HANA comes with an embedded business warehouse that you can use for reporting instead of (or in conjunction with) the embedded analytics provided by SAP S/4HANA.

Depending on the project architecture, you can choose from various frontend components, which we'll discuss in the following sections.

7.6.1 SAP GUI

SAP's graphical user interface, also known as the SAP GUI, represents the client in SAP's three-tier architecture of application server, database, and client. SAP GUI works across platforms and supports different operating systems such as Windows, Unix, etc. SAP GUI is a thick (non-browser) client and is subject to patches like any other software from SAP.

One advantage of using SAP GUI is that it can work across many SAP platforms and can establish secure network connections, thus adding a security layer between the client and backend servers. SAP GUI must be installed on each end user's laptop or a desktop to allow the user login to be authenticated. SAP GUI can also be used to launch Web Dynpro, a web-based user interface required by some SAP applications.

While SAP GUI is available for ABAP and Java stacks, you do need to consider the deployment approach and versions to be installed early on in the project cycle. In addition, not all applications (e.g., SAP BW reports) can be accessed by end users using SAP GUI. An older user experience, you can still enhance SAP GUI using GuiXT for SAP Screen Personas, which allows the user interface to be customized.

7.6.2 SAP Fiori

SAP Fiori is the name of SAP's user experience (UX). Simple to use, SAP Fiori comprises a range of tasks, from approvals workflow to monitoring to generating postings. SAP Fiori is available for use with Central Finance as delivered with the standard SAP S/4HANA core. By design, SAP Fiori is device independent and can work across workstations, tablets, laptops, and mobile phones. The user experience is maintained automatically through its responsive design.

Most processes in SAP S/4HANA are delivered as SAP Fiori apps. For Central Finance, you can deploy all SAP Fiori apps related to line of business finance on the core SAP

S/4HANA instance. Unlike SAP GUI, SAP Fiori comes with a URL/web link; thus, SAP Fiori can be deployed quite easily as part of user enablement. Of course, when SAP Fiori is introduced into the Central Finance architecture, training and change management will still be required.

In terms of technical architecture, SAP Fiori can be deployed within the SAP S/4HANA gateway for light use. If heavy use is expected, for enhanced performance, you should deploy SAP Fiori on own server. Your SAP Basis teams must understand the technical architecture of SAP Fiori, as shown in Figure 7.14, to correctly identify, install, and execute software packages. SAP Fiori can be deployed in the same instance of SAP S/4HANA as Central Finance or on a separate server. We recommend using a separate server for the production environment of your landscape, as a minimum, to ensure performance.

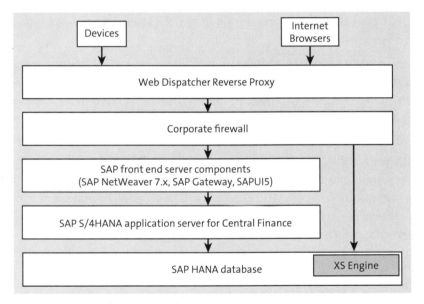

Figure 7.14 Central Finance and SAP Fiori

SAP Fiori components require an SAP HANA database for the SAP S/4HANA core and at least one primary application server (PAS) for Central Finance. The gateway where SAP Fiori is deployed must have the correct software, and SAP Fiori content must be imported.

SAP Fiori is based on HTML5 and jQuery, which are both open source. SAP delivers some themes that can be revised to create a more specific corporate look. SAP Fiori app development can be carried out using SAP Cloud Platform for cloud and on-premise solutions. You'll need to customize some development framework and servers for SAP Fiori apps as part of the technical architecture and should consider such topics as OData, SAP Web IDE, and code repositories such as Git. These specific topics are beyond the scope of this book.

7.6.3   SAP Analysis for Microsoft Office

SAP S/4HANA combines analytics capabilities with process enablement in Central Finance. In addition, many ABAP reports are provided by SAP using the SAP GUI. However, embedded analytics is now available with the new user experience (UX) using SAP Fiori. However, SAP recognizes that some customers may still want to use an Excel-like frontend to analyze processes for Central Finance and has developed a tool called SAP Analysis for Microsoft Office. The main advantages of using this tool include the following:

- Offers a familiar user interface with the most modern features of Excel
- Can be used with embedded SAP Business Warehouse (SAP BW), which comes with SAP S/4HANA
- Builds powerful features on top of data with customized workbooks and calculations
- Integrates PowerPoint with data coming from SAP S/4HANA
- Slices and dices data with attributes implemented using Central Finance

Working with an Excel-based solution should be used sparingly within the context of Central Finance because all the data is available real-time in Central Finance using built in-reports and the SAP Fiori user experience at the lowest granular level with context-based drilldown capability. As Central Finance is Excel based, you can manipulate the data and set the data architecture at transaction and master data level.

7.6.4   SAP Analytics Cloud

Finance transformation architecture is driven by business needs, which usually translates into a technical architecture that can allow connectivity to the SAP Analytics Cloud. Although all financial data could potentially be replicated into the Central Finance instance, some data may require an additional activity in the implementation project; this data could be sent via cloud connectivity for both planning and actual purposes. As a result, the technical architecture must take into account the type, level, and method of data being transmitted to SAP Analytics Cloud from Central Finance.

SAP Analytics Cloud follows the software as a service (SaaS) model, and its place in the overall Central Finance technical architecture requires the following minimal considerations:

- Security Assertion Markup Language (SAML) to ensure user authentication and authorization
- Secure Socket Layer (SSL) certificates
- Connectivity layer and its security, including encryption of data
- How the technical architecture will handle a live connection with Central Finance in terms of data volume vs. content needs of the storyboards in SAP S/4HANA Cloud
- Whether users will access SAP Analytics Cloud from within the customer domain or from outside the customer domain. Figure 7.15 shows a technical model assuming the user exists on the customer domain.

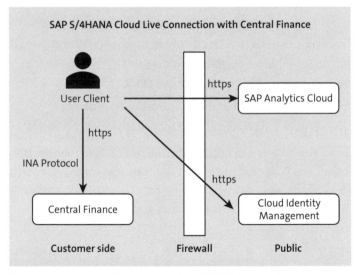

Figure 7.15 Central Finance and SAP S/4HANA Cloud

In this basic technical model, a user request reaches the cloud identity server using SAML, and then metadata is passed to the SAP S/4HANA Cloud server. The benefits of using SAP S/4HANA Cloud are many in terms of technical architecture but one benefit that stands out in particular is the overall simplification of the architecture for planning, actuals, and storytelling for the finance function in a single place at an aggregate level bearing in mind potential volume constraints for live data transmission. As a result, no additional devices are needed as prerequisites because access is through a web browser with cross-origin resource sharing (CORS).

7.6.5   SAP Business Client

Some consultants and business users prefer to use the desktop-based SAP Business Client as part of the frontend technical architecture. This option is particularly common if you want side panels to view data within the Central Finance instance beyond what is delivered by the replication of transaction data from source systems. Alternatively, you may prefer to use the SAP Business Client for master data governance roles rather than the other frontends, such as SAP GUI with Web Dynpro.

The choice of tool directly depends on your deployment strategy for processes and analytics. Figure 7.16 shows the basic setup with no consideration for security in terms of login, data encryption, network transmission, etc. Such protocols must be bundled into individual tools and their capabilities.

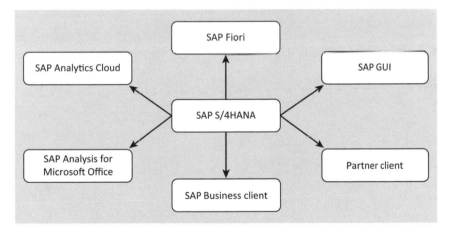

Figure 7.16 Central Finance Frontend Tools Sample

7.7   Summary

In this chapter, we walked through the most common architectural components that your architecture team must consider when undertaking a new Central Finance project. While not an exhaustive list, we hope we've provided a solid foundation for developing your own working model and procure the infrastructure, software, components, and integration required to deliver a working Central Finance system.

System architecture is a mandatory prerequisite to ensure the speedy and smooth deployment of Central Finance. System architecture drives, not just the software needed, but how the software will be used at each phase of the Central Finance implementation project, which we'll discuss further in the next chapter.

Chapter 8
Implementing Central Finance

*Successful organizations understand the importance of implementa-
tion, not just strategy, and, moreover, recognize the crucial role of
their people in the process.*
—*Jeffrey Pfeffer, professor of organizational behavior at Stanford*

8

In this chapter, we'll provide step-by-step instructions for your Central Finance implementation project. Our focus in this chapter will be on the technical steps for system setup, data integration, replication, and master data. In this chapter, we'll begin
by helping you define your rollout type and define a roadmap before moving on to
describing the more technical steps.

8.1 Rollout

How ERP projects are deployed is largely influenced by the rollout type, the key milestones, and the scope. Rolling out an SAP system means that, after the initial setup,
also known as a *template*, the system is replicated.

8.1.1 Iterative Rollout versus Big Bang

Whether you decide to implement Central Finance as a single large project or as a
sequence of smaller projects is mostly influenced by your source systems, which are
defined by certain characteristics, such as:

- **Source types**
  A large portion of the implementation time will be spent connecting, mapping,
  and reconciling your local source systems to the Central Finance system. If your
  organization is leveraging a mix of SAP and non-SAP source ERPs and versions as
  the source systems, we recommend phasing the implementation of these source
  systems by software vendor and version.

- **Source systems**

  Should all source systems be implemented at once or one after the other? How you answer this question usually depends on how much of your business is contained in each source system. For instance, a company that has historically grown through mergers and acquisitions might end up with one ERP supporting 80% of the revenue while the remaining 20% is shared across a handful of other ERPs. In this case, you might choose to start with the larger and more complex system, expecting more value when the system is live, or you might start with a smaller system as a pilot, expecting a shorter implementation period for the system to go live.

- **Source company codes**

  The most granular organizational structure in Central Finance is the company code. Once you've selected and prioritized your key source systems, you can include all company codes or restrict the implementation to only certain company codes. Be aware that merging a few company codes from different source systems is much more complex than merging many company codes from the same source system. This consideration stems from the integrated nature of SAP ERP systems: A single source system will have more similar organizational structures, like controlling areas, company codes, charts of accounts, etc.

- **Level of granularity**

  Something to keep in mind when integrating non-SAP systems is that not all ERP systems work on the same level of granularity. For instance, simpler software packages might not have objects corresponding to sales orders or internal orders. Thus, when performing sales, you might not be able to extract some information, such as volumes, unit prices, or cost components. In addition, some basic configurations might differ, such as units of measure, fiscal periods, or currency conversions. These aspects must be taken into account when considering the integration of non-SAP source systems.

An iterative rollout starts from a core template, usually centered on headquarters (more value) or a small country (less risk), before being extended to additional countries, with variations for localization. This approach is preferred for large and/or complex implementations.

On the other hand, a big bang approach implements the ERP system for the whole organization, including all countries and subsidiaries at once. However, this approach is more suitable for smaller organizations.

8.1.2 Milestone-Based Rollout

As described in previous chapters, Central Finance can be used for different scenarios. When implemented as the underlying platform for real-time consolidation, planning with embedded SAP Business Planning and Consolidation (SAP BPC), or machine learning, key milestones must be deployed and validated before the next layer of applications can be addressed. A typical strategy starts with setting up Central Finance as a foundation layer running in parallel to the source ERP until the data in Central Finance is considered reliable. Only then can project teams build upon the platform and use Central Finance itself as a source for additional applications.

Examples of milestones are:

- Creating a foundation layer with a new information model
- Using Central Finance for reporting
- Replacing integration between local systems and the data warehouse and connecting with the central system
- Expanding scope to budgeting/forecasting or consolidation on Central Finance
- Improved reporting with SAP Analytics Cloud connected to the source system
- Activating accounts payables (AP), accounts receivables (AR), or treasury functionality on top of the central system
- Activating applications like SAP In-House Cash

By adopting a milestone-based approach, as opposed to the big bang approach, project teams can deliver value to your business and justify the budget for additional scope.

8.1.3 Process Selection

When implementing Central Finance, you must understand the interdependency among some Central Finance processes. As shown in Figure 8.1 and Figure 8.2, processes are built on top of other processes, starting with the reporting hub at the bottom, leading up to more complex processes like treasury or consolidation. These core finance processes must be up and running before logistics processes can be implemented.

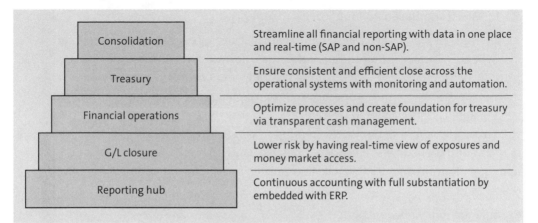

Figure 8.1 Scope Pyramid for Finance

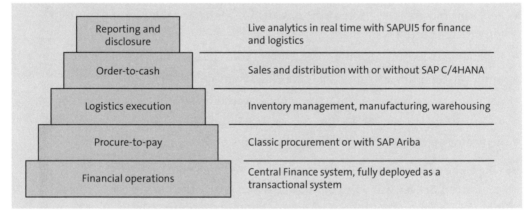

Figure 8.2 Scope Pyramid for Logistics

8.2   Roadmap

Once you've defined a rollout strategy, your team can start grouping tasks into *waves*. A wave is a project subphase, with a clear scope, timeline, and resource plan.

8.2.1 First Wave

The first wave will build the foundation of your organization's Central Finance platform. This phase will require the most coordination and preliminary work, as most of the decisions made at this stage will be difficult to change in subsequent waves.

Before starting, for each source system, your project team should inventory:

- **End-to-end processes**
  Which processes are currently run in the source system (i.e., core finance, core HR, procure-to-pay, plan-to-product, order-to-cash, record-to-report, etc.)?

- **Reports**
  What are the critical key performance indicators (KPIs)? Which key reports need to be considered? What is the source for these KPIs and reports (e.g., SAP ERP, SAP Business Warehouse [SAP BW], Excel)? How frequently are they run?

- **Users**
  What are the profiles of the users that run end-to-end processes? Which profiles need access to the Central Finance system? How will functional or technical users access the various systems? What are the security requirements?

- **Dependent systems**
  Which systems consume information from the source systems (e.g., SAP BW, SAP Supplier Relationship Manager [SAP SRM], SAP Customer Relationship Management [CRM], SAP Ariba, SAP BusinessObjects)? How is the data transferred (e.g., flat files, extractors, direct connections, integration)? Are these dependent systems the same across multiple source systems? Should these systems consume data from Central Finance? Should these systems be retired?

8.2.2 Subsequent Waves

In subsequent waves, the Central Finance platform delivered in the first wave will be expanded in these ways:

- **Expanded scope**
  New elements are added to the scope pyramid.

- **More sources**
  Additional company codes are imported from already connected systems, or additional source systems are connected to the Central Finance system.

In addition, after running the source system and the Central Finance system in parallel for some time, landscape transformation can begin, in which you'll perform two more tasks:

- Retire source systems
- Redirect the integration of dependent systems from your source systems to your Central Finance systems

8.2.3 End State

At the end of the Central Finance implementation journey, the original objective(s) should be met as well as the following:

- All selected processes are running across the source systems and the Central Finance system.
- Users have adopted the Central Finance system for their relevant reporting and operational tasks.
- All integration points, inbound and outbound, have been optimized.
- Systems that are no longer needed have been retired.

8.3 System Setup

Unlike many projects, the Central Finance application requires a full environment of systems to function. As shown in Figure 8.3, the main components are the Central Finance instance, the SAP Landscape Transformation Replication Server (SAP LT Replication Server) system, the SAP source system(s), the non-SAP source system(s), and an optional SAP Master Data Governance (SAP MDG) system. We'll discuss each component in turn in this section, but let's start with an overview of your system landscape to put all these components into context.

> **Important**
>
> Before starting the Central Finance system setup process, be sure you review the latest release notes:
>
> - SAP Note 2148893: Central Finance: Implementation and Configuration
> - SAP Note 2184567: Central Finance: Frequently Asked Questions
> - SAP Note 2323494: Overview of Notes Relevant for Source System

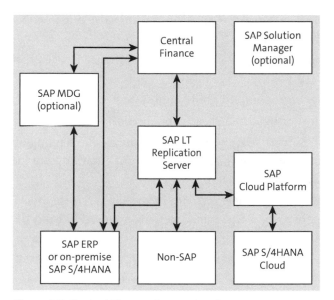

Figure 8.3 Central Finance System Landscape

8.3.1   Landscape

To properly evaluate and configure your Central Finance system, we recommend leveraging a source system containing the maximum amount of data covering as many scenarios as possible. In an ideal setup, the source system in the development environment is a recent copy of a source quality system or even a production system. Since some processes like the initial load can be demanding in terms of processing power and memory, we recommend setting up a new sandbox/development/quality environment for each source system.

As much as possible, as shown in Figure 8.4, the system setup should follow this sequence:

❶ Sandbox/source system: Copying the current production system or a recent quality system

❷ Sandbox/SAP LT Replication Server: Setting up a new instance or extending an existing sandbox instance

❸ Sandbox/Central Finance: Setting up a new instance of the latest release of SAP S/4HANA

❹ Development/source system: Copying the current production system or a recent quality system

❺ Development/SAP LT Replication Server: Setting up a new instance or extending an existing development instance

❻ Development/Central Finance: Setting up a new instance of the latest release of SAP S/4HANA

❼ Quality/source system: Copying the current production system

❽ Quality/source system: Transporting add-ons and configuration

❾ Quality/SAP LT Replication Server: Setting up a new instance or extending an extension of an existing quality instance and transporting configuration from the development SAP LT Replication Server system

❿ Quality/Central Finance: Setting up a new instance of the same release of SAP S/4HANA as the development system and transporting configuration from the development system

⓫ Production/source system: Transporting add-ons and configuration to the existing production system

⓬ Production/SAP LT Replication Server: Setting up a new instance extending the existing production instance and transporting configuration from the quality SAP LT Replication Server system

⓭ Production/Central Finance: Setting up a new instance of the same release of SAP S/4HANA as the quality system and transporting configuration from the quality system

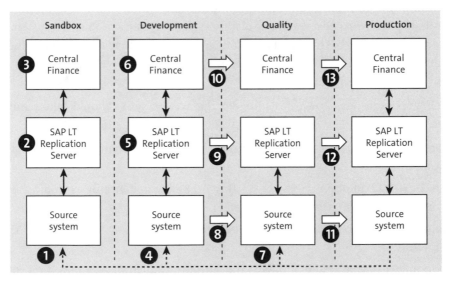

Figure 8.4 Simplified Architecture and Deployment Strategy

Note that Figure 8.4 doesn't reflect the optional addition of SAP MDG. In such a complex landscape, we recommend leveraging the SAP Solution Manager.

In the sandbox, development, and quality systems, keep in mind that the source system will not be live. Thus, testing real-time replication will require either manual input, automated testing, or robotic process automation (RPA) in the source system. The administration guide discusses the option of connecting quality systems to a productive source system, but for security reasons, this option should be considered with caution.

8.3.2   Central Finance Instance

As shown in Figure 8.5, Central Finance is delivered standard starting with SAP ERP 6.0—no need to install additional components. However, we recommend leveraging the latest SAP S/4HANA release and feature pack as the base for your Central Finance instance. The figures in this section were taken from the latest release available at the time of this writing: SAP S/4HANA 1709 FPS 01 with SAP GUI 7.50.

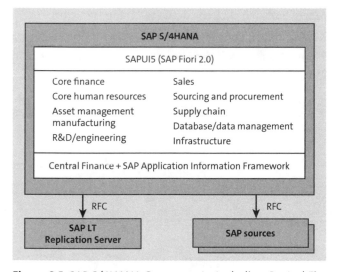

Figure 8.5 SAP S/4HANA Components, Including Central Finance and SAP Application Integration Framework

At the time of this writing, SAP S/4HANA Cloud cannot be used as a Central Finance instance. However, on-premise SAP S/4HANA can always be set up in the cloud through a hosting service. This configuration is particularly advantageous for proof of concept or pilot projects.

From a high-level perspective, these steps need to be configured:

- Activating business functions
- Activating the Web Dynpro application
- Updating security roles
- Creating RFC (Remote Function Call) users and destinations
- Defining logical systems
- Assigning RFC destinations
- Checking logical system assignment for the Central Finance client
- Creating and assigning an SAP Application Integration Framework runtime configuration group

Activating Business Functions

Once the central system is available, the business function FINS_CFIN must be activated. Open IMG Customizing (**Transaction SPRO**) • **Business Switch Framework Activation** (**Transaction SFW5**). Select the **Enterprise Business Functions** folder, select the **FINS_CFIN – Central Finance** checkbox, and click the **Activate Changes** button.

If the activation was successful, the lightbulb icon in front of business function FINS_CFIN should be on, and the **Planned Status** column should show **Business func. will remain activated**, as shown in Figure 8.6.

Name	Description	Planned Status	Depend...	Docum...	Software C...	Release	Application C...
ERP_IPC_INT_PRC	Price Summary on the Produc...			i	S4CORE	100	CA
ERP_IPM_BACKEND_1	IPM, Industry-Independent Ba...			i	S4CORE	605	SD
ERP_IPM_BACKEND_2	IPM, Download to CRM of Mat...			i	S4CORE	605	SD
ERP_MATERIAL_SOA	Master Data Governance for M...			i	MDG_APPL	607	CA-MDG-AP...
ERP_NWBC_ROLES	ERP, Roles for SAP NetWeav...			i	S4FND	702	CA-EPT-BRC
ERP_WEB_CHANNEL_1	SAP Web Channel Experienc...			i	S4CORE	605	CA
ERP_WEB_CHANNEL_2	SAP Web Channel Experienc...			i	S4CORE	605	CA
ERP_WEB_CHANNEL_3	SAP Web Channel Experienc...			i	S4CORE	605	CA
ESOA_OPS01	Enhancement Package 2 - Se...			i	S4CORE	602	CA
FICA_FSCM_CRM_DISPUTE	Integration FICA Dispute / CR...			i	S4FND	701	CA-EPT
FINS_CFIN	Central Finance	Business func. will remain activated		i	S4CORE	100	FI-CF-INF
FINS_CO_ICO_PROC_ENH_101	Intercompany Process Enhan...			i	S4CORE	101	CO-OM
FIN_AA_CI_1	FI-AA, Asset Accounting - Ob...	Business function is obsolete and c...			S4CORE	100	FI-GL
FIN_AA_PARALLEL_VAL	FI-AA, Parallel Valuation			i	S4CORE	617	FI-AA
FIN_ACC_GC_ALLOC	Financials, Group Close, Alloc...			i	S4CORE	747	FIN-SEM-BCS
FIN_ACC_GC_ASTHFS	Financials, Group Close, Asse...			i	S4CORE	605	FIN-SEM-BCS
FIN_ACC_GC_BCOMB	Financials, Group Close, Busi...			i	S4CORE	605	FIN-SEM-BCS
FIN_ACC_GC_CHKDGT	Financials, Group Close, Chec...			i	S4CORE	748	FIN-SEM-BCS
FIN_ACC_GC_RESTAT	Financials, Group Close, Rest...			i	S4CORE	736	FIN-SEM-BCS
FIN_ACC_GC_TAXRATECHG	Financials, Group Close, Adju...			i	S4CORE	604	FIN-SEM-BCS

Figure 8.6 Activation of Business Function FINS_CFIN in the Switch Framework (Transaction SFW5)

Activating a business function deploys coding, tables, and new configuration to an SAP system. Figure 8.7 shows the new Central Finance Customizing (Transaction CFINIMG) enabled by business function FINS_CFIN and which collects all configuration steps relevant to the Central Finance instance.

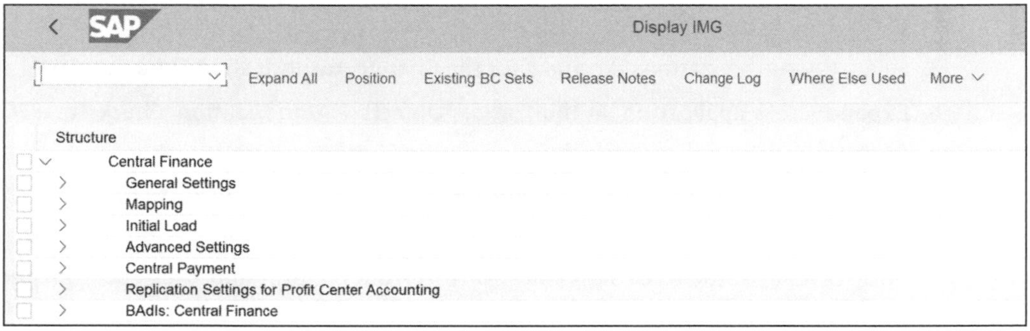

Figure 8.7 Transaction CFINIMG Showing Central Finance Customizing Steps

Activating the Web Dynpro Application

Some content delivered with the business function is not active by default. In particular, service MDG_BS_WD_ID_MATCH_SERVICE must be activated to enable data mapping for customers, suppliers, business partners, materials, financials, and custom objects. Enter Transaction SICF (Maintain Services), and in the **Hierarchy** field, enter "SERVICE." Enter the service name and click the **Execute** button. Select **Service/Host • Activate**, as shown in Figure 8.8. Note that the service cannot be deactivated later.

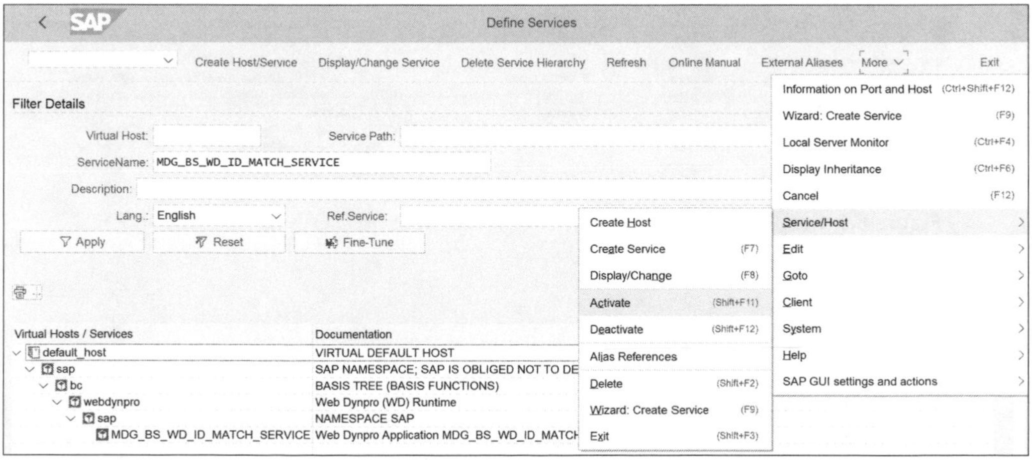

Figure 8.8 Activate Service MDG_BS_WD_ID_MATCH_SERVICE in Transaction SICF

Updating Security Roles

For security, the role SAP_IUUC_REPL_REMOTE must be updated to include RFC name BDCH in the white list. Follow these steps:

1. Start Transaction PFCG (Role Maintenance).

2. In the **Role** field, enter "SAP_IUUC_REPL_REMOTE" and click the **Change** button.

3. Select the **Authorizations** tab and click the **Change Authorization Data** button.

4. Expand **Cross-application Authorization Objects** • **Authorization Check for RFC Access**.

5. Click the **Change** button for the **Name (Whitelist) of RFC Object** (RFC_NAME) field.

6. Add "BDCH" to the existing values for the **From** column and click the **Transfer** button.

7. Click the **Generate** button.

The results are shown in Figure 8.9 and Figure 8.10. You'll need to repeat these steps in all on-premise SAP source systems.

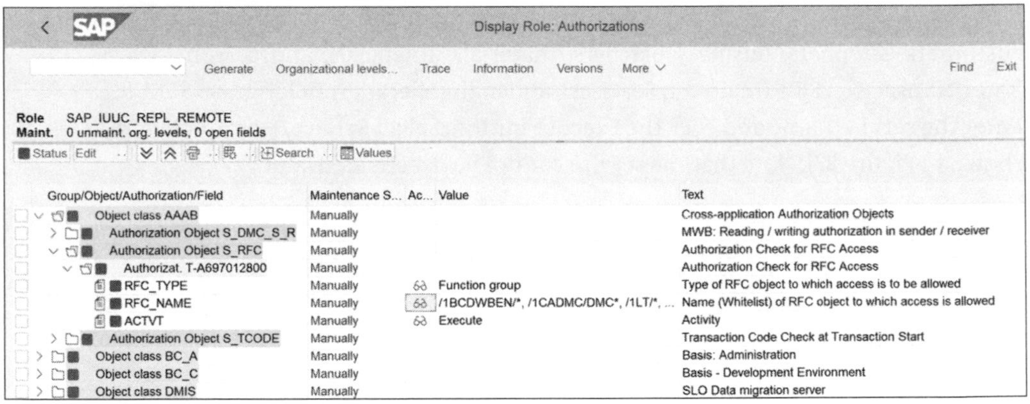

Figure 8.9 Result of Changes to Role SAP_IUUC_REPL_REMOTE in Transaction PFCG

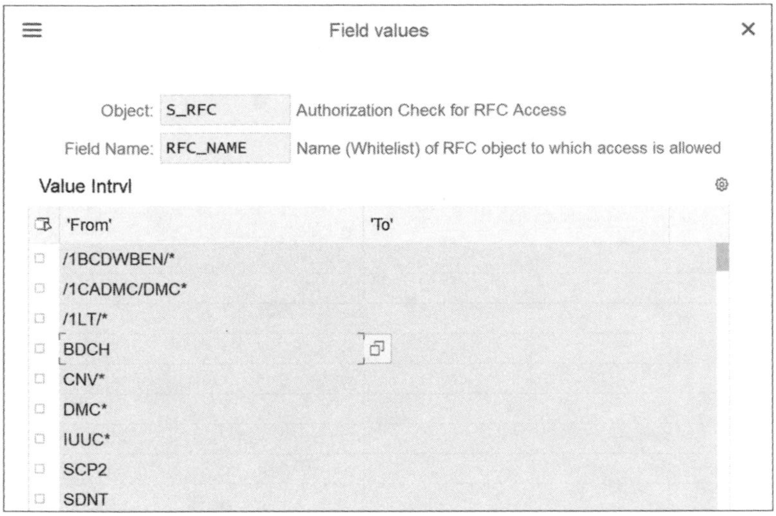

Figure 8.10 Result of Changes to Role SAP_IUUC_REPL_REMOTE in Transaction PFCG (Cont.)

The SAP Application Integration Framework also requires a security update. A new role must be created from template SAP_AIF_PROCESSING by following these steps:

1. Start Transaction PFCG (Role Maintenance).

2. In the **Role** field, enter a new role (e.g., "Z_SAP_AIF_PROCESSING") and click the **Create** button.

3. Select the **Authorizations** tab and click the **Change Authorization Data** button.

4. In the **Choose Template** popup, select **SAP_AIF_PROCESSING** and click the **Apply Template** button.

5. Click the **Save** button.

6. In the **Assign Profile Name for Generated Authorization Profile** popup, click the **Execute** button.

7. Click the **Generate** button.

The results are shown in Figure 8.11 and Figure 8.12. Unlike the earlier process for security role SAP_IUUC_REPL_REMOTE, you don't need to repeat these steps in all source systems.

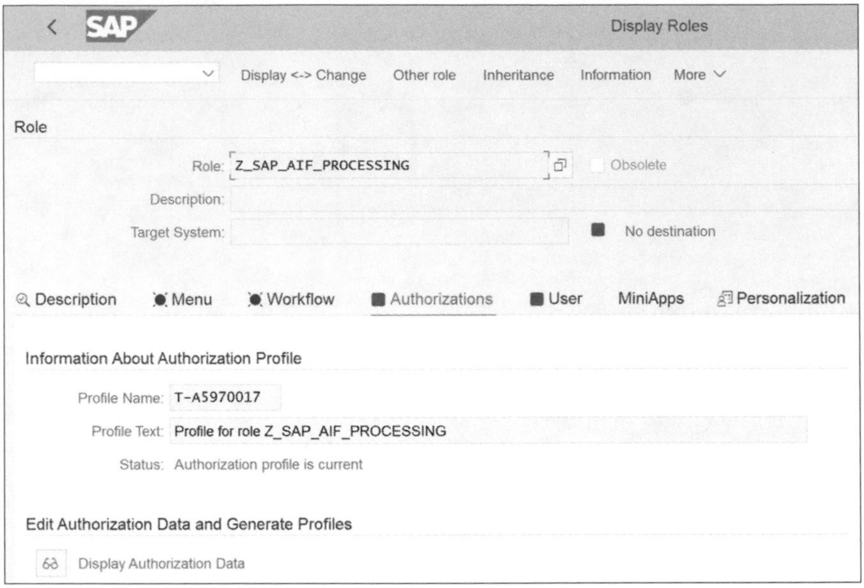

Figure 8.11 Result of Creating a New Role from Template SAP_AIF_PROCESSING in Transaction PFCG (Part 1)

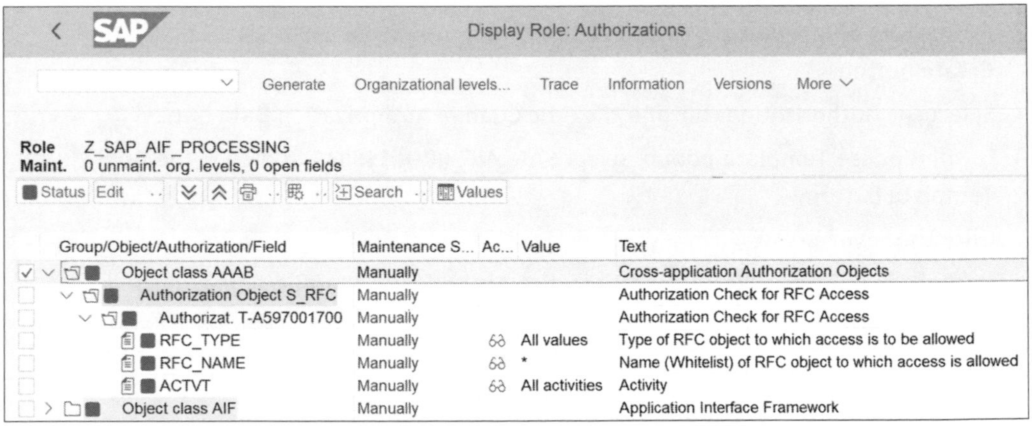

Figure 8.12 Result of Creating a New Role from Template SAP_AIF_PROCESSING in Transaction PFCG (Part 2)

Creating RFC Users and Destinations (Source Systems)

The communication between SAP on-premise systems is performed via RFCs. Before setting up the required RFC destinations, a user must be created with type C

(Communication) in the source systems with Transaction SUO1. That user also must be assigned the authorizations corresponding to the scenarios selected. You'll need to perform a number of steps for this setup:

1. **Initial load/replication in the SAP LT Replication Server**
   Assign roles SAP_MWB_PROJECT_MANAGER and SAP_IUUC_REPL_REMOTE. Note that this last role will only be available in the SAP LT Replication Server and the SAP source systems after the Data Migration Server (DMIS) is installed on these instances (for details, Section 8.3.3).

2. **Extracting data for financial accounting**
   Assign authorization object S_RFC with the following settings:
   - RFC_TYPE = FUGR (Function Group)
   - RFC_NAME = FIN_CFIN_INITIAL_LOAD, FIN_CFIN_CLEARING, FIN_CFIN_RESET_CLEARING
   - ACTVT = 16 (Execute)

3. **Extracting data for management accounting**
   Assign authorization object S_RFC with the following settings:
   - RFC_TYPE = FUGR (Function Group)
   - RFC_NAME = FIN_CFIN_CO, FIN_CFIN_CO_SIMULATE
   - ACTVT = 16 (Execute)

4. **Manage mappings**
   Assign authorization object S_RFC with the following settings:
   - RFC_TYPE = FUGR (Function Group)
   - RFC_NAME = FIN_CFIN_MAPPING_RFC
   - ACTVT = 16 (Execute)

5. **Comparison reports**
   Reports cannot be displayed with just a communication user. In this case, existing users of type A (Dialog) can be used, or you can create a new user of type A (Dialog). Users will require authorizations for:
   - Authorization object S_TCODE with the following settings:
     - TCD (Transaction Code) = FBO3, KSB5
   - Authorization object S_RFC with the following settings:
     - RFC_TYPE = FUGR (Function Group)
     - RFC_NAME = FIN_CFIN_DFV
     - ACTVT = 16 (Execute)
   - Authorization objects F_BKPS_BUK, K_VRGNG, K_TP_VALU, F_BKPF_KOA, and F_FAGL_LDR.

6. **Central payments**

   As with reports, performing central payments requires a dialog user (type A) with authorization for authorization object S_RFC with the following settings:

   - RFC_TYPE = FUGR (Function Group)
   - RFC_NAME = FIN_CFIN_APAR_CPAY, FIN_CFIN_APAR_SEPA, FIN_CFIN_APAR_CCARD
   - ACTVT = 16 (Execute)

7. **Displaying objects from the source system using the document relationship browser**

   In this step, we recommend using the current user in the RFC destination to restrict users' access only to documents they are authorized to access in the connected system.

Once users are created in the relevant systems, RFC destinations of type 3 (ABAP Connections) can be created in Transaction SM59 (RFC Destinations), as shown, for example, in Figure 8.13. Destinations exist between the central system and the SAP LT Replication Server system with a communication user and between the central system and the source system with a dialog user.

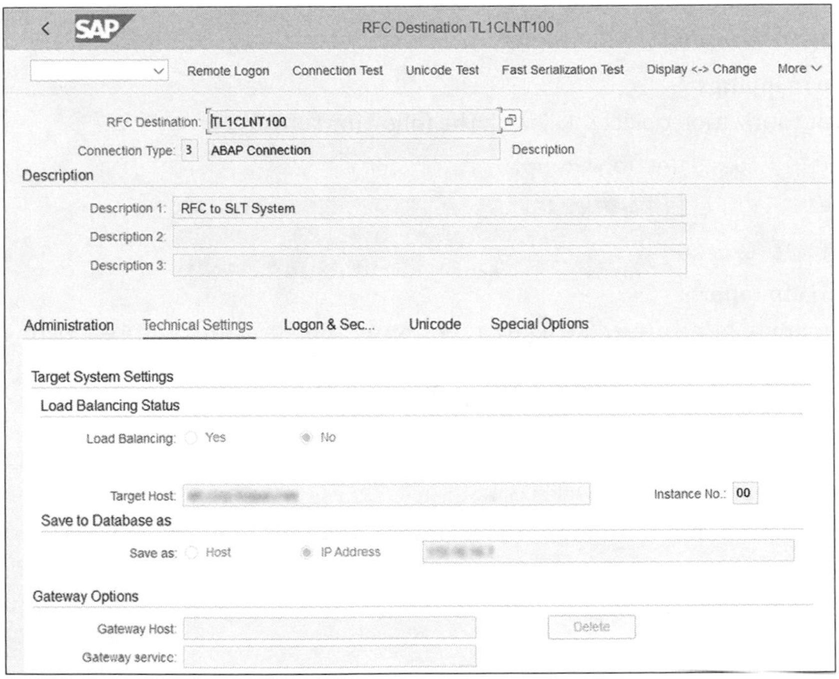

Figure 8.13 Setting Up an RFC Destination (Transaction SM59)

> **RFC Naming Convention**
>
> We recommend adhering to the standard naming convention for RFC destinations: <system ID> CLNT <client number>, for example, IADCLNT100.
>
> For RFC destinations set up with an empty user on the **Logon & Security** tab, the standard naming convention is <system ID> CLNT <client number> _DIALOG, for example, IADCLNT100_DIALOG.

Defining Logical Systems (Central System)

A *logical system* is an alias representing the source system in configuration and in accounting documents. Perform the configuration in Central Finance Customizing (Transaction CFINIMG), under **General Settings • Define Logical System for Source System and Central Finance Systems** to create at least two logical systems, as shown in Figure 8.14:

- One logical system representing the current Central Finance system
- One logical system for each source system

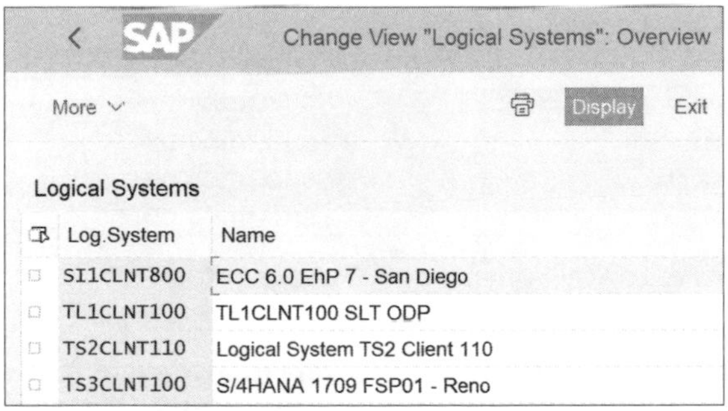

Figure 8.14 Defining Logical Systems

Assigning RFC Destinations (Central System)

You'll assign RFC destinations in Central Finance Customizing (Transaction CFINIMG), under **General Settings • Maintain Source Systems and RFC Assignments**. For each logical system, specify whether the source is an SAP (ensure the **Third-Party** checkbox is not selected) or non-SAP (select the **Third-Party** checkbox) system.

Then, and only for the SAP sources, select the line for the logical system and click on the **RFC Destinations** folder to assign an RFC destination for each scenario, as shown in Figure 8.15:

- **Extracting Data for Financial Accounting**
- **Extracting Data for Management Accounting**
- **Extracting Data for Commitment**
- **Manage Mappings**
- **Comparison Reports**
- **Central Payment**

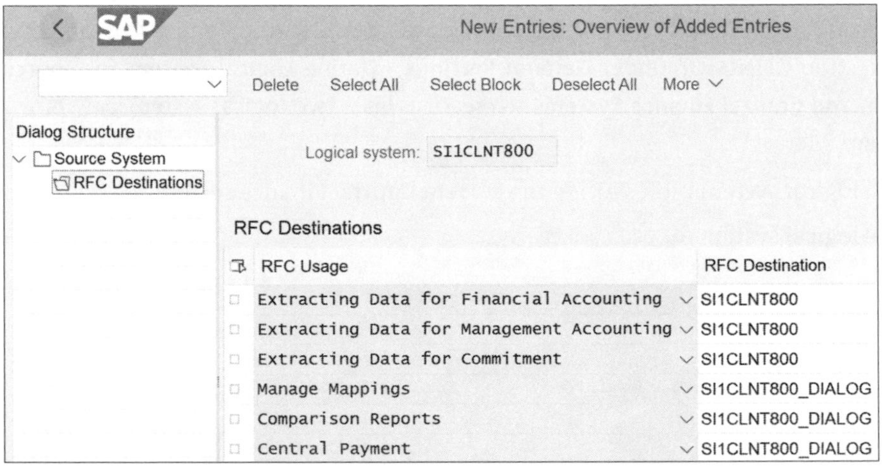

Figure 8.15 Assigning RFC Destinations to Logical Systems by RFC Usage

When displaying financial accounting documents in the Central Finance system, the reference source system and document numbers are saved to enable drilldown to the source. This capability requires configuring Central Finance Customizing (Transaction CFINIMG), under **General Settings • Assign RFC Destination for Displaying Objects from Source System**. Then, select the source system and follow the menu path **Assign Destination for Special Method**. Enter "DRB" in the **Object Type** field and "ObjectDisplay" in the **Method Object** field. Select an RFC destination, as shown, for example, in Figure 8.16. To restrict access to only authorized documents, remember to set up the RFC destination with the **Current User** checkbox selected.

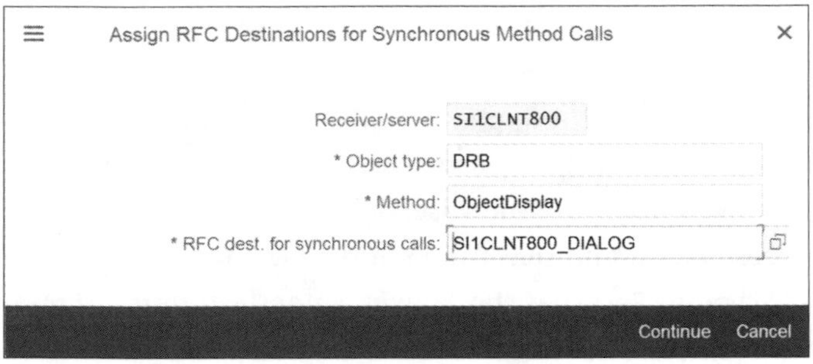

Figure 8.16 Assigning an RFC destination for Displaying Objects from Source System

Checking Logical System Assignment for the Central Finance Client (Central System)

The Central Finance system is itself referenced as a logical system. This link is created in Central Finance Customizing (Transaction CFINIMG), under **General Settings** • **Check Logical System Assignment for Central Finance Client**. Select the current client and click on the **Details** button. Enter a logical system in the corresponding field, as shown, for example, in Figure 8.17. Save these changes.

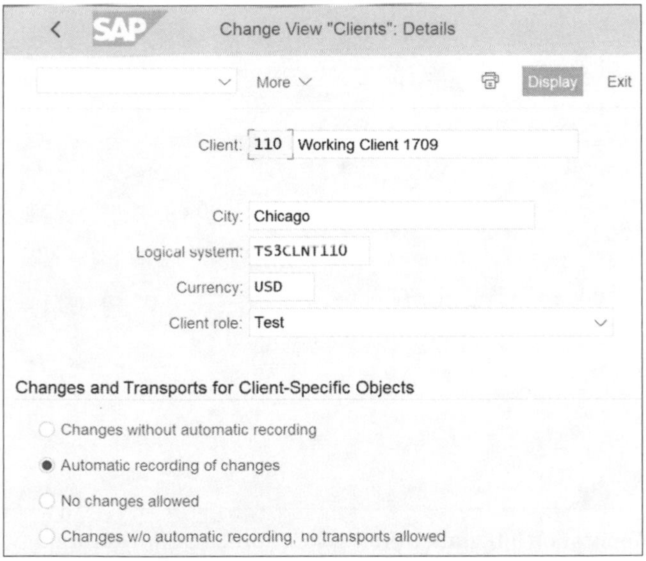

Figure 8.17 Assigning a Logical System to the Central Finance Client

Creating and Assigning a Runtime Configuration Group (Central System)

SAP Application Integration Framework requires a configuration group to define how messages should be processed. Use the application Maintain Runtime Configuration Group (Transaction /AIF/PERS_CGR) for namespace /FINCF. If a configuration group doesn't exist, click on **New Entries**. Otherwise, double-click on the **Runtime Configuration ID**. Enter a **Description** and select the **Runtime Configuration Group Active**, **Run Scheduled**, and **Schedule Packages** checkboxes. Enter the number of **Messages Per Package** and **Messages per Run** parameters, as shown, for example, in Figure 8.18. Save these changes.

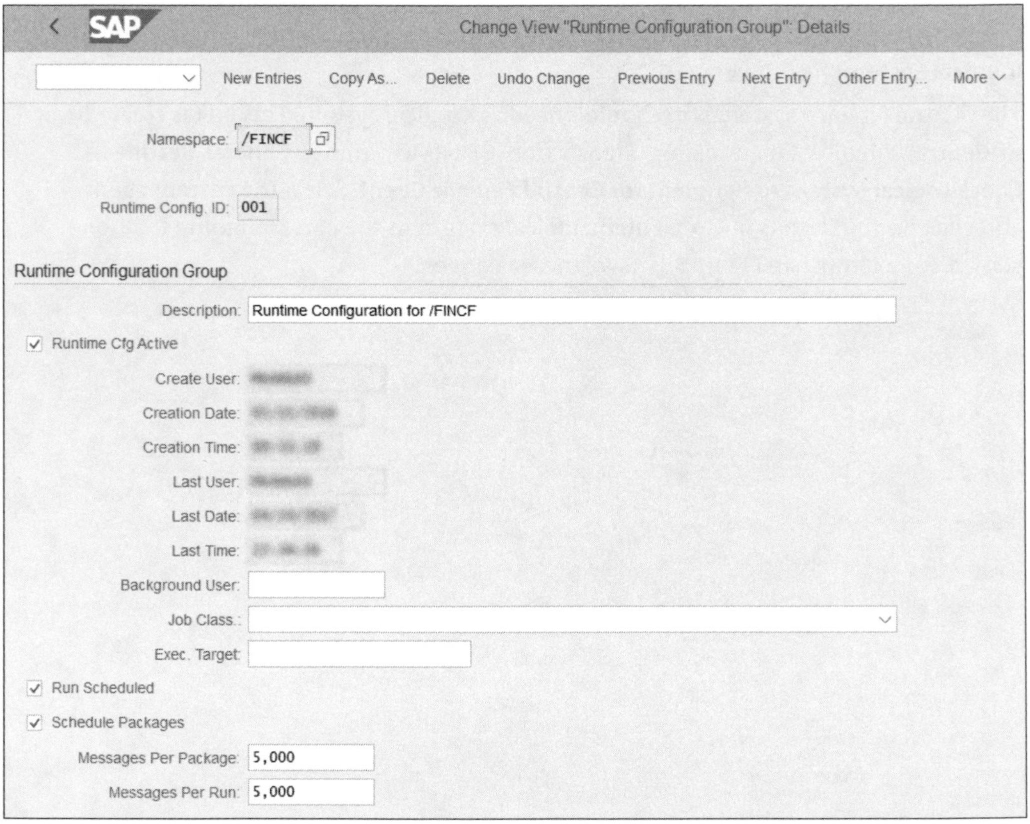

Figure 8.18 Creating an SAP Application Integration Framework Runtime Configuration Group

After the runtime configuration group has been created, you can assign it to a replication object in Central Finance Customizing (Transaction CFINIM), under **General Settings • Assign AIF Runtime Configuration Group to Replication Object**. For each configuration object—i.e., Finance (FI) and Controlling (CO) postings, CO internal postings, cost objects, CO-PA postings, and commitment postings), choose an SAP Application Integration Framework namespace (e.g., /FINCF) and a runtime configuration ID (e.g., 001), as shown, for example, in Figure 8.19. Save these changes.

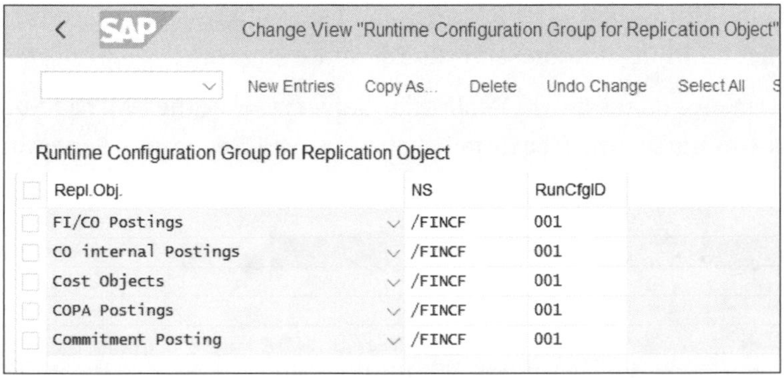

Figure 8.19 Assigning an SAP Application Integration Framework Runtime Configuration Group to Replication Objects

---

Note on Background Jobs

The Central Finance instance relies on an SAP S/4HANA setup, which is usually optimized for end-user performance. However, in a Central Finance context, and especially during the discovery or pilot phase, only a few users will access the system to launch resource-intensive background processes like the initial load.

In this context, we recommend enabling as many background work processes (BAT) as possible, even if doing so means reducing the number of dialog work processes (DIA).

The number and types of work processes across application servers can be checked with Transactions SM50 (Work Processes) and SM51 (Application Server Instances). Be aware that changing the work process distribution requires you restart each instance.

8.3.3   SAP Landscape Transformation Replication Server

The SAP LT Replication Server handles the initial load and replication of data from the local system(s) into the Central Finance system for FI and CO objects and documents. After the initial load, the SAP LT Replication Server will monitor database triggers on the source system, save these changes to logging tables, and propagate these changes to the target system.

In a Central Finance scenario, the SAP LT Replication Server system can be installed on the same instance. However, for performance and flexibility reasons, we recommend installing the SAP LT Replication Server as a separate server.

To enable Central Finance on the SAP LT Replication Server system, the DMIS add-on (version 2011_1_700 or higher) must be installed on the SAP LT Replication Server, as shown in Figure 8.20.

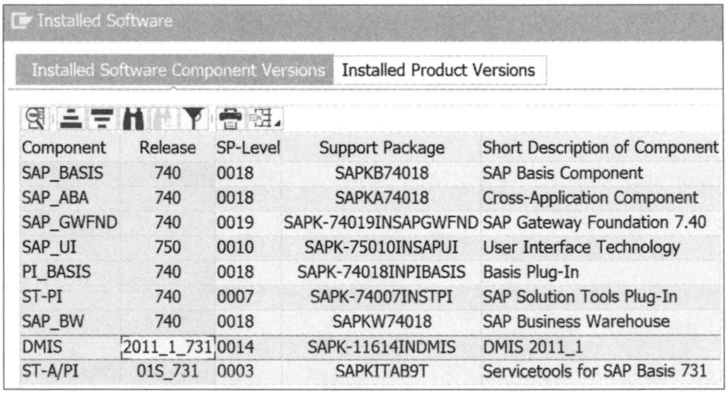

Component	Release	SP-Level	Support Package	Short Description of Component
SAP_BASIS	740	0018	SAPKB74018	SAP Basis Component
SAP_ABA	740	0018	SAPKA74018	Cross-Application Component
SAP_GWFND	740	0019	SAPK-74019INSAPGWFND	SAP Gateway Foundation 7.40
SAP_UI	750	0010	SAPK-75010INSAPUI	User Interface Technology
PI_BASIS	740	0018	SAPK-74018INPIBASIS	Basis Plug-In
ST-PI	740	0007	SAPK-74007INSTPI	SAP Solution Tools Plug-In
SAP_BW	740	0018	SAPKW74018	SAP Business Warehouse
DMIS	2011_1_731	0014	SAPK-11614INDMIS	DMIS 2011_1
ST-A/PI	01S_731	0003	SAPKITAB9T	Servicetools for SAP Basis 731

Figure 8.20 Component DMIS with Version 2011_1_700 or Higher Installed

> **Replication Content Update**
>
> Predelivered replication content might not be compatible with the specific releases of your Central Finance system and the SAP LT Replication Server system. Check Note 2154420: SAP LT Replication Server for Central Finance to download and install the most relevant version of the replication content.

The SAP LT Replication Server configuration requires fewer steps but can still be challenging. From a high-level perspective, the configuration consists in:

- Defining RFC destinations
- Defining configuration

Defining RFC Destinations

The SAP LT Replication Server system sits between the source system and the central system. Even when installed on the same server as the source or target system, the SAP LT Replication Server component communicates with RFC destinations.

As described earlier in Section 8.3.2, use Transaction SM59 to create RFC destinations:

1. Between the SAP LT Replication Server system and the source system(s)
2. Between the SAP LT Replication Server system and the central system

Defining Configuration

The SAP LT Replication Server will connect the source system with the central system. This link is called a *destination*. Destinations are configured in the Configuration and Monitoring Dashboard (Transaction LTRC), as shown in Figure 8.21.

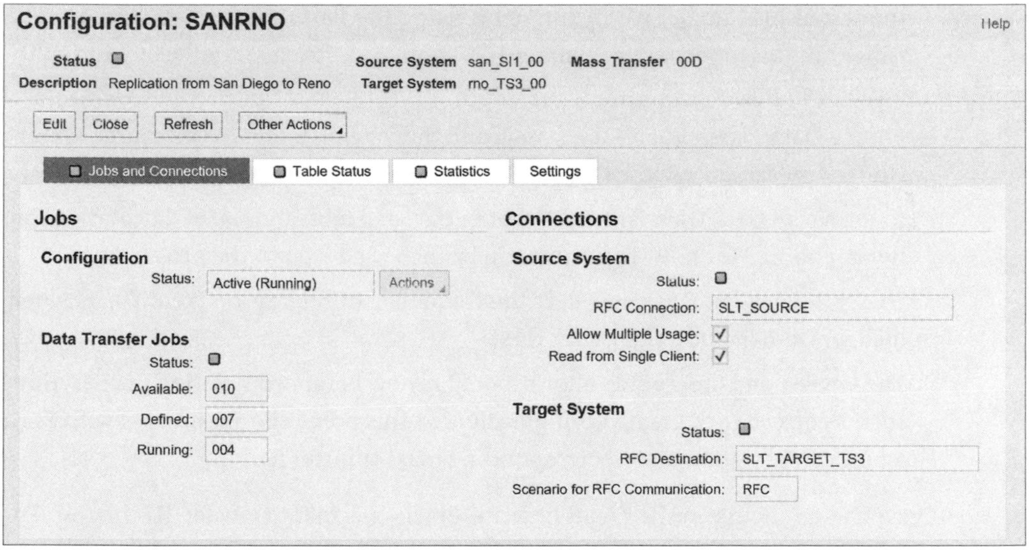

Figure 8.21 Example Configuration in the SAP LT Replication Server between an SAP ERP Source and an SAP S/4HANA Central Finance Target

To start defining configuration, follow these steps:

1. Click on the **New** button to create a new configuration. A new window will open that will guide you through the steps.

2. Enter a **Configuration Name** (e.g., <source>_<target>), **Description**, and **Authorization Group** (can be left blank) and then click **Next**.

3. Under **Specify Source System**, select **RFC Connection** and enter an RFC destination to the source system. The **Allow Multiple Usage** checkbox must be selected if data must be replicated via the SAP LT Replication Server from the same source system. This selection enables multiple configurations to use the same source system. If the SAP LT Replication Server is only used for Central Finance, this option is not necessary. Otherwise, other configurations need to be considered, including potential future use. The **Read from Single Client** checkbox should be selected if the client is already specified in the RFC destination. Click **Next**.

4. Under **Specify Target System**, enter the data corresponding to the central system. Click **Next**.

5. The **Specify Transfer Settings** step collects information related to data transfer for the initial load mode. We recommend using the **Performance Optimized** mode. However, this mode requires about 10% more disk space for buffering during the initial load phase.

6. Enter a **Data Class of Tablespace** to group the logging tables in the source system. Under **Application**, choose **Central Finance • Business Integration (CFIN_PI)**.

7. In the **No. of Data Transfer Jobs**, **No. of Initial Load Jobs**, and **No. of Calculation Jobs** fields, choose **1** for now. This value can be increased later in the project.

8. Under **Replication Options**, select the frequency of replication (**Real Time**, **Scheduled**, or **On-demand**). Then, click **Next**.

9. The **Review and Create** step allows a final review before completion. If everything seems correct, click **Create Configuration**. At this point, the application will create a new configuration and a corresponding mass transfer ID.

Once the configuration is created, write down the mass transfer ID. In the data browser (Transaction SE16), open table DMC_MT_GEN_EXIT. Create three new entries, as shown in Figure 8.22.

MT_ID	TABNAME	MODULE_TYPE	INCL_NAME_REPL
<Mass Transfer ID>	CFIN_ACCHD	OLI	IUUC_CFIN_REM_PROC_CFIN_ACCHD
<Mass Transfer ID>	AUFK	OLI	IUUC_CFIN_REM_PROC_AUFK
<Mass Transfer ID>	COBK	OLI	IUUC_CFIN_REM_PROC_COBK

Figure 8.22 Entries in Table DMC_MT_GEN_EXIT Supporting the Central Finance Business Integration (CFIN_PI) Scenario

The SAP LT Replication Server system is now ready for the initial load and replication. More configuration steps will be required once the source systems and the central system are ready.

8.3.4   SAP Source Systems

As detailed in Chapter 6, SAP source systems need to be distinguished between on-premise and cloud *editions* even though these editions are mostly configured in the same way.

On-Premise

Any recent on-premise SAP ERP solution requires only few updates to serve as a source system for Central Finance, as follows:

1. **Install the Data Migration Server**
   Like the SAP LT Replication Server system, the DMIS add-on (version 2011_1_700 or higher) must be installed on the local server(s).

2. **Update the security role**
   As described earlier in Section 8.3.2, update the RFC white list for security role SAP_IUUC_REPL_REMOTE.

In the Cloud

At the time of this writing, SAP S/4HANA Cloud 1805 is the most current release, which can serve as source system for Central Finance, but not as central system.

With quarterly updates, we recommend checking the latest SAP Best Practices available with SAP Activate by following these steps:

1. Open a web browser to *https://rapid.sap.com/bp*.

2. Select **Solutions Packages for SAP S/4HANA**.

3. Select **SAP S/4HANA Cloud**.

4. Select **SAP Best Practices for SAP S/4HANA Cloud**.

5. In the **Version** dropdown, select the country version (e.g., USA).

6. Under **Scope Item Groups**, open **Finance, Accounting, Subsidiary Integration of SAP S/4HANA Cloud to Central Finance (1W4)**.

The direct link to this scope item is: *https://rapid.sap.com/bp/scopeitems/1W4*.

The latest setup instructions and test scripts will be accessible in the **Details** section.

8.3.5   Non-SAP Source Systems

For legal reasons, SAP cannot provide standard connectivity to third-party systems. However, simplified staging tables can be created to receive data extracted and loaded from non-SAP source systems via the SAP LT Replication Server, as shown in Figure 8.23.

> **Replication Content for Third-Party Systems**
>
> Replication content for third-party systems is not available by default but can be downloaded from SAP Note 2481900: SAP LT Replication Server for Central Finance – Third-Party System Integration.

Download the latest version of the replication content from Note 2481900 and upload the content into the SAP LT Replication Server using program DMC_UPLOAD_OBJECT.

Create a custom program called ZCFIN_EX_CREATE_SLT_TAB. Copy the source code from the same Note 2481900, activate the changes, and execute the new program to generate the following staging tables:

- Table /1LT/CF_E_HEADER (Document Header)
- Table /1LT/CF_E_ACCT (Accounting Items)
- Table /1LT/CF_E_DEBIT (Debtor Items)
- Table /1LT/CF_E_CREDIT (Creditor Items)
- Table /1LT/CF_E_PRDTAX (Product Tax Items)
- Table /1LT/CF_E_WHTAX (Withholding Tax Items)

- Table /1LT/CF_E_EXTENT (Customer Extension on Header Level)
- Table /1LT/CF_E_EXT_IT (Customer Extension on Item Level)

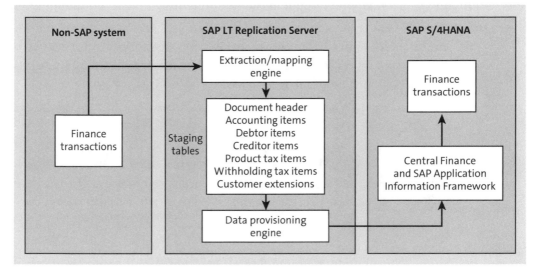

Figure 8.23 Data Flow from Non-SAP System to Central Finance through the SAP LT Replication Server Third-Party Staging Tables

8.3.6   SAP Master Data Governance System

Central Finance leverages SAP MDG tools for master data mapping. If only the mapping services are used, no license for SAP MDG is required. However, a license is required for other tools like master data distribution, business rules, workflow, data governance, etc.

There are two types of mappings, depending on the lifecycle of the master data:

- For long-lifecycle master data like general ledger (G/L) accounts, customers, and vendors, use either manual mapping or SAP MDG (recommended).
- For short-lifecycle master data like internal orders or production orders, use the cost object mapping framework.

If only the standard data mapping is used, no further installation is required. If the full SAP MDG solution is in use, carry out the SAP MDG-specific installation process.

8.4   Data Integration Framework

The goal of a Central Finance system is to replicate documents from one or more source systems. Contrary to traditional solutions like data warehouses, data hubs, or data lakes, the Central Finance system is a full ERP system. As a result, data is not simply copied from the source system and pasted into a database. Documents are re-created as if the transaction was posted again, which ensures complete data integrity and creates a platform for central operations.

> **Real-Life Example**
>
> During a project, let's say inconsistencies were found between the source system and the Central Finance system, specifically different balance amounts. Upon investigation, a custom integration program in the source system was identified as the cause: Taxes had not been recalculated in the source system but had been in the Central Finance system.

To ensure consistency between source systems and Central Finance systems, data must be segregated into different work streams: master data, transactional data, SAP source data, non-SAP source data, and the third-party interface.

8.4.1   Master Data

First, a note on master data: With the SAP LT Replication Server, the replication process supports the transfer of financial transactions between a non-SAP system and a Central Finance system. This process does *not* support the replication of master data. Other solutions like SAP MDG or third-party applications must be set up and configured to support master data synchronization.

Initial Configuration: Definition

The Central Finance system is an ERP system that requires initial configuration. This step is often overlooked because users tend to take for granted configuration that was performed 5, 10, or 15 years earlier and that now follows a well-organized process. However, in most cases, the central instance will be a greenfield system only populated with some predelivered content, called the SAP Model Company.

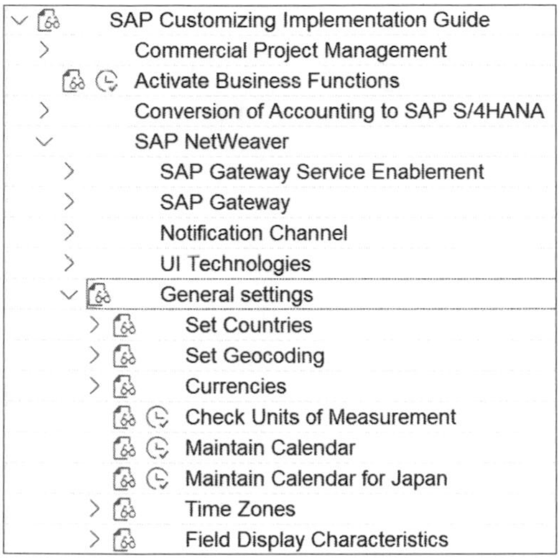

Figure 8.24 Customizing Steps for General Settings

The following initial configuration steps, partially shown in Figure 8.24, need to be performed manually or these configuration settings imported with Transaction SPRO:

- **SAP NetWeaver • General Settings**
  - Set Countries
  - Set Geocoding
  - Time Zones
  - Currency Codes
  - Currency Rate Types
  - Currency Rates
  - Check Units of Measurements
  - ISO Codes
  - Dimensions
- **Enterprise Structure • Definition**
  - Company
  - Company Codes
  - Business Area Functional Area
  - Controlling Area
  - Operating Concern

- Plant
- Sales Organization
- Distribution Channel
- Purchasing Organization

■ Enterprise Structure • Assignment
- Assign Company Code to Company
- Assign Company Code to Controlling Area
- Assign Controlling Area to Operating Concern
- Assign Plant to Company Code
- Assign Sales Organization to Company Code
- Assign Distribution Channel to Sales Organization
- Assign Purchasing Organization to Company Code

■ Financial Accounting
- Ledgers
- Fiscal Year
- Posting Periods
- Document Types
- Number Ranges for Documents
- Copy to Company Code
- Copy to Fiscal Year

■ General Ledger Accounting
- G/L Accounts
- Chart of Accounts
- Assign Company Code to Chart of Accounts

■ Controlling
- Number Ranges for Orders
- Number Ranges to Controlling Documents
- Cost Center Categories

■ Accounts Payables/Account Receivables
- Number Ranges for Customer Account Groups
- Number Ranges for Vendor Account Groups

This list is not exhaustive but should serve as a basis for evaluating whether the merger of multiple systems or changes to the business processes will impact the new information model.

Figure 8.25 shows the links between some of the most important elements for the financial information model inside an SAP ERP system. As an integrated solution, the whole model must be consistent for business processes to be performed with the necessary data integrity.

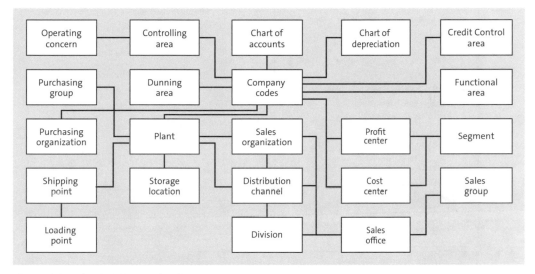

Figure 8.25 The SAP Enterprise Structure

Initial Configuration: Compare with SAP Source System

If the source system is provided by SAP, you can easily compare the configuration by, for example, following these steps:

1. Go to IMG Customizing (Transaction SPRO), under **Enterprise Structure • Definition • Financial Accounting • Define Business Area**.

2. In the menu, select **Utilities • Adjustment**.

3. Select the RFC destination pointing to the source system and click **Choose**. The program will show a comparison between the logon client (the Central Finance instance) and the comparison client (the source system). The layout is easier to understand with the legend, which is accessible with the menu labeled **Legend**.

4. Select the entries marked with **R** (**Entry only in the comparison client**) that need to be imported into the central instance and choose **Adjust** in the menu. The selected entries will be copied from the source system into the central system.

5. Save these changes.

Additional comparison/adjustment tools are available with Transactions SCMP, SCUO, or OY19. Figure 8.26 shows the comparison function.

		BusA	Business area description
☑	R	EDU	
☑	R	IN47	India Business area
☐	ML	IS00	New
	MR	IS00	Internal Service Group 00
☑	R	LS01	Legal Services
☑	R	RETL	Retail
☑	R	SSS	
☑	R	WSLE	Wholesale
☐		Z001	Cloud Services
☐		Z002	Consulting Services
☐		Z003	Hosting
☐		Z004	Knowledge Transfers
☐		Z005	Corporate Other
☐		Z006	Solution Delivery

Color	Description
	View/table entry differences
	Field contents differences
	Entry only exists in logon client
	Entry only in comparison client
	Identical entry
	Identical entry

Code	Description
ML	Differences, logon client entry
MR	Differences, comparison client entry
L	Entry only exists in logon client
R	Entry only exists in comparison client
	Identical entries
(M)	Differences only in hidden fields

Figure 8.26 Using the Adjustment Function to Import Configuration from the Source System into the Central System

Initial Configuration: Import with BC Sets

When you need to clean up configuration or when you need to merge configurations from multiple systems, we recommend using Business Configuration sets (BC sets). This method allows you to:

1. Select and export configuration from an SAP source system into files.

2. Manipulate the files outside the systems.

3. Import the configuration files into the central system.

4. Activate/group the configuration as needed.

First, you'll export a BC set: In the source system, open the BC set transaction from the SAP Menu: **Tools • Customizing • Business Configuration Sets • Display and Maintain BC Sets** (Transaction SCPR3). In the toolbar, click on the **Create BC Set** button. Enter a name, description, and software component, as shown in Figure 8.27. Select the **Create BC Set from … IMG Hierarchy** radio button. Click the **Continue** button.

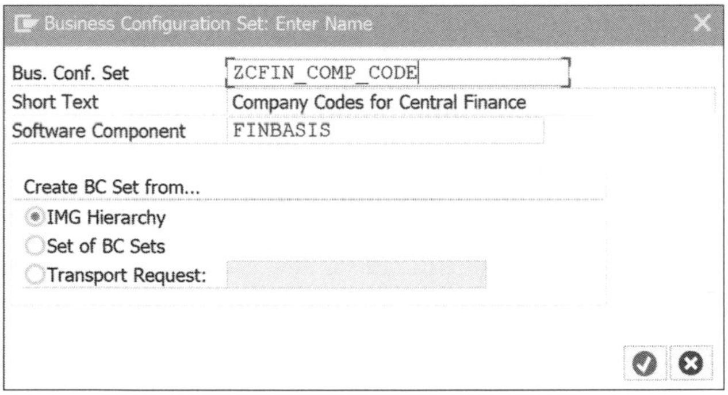

Figure 8.27 Creating a Business Configuration Set (BC Set)

The IMG will be displayed in the window. Select the configuration step that needs to be exported, from the menu path, for instance, **Enterprise Structure • Definition • Financial Accounting • Edit, Copy, Delete, Check Company Code**. Next, in the **Tables and Views for Selected Customizing Object** panel, double-click on the name of a table to be exported, for instance, table V_T001 (Company Code). In the **Table View** panel, select one or more entries to be exported: As shown in Figure 8.28, we selected 1000 (BestRun Germany), 2000 (BestRun U.K.), and 2200 (BestRun France). Click the **Save** button. In the transport window, click on the **Local Object** button since this configuration will not be moved from system to system, but moved through files instead. Finally, click the **Download BC Set** button from the toolbar and save the generated file to your desktop.

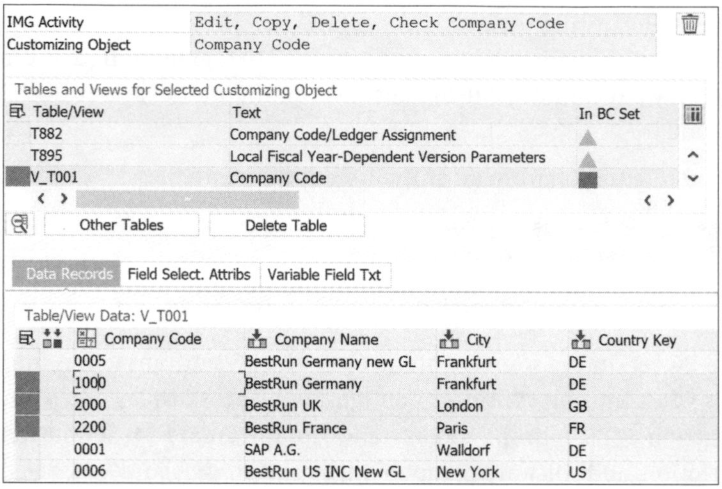

Figure 8.28 Selecting IMG Activity, Tables/Views, and Entries to Be Exported as a BC Set

Now that the configuration entries are saved as a BC set file, you can manipulate them locally with any text or spreadsheet editor. However, since the format of BC sets is rather specific, usually BC set files are imported as-is.

In the central system, open the BC set transaction from the SAP Menu by navigating to **Tools • Customizing • Business Configuration Sets • Display and Maintain BC Sets** (Transaction SCPR3). In the toolbar, click on the **Upload BC Set** button and select the file that was previously saved. Choose a transport request or save a local object. Review the configuration before saving it. Several options are available from the menu. For instance, **Compare with Customizing Tables** executes a report similar to the adjustment report presented earlier in this section.

At this point, the configuration is available but not active in the central system. To activate, either stay in the Transaction SCPR3 and follow the menu path **Goto • Activation Transaction**. Or, from the SAP Menu, follow the menu path **Tools • Customizing • Business Configuration Sets • Activation of BC Sets** (Transaction SCPR20). Next, select the BC set and click the **Activate BC Set** button in the toolbar. Select or create a customizing transport request. Click the **Continue Activation** button. Upon completion, the message **Activation successfully completed** should appear.

Master Data Upload

Depending on the scope, several master data object types are required for Central Finance processes to work. For instance, you'll need the following master data:

- Profit centers/profit center standard hierarchy
- Cost centers/cost center standard hierarchy
- Activity types
- Business partners (customers and vendors)
- Materials

These object types can be covered by SAP MDG if available in the landscape. If not, you'll need to manually upload these object types, and master data maintenance processes will need to be redesigned. The initial upload can be supported with the Landscape Transformation Migration Cockpit delivered with SAP S/4HANA. Other alternatives like SAP Data Services, third-party solutions, or custom programs can be used. For more information about master data management, see Chapter 10.

Initial Configuration: Import with Migration Cockpit

In the Central Finance system, open the Landscape Transformation Migration Cockpit (Transaction LTMC). Click the **Create** button to create a migration project, see Figure 8.29. Enter a name and then select **Transfer Data from File** and **Default View = On-premise – Enterprise Management Scope**. Click the **Create** button.

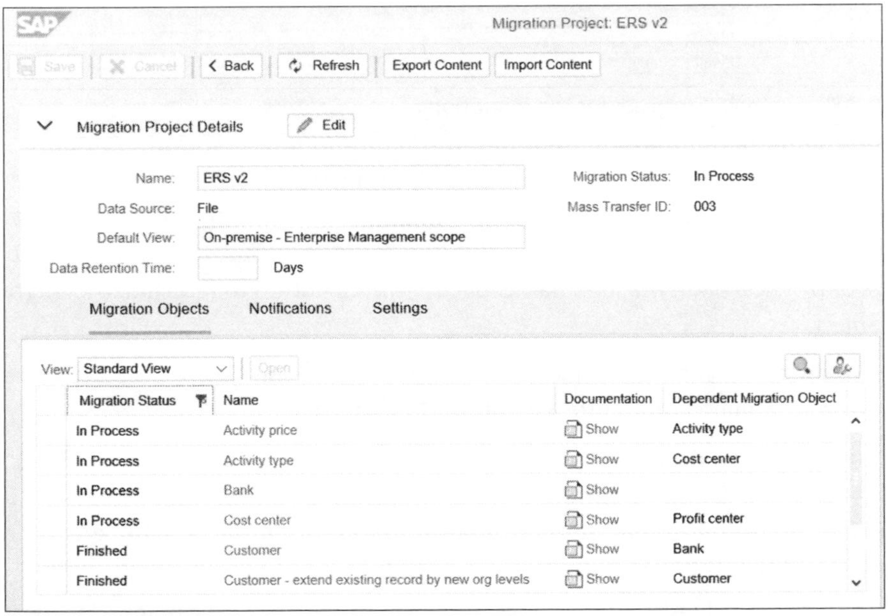

Figure 8.29 The Landscape Transformation Migration Cockpit Supporting Objects Like Activity Types, Cost Centers, or Customers

The migration project will show a list of migration objects, including the ones shown in Figure 8.30. For now, click on **Cost Centers**. In the migration object details view, review the documentation before clicking the **Download Template** button. The downloaded file has the .xml extension but can be opened with a spreadsheet application, as shown in Figure 8.30. The **Introduction** tab in the template describes how the file should be used. The **Field List** tab lists all fields, including their importance and technical length. The last tab, **Cost Center Master Record** in this case, is where the data is maintained. Make sure you follow the instructions from the first tab, as some functions like copy/paste or search/replace may damage the file.

Source Data for Migration Object: Cost center			
Version S4CORE 102 – 04.26.2018 © Copyright SAP SE. All rights reserved.			
Main data			
Controlling area*	Cost center*	Valid-from date*	Valid-to date*
0001	110518	01.06.1998	28.05.2000
0001	110518	29.05.2000	27.05.2001
0001	144471	30.05.1994	28.05.1995
0001	144471	29.05.1995	26.05.1996
0001	144471	27.05.1996	25.05.1997
0001	144471	26.05.1997	31.05.1998
0001	144471	01.06.1998	30.05.1999
0001	144505	31.05.1999	28.05.2000
0001	144505	29.05.2000	27.04.2003
0001	144505	28.04.2003	25.05.2003
0001	144505	26.05.2003	28.05.2006

Figure 8.30 Example Template for the Migration of Cost Centers

Once the data has been entered in the last tab of the template, save these changes. Back in the migration cockpit, click on **Upload File**. Choose the file and enter a description. Click the **Upload** button. After the file is uploaded, the content can be reviewed by clicking on the file's name. Click the **Back** button to return to the migration object.

Now, select the line for the file that needs to be transferred and click the **Start Transfer** button. The guided procedure will follow these steps:

1. In the **Data Validation** step, the program will confirm that all required fields are populated and that all values are technically correct. Errors will need to be fixed in the file and the file uploaded again. Repeat the validation step until all errors are solved and click the **Next** button.

2. In the **Convert Values** step, the values from the file will need to be mapped to existing values in the central instance. For instance, the controlling area can be mapped

one-to-one, while country or language keys might need mapping from "USA" to "US" or from "E" to "EN." All errors must be corrected in the source file and the file reuploaded. Once all the errors are fixed, click the **Next** button.

3. In the **Simulate Import** step, the program will execute the import in test mode to evaluate inconsistencies between the upload file and the system. This process might take some time and can be run as a background job. No master data will be saved into the target system at that point.

4. If all the previous steps are successful, move to the **Execute Import** step. If successful, the data will be saved into the central system. If the import is not completely successful, entries without errors will be saved, and a delta file containing the entries that failed will be generated.

Best Practice for Customer and Vendor Numbers

For migration objects that rely on autogenerated number ranges (as opposed to external numbering), like customers or vendors, a downstream requirement is to map the ID from the source system with the ID in the central system. Rather than keeping this mapping in spreadsheets, we recommend using a custom field to store reference IDs.

In addition, customers and vendors could be using the head office/branch concept. For instance, let's say your organization orders from a local warehouse supplier but pays the invoice to the supplier's headquarters. This relationship requires a link between the master data of both the branch vendor ID and the head office vendor ID. If the IDs are autogenerated, the head office and branch IDs must be mapped back and uploaded subsequently. If the IDs don't match, the error **Relationship between branch/head office has changed** may occur during the initial load process.

The example shown in Table 8.1 shows how the head office ID (130100) is stored as a characteristic of the branch. Table 8.2 shows the potential error caused by transferring incorrect master data: The old reference number 130100 is kept instead of being replaced with a new reference number 130001, as shown in Table 8.3.

	Source System	
	Branch	Head Office
Head Office ID	130100	
Vendor ID	130200	130100

Table 8.1 Original Master Data

	Target System	
	Branch	Head Office
Vendor ID	130002	130001
Head Office ID	130100	
Legacy ID	130200	130100

Table 8.2 Potential Error

	Target System	
	Branch	Head Office
Vendor ID	130002	130001
Head Office ID	130001	
Legacy ID	130200	130100

Table 8.3 Expected Master Data

8.4.2   Transactional Data

Once the configuration for finance and controlling has been carried out, and after the required master data has been uploaded, the central system is ready to receive the transaction data. As mentioned earlier, the transaction will be reposted as opposed to simply copying data from table to table. However, errors might occur during the posting, and documents may have to be reprocessed. To facilitate this procedure, the Central Finance application relies on the SAP Application Integration Framework.

This configuration consists in the following steps: activation of the SAP Application Integration Framework, setup of SAP Application Integration Framework users, technical settings for business systems, and mapping actions for mapping entities.

Activation of the SAP Application Integration Framework

In the central instance, install the following BC sets:

- FINS_CFIN_AIF_GEN: Central Finance AIF configuration - General
- FINS_CFIN_AIF_CO: Central Finance AIF configuration - CO Objects and Documents

- `FINS_CFIN_AIF_DOC_POST`: Central Finance AIF configuration - Document Posting
- `FINS_CFIN_AIF_DOC_CHG`: Central Finance AIF configuration - Document Changes
- `FINS_CFIN_AIF_CMT`: Central Finance AIF configuration - Commitment Documents

Predelivered BC sets can be found in the SAP Menu by following the menu path **Tools •
Customizing • Business Configuration Sets • Activation of BC Sets** (Transaction
SCPR20). Simply input the BC set name and click the **Enter** button to confirm its availability. In the menu, choose **Activate BC Set** ⌷F7⌷. Select a customizing transport
request and click **Enter**. Repeat these steps for all BC sets.

Once these steps are done, open Transaction FINS_CFIN_AIF_SETUP (Central Finance:
AIF Integration Setup). Select **Complete Configuration** and click **Execute**.

Setup for SAP Application Integration Framework Users

SAP Application Integration Framework will generate and collect the transaction
errors during the initial load and replication jobs. Users should monitor and dispatch
these errors depending on their root cause: incomplete master data, missing configuration, missing mapping, etc. Such errors should hold authorizations copied from
the template SAP_AIF_USER, which will grant these users access to the Interface
Monitor (Transaction /AIF/IFMON).

At this point, if users try to access the Interface Monitor, they should receive the error
No Recipient Assigned. Further authorizations for specific scenarios must be assigned,
as shown in Figure 8.31. In the SAP Menu, under **Cross-Application Components • SAP
Application Interface Framework • Administration Configuration Recipients of a User**
(Transaction /AIF/RECIPIENTS), click on the **New Entries** button and then enter a new
line and enter the following values for the relevant fields:

- **Namespace** = "/FINCF"
- **Recipient** = "CFIN_RECIPIENT'"
- **Message Type** = Application Error or Technical Error

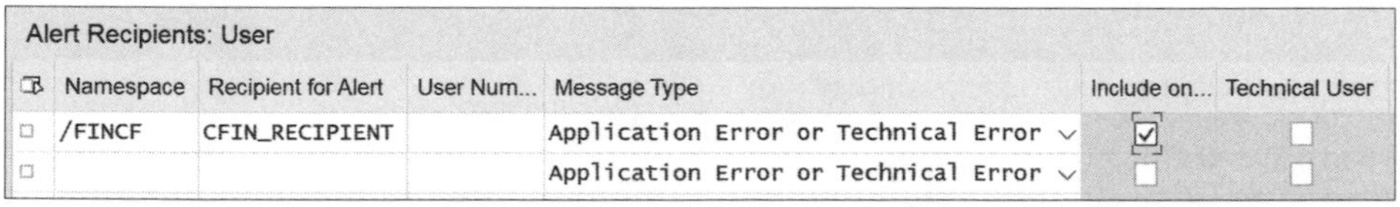

Alert Recipients: User						
	Namespace	Recipient for Alert	User Num...	Message Type	Include on...	Technical User
☐	/FINCF	CFIN_RECIPIENT		Application Error or Technical Error ∨	☑	☐
☐				Application Error or Technical Error ∨	☐	☐

Figure 8.31 Maintenance of Application Framework User (Transaction /AIF/RECIPIENTS)

Now, select the **Include on Overview Screen** checkbox. Click the **Save** button. The
selected user should now have access to the Interface Monitor.

Technical Settings for Business Systems

Master data is represented as business object types in the SAP MDG part of the Central Finance system. These object types must be mapped between your business systems. This step is usually performed in the System Landscape Directory (SLD) of SAP NetWeaver, but you can also use Central Finance Customizing (Transaction CFIN-IMG), under **Mapping • Define Technical Settings for Business Systems**. Create a **Business System** for the Central Finance system and one for each source system. Select the corresponding logical system and RFC destination. Enter a logical file path (e.g., "/AIF/LFA").

When done, select the line and double-click on the **Define Business Systems • BOs** folder in the menu on the left. For each business system and business object type, define the corresponding output mode. Typical business object types include:

- FIN_0001: Activity Type
- 154: Company
- 158: Cost Center
- 983: Cost Element
- 159: Customer
- 979: Purchasing Organization
- 892: General Ledger Account
- 194: Material
- FIN_0003: Tax Jurisdiction Code
- 464: Plant
- 229: Profit Center
- FIN_0002: Production Version
- 980: Sales Organization
- FIN_0004: Statistical Key Figure
- 266: Vendor

For the output mode, choose between:

- **Direct Output**
  Changes in the source system are directly transferred to the central system.

- **Pooled Output**
  Changes in the source system are collected and subsequently processed in batch. This is convenient for frequently changing materials.

- **Object-Dependent Default**
  Direct output for all objects except materials and pooled output for materials.
  Object-Dependent Default is recommended for Central Finance.

Finally, for each business system and business object type combination, double-click on the **Define Business Systems • BOs • Communication Channels**. Next, choose the mapping behavior for each communication channel. For instance, if using reliable sources, you could set **Replication via IDoc** or **Replication via RFC** as **Harmonized IDs (no Key Mapping)**. Data coming from less controlled systems should be set as **Key Mapping.**

Mapping Actions for Mapping Entities

Like the business object types in the SAP MDG engine, mapping entities must be set up and their behavior defined in Central Finance Customizing (Transaction CFIN-IMG), under **Mappings • Define Mapping Actions for Mapping Entities**. Create a line for each mapping entity, for example:

- BLART: Document Type
- ACTIVITY_TYPE_ID: Activity Type
- BUKRS: Company Code
- COST_CENTRE_ID: Cost Center
- COST_ELEMENT_ID: Cost Element
- CUSTOMER_ID: Customer
- EKORG_ID: Purchasing Organization
- GENERAL_LEDGER_ACC_MASTER_ID: General Ledger Account
- MATERIAL_ID: Material
- TXJCD: Tax Jurisdiction Code
- PLANT_ID: Plant
- PROFIT_CENTRE_ID: Profit Center
- PRODUCTION_VERSION_ID: Version
- SALES_FUNCTIONAL_UNIT_ID: Sales Organization
- STATISTICAL_KEY_FIGURE_ID: Statistical Key Figure
- SUPPLIER_ID: Vendor

For each mapping ID, create an entry for each business system and select a mapping action:

- **Keep Data**
  The value from the source system is taken as-is into the target system. No mapping is needed.

- **Mapping Obligatory**
  The sources values are mapped, and if no mapping is found, an error is raised.

- **Map if Possible**
  The source values are mapped, and if no mapping found, no error is raised, and the source value is transferred as-is to the target.

- **Clear Data**
  The source value is cleared before moving to the target.

8.4.3   SAP Source Data

SAP source data must be maintained, specifically because reference numbers can be either kept or new ones can be created. In both cases, a mapping will be necessary.

To create a mapping, the following tools are available: individual maintenance, mass maintenance, or additional transactions.

Key Mapping: Individual Maintenance

Individual objects may have different IDs between the source system(s) and the Central Finance system. The mapping between the source ID and the target ID is performed in Central Finance Customizing (Transaction CFINIMG), under **Mapping • Define Key Mapping (ID Mapping) • Create and Edit Key Mapping** (Transaction MDG_ KM_MAINTAIN). The web interface allows the selection of a business object type (e.g., cost center); a business system; and an object type/object ID. Enter the key values representing the target object ID and click the **Show** button. Click **Add Row** to enter the corresponding source IDs. Several source IDs can be mapped to a single target ID. This function is convenient during the pilot phase, when all master data may not be available and can be replaced with dummy objects. Click **Save** to save these changes.

As shown in Figure 8.32, some objects like cost centers are compound IDs that consist of the controlling area ID concatenated with the cost center ID. In the **Mapped Objects** tables, click on the **Object ID** to show the individual fields.

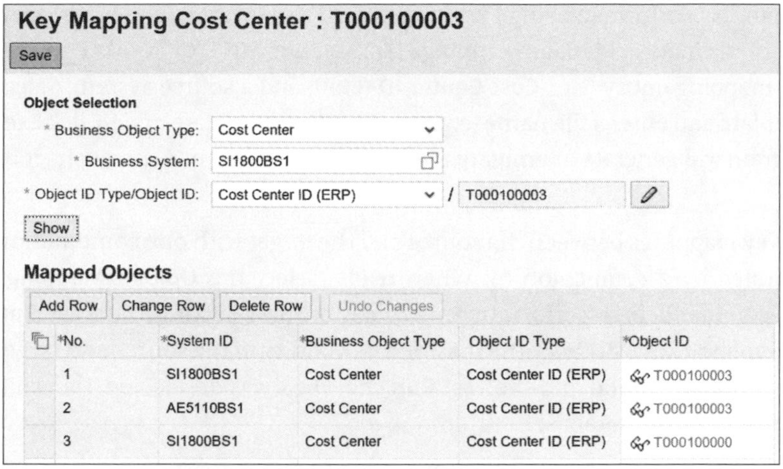

Key Mapping Cost Center : T000100003

Save

Object Selection

* Business Object Type: Cost Center
* Business System: SI1800BS1
* Object ID Type/Object ID: Cost Center ID (ERP)   /   T000100003

Show

Mapped Objects

Add Row | Change Row | Delete Row | Undo Changes

	*No.	*System ID	*Business Object Type	Object ID Type	*Object ID
	1	SI1800BS1	Cost Center	Cost Center ID (ERP)	T000100003
	2	AE5110BS1	Cost Center	Cost Center ID (ERP)	T000100003
	3	SI1800BS1	Cost Center	Cost Center ID (ERP)	T000100000

Figure 8.32 Example Key Mapping for Cost Centers

Key Mapping: Mass Maintenance

The web interface is fine for the individual maintenance of a few objects like controlling areas or company codes but is limited when many object keys must be mapped, like cost centers, customers, or vendors. Thus, a mass maintenance transaction, shown in Figure 8.33, is more appropriate.

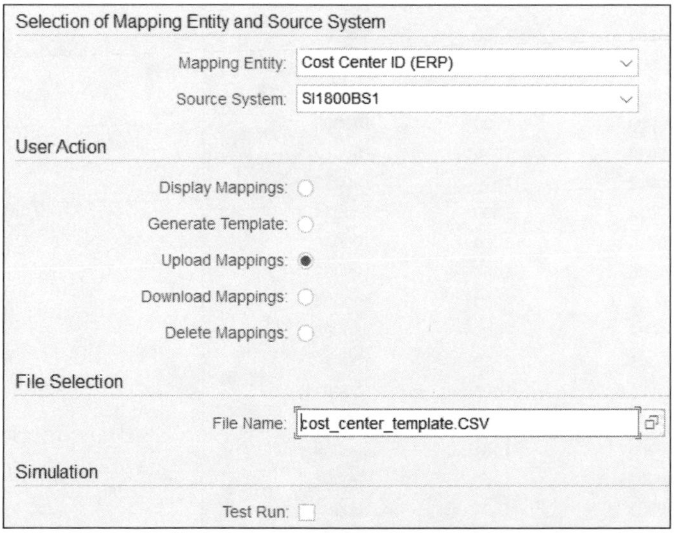

Selection of Mapping Entity and Source System

Mapping Entity: Cost Center ID (ERP)

Source System: SI1800BS1

User Action

Display Mappings: ○
Generate Template: ○
Upload Mappings: ●
Download Mappings: ○
Delete Mappings: ○

File Selection

File Name: cost_center_template.CSV

Simulation

Test Run: ☐

Figure 8.33 Managing Mappings (Transaction FINS_CFIN_MAP_MANAGE)

Mass maintenance is performed using Excel templates. To generate a template, open application Central Finance: Manage Mappings (Transaction FINS_CFIN_MAP_MAN-AGE). Select a mapping entity (e.g., **Cost Center ID (ERP)**) and a source system. Select **Generate Template** and enter a file name (e.g., "cost_center_template.csv"). Click **Execute**. The program will generate a template file that can be edited in a spreadsheet or text editor.

Maintain the key mappings between the source and the target with one combination per line, separated by a semi-colon (;). When ready, select the **Upload Mappings** option. We recommend first performing a simulation by selecting the **Test Run** checkbox. The application will check the master data validity in the source and target systems. If no errors are found and the **Test Run** checkbox was deselected, the valid entries will be saved to the database.

You can also display a list of all the mappings already saved for a given mapping entity, as shown in Figure 8.34. Simply select a mapping entity (e.g., **Cost Center ID (ERP)**) and a source system. Select **Display Mappings** and click **Execute**. The program will generate a list of all existing mappings between source objects and target objects.

Src Sys	Source: CO Area	Source: Cost Center	Target: CO Area	Target: Cost Center
SI1800BS1	T000	100000	T000	100003
SI1800BS1	T000	100001	T000	100001
SI1800BS1	T000	100002	T000	100001
SI1800BS1	T000	100003	T000	100003
SI1800BS1	T000	100005	T000	100005
SI1800BS1	T000	100006	T000	100006
SI1800BS1	T000	100007	T000	100007
SI1800BS1	T000	100009	T000	100009
SI1800BS1	T000	100010	T000	100012
SI1800BS1	T000	100012	T000	100013
SI1800BS1	T000	100013	T000	100014
SI1800BS1	T000	100016	T000	100016
SI1800BS1	T000	200000	T000	100002
SI1800BS1	T000	200001	T000	100004
SI1800BS1	T000	200002	T000	100008
SI1800BS1	T000	200003	T000	100010
SI1800BS1	T000	1000011	T000	1000011
SI1800BS1	T000	1000015	T000	100005
SI1800BS1	T001	100000	T001	100000
SI1800BS1	T001	100001	T001	100001
SI1800BS1	T001	100002	T001	100002
SI1800BS1	T001	400001	T001	400001

Figure 8.34 Displaying Mass Mappings

Key Mapping: Additional Transactions

Additionally, the SAP MDG program Search Key Mapping (Transaction MDG_ANA-LYSE_IDM) can be used to search and analyze key mappings. Enter a business object type (e.g., cost center) and click the **Start Search** button. The program will display a list of object IDs and the mappings that exist between a source business system and the central system, as shown in Figure 8.35.

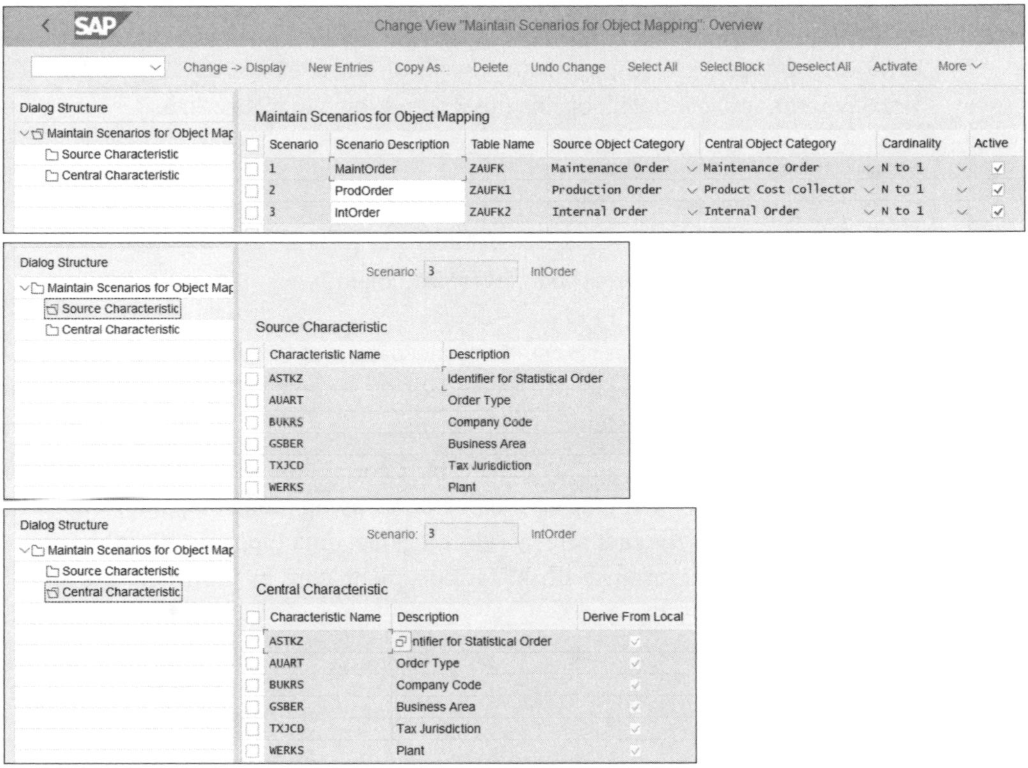

Figure 8.35 Searching Key Mappings with Transaction MDG_ANALYSE_IDM

8.4.4   Non-SAP Source Data

When migrating data from a non-SAP source system, some codes from Customizing might be quite different, like the controlling area of the accounting principle. These objects are called global data types (GDTs) and can be mapped to SAP entities, and their potential values can be included in the mapping. You can use this principle to extend data from SAP systems with custom fields and values.

First, check the available GDTs in Central Finance Customizing, under **Advanced Settings • Define Mapping Entities (Enhanced Configuration)**. On this screen, note the mapping entity, the type, and the corresponding global data type. For instance, BLART (Document Type) is defined as a data element from type BLART.

Then, still in Central Finance Customizing (Transaction CFINIMG), under **Mapping • Define Value Mapping (Code Mapping) • Assign Code Lists to Elements and Systems**. Click on **New Entries** and enter a type (e.g., "Data Element"); a global data type (e.g., "BLART"); and a business system (e.g., the source system). Give the list an ID (e.g., "BLART"); a list agency ID (e.g., the source system); and a list version ID (usually "01"). Click **Save**. The result should look like the screen shown in Figure 8.36.

Assign Code Lists to Elements and Systems						
Type	Global Data Type	Internal List ID	Business System	List ID	List Agency ID	List Version ID
Data Element ∨ BLART			SI1800BS1	BLART	SI1800BS1	01

Figure 8.36 Assigning an External Code List for Document Types

With this step, the system has reserved a namespace, also known as an external code list, for a list of values coming from a specific source system, to be mapped with value from the Central Finance system.

Now, values can be mapped at the field level in Central Finance Customizing (Transaction CFINIMG), under **Mapping • Define Value Mapping (Code Mapping) • Maintain Value Mapping**. From the first screen, select a global data type and click the **Display Mapping Relations**, for instance, **BLART** for **Document Type**, as shown in Figure 8.37.

Maintain Value Mapping Fields								
Object Type	Global Data Type	Name	Nav...	GDT Default	Client Dep	Context Structure	Input Help	Mapping Class
Data Eleme.. ∨	ABTNR				✓		CL_MDG_CODE_LIST_PROVIDER	
Data Eleme.. ∨	ACCOUNTING_PRINCIPLE				✓		CL_FINS_CFIN_CODELIST_ACC_PRPL	
Data Eleme.. ∨	ACTIVITY_PROFIL				✓		CL_MDG_CODE_LIST_PROVIDER	
Data Eleme.. ∨	AKVER				✓		CL_MDG_CODE_LIST_PROVIDER	
Data Eleme.. ∨	AM_UMWKZ				✓		CL_FINS_CFIN_CODELIST_PROV	
Data Eleme.. ∨	ASSIGN_TEST				✓		CL_MDG_CODE_LIST_PROVIDER	
Data Eleme.. ∨	AUFNR						CL_MDG_CODE_LIST_PROVIDER	
Data Eleme.. ∨	AUFSD_X				✓		CL_MDG_CODE_LIST_PROVIDER	
Data Eleme.. ∨	BLART				✓		CL_FINS_CFIN_CODELIST_BLART	

Figure 8.37 Maintaining Value Mappings for External Code Lists

If more than one code list has been created, they will appear on the next screen. Select the relevant code list and click on the **Define Value Mapping** folder. In the table, values can be mapped between internal code and external code, as shown in Figure 8.38. When the mapping is many-to-one or one-to-many, select the **Inbound Default** and

Outbound Default checkboxes to define which value should be used. When a code list is long, you can import a mapping from XML or CSV files with the **Connect to External Codelist** button. Save these changes before leaving the transaction.

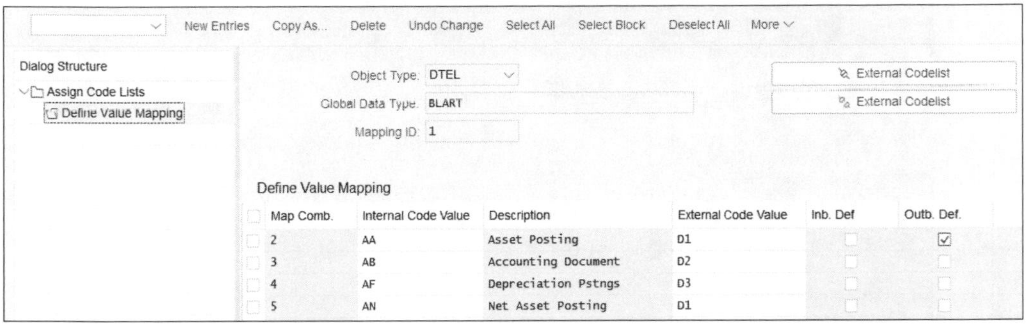

Figure 8.38 Mapping External Codes Values to Internal Code Values

8.4.5 Third-Party Interface

Once the staging tables are generated, the data can be extracted and mapped into the central system. Use the interface description file provided in Note 2481900 to perform the extraction and mapping of the source data into the staging tables. Make sure you load the item data *before* the header data, as changes to the headers triggers the data replication.

The third-party interface supports the reversal of financial documents as long as the fields for **Reference Transaction** (BKPF-AWTYP) and **Reference Key** (BKPF-AWKEY) are recognized. To facilitate this process, make sure that the **Document Number of an Accounting Document in Sender System** (BELNR_SENDER) field is filled in with the document number from the source system.

The reversal process comes in two variants:

- If only the document headers are transferred, the function module BAPI_ACC_DOCUMENT_REV_POST will be executed, and the original document will be reversed.
- If the document headers and items are transferred, the function module BAPI_ACC_DOCUMENT_POST will be executed, and an inverse posting will be created.

As mentioned earlier, document items must be loaded before their corresponding headers. Otherwise, you run the risk that only the headers are passed, and inverse postings are created instead of reversing documents. Table 8.4 and Table 8.5 show that, if the resulting balance is the same for reversal postings and negative postings, the totals are different. This difference could influence reporting or decision-making because some incorrect postings could be interpreted as cash flow.

	Account: Customer		Account: Bank	
	Debit	Credit	Debit	Credit
Incorrect Posting		$1,000	$1,000	
Reversal Posting	$1,000			$1,000
Correct Posting	$1,000			$1,000
Total	$2,000	$1,000	$1,000	$2,000
Balance	$1,000			$1,000

Table 8.4 Reversal Posting

	Account: Customer		Account: Bank	
	Debit	Credit	Debit	Credit
Incorrect Posting		$1,000	$1,000	
Negative Posting		$(1,000)	$(1,000)	
Correct Posting	$1,000			$1,000
Total	$1,000	$ -	$ -	$1,000
Balance	$1,000			$1,000

Table 8.5 Negative Posting

Load Strategy

In the discovery or pilot phase, the project team's goal should be to learn how the source systems, the SAP LT Replication Server, and the central system work together. Experience shows that jumping directly into the initial load can be overwhelming because millions of errors can be generated by simple missing configurations like number ranges. Our recommended strategy is to use an agile approach to optimize learning by gradually increasing the number of replicated documents. For instance:

1. Start with a single source system, a single company code, or empty initial load. Perform initial configuration with BC sets (fiscal year, fiscal period, number ranges,

etc.). Enable online replication. Map to dummy master data like cost centers, G/L accounts, customers, and vendors. Manually create documents in the source system to be replicated into Central Finance.

2. Expand the scope to increase to manually created master data. Validate system behavior against valid and invalid master data.

3. Start analysis based on reconciliation reports.

4. Start mass upload of master data for G/L accounts, cost centers, customers, and vendors.

5. If part of scope, activate reporting.

6. Expand to managerial accounting documents. Map all cost objects to a dummy internal order.

7. Expand internal orders to 1:1 and keep all other order types mapped to internal orders.

8. If part of scope, expand to more than one source system with a single company code and empty initial load.

9. If part of scope, expand to replication of non-SAP source system.

10. Expand to multiple company codes and validate intercompany postings.

11. If part of scope, expand to Profitability Analysis (CO-PA) mapping and postings.

12. If part of scope, expand to logistics. Perform corresponding configuration (e.g., plants) and upload material masters.

13. Configure and execute initial load (extract, simulate, then post).

14. Drop the Central Finance and reload, including initial balances.

15. If part of scope, configure and test central operations.

8.5   Replication Setup

Data replication is the heart of Central Finance and consists of two main parts: the initial load and online replication. You'll use the SAP LT Replication Server to set up data replication, and the procedure is slightly different depending on whether the source is an SAP system or not. Any user with authorizations based on template SAP_AIF_PROCESSING can use the SAP LT Replication Server for these tasks.

The configuration will differ based on the source system (SAP versus non-SAP), as well as depending on the phase (preliminary check, test load, initial load, and online replication).

8.5.1   SAP Source Systems

The setup of replication objects is facilitated by templates for table AUFK (Order Master Data), table CFIN_ACCHD (Finance Document Transfers), table COBK (CO Document Headers), and table CFIN_CMT_H (Commitment Document Transfers).

Start program IUUC_REPL_PREDEF_OBJECTS and select the mass transfer ID created earlier. Click on **Copy Predefined Objects** button. In the **Project** and **Subproject** fields, enter "REPL_CFIN." Under **Predefined Objects**, use the value help by pressing F4 to list all possible options. Depending on your progress in the project, select the relevant migration object. For instance, for table AUFK, you'll want the following objects:

- CFI_SIM_AUFK_L: Simulate Load
- CFI_AUFK_L: Load
- CFI_AUFK_R: Replicate

Under **Target Object**, enter the table name corresponding to the selected source object (e.g., "AUFK") and choose between **Load** and **Replication**. Click **Continue**, as shown in Figure 8.39.

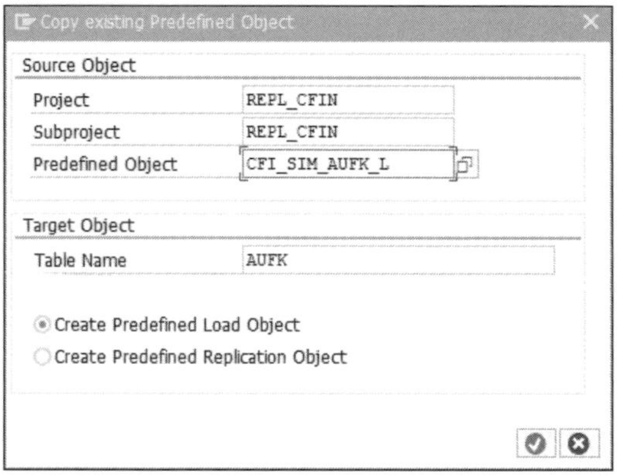

Figure 8.39 Creating a Load Object from a Template for an SAP Source

---

Simulation of CO Objects

During the discovery or pilot phase, we recommend using simulation replication objects CFIN_SIM_AUFK_L and CFIN_SIM_COBK_L instead of CFIN_AUFK_L and CFIN_COBK_L. The recommended simulation objects do not need a replication object, which is preferred at this stage.

More information can be found in Note 2154420.

Repeat the process for the other tables, for both the load objects (ending in "_L") and replication objects (ending in "_R"). Once the load and replication objects are configured, set their status to **Active,** as shown in Figure 8.40.

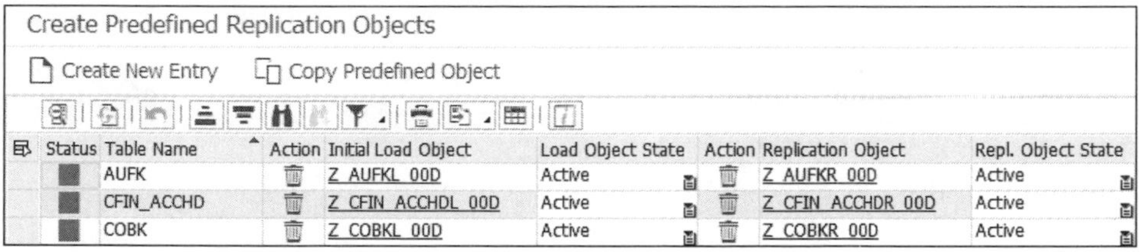

	Status	Table Name ▲	Action	Initial Load Object	Load Object State	Action	Replication Object	Repl. Object State
		AUFK	🗑	Z_AUFKL_00D	Active	📄 🗑	Z_AUFKR_00D	Active	📄
		CFIN_ACCHD	🗑	Z_CFIN_ACCHDL_00D	Active	📄 🗑	Z_CFIN_ACCHDR_00D	Active	📄
		COBK	🗑	Z_COBKL_00D	Active	📄 🗑	Z_COBKR_00D	Active	📄

Create Predefined Replication Objects

📄 Create New Entry   📋 Copy Predefined Object

Figure 8.40 Replication Objects Created and Active for an SAP Source

8.5.2 Non-SAP Source Systems

When using the third-party interface, the source tables are not AUFK, CFIN_ACCHD, or COBK, but instead, the staging tables /1LT/CF_E_ACCT, /1LT/CF_E_CREDIT, /1LT/CF_E_DEBIT, /1LT/CF_E_EXTENT, /1LT/CF_E_HEADER, /1LT/CF_E_PRDTAX, and /1LT/CF_E_WHTAX are used.

Start program IUUC_REPL_PREDEF_OBJECTS and select the mass transfer ID. Click the **Copy Predefined Object** button. Under **Source Object,** enter "REPL_CFIN" in the **Project** field and "REPL_CFIN_ST" in the **Subproject** field. Choose the **Predefined Object**: either **CFIST_ACDOC_L (Load)** or **CFIST_ACDOC_R (Replication)**. Under **Target Object,** enter "/1LT/CF_E_HEADER" in the **Table Name** field and choose between **Load** and **Replication.** Click **Continue,** as shown in Figure 8.41.

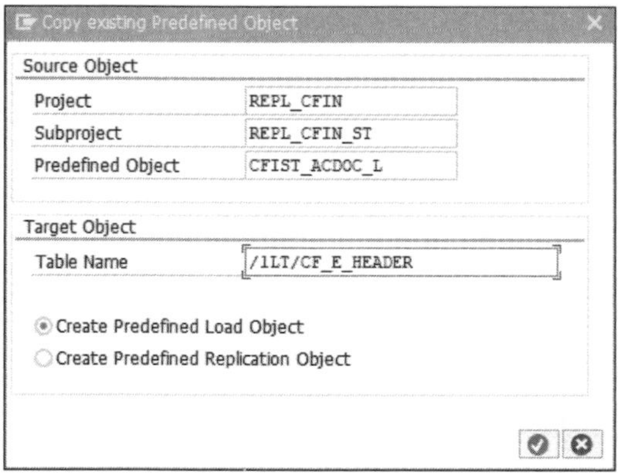

Source Object

Project	REPL_CFIN
Subproject	REPL_CFIN_ST
Predefined Object	CFIST_ACDOC_L

Target Object

Table Name	/1LT/CF_E_HEADER

◉ Create Predefined Load Object
○ Create Predefined Replication Object

Figure 8.41 Creating a Load Object from a Template for a Non-SAP Source

Once the load and replication objects are configured, set their status to **Active**, as shown in Figure 8.42.

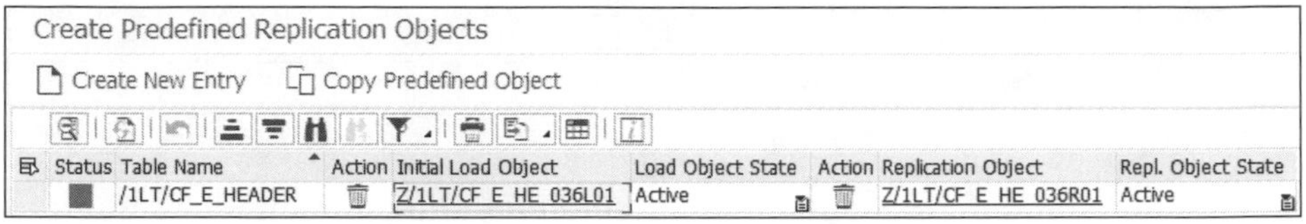

Figure 8.42 Replication Object Created and Active for a Non-SAP Source

Note that, for non-SAP source systems, only the header staging table needs to be set up as load and replication objects. The process will automatically read the other tables based on the header number, which is why line items must be loaded into the staging table *before* the header information.

8.5.3   Pre-Implementation Assessment

The initial load re-creates all selected financial and controlling documents. This process can be time-consuming. Before starting this process, we recommend evaluating the following decision criteria:

- Which company codes should be replicated? From which sources?
- Which fiscal year and fiscal periods should be included in the initial load as opposed to balances only?
- Should the CO objects be replicated? Which ones?

In addition, certain document types are not included in the initial load and online replication:

- G/L reconciliation postings
- Year-end closing postings with data elements AWTYP (Reference Transaction) and GLYEC (Year-End Closing Doc)
- Clearings and clearing resets, which can be enabled with Notes 2147776 and 2292043
- Recurring entries
- Sample documents
- Noted items

- Parked documents

- Balance carry-forward items

- Closing operations

Some of these decision criteria might be difficult to answer at the beginning of the project. Therefore, we highly recommend an initial discovery or pilot phase in which a minimal scope should be covered and gradually extended.

Once the replication objects have been configured, the initial load and replication still need to be triggered. Open the SAP LT Replication Server Cockpit (Transaction LTRC). Select the mass transfer ID.

To enable the replication or initial load, in the **Table Overview** tab, click the **Data Provisioning** button. Enter the table name (e.g., "AUFK"); select the replication step (e.g., **Start Load**); and click the **Execute** button, as shown in Figure 8.43.

SAP LT Replication Server - Cockpit: SANRNO (00D)

Refresh   Data Provisioning   [?]

| Administration Data | Processing Steps | Table Overview | Data Transfer Monitor | Application Logs | Load Statistics | Expert Functions |

No.Tables	Failed	In Process	Initial Load	Replication	LogTab	No LogTab	Trg. Active	No Trg. Act.
4				4	4		4	

View Errors   Actions

Table Name in Database	Logging Table	Failed	In Process	Current Action	Tab. Cat.	Pool/cluster	Log. Tab. Created	Trigger Status	Proxy Table	Tab. in Target Sys.	Syn. in Target Sys.
CFIN_ACCHD	/1CADMC/00000222			Replication	TRANSP		X	Activated	n/a	n/a	n/a
T001	/1CADMC/00000321			Replication	TRANSP		X	Activated	n/a	n/a	n/a
AUFK	/1CADMC/00000221			Replication	TRANSP		X	Activated	n/a	n/a	n/a
COBK	/1CADMC/00000261			Replication	TRANSP		X	Activated	n/a	n/a	n/a

Figure 8.43 Starting Initial Load and Replication with Data Provisioning

The same transaction can be used to monitor the data transfer (**Data Transfer Monitor** tab) or view the logs (**Application Logs** tab).

To easily monitor the data transfer, the SAP LT Replication Server can be connected to an SAP Solution Manager instance. More information on this topic can be found in SAP Notes 1558756 and 1558756.

8.5.4   Test Data Load

If the configuration has been done correctly, data should start flowing from the source system to the central system via the SAP LT Replication Server. You can monitor this process through the Interface Monitor (Transaction /AIF/IFMON) in the central instance, as shown in Figure 8.44.

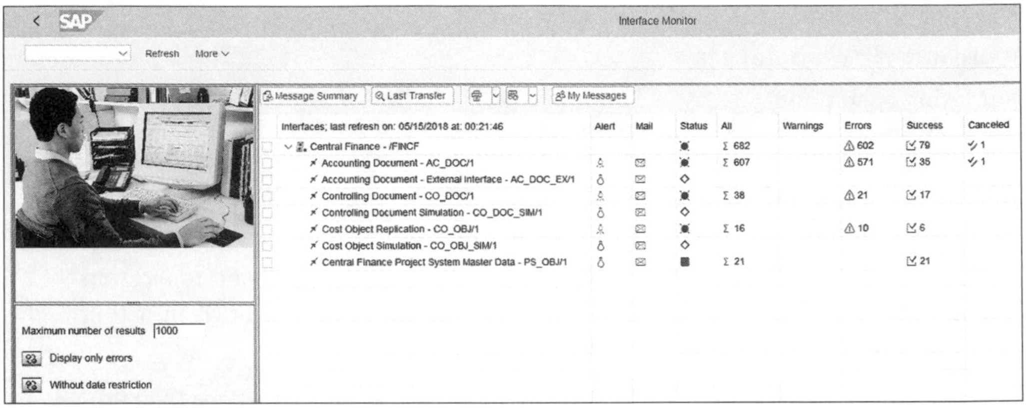

Figure 8.44 Analyze Data Replication with the Interface Monitor

The Interface Monitor serves as a dashboard with an overview the error handling process and supports advanced features.

Error Handling with the Interface Monitor

The Interface Monitor groups messages by steps (e.g., cost object simulation versus cost object replication) and message type. The steps are represented by interfaces and are linked to the source tables as shown in Table 8.6.

Interface Name	Source Table
AC_DOC, AC_DOC_CHG	CFIN_ACCHD
AC_DOC_EX	/1LT/CF_E_HEADER
CO_DOC, CO_DOC_SIM	COBK
CO_OBJ, CO_OBJ_SIM	AUFK

Table 8.6 Link between Interface and Source Table in the Interface Monitor

The goal of the Interface Monitor is to facilitate the analysis and dispatching of the errors. Select a line (e.g., cost object replication) and click the **Message Summary** button. The message summary will group the messages and indicate the number of occurrences, as shown in Figure 8.45.

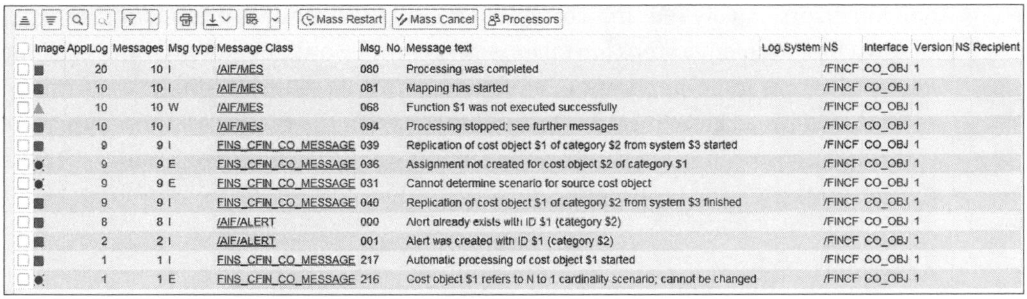

Image	AppiLog	Messages	Msg type	Message Class	Msg. No.	Message text	Log.System NS	Interface	Version NS Recipient
■	20	10 I	/AIF/MES	080	Processing was completed	/FINCF	CO_OBJ	1
■	10	10 I	/AIF/MES	081	Mapping has started	/FINCF	CO_OBJ	1
⚠	10	10 W	/AIF/MES	068	Function $1 was not executed successfully	/FINCF	CO_OBJ	1
■	10	10 I	/AIF/MES	094	Processing stopped; see further messages	/FINCF	CO_OBJ	1
■	9	9 I	FINS_CFIN_CO_MESSAGE	039	Replication of cost object $1 of category $2 from system $3 started	/FINCF	CO_OBJ	1
●	9	9 E	FINS_CFIN_CO_MESSAGE	036	Assignment not created for cost object $2 of category $1	/FINCF	CO_OBJ	1
●	9	9 E	FINS_CFIN_CO_MESSAGE	031	Cannot determine scenario for source cost object	/FINCF	CO_OBJ	1
■	9	9 I	FINS_CFIN_CO_MESSAGE	040	Replication of cost object $1 of category $2 from system $3 finished	/FINCF	CO_OBJ	1
■	8	8 I	/AIF/ALERT	000	Alert already exists with ID $1 (category $2)	/FINCF	CO_OBJ	1
■	2	2 I	/AIF/ALERT	001	Alert was created with ID $1 (category $2)	/FINCF	CO_OBJ	1
■	1	1 I	FINS_CFIN_CO_MESSAGE	217	Automatic processing of cost object $1 started	/FINCF	CO_OBJ	1
●	1	1 E	FINS_CFIN_CO_MESSAGE	216	Cost object $1 refers to N to 1 cardinality scenario; cannot be changed	/FINCF	CO_OBJ	1

Figure 8.45 Message Summary Groups and Error Counts

To assign a user to a particular message type, select the corresponding line and click the **Processors** button. On the next screen, choose **Assign User** from the **Assign Processors** dropdown list. Messages can also be assigned a status: **Assigned**, **Unassigned**, **Waiting for Input**, **OK to restart**, **OK to cancel**, **Confirmed/Solved**, or **Canceled**. These features prevent multiple users from wasting time focused on the same error.

Back in the message summary, you can click on the link in the message class. The program will list all documents that encountered the selected error (up to a limit; 10,000 by default). Double-click on a document in the top-left corner. The corresponding error messages will be listed in the top-right corner. The bottom-left corner lists all relevant tables. Double-click on each table to display corresponding values in the bottom-right corner, as shown in Figure 8.46.

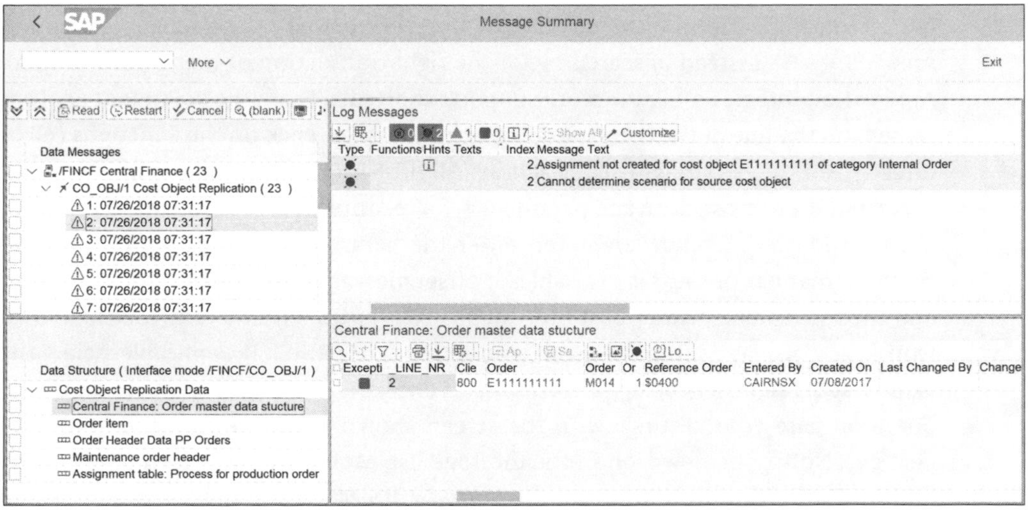

Figure 8.46 Analyzing Errors Related to Individual Documents

Solving errors usually requires correcting missing master data or updating configuration. Once corrective steps are taken, select the relevant document(s) and click the **Restart** button. In an application, all documents affected by a single error can be reprocessed by clicking the **Mass Restart** button from the message summary screen. If the error has been solved and the document doesn't need reprocessing, click the **Cancel** or **Mass Cancel** buttons.

Advanced Features

After several iterations of a data load, separating old error messages still being worked on from new error messages might be confusing. From the first screen of the Interface Monitor, click the **Without Date Restriction** button. Pick any date or date range from the displayed calendar.

Sharing knowledge is crucial in all Central Finance projects, which usually involve members from several teams, like business, master data, or IT. SAP Application Integration Framework supports the simple yet powerful documentation of error messages. From the document analysis screen, on the line with an error message, click on the **Hints** cell or call this popup directly from Transaction /AIF/CUST_HINTS. In the popup, enter the relevant document and choose a tooltip. We recommend adopting a common schema for all hints, for instance, symptom/root cause/resolution. Once the changes are saved, notice the new icon in the **Hints** column. Mouse over the icon to display the tooltip. Click on the icon to access the long text.

As the project progresses, some functions might become repetitive. For instance, new materials could be missing or may have not been extended to a new plant (error message M3 – 305). Instead of searching for the right transaction or menu path, the SAP Application Integration Framework supports shortcuts. From the document analysis screen, on the line of the corresponding error message, click on the **Functions** cell or directly call the popup with Transaction /AIF/CUST_FUNC. In the popup, enter the corresponding transaction and parameters, for example, Transaction MM03 (Display Material Master). Under **Parameter,** enter the parameter ID (e.g., "MAT"); the fill method (manual, or message variable, or offset message variable, or value mapping); and the filled value. Under **Custom Function Attributes,** enter a text/tooltip and an icon (e.g., "Display Material Master" and ICON_MATERIAL). If applicable, select the **Skip First Screen** checkbox. We recommend checking the **Start New Session** checkbox. Compare your settings with the screen shown in Figure 8.47 and save your changes. Notice the new icon in the message list. Mouse over the icon to check the tooltip. Click on the icon to open a new window directly to the right transaction with relevant information prefilled, like the material master with a material ID.

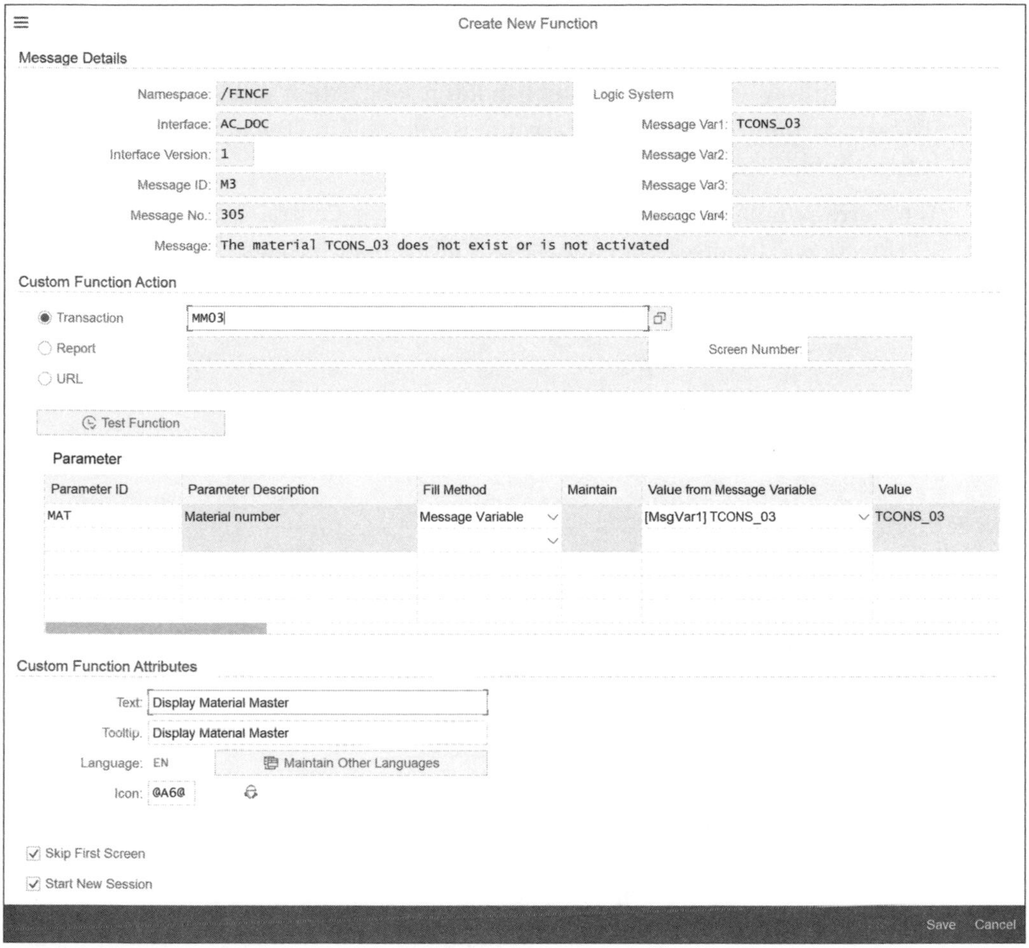

Figure 8.47 Creating a Custom Function to Create Material Master Data

> **Note**
>
> For more information on the SAP Application Interface Framework 3.0, go to the SAP Help Portal at *http://help.sap.com/aif*.

8.5.5   Initial Data Load

During the initial load, the Central Finance system creates financial postings. When the balances are handled, the program needs an offset account for each company code. At the end of the initial load process, the migration clearing account should balance back to zero.

In a similar way, when the program handles reconciliation accounts and open-item manager accounts, a substitution account is needed. After the initial load, the substitution should balance back to zero.

The corresponding configuration is performed in Central Finance Customizing (Transaction CFINIMG), under **Initial Load • Initial Load Settings • Define Clearing and Substitution Accounts**, as shown in Figure 8.48.

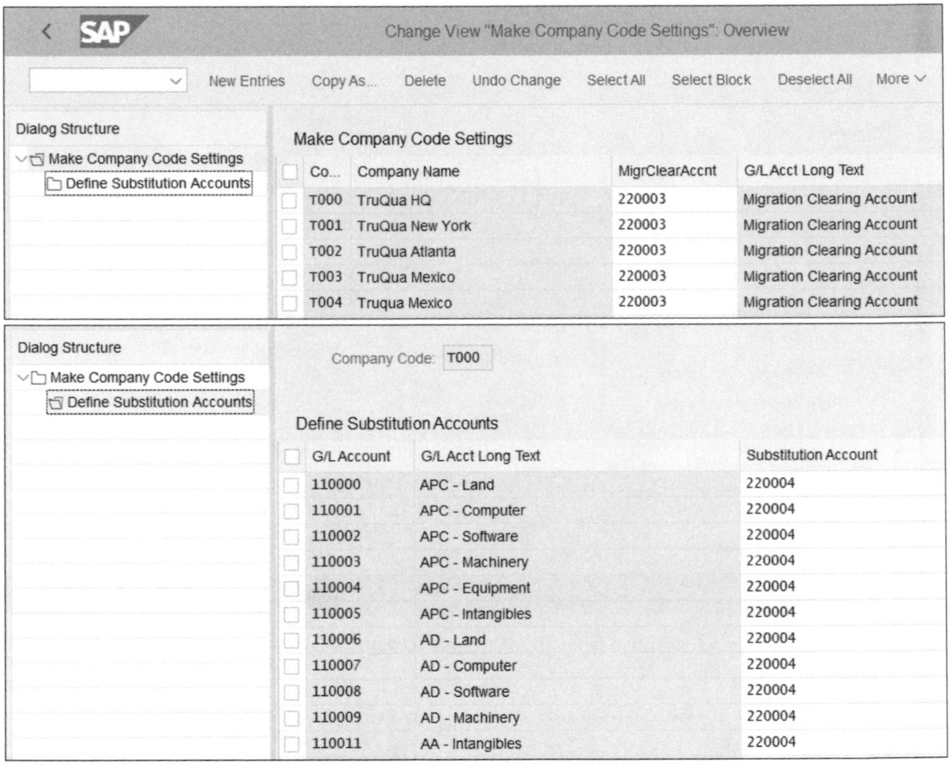

Figure 8.48 Define Clearing and Substitution Accounts

8.5.6   Online Replication

Depending on the project strategy, you may be able skip the initial load and move directly to online replication, an excellent way to monitor small numbers of documents being replicated from the source to the target.

To enable online replication, in the source system, use Transaction SM30 to maintain view VCFIN_SOURCE_SET. For the relevant company codes, enter a future year in the **Start – Balances** columns. With this setting, the selection of balances to load will not return any data.

8.6   Process Design

The Central Finance platform can be used for many scenarios, ranging from decision support, to data integration, all the way to shared services for finance and logistics, as shown earlier in Figure 8.1 and Figure 8.2. Moving from a reporting and integration hub to central processing requires specific design and configuration considerations. In particular, the notion of a *system of record* needs to be revisited.

The definition of a system of record is quite vague. Bill Inmon, known as the father of data warehousing, defines it as "the place where there is a definitive value for some unit of data." More interestingly, Sandy Kemsley, BPM architect and industry analyst, declares: "When data is replicated between systems, the notion of the [system of record], or 'golden copy', of the data is often lost, the most common problem being when the replicated data is updated and never synchronized back to the original source." A Central Finance system qualifies for internal and external audits as it supports the traceability of transactions, the creation of audit trails, and the segregation of duties. When the central system is only used for reporting, the system(s) of record can be either the source system(s) or the central system. The central system will be easier to audit than multiple source systems. However, as soon as processes, such as central payments or company closings, are executed in the central system, that system becomes the *de facto* system of record. This shift may or may not have an impact on your organization.

Beyond designating systems of record, process design can be separated between the process settings (functional) and the configuration (technical).

8.6.1   Process Settings

This section defines the basic settings required for data management, three-way matching, payables, receivables, taxes, and period close.

Data Management Process

Master data management for Central Finance will be described in more detail in the next chapter. However, during the design phase, the master data management process must be defined, leading to the potential selection of a master data management solution.

Most discovery or pilot phases start with manual maintenance and the synchronization of master data objects like customers, vendors, and G/L accounts. Once the project is extended to larger volumes, the manual process becomes cumbersome. Several options for managing large data volumes are possible, including:

- Manual processing
- IDocs
- Magnitude SourceConnect accelerator
- SAP Master Data Governance (SAP MDG)

Which solution you select will depend on the availability your landscape, license costs, compatibility with your source system, and reusability in other projects, as shown in Figure 8.49.

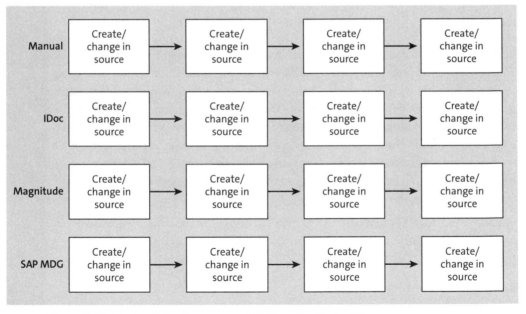

Figure 8.49 Master Data Management Options for Central Finance

Three-Way Matching Process

Three-way matching is a process involving documents from purchase orders, goods receipts, and invoice receipts. The goal is to avoid incorrect payments or even fraudulent requests for payment. These documents are matched based on ordered quantities, received quantities, invoiced quantities, price per unit, taxes, and total amounts.

The process covers both direct procurement (materials involved in the manufacturing, such as raw materials or packaging) and indirect procurements (goods and services supporting the organization, such as hardware, software, utilities, or services), as shown in Figure 8.50.

In the context of Central Finance, multiple options are available, based on where the process takes place (i.e., decentralized in local systems or centrally by shared services). The systems involved are:

- Source system material master
- Central Finance material master
- SAP Ariba connected to the local systems and/or the central system
- Manual invoicing in Central Finance
- OpenText Vendor Invoice Management for SAP Solutions (VIM)

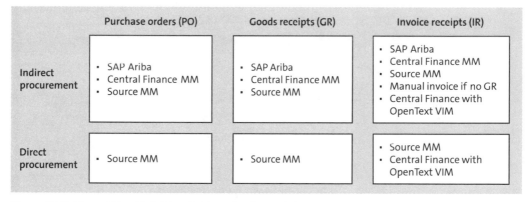

Figure 8.50 Three-Way Matching Options for Central Finance

Payables Process

The payables process can be handled locally or centrally. When handled locally, the accounting documents are replicated from the local system into the central system, while payment and bank reconciliation occur in the local system.

If the payables process is handled centrally, typically by a shared service center, the system of record becomes the central system. Purchase orders, goods receipts, and invoice receipts can be performed in the local system, the SAP Ariba system, or the central system. If the process is started locally, documents are automatically cleared during the replication process to avoid payments from the local system. Information from the central system does not need to be retracted from the local system because the system of record is now the central system. Follow-up steps—payment, bank reconciliation, and reporting—are performed in the central system. Additional applications like payments on behalf of others (POBO), real-time cash management, or machine learning for cash applications can be installed on top of the central system. The local and central processes are shown in Figure 8.51 and Figure 8.52, respectively.

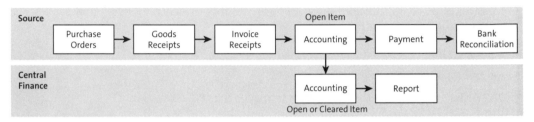

Figure 8.51 Payables Process with Central Finance and Local Payment

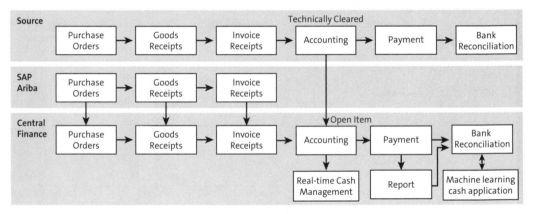

Figure 8.52 Payables Process with Central Finance and Central Payments

Receivables Process

Like the payables process, the receivables process can be performed locally or centrally. When performed locally, the process stays unchanged until reporting is executed in the central system. When performed centrally, local systems can benefit from a central credit management option, which prevents customers that are bad creditors in one region/local system from getting goods or services from another region/local system. Similar to payables, local documents become technically completed after replication to the central system. Again, information from the central system does not need to be retracted from the local system because the central system is now the system of record. In addition, features like central disputes, collections on behalf of others (COBO), real-time cash management, or machine learning for cash applications can be enabled in the central system, as shown in Figure 8.53 and Figure 8.54.

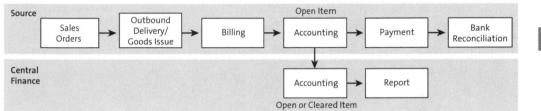

Figure 8.53 Receivables Process with Central Finance and Local Payment

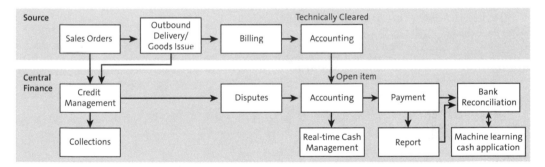

Figure 8.54 Receivables Process with Central Finance and Central Payments

Tax Process

At the time of this writing, the topic of tax on sales and purchases, also called *input tax* and *output tax*, as opposed to corporate tax, is still on the roadmap but has not yet been released. You can choose between using SAP solutions for tax calculation or connecting to third-party applications like Vertex. Note that Vertex is being certified for SAP S/4HANA 1709 but not yet for Central Finance.

In principle, the tax amounts and breakdowns should be calculated in local systems and the results passed to the central system. However, as soon as receivables or payables processes are activated in the central system, not only should the taxes be calculated centrally, but the history of taxes invoiced and collected is also necessary to support disputes, returns, or partial and full payments.

If performed centrally, additional configuration and master data like tax codes, tax jurisdictions, or tax rates need to be synchronized between the local systems and the central system to ensure that all systems output the same tax amounts.

Closing Process

Depending on which system is the system of record, some closing steps can be handled in the local system or moved to the central system, as shown in Figure 8.55.

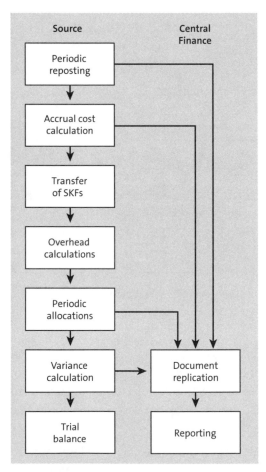

Figure 8.55 Period-End Closing Process with Local Processing

8.6.2   Configuration

Once the functional part of the process design has been completed, the technical configuration can be implemented.

Central Tax Reporting

Before activating central tax reporting, please refer to SAP Note 2509047: Central Finance: Required SAP Notes to support Tax Reporting out of the Central Finance System.

Also, enhanced tax checks must be active far enough ahead of activating central payments to be able to collect relevant tax information.

In addition, Central Finance does not currently support the concept of official document numbering. Therefore, tax reporting for countries where official document numbering is a legal requirement is not supported.

Finally, central tax reporting only applies to the fiscal periods where documents and line items are replicated, as opposed to only balances and open items. For these periods, the tax reporting must be carried out in the source system(s).

When central payments is active, tax reporting also must be performed on the central system, which is the only system that contains tax information from all source systems, as well as from the central system itself.

In Central Finance Customizing (Transaction CFINIMG), under **Central Payment •
Activate Central Payment for Company Codes**, click on **New Entries**. For each combination of **Logical system** and **Source Company Code**, select a **Central Company Code** and choose **VAT Configuration Check Active** in the **Scope** column. Save these changes. The result should look like the screen shown in Figure 8.56.

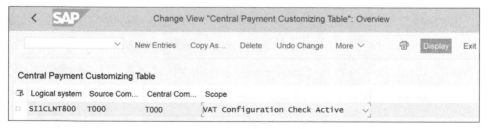

Figure 8.56 Activation of VAT Configuration Check for Central Tax Reporting

Now, the central system will perform additional checks each time a tax-relevant posting is posted from a relevant source system/company code. The errors are collected in SAP Application Integration Framework.

You'll also need to enhance the SAP LT Replication Server with a new set of load (`CFI_<table_name>_L`) and replication (`CFI_<table_name>_R`) objects. Table 8.7 shows tables you'll need to replicate from the source system to the central system.

Table in Source System	Table in Central System
T000F (Cross-Client FI Config.)	FINS_CFIN_T000F
T001 (Company Code)	FINS_CFIN_T001
T005 (Country Code)	FINS_CFIN_T005
T007A (Tax Code)	FINS_CFIN_T007A
T007B (Tax Processing Key)	FINS_CFIN_T007B
TTXD (Tax Jurisdiction Code)	FINS_CFIN_TTXD

Table 8.7 Tables Relevant for Central Tax Reporting and Replicated from Source System into the Central System

For a complete list of tables and checks, refer to SAP Note 2494127: SAP LT Replication Server for Central Finance - VAT Configuration Check for Company Codes.

The reports in Table 8.8 are currently supported (elements with * have restrictions).

Technical Name	Description
RFUMSV00 (*)	Advance Return for Tax on Sales/Purchases
RFUVDE00 (*)	Print Program: Advance Return for Tax on Sales/Purchases (Germany)
RFUMSV10 (*)	Additional List for Advance Return for Tax on Sales/Purchases
RFID_PTVPRADPRC00 (*)	Pro-Rata Adjustments Due to PR Calculation
RFID_PTVPRADPRV00 (*)	Pro-Rata Adjustments due to PR Variation
RFUMSRVG00 (*)	VAT Refund
RFUMSV35 (*)	Tax Adjustment
RFASLM00 (*)	EC Sales List
RFASLD20 (*)	EC Sales List in Data Medium Exchange Format

Table 8.8 List of Standard Tax Reports Supported in Central Tax Reporting

Technical Name	Description
SAP Fiori App	Tax Reconciliation Account Balance
SAP Fiori App	Tax Declaration Reconciliation

Table 8.8 List of Standard Tax Reports Supported in Central Tax Reporting (Cont.)

Refer to the Central Finance documentation for an updated of list supported and non-supported tax operations and corresponding restrictions.

Central Payments

Before trying to activate central payments, please refer to SAP Note 2346233: Central Payment for Central Finance: Pilot Note for Activation of Central Payment. Then, create an SAP Support message under component FI-CF-APR to request product activation.

The activation of central payments is done by company code and is only compatible with SAP source systems. The following steps assume that the preliminary configuration has been carried out in Central Finance Customizing (Transaction CFINIMG), under **Set Up Systems • Define Logical System for Source and Central Finance Systems**. Select **All Mappings**.

Now, open the ABAP Editor (Transaction SE38) in the central system and execute program FINS_CFIN_APAR_CPAY_SWITCH.

Then, open Central Finance Customizing (Transaction CFINIMG), under **Central Payment • Activate Central Payment for Company Codes**, or directly open central payment Customizing (Transaction CFIN_CPAY_CUST). Click on **New Entries** and enter the relevant combination of **Logical System**, **Source Company Code**, and **Central Company Code**. Select the **Scope** as **Central Payment with VAT Configuration Check Active**. Repeat the process for each combination of logical system and source company code. Before saving, compare with the screen shown in Figure 8.57 and make sure your entries are correct because they cannot be changed later.

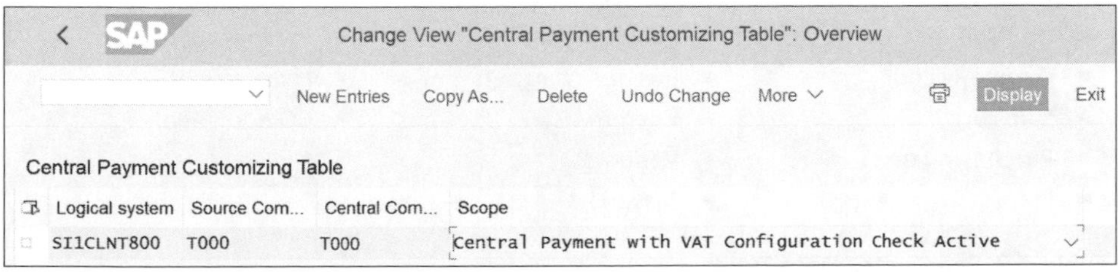

Figure 8.57 Customizing for Central Payments

This customizing is saved in the central system and sent to the relevant source system(s). Check that the customizing is in sync by calling central payment Customizing (Transaction CFIN_CPAY_CUST) in the source system. Click the **Reconcile** button to display a comparison of the customizing in the source and central systems, and master data governance if applicable. If any entry is highlighted in red, select the entry and click the **Sync** button. Save these changes.

From this point, invoices posted in the source system from the configured company codes will be automatically replicated to the central system and marked as **Technically Completed.** These invoices will not be considered for payment or clearing. The corresponding invoices posted in the central system will be marked as **Open.** You'll need to process payments and clearings in the central system.

Invoices for company codes not configured for central payments will still be replicated to the central system but not set to **Technically Completed.** You'll need to process payments and clearings in the source system for these invoices.

8.7   Master Data

By its nature, the Central Finance platform needs lots of master data. In addition, master data objects could be coming from multiple source systems, SAP and non-SAP.

Different strategies should be evaluated to handle the master data objects, their harmonization, and their hierarchies.

8.7.1   Master Data Objects

The priority is to segregate data between configuration data, static data, and dynamic data.

Configuration Data	Static Data	Dynamic Data
■ Operating concern ■ Controlling area ■ Company codes ■ Sales org. ■ Purchasing org. ■ Plants	■ Cost centers ■ Activity types ■ Business partners ■ Customers ■ Vendors ■ Materials	■ Internal orders ■ Purchasing orders ■ FI document ■ CO document

Table 8.9 Segregated Data Types

We'll look at each type of data in the following sections.

Configuration Data

The configuration data is set up once and is not expected to change much during the year. In the case of Central Finance, the configuration data is usually related to the organization's structure: operating concern, controlling area, company code, sales organization, purchasing organization, plant, cost center, activity type, etc. Not only should you consider individual data objects, but also their assignments, like company code to controlling area.

For these data points, the following questions should be answered:

- Should all data be transferred to Central Finance?
- Does semantic data (the same physical plant in two systems) overlap with technical data (the same plant number in two systems), or vice versa?
- Should the original data IDs be kept or re-created with new IDs?
- If conflicts exist, should one configuration take precedence, or should configurations be merged?
- What are the mapping implications?
- What's the best way to transfer the configuration (direct BC sets, modified BC sets, manual configuration)?

Static Data

Static data is master data that changes slowly, such as cost centers, activity types, business partners, customers, vendors, materials, etc. Static data is expected to change during a single period. Most of this data have validity dates to track changes or characteristics.

In a Central Finance project, the following topics must be resolved:

- Which static data objects should be considered in scope? Not in scope?
- For each object type, do all objects need to be represented in Central Finance?
- How much master data history is required?
- When objects are shared across systems, should one object take precedence, or should they be merged?
- Does semantic data (the same physical cost center in two systems) overlap with technical data (the same cost center number in two systems), or vice versa?

- What are the mapping implications?
- What's the best way to transfer the static data (migration cockpit, Landscape Transformation Migration Cockpit, manual creation, third-party software)?
- What is the governance related to creation, update, deletion, and broadcasting of static data?
- Is a master data management or governance solution required?

Dynamic Data

Unlike configuration or static data, dynamic data has a short lifecycle and includes most orders and documents, for example, internal orders, purchasing orders, FI documents, CO documents, etc.

In this context, the following points must be addressed:

- Which dynamic data objects should be included in the scope? Excluded?
- For each object type, do all objects need to be represented in Central Finance? Should some object types be merged? For example, can production orders be represented as internal orders to avoid having logistics master data in Central Finance?
- How much data history is required?
- When objects are shared across systems, should one object take precedence, or should they be merged?
- Do number ranges overlap? Should new number ranges be used?
- What are the mapping implications?
- What's the best way to transfer the dynamic data (standard SAP LT Replication Server or third-party interface)?

8.7.2   Harmonization (Golden Record Creation)

Master data is significant enough in Central Finance projects form its own workstream. The level of effort ranges from small (a single SAP ERP system, one-to-one mapping) to very large (multiple ERPs from different vendors, inherited through mergers and acquisitions, no master data governance).

Several solutions exist to facilitate the load, merge, and purge process, for example, SAP MDG, SAP Data Services, or third-party software.

If your source system is an SAP ERP system, you should consider using a special strategy, customer/vendor integration (CVI), which can be performed in the source system, independently of the Central Finance project. Since CVI is a prerequisite for an SAP S/4HANA migration, you can execute a CVI project earlier than planned to simplify mapping and reconciliation.

Real-Life Example of Integration

In this example, a Central Finance project involved connecting a single source system but required customer/vendor integration into business partners. As a B2B organization, the company's business partners were mostly vendors, rather than customers, with little to no overlap. A strategy was adopted that loaded vendors first and customers second. If customers overlapped with vendors, new master data was created.

Real-Life Example of New IDs

A consumer packaged goods (CPG) company was merging two systems—one international, one domestic—into Central Finance. After analysis, only a few customers and vendors overlapped, so this data was merged and migrated to Central Finance with new IDs. A master data governance solution is being considered to support ongoing data maintenance.

8.7.3 Hierarchies

Master data can require a lot of effort and cause a lot of pain, but hierarchies can be even more important than individual master data objects, because most reports start with data aggregated by a hierarchy, for example, cost center groups, profit center groups, customer hierarchies, vendor hierarchies, etc. Further, hierarchies can change over time.

A particular discussion point in Central Finance design revolves around how much data will be saved to the database (also known as a *stamping strategy*) as opposed to being left to hierarchies and reports (also known as an *atomic strategy*).

Let's look at an example. Suppose our organization has defined the following initial customer hierarchy:

- **0 – Global**
  - 10 – North America
    - 10010 BestCustomer US
    - 10020 BestCustomer Canada
    - 10030 BestCustomer Mexico
  - 20 – South America
    - 10040 BestCustomer Brazil
    - 10050 BestCustomer Colombia
    - 10060 BestCustomer Argentina

Over time, the organization needs to be reorganized as follows:

- **0 – Global**
  - 10 – North America
    - 10010 BestCustomer US
    - 10020 BestCustomer Canada
    - 10030 BestCustomer Mexico
  - 20 – South America
    - 10040 BestCustomer Brazil
    - 10060 BestCustomer Argentina
  - 30 – Central America
    - 10050 BestCustomer Colombia
    - 10070 BestCustomer Costa Rica

Table 8.10 shows how financial data could be saved in table ACDOCA. Note the additional customer hierarchy attributes Hry-L1 and Hry-L2, which are saved in the table ACDOCA to facilitate reporting, as seen in Table 8.10.

Period	Hry-L1	Hry-L2	Customer	Amount	Curr.
01	0	10	10010	14,964,372.00	USD
01	0	10	10020	1,613,464.42	USD
01	0	10	10030	1,051,128.60	USD
01	0	20	10040	2,208,871.65	USD

Table 8.10 Data in Table ACDOCA

Period	Hry-L1	Hry-L2	Customer	Amount	Curr.
01	0	20	10050	287,018.18	USD
01	0	20	10060	423,627.42	USD
02	0	10	10010	18,624,475.00	USD
02	0	10	10020	1,535,767.74	USD
02	0	10	10030	1,046,922.70	USD
02	0	20	10040	1,796,186.59	USD
02	0	20	10050	282,462.55	USD
02	0	30	10060	545,476.10	USD
02	0	30	10070	57,435.51	USD

Table 8.10 Data in Table ACDOCA (Cont.)

As shown in Figure 8.58, a report is created out of table ACDOCA.

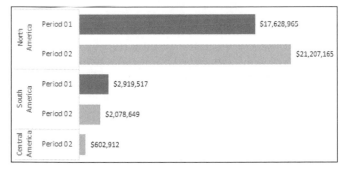

Figure 8.58 Report with Hierarchy as of Period 02

However, notice how the report shows how the South America group lost close to a million dollars. Seeing this loss, the manager of South America might ask to see Q2 values displayed with a Q1 hierarchy to show the true evolution, as shown in Figure 8.59. This comparison shows that the South America group in reality lost less than $300k. The rest was due to the reorganization moving BestCustomer Colombia from South America to Central America.

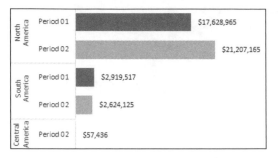

Figure 8.59 Report with Hierarchy as of Period 01

As shown in this example, Central Finance projects should start by considering reporting needs to define the information model requirements. Consequently, the best strategy to combine the two views, which we'll discuss in Section 8.8, consists in combining the stamping of data. This can be done through the Universal Journal coding block or CO-PA characteristics, and allows for standard reporting in the SAP GUI or SAP Fiori. It relies on atomic data from the Universal Journal together with time-based hierarchies, to support flexible reporting, planning, and simulation.

8.8   Business Mapping

While master data mapping might be a familiar concept, business mapping is a concept specific to SAP. In this ERP system, transactions are represented as objects, like orders, that collect multiple types of information like master data and key figures. If the source system is an SAP system, Central Finance offers the option of replicating these business objects.

Let's go over the available master data objects and strategies for their replication.

8.8.1   Master Data Objects

The Central Finance system replicates documents from the source system. In finance and controlling, the main objects are:

- **Production orders**
  Collect actual and plan costs related to a material, plant, date, and quantity. Necessary bills of materials (BOMs) and routings are copied to the production order to determine the list and quantities of raw and semifinished materials, as well as activities.

- **Product cost collectors**
  Collect actual costs related to the manufacturing of a material, especially in order-related production, process manufacturing, or repetitive manufacturing.

- **Internal orders**
  Collect actual and plan costs related to an internal job or task, usually representing assets or overheads. At the end of its life, an internal order is settled at month end to assets, projects, or cost/profit centers.

- **Maintenance orders**
  Collect actual and plan costs related to the upkeep of an asset. At month-end, the maintenance order is settled to a cost center or G/L account.

- **Quality management orders**
  Collect actual and plan costs related to quality management (i.e., operations on materials or inspection lots). These costs are settled at the end of the period to a cost/profit center, internal order, profitability segment, or asset.

- **Process orders**
  Collect actual and plan costs related to the manufacturing of a product or the execution of a service with specific quantity and date. Processes consist of operations and use materials and/or resources. At period end, process orders can be settled to a G/L account.

A special type of cost object is a CO-PA segment. This unique combination of characteristics is used to analyze results with more granularity. This object can also be used as a receiver of settlement or in overhead allocations like top-down distributions.

8.8.2   Strategies

Depending on the scope of the Central Finance environment, the central system may or may not hold the master data necessary for replicating these master data objects. For instance, production orders require master data for plant, materials, BOMs, routings, work centers, etc. If a quality management order is settled to a profitability segment, it should be configured in CO-PA.

Cost Object Mapping Scenarios

To avoid having to replicate all master data, Central Finance supports two cost object mapping strategies:

- **Order type mapping**
  An order type that requires material master data can be converted into an internal order, which only requires cost center master data.

- **Many-to-one mapping**
  All orders of the same type can be mapped to a dummy object. For instance, all internal orders can be mapped to a dummy cost center.

The scenario mapping is performed in Central Finance Customizing (Transaction CFINIMG), under **Mapping • Cost Object Mapping • Define Cost Object Mapping • Define Scenarios for Cost Object Mapping**.

The templates in Table 8.11 can be used to facilitate the maintenance.

Scenario Template	Cost Object in Source System	Cost Object in Central System	Cardinality
SAP001	Production Order	Product Cost Collector	N:1
SAP002	Product Cost Collector	Product Cost Collector	1:1
SAP003	Internal Order	Internal Order	1:1
SAP004	Service Order (PM Order)	Service Order (PM Order)	N:1
SAP005	QM Order	QM Order	N:1

Table 8.11 Scenario Templates Available for Cost Object Mapping

In the maintenance transaction, click on **New Entries.** Enter a scenario, scenario description, table name, source object category, target object category, and cardinality. Make sure the scenario is set to **Active**.

Select the scenario and click on the **Source Characteristics** folder. Click on **New Entries** and choose from the predefined list. Repeat the process with the **Target Characteristics.** Select the **Derive from Local** checkbox if you want to use predefined mappings instead of a fixed value.

Save the scenario. The program will generate the required mapping tables. Note that each scenario can only have one source cost object category, but several scenarios can have the same source cost object category, as shown, for example, in Figure 8.60.

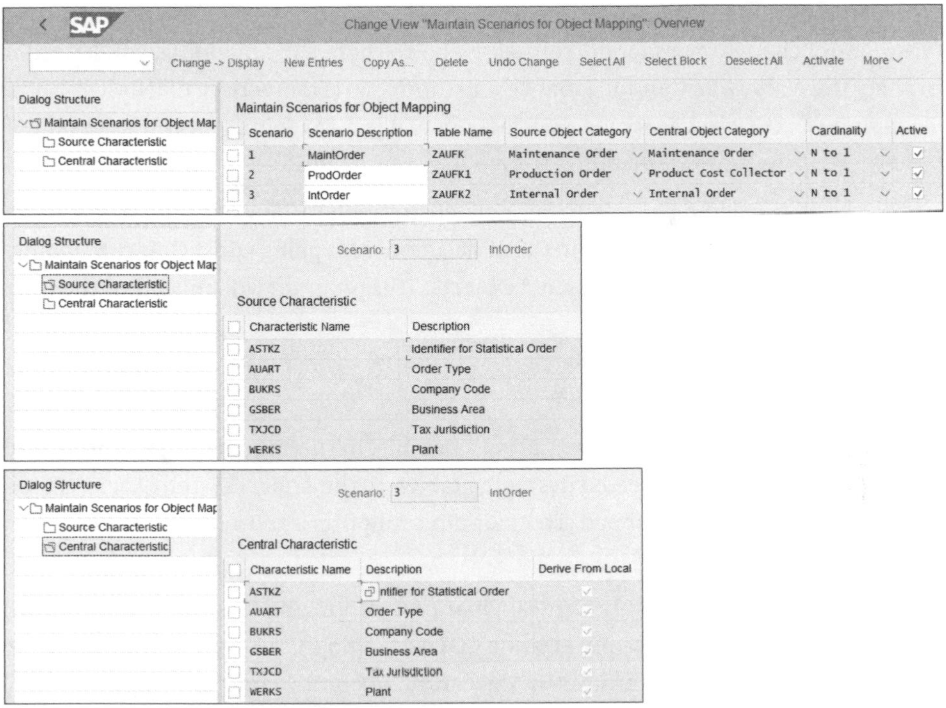

Figure 8.60 Maintain Cost Object Category Mapping

Cost Object Mapping Rules

Once the cost object category scenarios are defined, the mappings can be maintained in the generated tables. This definition is performed in Central Finance Customizing (Transaction CFINIMG), under **Mapping • Cost Object Mapping • Define Mapping Rules for Cost Object Mapping Scenarios**. Select a scenario and click **Execute.** As shown in Figure 8.61, enter mapping rules for the source characteristic values and the target characteristic values that are not **Derived from Local.** Save these changes.

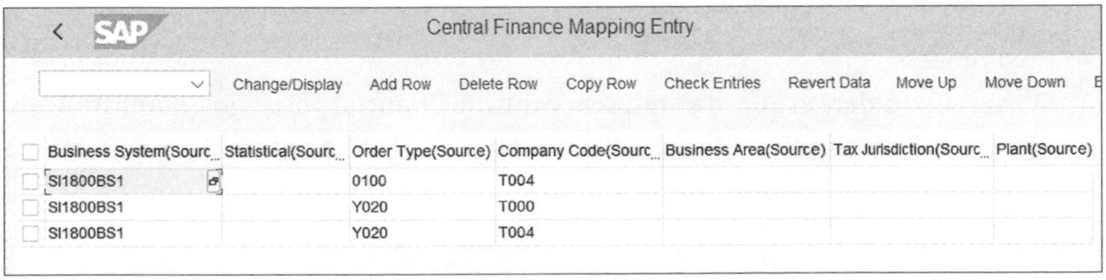

Figure 8.61 Maintain Mapping Rules for Cost Object Category Scenarios

The mapping will be used during the initial load and online replication processes, but you cannot change the mapping retroactively. To change the mapping, you'll need to remap the values in Central Finance Customizing (Transaction CFINIMG), under **Mapping • Cost Object Mapping • Correct Cost Object Mapping**. This program allows you to perform a mass remapping from old to new values.

Similarly, if a mapping needs to be deleted to apply a new strategy, use Central Finance Customizing (Transaction CFINIMG), under **Mapping • Cost Object Mapping • Delete Cost Object Mapping and Cost Objects**. This program will only allow the mass deletion of cost objects.

CO-PA Mapping

The replication of CO-PA segments is very flexible. In the source system, the characteristics and values are collected in staging tables. In the central system, these characteristics and values are mapped. The mapping supports one-to-one or many-to-one combinations.

Configuration is performed in Central Finance Customizing (Transaction CFINIMG), under **Mapping • COPA Mapping • Define COPA Mapping**. Click **New Entries** and enter the central **Operating Concern.** Select the central operating concern and double-click on the **Operating Concern in Source System** folder. Select the local operating concern and double-click the **Characteristics Mapping.** Map the local characteristics to the central characteristics. Repeat the process with the **Value Fields Mapping.** If the operating concern configuration changes in the source or central systems, use the **Sync Structure** button. Save these changes. Once all cost objects are mapped, the system should be ready for the initial load.

8.9   Initial Data Load

The initial data load is handled three different types of objects:

- **Cost objects**
  Objects like orders are used as reference during financial postings. Therefore, these objects must be replicated in the Central Finance system before the replication of financial postings. The replication of cost objects is performed from the SAP LT Replication Server, instead of Central Finance.

- **Financial (FI) postings**
  The initial load of financial postings replicates historic documents from the source system. The configuration is performed in the source system for SAP sources. The initial load only occurs if all master data is present in the central system. Online replication can only start after the initial load, even if the initial load was empty.

- **Controlling (CO) postings**
  This portion of the initial load replicates the postings that are only relevant to CO and not to FI, for instance, for overhead cost allocations. Like cost objects, customizing is performed in the SAP LT Replication Server.

In the following sections, we'll cover the steps required configuring the initial load: prerequisites, source system, CO postings, FI postings, and final steps.

8.9.1   Prerequisites

Before you begin, you should reduce the activity in the source system as much as possible to minimize conflicts. Some actions could be:

- Executing all scheduled jobs and not scheduling new jobs
- Performing closing for periodic asset postings (program RAPERB2000)
- Executing the periodic depreciation posting run (program RAPOST2000)
- Checking for and correcting any update terminations
- Locking all periods, apart from the current period, in FI and CO (plan or actual)

We also recommend that you run a number of consistency checks, as follows:

- Running the consistency check process (report RFINDEX) with, as a minimum, the following checks:
  - Documents against indexes
  - Documents against transaction figures
  - Indexes against transaction figures
- Running the consistency check process (report RFINDEX) for all fiscal years in the system. Restrict the selection to the relevant company codes.
- If you're using the new G/L account, execute reconciliation for the GL and the subledgers by either running the report TFC_COMPARE_VZ or opening Transaction FAGLF03.

- If you're using the new G/L account, compare the ledgers by either running the report RGUCOMP4 or opening Transaction GCAC. Restrict the selection to the relevant company codes.

- Reconciling Materials Management (MM) with the G/L by running the report RM07MBST/RM07MMFI. Restrict the selection to the relevant company codes.

Finally, you should perform business reconciliation, as follows:

- Carry forward balances again for all currencies and all ledgers to ensure that all balance carry-forwards are complete and consistent. For account payables and account receivables, run report SAPF010. For G/L accounts, open Transaction FAGLGVTR.

- Create the closing documentation. Restrict the selection to the relevant company codes. We recommend running the following reports:
  - Financial Statements (program RFBILA00)
  - Totals for Cost Centers (Transaction S_ALR_87013611)
  - The G/L Account Balance List (report RFSSLD00)
  - The Compact Document Journal (report RFBELJ00)

8.9.2   Configuration in Source System

To customize financial postings in an SAP source system, open Transaction SM30 for view VCFIN_SOURCE_SET, as shown in Figure 8.62, and click the **Maintain** button. For every relevant company code, maintain the following fields:

- **Start – Balances**
  The starting fiscal year for the balances to be included in the initial load.

- **Start – Documents**
  The starting fiscal year for the accounting documents to be included in the initial load.

- **Period – Documents**
  The starting fiscal period for the accounting documents to be included in the initial load.

- **Periods**
  The number of financial periods to keep and not delete. Report RFIN_CFIN_CLEANUP uses this field to clean data in the transfer tables.

- **GL Reconciliation**

  Select this checkbox if G/L reconciliation postings from CO should also be replicated during the initial load. If CO replication is active, *do not select this checkbox* because documents would be posted twice.

- **Initial Load Finished**

  Select this checkbox if the initial load has been completed.

- **Package Size**

  The number of documents to be included in each transfer package during the initial load.

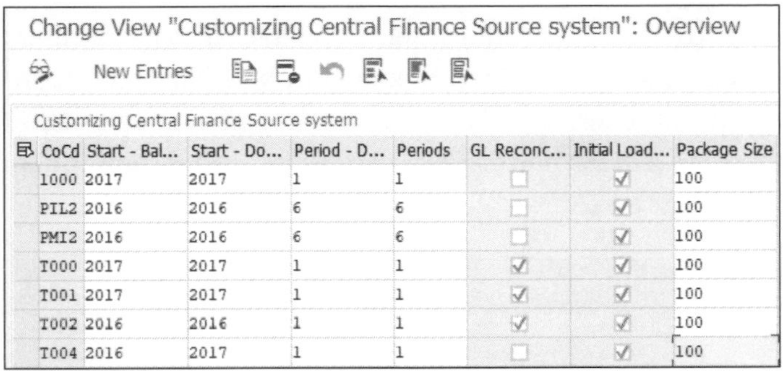

Change View "Customizing Central Finance Source system": Overview

⚙   New Entries   📄 📑 ↰ 📰 📰 📰

Customizing Central Finance Source system

CoCd	Start - Bal...	Start - Do...	Period - D...	Periods	GL Reconc...	Initial Load...	Package Size
1000	2017	2017	1	1	☐	☑	100
PIL2	2016	2016	6	6	☐	☑	100
PMI2	2016	2016	6	6	☐	☑	100
T000	2017	2017	1	1	☑	☑	100
T001	2017	2017	1	1	☑	☑	100
T002	2016	2016	1	1	☑	☑	100
T004	2016	2017	1	1	☐	☑	100

Figure 8.62 Initial Load Settings in Source System

Corresponding customizing must be configured in the central system. Under Central Finance Customizing (Transaction CFINIMG), open **Initial Load • Initial Load Settings • Choose Logical System**. For each source system, enter the package size, which corresponds to the number of documents per data load package.

8.9.3   Initial Load of CO Postings

As we've mentioned earlier, CO master data and postings must occur before FI postings. At this point, the CO master data should have been replicated via the SAP LT Replication Server. Now, let's carry over CO postings from the source systems into the Central Finance staging tables.

First, check that the following prerequisites have been met:

- An SAP Application Integration Framework runtime configuration group has been assigned to the replication object.

- An RFC destination for the source system has been set up.

- The logical system for the source and Central Finance systems has been defined.
- An RFC destination to the logical system for the source system has been assigned.
- The logical system assignment for the Central Finance client has been checked.
- Initial **Load Settings • Choose Logical System** has been checked.
- Initial **Load Settings • Make Configuration Settings** in the source system has been checked.
- The initial load of the CO postings has not been performed yet.

Once these prerequisites have been met, go to Central Finance Customizing (Transaction CFINIMG), under **Initial Load • Initial Load for Management Accounting • Prepare for and Monitor the Initial Load of CO Postings**. Select the logical system, enter a **Number of Background Jobs**, and click the **Execute Run** button. A call to the source system will be triggered that will generate background jobs for each company code to load the necessary data. Use the **Refresh** button until all company codes show the **Finished** (F) status, as shown in Figure 8.63.

CO Area	Company Code	Run Mode	Run Mode Description	Status	Status Description	Progress	No. of Aborted Jobs
T001	T004	F	First Run	F	Finished	100.00%	
T000	T002	D	Delta Run	F	Finished	100.00%	
T000	T002	F	First Run	F	Finished	100.00%	
6000	PMI2, PIL2	D	Delta Run	F	Finished	100.00%	
6000	PMI2, PIL2	F	First Run	F	Finished	100.00%	
1000	1000	D	Delta Run	F	Finished	100.00%	
T000	T001, T000	D	Delta Run	F	Finished	100.00%	
1000	1000	F	First Run	F	Finished	100.00%	
T000	T001, T000	F	First Run	F	Finished	100.00%	

Figure 8.63 Preparing the Initial Load of CO Secondary Postings

In case of failure, the status will be set to **Aborted** (A). Check tables for table CFIN_MIG_LOG_CO (Log of Migration Status for CO) and table CFIN_JOB_LOG_CO (Detail Job Log for CO) in the source system to identify the cause. When errors are resolved, restart the transaction by clicking the **Restart** button.

Once the data has been staged, the system is ready to replicate the CO postings. We recommend starting with a simulation to identify and fix mapping errors more quickly than during a full replication. Make sure that the SAP LT Replication Server is configured with initial load object CFI_SIM_AUFK_L instead of object CFI_AUFK_L. You don't need to provide a replication object yet (see SAP Note 2154420 for more details).

Since the CO object replication is handled by SAP LT Replication Server, the process should be monitored with the Interface Monitor (Transaction /AIF/IFMON) under interface Cost Object Simulation (CO_OBJ_SIM). The error handling is similar to what we described earlier in Section 8.4.

When errors messages are identified in the Interface Monitor and once the necessary corrections have been taken, you don't always have to run the whole package again. Simply perform a smoke test in Central Finance Customizing (Transaction CFINIMG), under **Initial Load • Initial Load Preparation for Management Accounting • Smoke Test for Cost Object Mapping and CO Document Replication**, as shown in Figure 8.64.

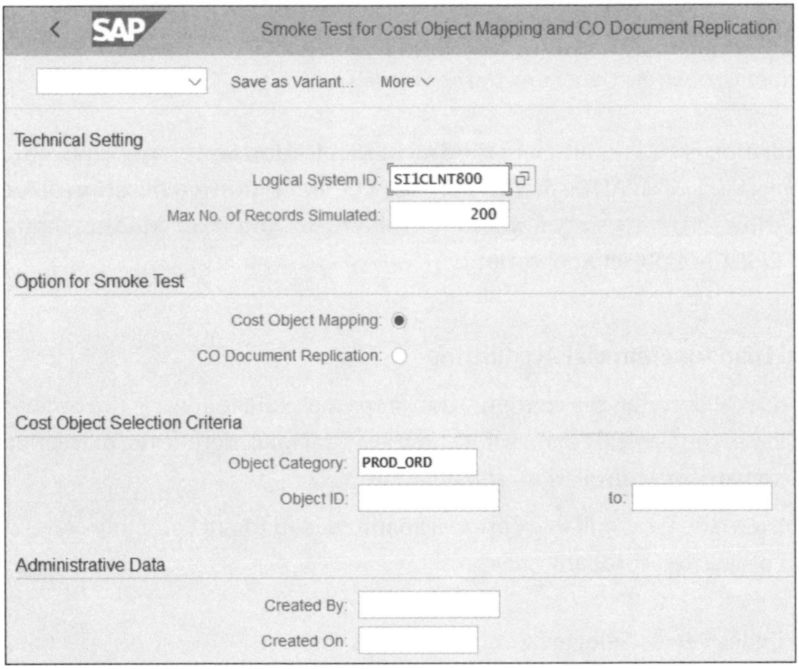

Figure 8.64 Performing a Smoke Test for Cost Object Mapping and CO Document Replication

On this screen, enter the **Logical System ID** and the **Max Number of Records Simulated.** Choose between **Cost Object Mapping** or **Document Replication**. If you choose **Cost Object Mapping,** select an **Object Category** (e.g., PROD_ORD) and an **Object ID** if applicable. Click **Execute.** In the document list, select an individual document and click **Simulate.**

Now, the application will perform a simulation of the replication for the selected document and present the same results as the Interface Monitor would produce, as shown in Figure 8.65. However, these messages won't be saved in the Interface Monitor. This process can be repeated until all errors are resolved. Then, the package can be reprocessed in the Interface Monitor.

Type Order		Message Text	LTxt
■	60003285	Replication of cost object 000060003285 of category Production Order from system SI1CLNT800 started	
●	60003285	Assignment not created for cost object 000060003285 of category Production Order	⑦
●	60003285	Simulation stage 1; scenario determination is finished with errors	
●	60003285	Cannot determine scenario for source cost object	⑦
■	60003285	Replication of cost object 000060003285 of category Production Order from system SI1CLNT800 finished	
■	60003285	Simulation of cost object 000060003285 finished	

Figure 8.65 Example of Errors Generated by the Smoke Test

After the simulation is successful, go to the SAP LT Replication Server and replace the initial load object CFI_SIM_AUFK_L with CFI_AUFK_L and set up a replication object CFI_AUFK_R. Now, error messages will be visible in the Interface Monitor under interface CO_OBJ (Cost Object Replication).

8.9.4 Initial Load for Financial Accounting

In this section, we'll describe the configuration steps in detail, following the order of their availability in the Central Finance IMG for the initial load: definition, extraction, monitoring, comparison, completion, and deletion.

First, let's look into the two available options: an initial load for all company codes or an initial load of selected company codes only.

All Company Codes versus Selected Company Codes

In Central Finance Customizing (Transaction CFINIMG), under **Initial Load • Initial Load Execution for Financial Accounting**, two options will be available: **Initial Load Execution for All Company Codes** and **Initial Load Execution for Selected Company Codes**. These two options perform the exact same series of steps, but grouped slightly differently. You cannot combine the two methods.

We recommend starting the discovery or pilot phase with an initial load of selected company codes, as this approach involves the selection, extraction, mapping, and posting of fewer documents based on their company codes. This strategy yields faster results in the execute/error analysis/resolution cycles. Still, in the realize phase or full project phase, we recommend choosing an initial load of all company codes, as this option supports extraction, mapping, and posting of cross-company documents.

For the remainder of this chapter, we'll describe the selected company codes approach.

Defining Initial Load Groups

You'll define initial load groups in Central Finance Customizing (Transaction CFIN-IMG), under **Initial Load • Initial Load Execution for Financial Accounting • Initial Load Execution for Selected Company Codes • Define Initial Load Groups**. As shown in Figure 8.66, click on **New Entries.** Enter a group ID and group description. Then, select a group ID and double-click on the **Assign Company Codes** folder. Next, click on **New Entries** and enter a combination of **Logical System** and **Source Company Code.** Save these changes.

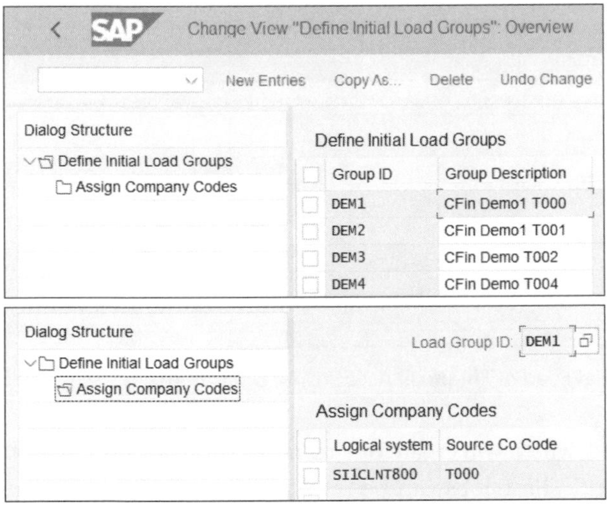

Figure 8.66 Defining Initial Load Groups

Any combination of logical system/source company code can be used in an initial load group. For instance, North American company codes from two different source systems can be grouped together to facilitate the validation of supplier and customer master data. However, any specific combination of logical system/source company code can only be used in a single initial load group.

In general, we recommend maintaining small initial load groups as much as possible, ideally a single combination of logical system/source company, to reduce processing time by running initial load groups in parallel.

Extracting Data for Initial Load

In this step, the FI documents staged in the source system will be transferred into the Central Finance staging tables in the central system.

You'll extract data for the initial load in Central Finance Customizing (Transaction CFINIMG), under **Initial Load • Initial Load of Initial Load Execution for Financial Accounting • Initial Load Execution for Selected Company Codes • Extract Data for Initial Load**. Enter a **Number of Batch Jobs** and select the **Company Code Specific Run** checkbox if applicable. Click **Execute.** The result is shown in Figure 8.67.

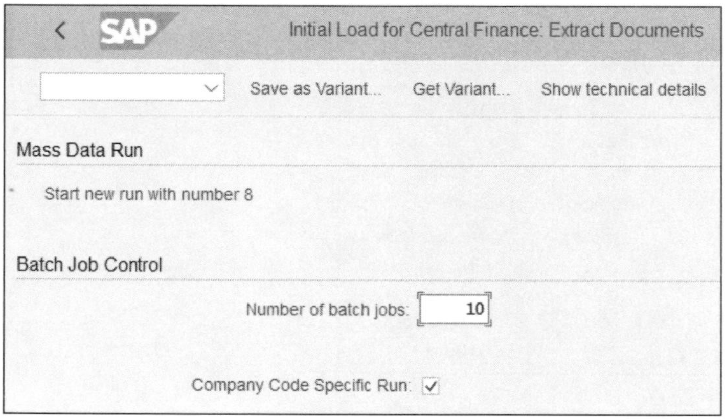

Figure 8.67 Extract Data for Initial Load of Financial Accounting Documents

A new **Run ID** will be generated, which will create one or more background jobs with names starting with "FINS_CJ1." These jobs can be monitored in the Job Overview (Transaction SM37) or in the next customizing step.

Note that the initial load group is not used at this point. Thus, all the FI data in the source systems, across all source systems and company codes, should have been configured and loaded into staging tables *before* this step is taken.

Monitoring the Data Extraction

You can monitor the data extraction process in Central Finance Customizing. In Transaction CFINIMG, follow the menu path **Initial Load • Initial Load of Initial Load Execution for Financial Accounting • Initial Load Execution for Selected Company Codes • Monitor Data Extraction**. All the runs executed previously will be listed. Use the **Refresh** button until the run receives status **Finished**, as shown in Figure 8.68.

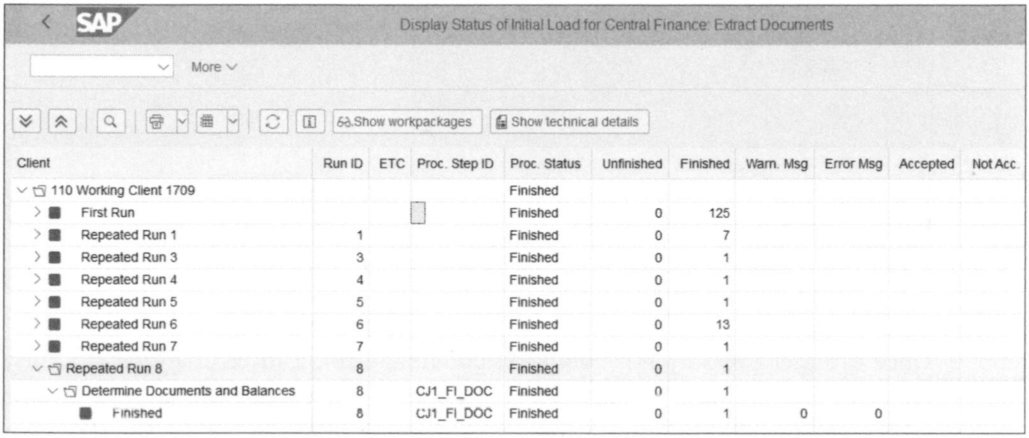

Client	Run ID	ETC	Proc. Step ID	Proc. Status	Unfinished	Finished	Warn. Msg	Error Msg	Accepted	Not Acc.
∨ ⊡ 110 Working Client 1709				Finished						
> ■ First Run				Finished	0	125				
> ■ Repeated Run 1	1			Finished	0	7				
> ■ Repeated Run 3	3			Finished	0	1				
> ■ Repeated Run 4	4			Finished	0	1				
> ■ Repeated Run 5	5			Finished	0	1				
> ■ Repeated Run 6	6			Finished	0	13				
> ■ Repeated Run 7	7			Finished	0	1				
∨ ⊡ Repeated Run 8	8			Finished	0	1				
∨ ⊡ Determine Documents and Balances	8		CJ1_FI_DOC	Finished	0	1				
■ Finished	8		CJ1_FI_DOC	Finished	0	1	0	0		

Figure 8.68 Monitor Data Extraction for Financial Documents

If errors occur, double-click on the number in the **Error Msg** column to analyze the messages (see **Monitor Initial Load Execution** for an example).

Executing the Initial Load for Initial Load Group

Once staged, the data can be mapped and posted in Central Finance Customizing (Transaction CFINIMG), under **Initial Load • Initial Load of Initial Load Execution for Financial Accounting • Initial Load Execution for Selected Company Codes • Execute Initial Load for Initial Load Group**, as shown in Figure 8.69.

First, select **Start Mapping Simulation** as the **Mass Data Run**. Enter a **Number of Batch Jobs** and an **Initial Load Group**. Click **Execute.** The program will generate batch jobs with a name starting with FINS_<load_group_number>, which you can monitor in the Job Overview (Transaction SM37) or in the next customizing step.

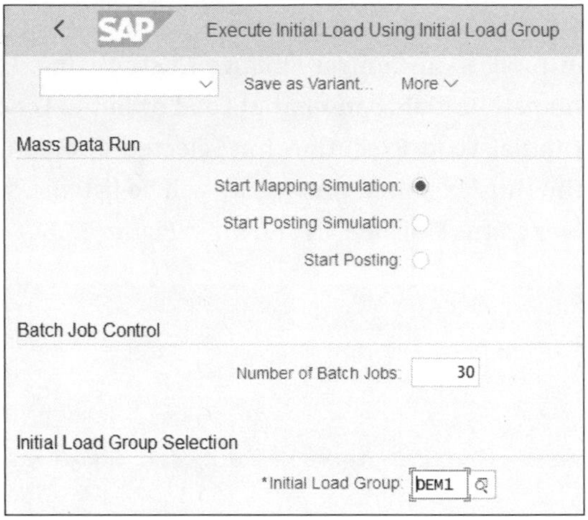

Figure 8.69 Executing Initial Load for Initial Load Group

Monitoring the Initial Load Execution for the Initial Load Group

Once the background job is complete, potential errors can be analyzed in Central Finance Customizing (Transaction CFINIMG), under **Initial Load • Initial Load of Initial Load Execution for Financial Accounting • Initial Load Execution for Selected Company Codes • Monitor Initial Load for Initial Load Group**, as shown in Figure 8.70. Make sure the selection parameters are the same as in the previous transaction.

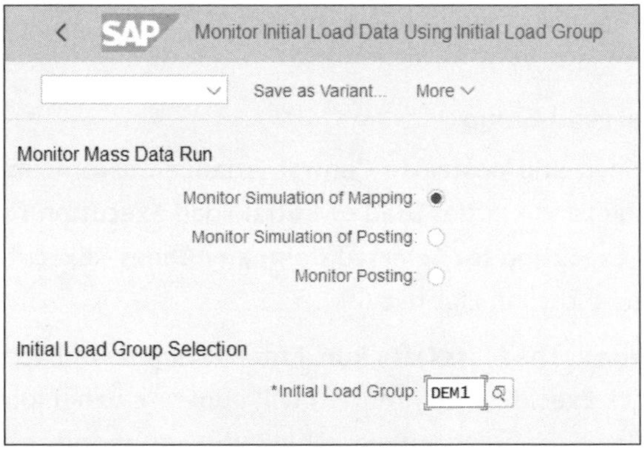

Figure 8.70 Monitoring the Initial Load Execution for Initial Load Group

For errors, double-click on the number of errors in the **Error Msg** column, as shown in Figure 8.71.

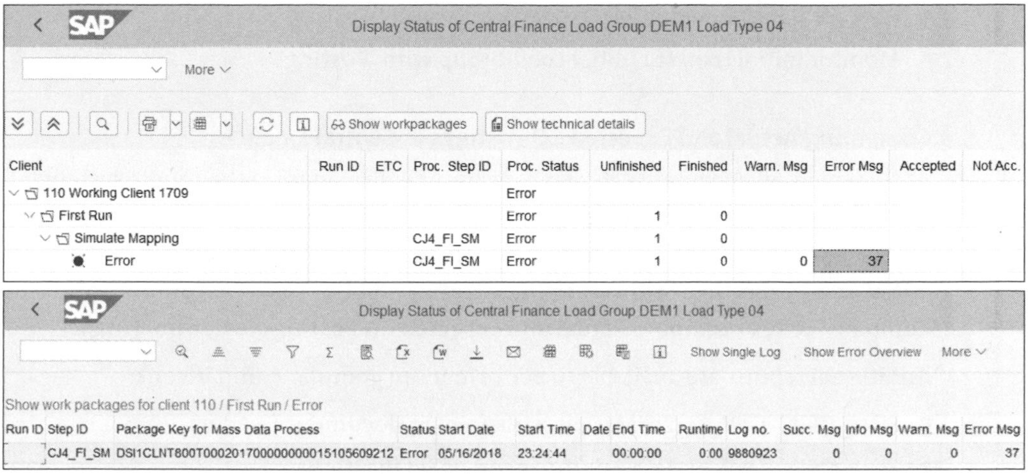

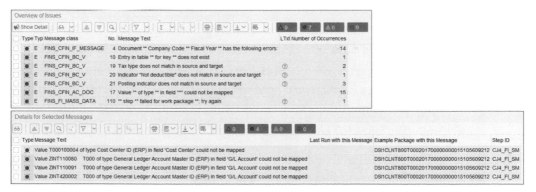

Figure 8.71 Status Shows Errors after Mapping Simulation

Click on the **Show Error Overview** button. Errors will be grouped by message type/ID. Select a message and click on the **Show Detail** button. All occurrences of the error will be listed. In the example shown in Figure 8.72, the mapping failed for one cost center and three G/L accounts, resulting in fifteen total errors.

Figure 8.72 Analyzing Mapping Errors

When all the mapping errors are solved, repeat the process with the following Central Finance Customizing paths:

- **Execute Initial Load for Initial Load Group with 'Simulate Postings'**
- **Monitor Initial Load for Initial Load Group with 'Simulate Postings'**

- **Execute Initial Load for Initial Load Group with 'Posting'**
- **Monitor Initial Load for Initial Load Group with 'Posting'**

Comparing Actual and Expected CO Postings in Central Finance

At this stage, all documents should have been replicated from the source system into the Central Finance system. You can confirm the number and balances of all documents in Central Finance Customizing (Transaction CFINIMG), under **Initial Load • Initial Load Execution for Financial Accounting • Initial Load Execution for Selected Company Codes • Compare Actual and Expected CO Postings in Central Finance**.

Additional reports are available to perform more granular comparisons:

- FINS_CFIN_DFV_FI_NUM: Comparison of FI Document Headers
- FINS_CFIN_DFV_FI_DOC: Comparison of FI Line Items

Completing the Initial Load

Once the initial load has been completed, the online replication should take over. To allow the SAP LT Replication Server system to start this process, in the source system, open Transaction SM30 for view VCFIN_SOURCE_SET and click the **Maintain** button. For every relevant company code, mark **Initial Load Finished** as **True**. Save these changes.

Deleting Initial Load Data

When configuration changes too much, or when moving between phases, restarting the project might be useful. You'll need to the initial load data to clear the database tables that were filled during extraction, posting, or simulation of the initial load.

Specifically, the following entries are deleted:

- Central Finance migration log table entries
- Central Finance replicated database table entries
- Messages in the application log

In the selection screen, as shown in Figure 8.73, select which data and logs should be cleared, as follows:

- Extracting and posting data (all or by load group)
- Mapping and posting simulation data (all or by load group)

Enter an **Initial Load Group** if applicable. Click **Execute.** The program will clear all temporary data from the extract, posting, mapping simulation, and posting simulation steps.

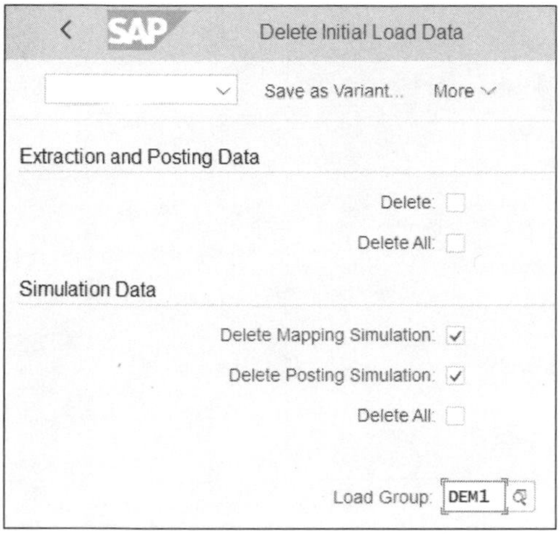

Figure 8.73 Parameters for the Deletion of Initial Load Data

> **Note**
>
> Only the initial data loaded in the Central Finance system will be deleted with the transaction above. For a complete reset of all initial load data from the source system, follow the instructions from SAP Note 2182309: Reset Initial Load not possible.

Deleting the Initial Postings

If the documents that were already posted also need to be deleted, use report Central Finance: Deletion of FI Documents (Transaction FINS_CFIN_DOC_DELETE). As shown in Figure 8.74, select a source system, one or more company code in the source system. Then, decide whether the processing should be a **Test Run** and validate the parameters for parallel processing. Click **Execute** or run the program in background.

If in test run mode, the application will list all documents that can be deleted and show errors for the others. If not in test run mode, the application will list all documents and validate which ones were successfully deleted and which ones were not.

For more information, see SAP Note 2329453: CFIN: Delete documents from G/L, CO, and FI, SAP Note 2548002: CFIN Deletion report, and SAP Note 2457869: How to delete FI/CO documents replicated to Central Finance.

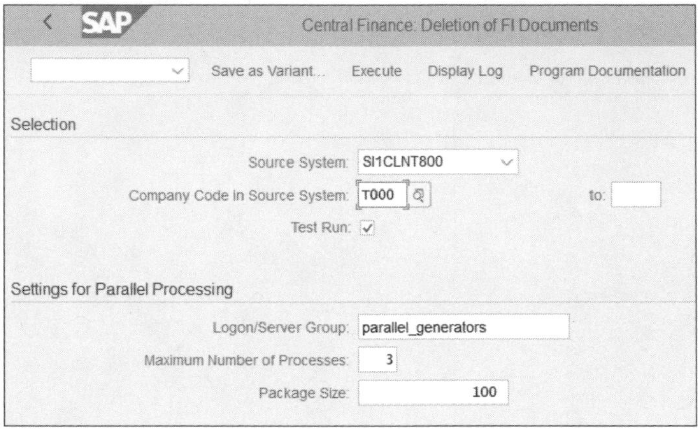

Figure 8.74 Deletion of FI Documents

In addition, the following tools could be used to clean up the data replicated from FI and CO as well as the master data:

- Implement SAP Note 2171525: Preparation for resetting Central Finance transaction data in the source system
- CO Initial Load Reset (FINS_CFIN_CO_DOCS_IL_RESET)
- CO Document Deletion (FINS_CFIN_CO_DOC_DEL)
- CO Central Reversal with Reposting (FINS_CFIN_CO_DOC_CRCT)
- Delete internal order (AUFK) using Transaction CFIN_CO_MAPPING_DEL
- Delete CO orders using Transaction OKO5
- Reset the number range for orders using Transaction KONK
- Reset the number range for CO documents using Transaction KANK
- Delete master data (G/L accounts, customer, vendor) with program SAPF019 (Transaction OBR2)

8.9.5   Final Steps

Once the initial load is complete, some final steps must be taken to start the ongoing replication.

Balances and Open Items

The number of fiscal years to carry only as balances is defined in view VCFIN_ SOURCE_SET in the source system configuration, as shown in Figure 8.62. For these years, documents will not be carried over to the Central Finance system, only their balances. However, be aware that all open item documents that fall in the balance-only period will be carried over as documents. The number of documents that are still open and that belong to the balance periods could significantly impact the performance of the initial load. We therefore recommend closing as many open items as possible.

To check the number of open items in an SAP ERP source system, use Transaction SE16 to count the number of entries for tables Accounting: Secondary Index for Vendors (table BSIK) and Accounting: Secondary Index for Customers (table BSID). These tables are usually cleared with matching transactions like:

- Clear Customer (Transaction F-32)
- Clear Vendor (Transaction F-44)
- Post with Clearing (Transaction F-51)
- Automatic Clearing without Currency (Transaction F.13)
- Post with Clearing (Transaction FB05)

When the clearing transactions still don't remove enough open items, the matching between transactions and payments must be improved. Machine learning applications delivered by SAP or by third-party software vendors can be used to improve the matching rate.

> **Note**
>
> More information on open item management can be found in the SAP documentation: *https://bit.ly/2N8CM7I*.

Line Items

Transferring individual documents and corresponding line items can be very time consuming, especially during the initial load. Therefore, we recommend keeping the window of document loads as short as possible. Also, whenever applicable, the document load should be lined up with the beginning of a fiscal year to facilitate reconciliation.

When reversal documents are selected for import, either during the initial load or during online replication, the Central Finance system will reach back into the source system to load the original document. This process could be time consuming if a single document reverts many source documents from different periods.

Retroactive History Load (Back-Load)

After the initial load is performed and the online replication is activated, a common question is "How can the data history be uploaded?" Let's say your balance load covers 2 years of data, and your organization wants to use Central Finance as the source for machine learning or for trend analysis. In this case, 3 to 5 years of data would be required. How can balances be uploaded for previous years?

Unfortunately, at the time this of writing, this feature is not available and is not on the roadmap. You'll need alternative methods to cover these requirements, for example:

- Loading Central Finance data into a data warehouse to be merged with historical data.
- Loading historical data into CO-PA only and then use CO-PA as the source.
- Using BAPIs/IDocs to generate historical balances in table ACDOCA. In this case, we recommend separating the data either via a new origin field or using the extended ledger functionality.

8.10   Summary

The various Central Finance deployment options serve multiple purposes, and implementation time can vary greatly depending on elements like:

- The number and types of source systems
- Data volume, data quality, and harmonization requirements
- Scope (i.e., reporting to central processing or as a stepping stone to SAP S/4HANA)

We recommend taking an agile approach and gradually building from a pilot project or from the discovery phase with a focus on learning how to combine the main components: your source system(s), the SAP LT Replication Server, SAP Application Integration Framework, and the central system. SAP recommends following the major phases of the SAP Activate methodology.

The project team will need to cover both technical and functional aspects of the environment, which can be divided into several streams:

- Infrastructure
- Data management
- Information model
- Business processes
- Reporting
- Project management and change management

Starting a Central Finance project can be overwhelming, but with the right team and the right methodology, your organization can soon benefit from a single platform to improve decision-making and support operations.

Chapter 9
Central Finance Operations

The first rule of any technology used in a business is that automation applied to an efficient operation will magnify the efficiency. The second is that automation applied to an inefficient operation will magnify the inefficiency.
—Bill Gates, founder of Microsoft

Once a Central Finance project is live, the run phase begins. During this phase, the actual operations of an active Central Finance implementation are conducted. Don't underestimate the required effort going forward. Successful organizations tend to be organized around a center of excellence with representatives from key teams: business, finance, IT, master data, and change management.

In the following sections, we'll briefly introduce you to the center of excellence paradigm before moving on to more specific finance operations: replication, managing master data, system onboarding and process onboarding as well as operations for mergers, acquisitions, and divestitures.

9.1 Centers of Excellence

If your organization adopts a center of excellence paradigm, as shown in Figure 9.1, the *lead* usually comes from an *architecture* background as he/she needs the skill to connect other modules, which affects the overall impact of the solution within the landscape and within the organization. The lead will also be responsible for communicating with and reporting, to both IT and finance upper management, the state of operations.

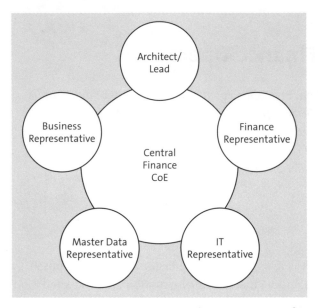

Figure 9.1 Key Resources in a Central Finance Center of Excellence

The rest of the center of excellence is composed of representatives, either part-time or full-time. The *finance representative* is responsible for ensuring consistency in the data that is replicated from source systems into the central system. He/she must ensure that the chart of accounts, the profit and loss (P&L) account, and balance sheet reflect the transactions occurring in the local systems and in the central system, as applicable. The finance representative also influences the design of the information model and contributes to other finance projects using Central Finance as source system, e.g., consolidation, planning, and budgeting.

The *IT representative* is the relay between the center of excellence and the rest of the IT technical team. He/she must ensure that other projects (system upgrades, downtimes, new implementations, etc.) will unexpectedly impact the operation of the Central Finance environment. If errors are identified, he/she serves as communication channel with the SAP support team and ensures the potential implementation of corrections. The IT representative also influences design and supervises the delivery of custom code, as applicable.

The *master data representative* is a key resource in the center of excellence. As mentioned in previous chapters, master data is crucial to the operation of a Central Finance environment. However, the topic is both so wide and so deep that a single dedicated person is not enough. Therefore, the master data representative will serve as the dispatcher for the master data team so that all the potential errors related to master data will be solved in a timely manner. The master data representative will also influence all master data projects that could impact the central system, for example, due to changes in the design of master data in source systems, or if the central system will serve as a source to an outbound system, or even while integration to/from Central Finance is being evaluated.

Last but not least, the *business representative* is responsible for ensuring the Central Finance project delivers the value expected from its business case. An indicator of this value is the adoption ratio. The business representative must work with the change management team to guarantee that the user community is well trained, that new procedures and trainings are well documented, and that operations run smoothly between systems.

Finally, in the worst-case scenarios, a shadow IT group may appear, and processes are run outside the Central Finance system. To avoid this situation, the center of excellence must handle ongoing replication, master data, onboarding, and changes to the architecture effectively.

9.2 Ongoing Replication

On the technical side, the online replication must be set up, which we've described in Chapter 8. Once this setup is complete, you'll still need to manage the process to handle incoming errors and validate results.

Figure 9.2 shows how data is replicated between a source system and the central system. The configuration is usually re-created either manually or via Business Configuration sets (BC sets), which are manually imported. Master data can also be handled manually but is usually re-created automatically through master data management solutions like SAP Master Data Governance (SAP MDG). Finally, transactional data can be replicated out of the box via SAP Landscape Transformation Replication Server (SAP LT Replication Server).

Figure 9.2 Central Finance Online Replication Process

9.2.1   Transaction Replication

In configuring the SAP LT Replication Server, you'll define how frequently the data should be replicated from the source system, usually in real time: The SAP LT Replication Server monitors the source database, and as soon as transactions are created, these transactions are transferred to the central system. This configuration can also be scheduled with time intervals, from minutes to hours or to days, as required. When master data replication process creates lags in the transaction process, we recommend this setup.

The SAP LT Replication Server constantly monitors source systems for any changes, which could have a negative impact on performance in the source system. To avoid performance issues, several parameters can be checked, as follows:

- **Background jobs**
  In a Central Finance-only scenario, the number of tables that must be monitored is usually less than 5. The SAP LT Replication Server system itself doesn't need many background jobs to trigger analyses, so make sure your system is set up with a minimum of background jobs.

- **Table logging**
  When searching for changes in source systems, the SAP LT Replication Server normally triggers a job in the source system for each identified table. In most cases, no changes have been identified. Nonetheless, the SAP LT Replication Server will continue to check if changes have been made.

  As of SP 15, the default behavior has been changed so that only logging tables that contain records are processed. This change has significantly reduced the impact on source system performance.

  For systems older than SP 15, go to the Replication Cockpit (Transaction LTRC), under **Utilities • Specify Option for Logging Tables**. In the popup, make sure that **Only Process Logging Tables with Records** is selected.

- **Memory size**
  Replicating transactions between the source systems and the target system can consume a great deal memory on the SAP LT Replication Server during the initial load. However, going forward, online replication requires much less memory.

  In the Replication Settings (Transaction LTRS), under **Performance Options**, the package size can be defined for both the initial load and online replication. The default value (blank) is 5,000 documents per package. Depending on the amount of available memory, you might increase the package size for the online replication and reduce it for the initial load.

- **Recovery/partial load**
  Unscheduled downtimes can disrupt a Central Finance environment, especially with three major systems involved (source, the SAP LT Replication Server, target), leading to systems becoming out of sync. In this case, you'll need to execute a partial load, which will involve creating additional replication objects with additional filters. The procedure is detailed in the recovery guide attached to SAP Note 2154420: SAP LT Replication Server for Central Finance.

For more information on using the SAP LT Replication Server for Central Finance, refer more generally to SAP Note 2154420: SAP LT Replication Server for Central Finance.

9.2.2 Error Correction

As transactions are replicated from the source into the central system, errors may occur. The role of the Central Finance center of excellence is not so much to solve these errors, but to dispatch errors and coordinate their resolution.

Representatives from multiple domains are required to sort through errors, which are usually related to the following areas:

- **Missing master data or missing mapping**
  The master data representative should help revise the master data management process to ensure that all necessary master data elements and their corresponding mappings are synchronized in the central system before the transactions are replicated.

- **Period handling**
  During period-end close in the source system, actions are taken to prepare the next period, for example, ensuring that the next fiscal period is open for posting. The finance representative should make sure that the period-end process is extended to either communicate with the center of excellence or to take direct actions in the central system to prepare for the next period.

- **Integration**
  The IT representative should ensure proper communication with the infrastructure group so that the center of excellence is aware of any downtime/upgrades to interfaces that could impact the central system.

- **Changes to the source system**

  The source system might change over time. The business representative and the architect should maintain close collaboration with the rest of the organization to anticipate changes in the configuration of inbound systems or their processes.

We recommend using the SAP Application Integration Framework notification features available in Transaction /AIF/RECIPIENTS to ensure that errors do not accumulate too quickly. Check the Master and Upgrade Guide for SAP Application Integration Framework for more details.

9.2.3   Data Reconciliation

Reconciliation between source and target system is required at least after each period is closed in the source system. We recommend performing regular checks during the period using the reconciliation reports described in Chapter 8.

From a high-level overview, the reconciliation process involves the following steps:

1. In the central system, execute report Central Finance Comparison for FI Document Headers (Transaction FINS_CFIN_DFV_FI_NUM), as shown in Figure 9.3. This report counts the number of relevant finance (FI) documents in the source system, the target system, or the SAP Application Integration Framework and highlights the number of missing documents.

2. List the missing documents (same report).

3. Click on the magnifying glass icon next to **Document not in Central Finance** to display a detailed list of missing documents. This list can be exported to Excel.

4. In the source system, list the missing documents (Transaction SE16).

5. Reuse the information from the comparison report to extract extended information on the missing documents from the table BKPF (Accounting Document Headers). This list serves as the root cause analysis. For instance, a document may have been missed, for example, if data is stored in the cross-company code column.

6. In the central system, compare line items.

7. Use the list of missing documents from the previous steps as parameters to run the report Central Finance: Comparison of FI Line Items (Transaction FINS_CFIN_ DFV_FI_DOC, as shown in Figure 9.4). Documents should contain line items. If the report shows no line items for the selected documents, these documents don't need to be transferred to Central Finance because they don't carry any balances, which is also true for clearing documents.

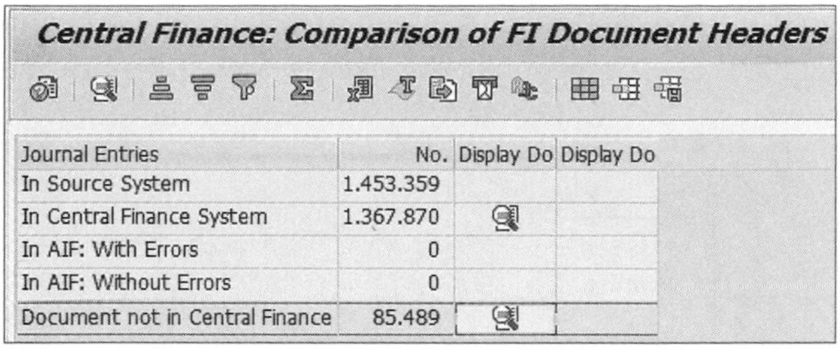

Central Finance: Comparison of FI Document Headers

Journal Entries	No.	Display Do	Display Do
In Source System	1.453.359		
In Central Finance System	1.367.870	🔍	
In AIF: With Errors	0		
In AIF: Without Errors	0		
Document not in Central Finance	85.489	🔍	

Figure 9.3 Central Finance Report: Comparison of FI Document Headers

Central Finance: Comparison of FI Line Items

Selection for Source System

Source System	ERP100

Parameters for Source System

Company Code	0001	to	
Document Number	1200091746	to	
Posting period	8	to	12
Fiscal Year	2018	to	
G/L Account		to	
Posting Date		to	
Entry Date		to	
Document type		to	

Currency Type for Comparison	Company Code Currency

☑ Show Errors Only

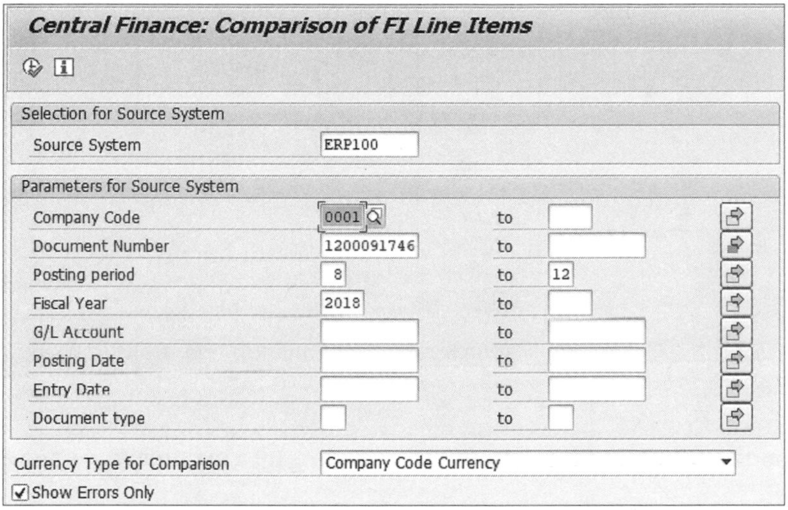

Figure 9.4 Central Finance Report: Comparison of FI Line Items

The process can later be augmented with custom reports developed in a data warehouse system or using reporting solutions to identify and prevent discrepancies between systems.

9.3   Master Data

As mentioned earlier in this chapter, master data must be present in the central system before the transaction replication. This requirement can have impact on existing master maintenance and governance.

Figure 9.5 shows how configuration, transaction data, and master data can flow from the source to the target, either manually, or through tools like the SAP LT Replication Server or SAP MDG.

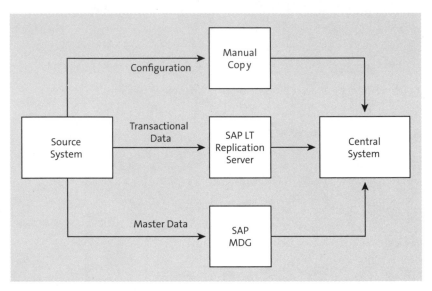

Figure 9.5 Typical Central Finance Replication Strategy for Configuration, Transactions, and Master Data

This architecture must be taken into account when setting up a maintenance or governance model.

9.3.1   Maintenance

In terms of maintenance, transactions must be considered separately from configuration and master data. In a Central Finance environment, transactions are replicated through the SAP LT Replication Server and should run smoothly so long as the required configuration and master data are ready.

The configuration should be segregated based on the frequency of change. For instance, currency conversion rates change on a regular basis. Therefore, the current update methods in your source systems must be extended to the central system. Slowly changing configuration, like new cost centers/profit centers, new plants, changes to general ledger (G/L) accounts, and account determinations should be considered on a case-by-case basis. Consider the following questions:

- **Is the configuration change in the source relevant to the central system?**
Some configuration to the logistics or human resources modules might not be relevant to the Central Finance system.

- **Is the configuration change compatible with the central system?**
If the central system is used as a finance transformation platform, significant changes have been made to its initial configuration that prevent simple copying/ pasting or transport of the new configuration. For instance, when merging several source systems, controlling area numbers may have been changed. As a result, new cost centers and profit centers will require a translation into the new controlling area.

- **Special case: Is this a one-to-one stepping stone?**
If the Central Finance system is used as a stepping stone to implementing SAP S/4HANA with a unique SAP source system, where all configuration has been maintained in a one-to-one relationship, you might be able to simply transport changes from the source system to the central system. These changes should still be validated, however, because some configurations, like G/L accounts, might not be compatible between SAP ERP and SAP S/4HANA.

Like configuration, master data must be synchronized between your source systems and the central system. This synchronization is best achieved with a dedicated master data management solution like SAP MDG, which we'll describe in more detail in Chapter 10.

9.3.2   Governance

Whether Central Finance is used only for reporting or also for operations, you'll still need to include it in the master data governance process and consider it as an input for master data management. This inclusion is especially important when defining a master data golden record and should include maintaining the master data mapping in the central system, which we'll describe in detail in Chapter 10.

9.4   System Onboarding

Frequently, Central Finance projects start with a limited scope, perhaps just a few company codes from a select few source systems. After the initial phase, additional company codes or source systems can be included. This process is relatively simple, assuming that functional scope has not changed and that no new source systems types (SAP ERP versus non-SAP ERPs) need to be considered.

Figure 9.6 shows the relative progression in complexity between the initial wave of a Central Finance project and its subsequent waves. For instance, maintaining the same scope but extending the solution to more company codes is likely to increase the *volume* of messages and potentially generate new errors from mapping or master data. On the other hand, extending source systems from SAP-only to non-SAP ERPs is mostly seen as an *integration* challenge, which requires, for instance, new channels for master data synchronization. Finally, increasing the *scope* from central reporting to central operations will require more teams involved in the platform. In terms of projects, these waves should be treated differently, especially with regard to change management.

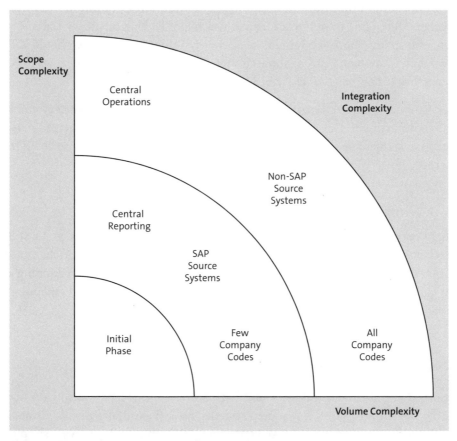

Figure 9.6 Complexity Progression for Central Finance Projects

To operationalize the process, the project team should start building a dedicated checklist:

- **Technical/security**
  - Are there any additional license requirements?
  - Does the source system need add-ons installed?
  - Have RFC (Remote Function Call) destinations been created?
  - Do open items need to be cleaned?
  - Have the security steps been taken in the source and central systems?
- **Functional/configuration**
  - Which company codes should be included?
  - How many years should be included in the initial load?
  - How many periods should be replicated as documents versus as balances?
  - Is the current configuration compatible with the central system?
- **Master data**
  - Is there an opportunity to clean master data?
  - Do we need new number ranges?
  - Does the prerequisite master data (company codes, plants, jurisdiction codes, etc.) exist?
  - Is the new source system included in the master data management process?
- **Transactional data**
  - Should new company codes be included in an existing load group or in a new load group?
  - Are there new types of objects to consider?
- **New company code**
  - Does the new company code belong to a different region/geography that requires additional configuration (e.g., country codes, jurisdiction codes, etc.)?
  - Does the existing master data cover the new company code, or does the master data need to be extended (e.g., G/L accounts, cost centers, profit centers, controlling area, etc.)?
- **New source system**
  - Are the users from non-SAP systems also users of the central system? Is there a license or security requirement for these users?

- How will master data be synchronized between the non-SAP system and the central system?
- What is the frequency of data replication between master data and transactional data?

- **Change management/timeline**
  - Is there an impact on the current period-end close process?
  - Are there any conflicting projects planned for the source system (e.g., upgrades)?
  - Are users available to support the adoption of Central Finance?

9.5   Process Onboarding

When moving from a central reporting strategy to central operations, frequently, you'll start with only a few company codes and gradually extend to more. However, before onboarding new company codes, several prerequisites must be fulfilled. Otherwise, your organization might have to reload of the initial data:

- **Start early with the replication of documents**
  At least one period of documents must be replicated prior to moving to operations to facilitate the potential reversal of documents like accruals.

- **Validate tax calculation**
  Tax calculation is not needed for central reporting but is required for central processing. You'll need to ensure that taxes are calculated the same way as in the source system to avoid issues with customers and vendors after the switch. In addition, taxes must be calculated for several periods before converting to central operations because the breakdown of taxes will be needed for tax reporting and operations like returns or partial payments.

- **Transfer the system of record**
  As soon as cash operations are performed in the central system, you should consider the central system the system of record for the selected company code(s). In some finance departments, this switch may find some resistance. The change management team will need to take extra steps to explain the rationale for this change and the expected benefits.

During the onboarding process, or transition to operations (as defined in the SAP Activate methodology), the following tasks must be prepared:

- **Realize**
  - Set up roles and authorizations
  - Validate support strategy
  - Establish support processes
  - Set up business process monitoring
- **Deploy**
  - Perform business validation and transition planning
  - Establish system administration and control
  - Establish security/role and authorization management
  - Establish a center of excellence
  - Execute transition to production support
  - Setup continuous improvement process
  - Complete transition to support organization
- **Run**
  - Set up and operate the center of excellence
  - Assess documentation
  - Assess template management
  - Assess test management
  - Assess change management
  - Assess process operations
  - Assess maintenance management
  - Assess upgrade management

9.6   Mergers and Acquisitions

Central Finance is particularly recommended for organizations relying on mergers and acquisitions for R&D or growth. During the due diligence phase, the finance and IT teams should evaluate the compatibility of the acquired company's ERP with the central system and determine whether the new source system should be kept separately in the long run. Alternatively, they may conclude that the integration to Central Finance can serve as a stepping stone for full integration into the larger organization's ERP, as shown in Figure 9.7. This decision depends on the scope currently available in the central system. For more information on mergers and acquisitions, see Chapter 11.

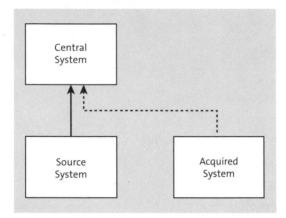

Figure 9.7 Merger and Acquisitions Strategy with Central Finance

9.7   Divestitures

Spin-offs and the selling off of entities are frequent strategies for many organizations. The selling organization must provide a fully running independent ERP to the acquiring or standalone company. This requirement is usually fulfilled with a carve-out from the existing ERP, as shown in Figure 9.8, but performing the required data deletion or masking could be complex.

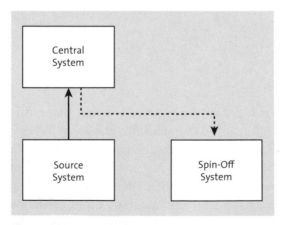

Figure 9.8 Divestiture Strategy with Central Finance

Another strategy consists in spinning off a new SAP S/4HANA system, either on-premise or in the cloud, and then integrating this system into the Central Finance system until hand-off. This two-tier strategy is especially beneficial if the business model of the new entity is significantly different from the original organization, for instance, just the service side of a manufacturing company or, on the contrary, just the manufacturing sites.

9.8   Summary

Switching from an initial project into operations requires changes in the organization. We recommend organizing support around a center of excellence with representatives from enterprise architecture, business, finance, IT, and master data. This team will resolve errors that arise from the online replication of transactional data, as well as guide the extension of the Central Finance platform to more company codes, more source systems, or additional scope, as needed.

Now that the Central Finance system is live, you should consider the system a key part of your corporate strategy for mergers, acquisitions, or divestitures.

In all cases, the Central Finance platform, including the source system, the SAP LT Replication Server and the target system, is part of a larger environment of solutions, all sharing critical master data. Unlike previous solutions, like data warehouses, the central system cannot run on imperfect master data. Thus, master data management should be considered as a workstream for every Central Finance project.

Chapter 10
Master Data Management

As data landscapes become increasingly complex, companies face the challenge of trying to manage the influx of both structured and unstructured data from multiple applications, files, databases, data warehouses, and data lakes. They need a solution that simplifies their landscape while also ensuring the highest levels of security.
— Bernd Leukert, member of the SAP Executive Board

If your goal is to replicate transactional data into Central Finance, you'll need the support of good master data management. The practice of creating, synchronizing, and updating master data across multiple systems is not easy and should not be underestimated, especially in the context of a Central Finance deployment.

In this chapter, we'll link Central Finance with master data management through the major steps of the project: data loads, master data processes, master data objects, and governance.

10.1 Data Loads

Transactional data replication from a source system to a Central Finance system is performed in two major steps: initial load and delta load. In parallel, master data maintenance must create a Golden Record.

10.1.1 Initial Data Loads

The initial data load is a critical phase in any Central Finance project. The best way to approach the initial data load is to plan for multiple data loads with a data drop in-between.

The reason is simple: Carrying a full data load for all company codes, including balances and document replication, could generate hundreds of thousands, if not millions, of error messages in the SAP Application Interface Framework. Solving so many error can be overwhelming, since resolution may require changes to both the configuration (number ranges, organizational structure, exchange rates, units of measures, etc.) and master data (chart of accounts, mappings, cost centers, etc.).

Instead of this big bang approach, an agile step-by-step strategy focused on learning is more effective and reliable. As shown in Figure 10.1, with a smaller number of transactions to replicate, these first steps will be faster. The number of error messages will be limited, and these errors will be easier to solve. As complexity increases, for instance, by adding company codes or including balances that were skipped initially, the team could experience a sense of progress while enhancing their learning. However, this best practice strategy requires a drop and reload of the data between each step.

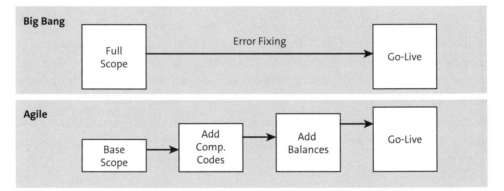

Figure 10.1 Big Bang versus Agile Approach to Initial Loads in Central Finance Projects

The initial load process loads the tables listed in Table 10.1 (in that order).

Document Type	Source Table	Communication Channel	Filter	Error Handling
Cost objects (orders)	AUFK	SAP Landscape Transformation Replication Server (SAP LT Replication Server)	SAP LT Replication Server rules	SAP Application Interface Framework

Table 10.1 Link between Document Types, Source Tables, Communication Channels, Filter Tools, and Error Handling Tools

Document Type	Source Table	Communication Channel	Filter	Error Handling
Finance and controlling (FI/CO) postings (balances, docs)	CFIN_ACCHD	RFC (Remote Function Call)	CFIN Customizing	Logs
CO secondary postings (documents)	COBK	SAP LT Replication Server	SAP LT Replication Server rules	SAP Application Interface Framework
Commitment postings	CFIN_CMT_H	SAP LT Replication Server	SAP LT Replication Server rules	SAP Application Interface Framework

Table 10.1 Link between Document Types, Source Tables, Communication Channels, Filter Tools, and Error Handling Tools (Cont.)

You'll need to execute the following configuration steps to perform the initial load (which we detailed in Chapter 8):

1. SAP LT Replication Server: Define a simulation of replication objects for table AUFK.

2. Central system: Perform smoke testing and/or simulating an initial load of cost object mappings.

3. Central system/SAP Application Interface Framework: Handle errors from table AUFK under CO_OBJ_SIM.

4. SAP LT Replication Server: Start the load and replication of table AUFK.

5. Central system/SAP Application Interface Framework: Handle errors from table AUFK under CO_OBJ.

6. Source system: Configure company codes in view VCFIN_SOURCE_SET.

7. SAP LT Replication Server: Define replication objects for table CFIN_ACCHD.

8. SAP LT Replication Server: the start load and replication of table CFIN_ACCHD.

9. Central system: Extract/monitor data for the initial load.

10. Central system: Extract/monitor delta load for the initial load.

11. Source system: Select the **Initial Load Finished** checkbox in view VCFIN_SOURCE_SET.

12. Central system: Simulate/monitor the mapping.

10

13. Central system: Execute/monitor the mapping.

14. Central system: Execute/monitor the postings.

15. Central system: Compare initial load postings for FI and CO.

16. SAP LT Replication Server: Activate replication for table `CFIN_ACCHD`.

17. Central system/SAP Application Interface Framework: Handle errors from table `CFIN_ACCHD` under `AC_DOC`.

18. Central system: Prepare/monitor the initial load of CO postings.

19. SAP LT Replication Server: Define replication objects for table `COBK`.

20. Central system: Perform smoke testing and/or simulation for CO document replication.

21. SAP LT Replication Server: Start the load and replication for table `COBK`.

22. Central system/SAP Application Interface Framework: Handle errors from table `COBK` under `CO_DOC`.

23. SAP LT Replication Server: Define replication objects for table `CFIN_CMT_H`.

24. Central system: Simulate/execute the initial load of commitments.

25. Central system/SAP Application Interface Framework: Handle errors from table `CFIN_CMT_H` under `CMT_DOC`.

26. Central system: Reconcile journal entries, balances, and line items for FI and CO.

10.1.2   Delta Loads

The initial load can take several hours, depending on the size and performance of your source systems and the central system. After the first initial load, you should always perform a second initial load (the *delta load* in step 10) to ensure that all documents have been selected and transferred.

After the delta load has completed, maintain the view VCFIN_SOURCE_SET in the source system and select the **Initial load finished** checkbox. Then, in the SAP LT Replication Server, start the load and replication for table `CFIN_ACCHD`. From this point on, all documents created in the source system will be automatically replicated in the central system.

10.1.3   Golden Record Creation

Nowadays, data is considered an enterprise asset. Its value is recognized when it supports operational and strategic business decisions. However, this value is directly correlated to its quality, measured in the accuracy, consistency, existence, integrity, and validity of the data.

The highest value is given to the Golden Record, the most complete combination of master data elements and hierarchies in an organization, combining information from multiple sources. The Golden Record is an important step in the quest for a single source of truth.

In the context of master data management in SAP, the term "Golden Record" usually applies to master data domains such as customers, vendors, or materials. By extension, this principle can be applied to the configuration domain, such as plants or controlling areas, and to transactions objects, such as sales orders, purchase orders, or journal entries.

As shown in Figure 10.2, an ideal environment would use a master data management solution like SAP Master Data Governance (SAP MDG) or use third-party software to integrate master data from multiple SAP and non-SAP sources. In a high-level overview, the following steps are undertaken:

❶ Synchronize the systems to match, merge, and purge the records.

❷ Create the Golden Record in the master data management solution.

❸ Create a corresponding record in the Central Finance system.

❹ Match the record from the central system to the golden record.

❺ Update the mapping table in the SAP MDG foundation in the central system.

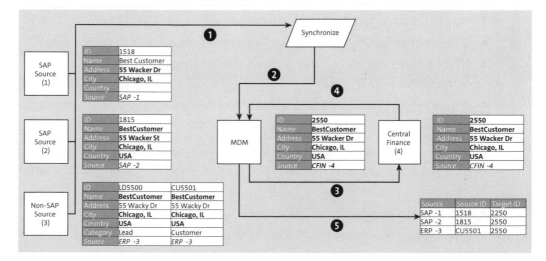

Figure 10.2 Golden Record Creation in a Central Finance Environment

10.2   Master Data Processes

Almost every organization has issues with master data. The lucky few spend a great deal of time dealing with master data issues. Master data is usually captured and managed in multiple business applications and/or manually. As a result, the data lacks consistency across the different applications. The chief financial officer is usually the owner of all the financial numbers used in and produced by multiple applications and their master data. The consistency of these numbers can be directly affected by the lack of synchronization of master data across multiple applications. Some key issues in master data processes that may directly impact data quality in Central Finance include the following:

- Lack of resources allocated to master data quality
- No business ownership with data quality being handled by IT and consultants
- Lack of adoption of best practices due to little or disconnected engagement with different parts of the business
- Starting a master data management process without understanding the underlying issues
- Trying to achieve too much too quickly due to lack of focus on key master data objects
- Choosing a generalist as a leader who does not fully understand how processes interact with each other

When managing master data, you'll choose from three basic choices:

- Leave the current way of managing the process as-is, even if it is not working
- Establish a manual process that allows you to determine who is doing what and to enforce manual governance
- Automate the process of governance for the core process involved in managing the master data

Automation is ideal because leaving the current process as-is could lead to issues in Central Finance after go-live that might manifest themselves in the following symptoms:

- Mapping errors appearing in SAP Application Interface Framework
- Missing master data in Central Finance even though the data had been mapped correctly
- Incorrect mapping between source and Central Finance master data

- High volume of errors caused by missing data or incorrect mapping during the initial load, the cutover period, and the real-time replication, after go-live

- Users in the source system creating their own master data without notifying Central Finance owners, which could affect reporting and/or operations in the central system

Controlling this master data process for Central Finance is essential for avoiding frequent, redundant errors and for establishing business control over the initial creation and sustainability of your master data. The recommended process encompasses at least four steps, as shown in Figure 10.3.

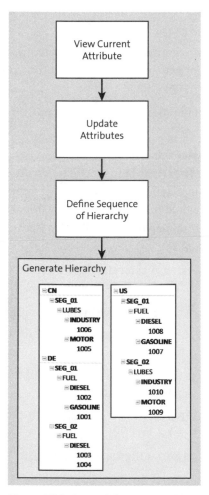

Figure 10.3 Central Finance Master Data Process Steps

Whether the process is manual or fully automated, the master data process must have at least these steps to reduce the number of errors after go-live. In the following sections, we'll describe each of these steps.

10.2.1   Request for Change

The change request must cover the creation, modification, deletion and the blocking of master data in accordance with SAP S/4HANA core master data operations. Mass create, change, delete, or block operations outside of core systems are optional, since these operations can be performed in a series. An additional task is that the change request will need to include whether the master data request requires any creation or changes to the mapping for Central Finance.

The mapping for Central Finance is a mandatory element in the change request because the mapping triggers alerts to users and/or executes an automated control in a tool, for example, a business rules framework in SAP MDG.

Once the change request is raised, key elements of the master data element must be added before the changed data can be validated.

The completion of the change request should trigger the validation of master data. This task must be given to an expert in the business process being facilitated by the given master data object. For example, the creation of general ledger (G/L) accounts must be checked by the finance department, who would fully understand the impact of the various settings. Giving this task to the wrong department will only lead to poor processes and increased errors and is wasted effort.

The validation of the data is the most critical step in a master data process. You'll need to perform the following checks:

1. Check whether the change or creation operation requires a change in the mapping.
2. Check that the attributes requested by the change request are relevant for Central Finance.
3. Check whether any attributes are inconsistent between the source system and the Central Finance system.
4. Check that the objects requested in the change request are consistent with the scope of Central Finance.
5. Check that the individual values for the attributes are configuration dependent.

6. Check whether the master data organizational assignments are the same or different in the source system and the Central Finance system.

7. Check which systems the master data requires be created, changed, deleted, blocked, etc.

This list of checks is not exhaustive but reflect the lessons we've learned from our customers that either have gone live or are in the project phase. The validation phase should belong to a data steward, even if only unofficially. When one or more checks are inconsistent with the process laid out for the relevant master data object, this change request should be returned to the person who initiated the change request.

In instances where the data steward can determine the values or corrective action for a change request, a modification should be made to the change request and resent to the person who initiated the change request to confirm the changes suggested by the data steward. While this step is not necessary, some organizations could improve data quality continuously by requiring the initiator of a change request ensure checks won't fail and to provide continuous feedback, which increases future accuracy.

10.2.2   Approval of the Request

Assuming the data steward, automated or manual, has carried out the validation steps with the requisite due diligence, the approval step should be a formality. However, this step represents the point of no return. The approver should understand the process, the systems, and the impact of a change while being accountable for the change request and its impact.

For Central Finance, an approval involves many facets of the master data process that have a direct impact on the replication process. The approver ideally is the owner of the object and someone who understands Central Finance design. The approver's tasks include the following:

1. Confirm that the data steward has completed or verified all the mandatory fields.

2. Check that optional fields have the correct values for the target system.

3. Check that mapping values exist when mapping for Central Finance exists.

4. Make final changes to values for any attributes.

5. Approve the change request.

> **Note**
>
> The data steward and the approver can be the same person for the purposes of Central Finance, but validation and approval processes should be segregated to ensure one final check before executing the change request.

Once the approval is granted, the given master data change operation (i.e., create, change, delete, block, mass change, etc.) is executed.

10.2.3 Execution of the Change Request

In execution, automation helps. Central Finance needs at least three events to occur to ensure the correct execution of master data changes, as follows:

- Always updating the Central Finance system first in the execution phase
- Updating the mapping engine for Central Finance next
- Carrying out the requested change in the source system if appropriate (i.e., create, change, block, etc.)

The exact method of execution depends on the scope of the project and the tools your organization uses to implement this process. Execution can take the form of a manual process at an offshore center or a completely automated web service that notifies all parties when a change request has been executed successfully. Figure 10.4 shows a high-level overview of the process for executing master data change requests.

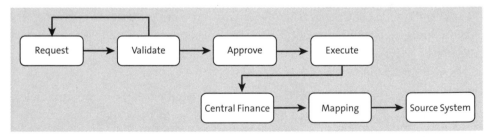

Figure 10.4 Master Data Execution for Central Finance

Where the process stops short of full execution, you should expect to receive error messages in SAP Application Interface Framework for Central Finance.

All master data objects are subject to the core process for managing data we've described in this section. However, so far, we've been focused on the process and should look at master data itself next.

10.3   Master Data Objects

Up to now, we've discussed the process for maintaining master data objects using tools from SAP and its partners (see Figure 10.5). In this section, we'll discuss the most common master data objects relevant to Central Finance.

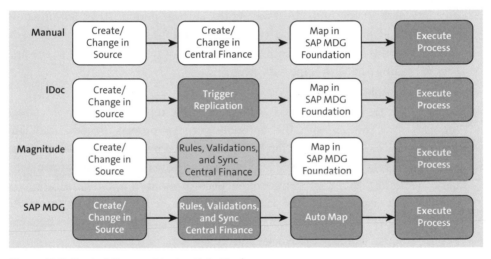

Figure 10.5 Central Finance Master Data Tools

At the time of this writing, Central Finance can automatically create orders based on order types maintained in configuration settings. In addition, as of SAP S/4HANA FPS 01, work breakdown structure (WBS) elements can be replicated into Central Finance for reporting purposes. For other master data, automatic replication does not exist as other tools already perform this function.

In general, four main tools for ensuring master data synchronization between your source systems and Central Finance are available:

- **Manual processes**
  In a manual process, you would use a CSV file that uses Central Finance mapping maintenance programs. The actual creation and change of master data between systems for most master data is manual. This process requires users to confirm

the output prior to posting a transaction. If a transaction is posted without the process being followed, the likelihood of an error arising is quite high.

- **Intermediate documents (IDocs)**
  IDocs could be used to send data from a source system to Central Finance, and vice versa. This method works well during the initial cutover, when harmonization is not critical for the relevant object. If harmonization is important, you would need to customize the IDoc. IDocs are a purely IT solution and does not help manage master data.

- **Third-party tools**
  A partner solution, such as those offered by Magnitude, could be used for SAP and non-SAP data for the initial load during the cutover period. This solution could also assist with profiling data and with removing duplicates in legacy data. In addition, Magnitude could handle both SAP and non-SAP systems to kickstart the process of loading data with some data cleansing.

- **SAP Master Data Governance**
  Using SAP MDG allows for initial loads and online replication based on change requests that comply with the optimal four-step process (request, validate, approve, and execute). In addition, SAP MDG is used by Central Finance to maintain the mapping. SAP MDG will also allow a full governance process for master data, including the creation of the Golden Record, replication, and notifications of changes to user groups. This tool is built and maintained by the IT department but owned and used by business users. Consider SAP MDG as just another business application that happens to manage master data.

10.3.1   Chart of Accounts

The central object in a finance transformation is a chart of accounts, which represents the basic recoding mechanism for accounting entries being fed from source systems. A chart of accounts is the number one prerequisite for implementing Central Finance from a business perspective and will drive many design decisions for finance functions. You don't have to wait until kicking off a Central Finance implementation project before creating a chart of accounts. Starting even months ahead could provide your organization the time to discuss the project and save resources in the long run. Up to three charts of accounts can exist for a company code, and each company code must have at least one chart of accounts, as a minimum, per SAP standards.

Within SAP S/4HANA, and thus within Central Finance, three charts of accounts exist: group, country, and operational. Each represents a different purpose, recording mechanism, and reporting capability. By default, implementing Central Finance implies commonality and harmonization among these objects from multiple source systems.

Often, but not necessarily, the Central Finance instance will contain a single operational chart of accounts. This chart of accounts will be used to make all the postings from the source system into SAP S/4HANA. The configuration of the Central Finance instance will be depend on this operational chart of accounts, as shown in Figure 10.6, and how this chart of accounts is set up directly impacts how Central Finance operates.

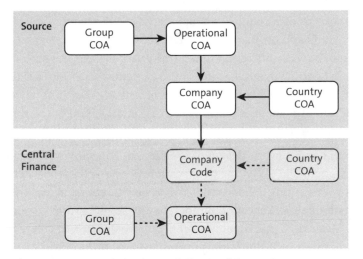

Figure 10.6 Central Finance and Charts of Accounts

Let's consider the context of different charts of accounts in Central Finance. As shown in Figure 10.6, the group chart of accounts is linked to the operational chart of accounts in the Central Finance instance. This optional chart of accounts and configuration element becomes important for three reasons: First, perhaps your organization wants to generate a consolidation feed from Central Finance or use embedded SAP consolidation software within the Central Finance instance. Second, you will also manage intercompany or intracompany transactions within the Universal Journal with Central Finance. Thirdly, using the reporting capabilities enabled by Central Finance using the group chart of accounts could assist with resolving preconsolidation or intercompany issues.

When Central Finance is used as a reporting or operational tool for local GAAP, then the country chart of account becomes relevant but is otherwise optional. If needed, this chart of account must be configured for each company code being transitioned into the Central Finance instance.

Normally, the chart of accounts would be directly configured within Central Finance Customizing in an early design step. Thereafter, many customizing settings will be a product of the operational chart of accounts, for example, the retained earnings account, the currency valuation, bank account link to the G/L account, etc.

10.3.2   General Ledger Account

The G/L account is part the chart of accounts. Two main types of G/L accounts will be set up: balance sheet accounts and profit and loss (P&L) accounts. You must create G/L accounts for each chart of accounts set up in Central Finance as per the project scope. Each G/L account in Central Finance has the same segments as SAP ERP 6.0 in terms of chart of account segment and company code segment. The key difference between SAP ERP 6.0 and a Central Finance instance is that Central Finance does not differentiate between G/L accounts and cost elements.

Therefore, you must understand how the design of G/L account will work with Central Finance given the differences between the two technologies as well as the existing differences between your various G/L accounts, which may be set up across the same technologies. For example, a G/L account number may be 7 digits in one system and 9 digits in another. Meanwhile, the organization may have decided to create a new G/L account structure based on 8 digits going forward.

Differences can arise in G/L account structure for the following reasons:

- Length of the G/L account
- Usage of the G/L account
- Settings of the G/L account
- Structure of the G/L account for non-SAP technologies
- Same G/L account usage with different codes
- Links between G/L accounts for country and group chart of accounts inconsistent at the operational level

This list represents just a few sample reasons why the harmonization of G/L accounts is a key activity in all implementations of Central Finance. Regardless of reason, the G/L account should be harmonized as a matter of best practice.

Like all other master data objects relevant for Central Finance, the G/L account may need to be mapped, as shown in Figure 10.7, from the source system to the SAP S/4HANA system where Central Finance is operational. Three options exist for mapping the G/L account:

- The G/L account number in the source system is the same as the G/L account number in Central Finance. In this case, no mapping is needed.

- One or more G/L account numbers in the source system have different numbers to one G/L account in Central Finance. In this case, mapping is needed.

- A rule does not exist for mapping on a 1:1 or N:1 basis. In this case, rule-based mapping is needed.

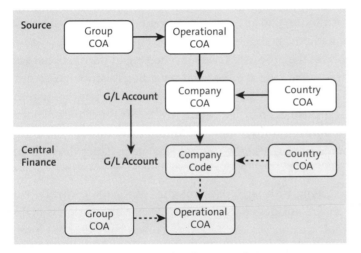

Figure 10.7 G/L Account Mapping for Central Finance

For each source system G/L account, the designer will need to establish the mapping options from a business perspective to ensure the correct working of the G/L account master data process. Note that the process of managing G/L accounts also requires that users understand how the design of this object has changed with SAP S/4HANA. In the following section, we'll cover the most salient changes.

10.3.3   Business Partners

One big change in SAP S/4HANA beyond the G/L account is the adoption of the business partner as the main functional object for customers and vendors. Business partners are probably the second most important objects in Central Finance, in terms of data volumes and impact, because most open items in Central Finance will be related to a business partner. While business partners are mandatory for Central Finance for payables and receivables reporting, for operational scenarios, or as a stepping stone to SAP S/4HANA logistics, customer and vendor objects will still be involved in these processes in SAP S/4HANA and, therefore, in Central Finance.

You should consider how business partners will be initially loaded into Central Finance, whether using a master data load tool described earlier or another method. Once the data is loaded into the Central Finance instance, the configuration must be set up appropriately to ensure customers and vendors are correctly created from business partners.

The process of creating customer and vendors requires you design and build business partner roles; their attributes; and any process-relevant data such as bank data, credit details, payment methods, etc. The scope of the business partner data is directly driven by the scope of the processes used for reporting or transactional scenarios. Once your data needs clearly determined and according to scope, customer/vendor integration (CVI) can be used to manage the process of maintaining customers and vendors through the business partner. Figure 10.8 shows the required movement set up as a process during the cutover and for ongoing maintenance. What tool used to maintain the source system and the Central Finance instance depends on your requirements.

Of course, manual tools dealing with large data volumes in a large company will require greater effort to ensure business partner and customer integration is maintained in Central Finance. For example, you'll need to ensure bank data is correct across the landscape, a prerequisite for payment factories to make payments, which may originate from more than one system, to vendors and to engage in multiple types of procurement categories.

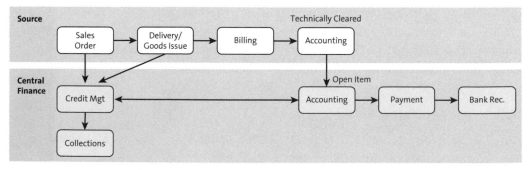

Figure 10.8 Central Finance and Business Partners

By understanding the management of the business partner process and its attributes during the project, the go-live will be smoother, and after go-live, maintenance will be easier. These organizational change management issues can cause symptoms in Central Finance's functional and technical operations.

10.3.4   Material Numbers

Whether you use the material master within Central Finance is optional. Replicated postings from SAP source systems will include the material number, which can then be used for market segment reporting within the Universal Journal within Central Finance. Another reason for maintaining the material master within Central Finance is to facilitate the execution of logistical processes that may be centralized, such as procurement.

When material master numbers differ across multiple source systems, SAP MDG key mapping can be used to manage their relationships. When deployed fully, SAP MDG can also be used to manage governance and distribution processes.

If the material master is not required within the scope of the project, a Central Finance BAdI (Business Add-In) will be required to remove the material master from the replicated accounting postings, which is a relatively easy task. Assuming the BAdI is no longer relevant and that the material master is no longer needed, the BAdI can be deactivated, and the code removed as a project activity. The flexibility is provided by the technical framework behind Central Finance.

10.3.5   Profit Centers

Profit centers are probably required within Central Finance because almost every connected system (both SAP and non-SAP systems) will use the concept of profit centers to manage overhead. Also, profit center codes may differ in the Central Finance system in order to introduce a single controlling area. SAP MDG key mapping would therefore be required to identify new values based on the source system, controlling area, and profit center.

As with financial master data objects, fully deployed, SAP MDG can centrally govern and distribute profit center records. SAP S/4HANA Finance provides SAP Fiori apps for the maintenance of profit centers (e.g., the Manage Profit Centers app). Profit centers within SAP S/4 HANA are linked to a "segment" as per the new G/L functionality, and document splitting can be performed for both profit centers and segments. If the

10

source system uses classic G/L, profit center master records will not contain this attribute. However, given the framework behind Central Finance, any classic G/L attributes can be determined using a BAdI based on business rules or default values, which could be a project activity.

Full P&L account reporting by profit center and profit center hierarchy will be available in the Central Finance instance using replicated and direct postings. Standard SAP Fiori apps (e.g., the Profit Centers – Plan/Actual app) are provided, together with queries and core data services (CDS) views. Queries and views can also be consumed within business intelligence tools such as SAP Analysis for Microsoft Office. You should also consider planning data since most profit center managers require actual and plan postings within a single report. Thus, building a centralized planning system using SAP S/4HANA optimized with SAP Business Planning and Consolidation (SAP BPC) may make sense since planning data is not replicated to Central Finance. Alternatively, SAP Analytics Cloud could also provide users the necessary planning capabilities.

10.3.6   Cost Centers

Cost centers are probably required within Central Finance process design because almost every connected system (both SAP and non-SAP systems) will use the concept of cost centers to manage overhead and operational expenses. Also, cost center codes may differ in the Central Finance system in order to introduce a single controlling area. SAP MDG key mapping is therefore required to identify the new values based on the source system, the controlling area, and the cost center. Like other financial master data objects, fully deployed, SAP MDG can centrally govern and distribute cost center records.

Central Finance provides SAP Fiori apps for maintaining cost centers (e.g., the Manage Cost Centers app). Cost centers may also be posted to directly within Central Finance because centralizing certain indirect business processes, e.g., connectivity with SAP Ariba and Concur, may make sense.

Full profit and loss reporting by cost center and cost center hierarchy will be available in the Central Finance instance using replicated and direct postings. Standard SAP Fiori apps (e.g., the My Spend app) are provided, together with queries and CDS views. Queries and views can also be consumed within business intelligence tools such as SAP Analysis for Microsoft Office. You should also consider planning data since most cost center managers require actual and plan postings within a single report. Thus, building a centralized planning system using SAP BPC optimized for SAP S/4HANA may make sense since planning data is not replicated to Central Finance. Like profit centers, SAP Analytics Cloud can also hold planning data and provide reporting capabilities.

10.3.7   Activity Types

Activity types are optional within Central Finance. If the connected SAP system performs activity type allocations (directly or indirectly), then these activities can be passed to Central Finance via the SAP LT Replication Server's CO document replication. Alternatively, allocations may be performed directly within Central Finance as a part of centralized closing activities.

If activity type allocations are being replicated to Central Finance, you may need to perform an SAP MDG key mapping to convert to a harmonized activity type code. Often, this mapping is necessary when the Central Finance design includes a single controlling area and the connected systems use multiple controlling areas. Like other financial master data objects, fully deployed, SAP MDG can centrally govern and distribute activity type records.

One dimension often overlooked regarding activity types is that, if direct activity type allocations are replicated, the activity type rate must exist within Central Finance. SAP S/4HANA Finance provides SAP Fiori apps maintaining activity types (e.g., the Manage Activity Type app).

10.3.8   Statistical Key Figures

Statistical key figures (SKFs) are optional within Central Finance. SKFs are generally used to support allocations within the CO module. For example, SKFs may be used within an assessment cycle to distribute costs from a central cost center to several receiver cost centers (e.g., based on floor space, employee headcount).

If central closing allocations are being performed within Central Finance, then SKFs can be defined. Like other financial master data objects, fully deployed, SAP MDG can centrally govern and distribute SKF records. Like other CO objects, SAP S/4HANA Finance provides SAP Fiori apps for maintaining SKFs (e.g., the Manage Statistical Key Figures app).

> **Flexible Hierarchies**
>
> Not strictly master data, flexible hierarchies need special mention as one of the key innovations from SAP that can be used when deploying Central Finance. Hierarchies,

for example, profit center and cost center hierarchies, are composed of master data exclusively. Since SAP S/4HANA 1709, you can create hierarchies and base their levels on cost center and profit center attributes.

End users can create these hierarchies and then use them on all data replicated via Central Finance in SAP S/4AHANA. Using Central Finance with flexible hierarchies can benefit business users by separating the process of managing hierarchies from the normal master data processes for cost centers and profit centers. Flexible hierarchies can use a harmonized model down to the profit center and cost center attributes, which in turn can be used in reporting based on different levels and the nature of the hierarchy.

10.4   Governance

Since a Central Finance system merges master data, configuration, and transactions from multiple systems, a question often arises: What happens when new data is created, updated, or even archived? This process requires proper governance.

The steps shown in Figure 10.9 follow the lifecycle of master data governance: extraction, harmonization, rationalization, dissemination, and maintenance.

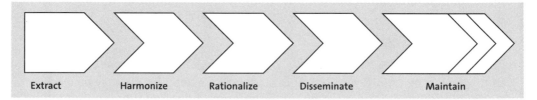

Figure 10.9 Master Data Maintenance Process

10.4.1   Master Data and Master Data Objects

The following domains should be considered in all Central Finance projects:

- Operating concern, controlling areas, company codes, plants
- Profit centers, cost centers, activity types, G/L accounts, and cost elements
- Customers, vendors, and business partners
- Projects and WBS elements
- Materials and characteristics

During the scoping phase, the following questions will have to be answered:

- Which domains are relevant to the selected scope? For instance, plants and materials might not be necessary if logistics and product profitability are not considered

- Which source system(s) contain the right master data? Are all characteristics necessary for the project? For example, material dimensions might not be required, but unit costs might.

- What software solutions are already in place that cover part or all of these domains?

- Are the master data objects time-dependent? How frequently are they created, updated, or archived?

- Is there a language component for the master data objects, e.g., cost center description in multiple languages?

- When a master data object is changed, how quickly does the change need to be replicated to the Central Finance system before a corresponding transaction is replicated?

- What are the security and authorization requirements?

- What are the audit or logging requirements?

- What is the incremental level of effort required for the initial load? For ongoing maintenance?

This list of questions should help you evaluate the need for a dedicated master data governance solution.

10.4.2   Dynamic Cost Object Creation

The following cost objects are supported in Central Finance:

- OR: Order
- KS: Cost Center
- KL: Cost Center/Activity Type
- EO: Profitability Segment (Account-Based)
- AO: Profitability Segment (Costing-Based)
- PR: Project (WBS Element)

Some cost objects, however, are not supported by the Central Finance system, but BAdIs are available to extend the solution, which is the case for:

- VB: Sales Order
- BP: Business Processes
- NV: Networks
- HP: Generic Cost Object
- I*: Real-Estate Object
- OP: Order/Line Item

For more information on supported cost objects, refer to SAP Note 2103482.

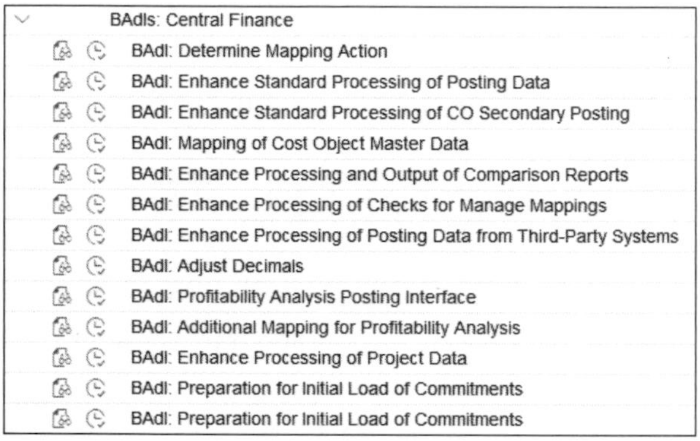

Figure 10.10 List of BAdIs Available for Central Finance

Figure 10.10 shows a list of all BAdIs available for Central Finance. Templates are available to facilitate these extensions. In general, you would follow these steps:

1. Open Central Finance Customizing (Transaction CFINIMG), under **BAdIs: Central Finance • BAdI: Enhance Standard Processing of CO Secondary Posting**.
2. Now, an implementation for BAdI `BADI_FINS_CFIN_CO_INTERFACE` of enhancement spot `ES_FINS_CFIN_CO_INTERFACE` will be created. Click **Continue**.
3. In the popup window, enter an **Enhancement Implementation** name and a **Short Text**.
4. Click **Creation of Enhancement**.
5. Select a transport package or choose **Local Object** if in a sandbox system.
6. Enter a name for the **BAdI Implementation** and the **Implementation Class**. Click **Continue**.
7. This step is important: Choose between **Create a new empty class**, **Copy one of the example classes**, or **Inherit from an example class not declared as final**. We recommend either copying the example or inheriting the class attributes from class `CL_FINS_CFIN_CO_INTERFACE_EXAM`. In this example, choose **Copy sample class**.

8. On the overview screen, click **Save** and then **Activate**.

In the implemented class, open method IF_BADI_FINS_CFIN_CO_INTERFACE~MAP_REPLACE_ CO_POSTING_DATA. Notice the call to object_handler_bp. In this private method, the technical object key is interpreted and available in field prznr. From this field, developers can map to a dummy business process, perform remote calls, or generate the necessary master data.

10.4.3   Extraction

Data extraction from SAP and non-SAP systems can be performed in three ways:

- Manually, through data file export
- With standard solutions like SAP MDG, SAP Data Services, or third-party software
- With custom programming

Which solution you choose will depend on the level of effort, the frequency of updates, and the solutions already in place. The solution could also handle the initial load and the ongoing operations differently.

> **Note**
>
> Before performing the extraction, always check for deletion flags because you don't need to extract and transfer master data that's marked for deletion, which is particularly relevant with materials (MARA-LVORM), customers (KNA1-LOEVM), or vendors (LFA1-LOEVM).

10.4.4   Harmonization

Multiple strategies are possible for master data harmonization, for example:

- Spending as little time as possible harmonizing data by only dealing with overlapping number ranges
- Focusing on attributes and characteristics like groups and only harmonizing the top elements (i.e., top 10% of customers by revenue or top 20% of raw materials by procurement volume)
- Performing an extensive harmonization process using matching algorithms and machine learning

When merging data from multiple source systems, especially in the case of customer/vendor integration (CVI), pay special attention to key IDs when these values are kept from the source systems. Watch out for the following:

1. Different elements representing different IDs

2. The same elements with different IDs

3. Different elements with the same IDs

4. The same elements with the same IDs

The only hard requirement is, if key IDs are kept from the source system, that the third case be avoided, which is possible with preliminary work.

Organizations usually worry about the second case. What if the same customer or supplier exists in different source systems but is represented as two different customers? The answer is to overlook the IDs and focus on customer attributes, groups, or hierarchies. If these elements are maintained correctly, reports will show these elements in the same group, and harmonization can be performed after the fact.

With harmonization, unfortunately, the return does not always match the level of the effort that team has put in, and the law of diminishing returns can certainly apply in this situation.

10.4.5 Rationalization

Over time, or through system integration, chances are that some pieces of master data will be duplicated. For example, a vendor could have different numbers in the procurement and ERP systems; a customer could be represented twice in CRM, ERP, or logistics due to multiple subsidiaries; a raw material could be represented differently in separate source systems, etc. The process of reducing the number of duplicates while ensuring better master data quality is called *rationalization*.

For master data rationalization, we recommend using standard taxonomies such as UNSPSC, NATO, or eClass to facilitate the rationalization process. These taxonomies are supported by most master data software.

Once duplicates have been identified, you'll need to determine which fields should be kept. This process can be done manually if the volume is reasonable. With larger datasets, the best strategy is to prioritize information based on source systems. For instance, a customer address is probably more reliable coming from the logistics system than from the CRM system. Another strategy would be to prioritize the most recent records.

10.4.6   Dissemination

The dissemination or synchronization of master data is the process of communicating the updated record back to the source systems. To maintain transactional integrity, the original element IDs should be kept and transferred together with the updated information. As much as possible, the dissemination process should update all systems at once to avoid discrepancies.

10.4.7   Maintenance

To reduce effort and provide a more reliable framework, we recommend setting up the same de-duplication rules during the initial load as in the ongoing replication. Master data management should be set up in such a way that exceptions will be raised, and the master data group should be notified. Then, an analyst can evaluate master data conflicts and either resolve these issues directly or dispatch issues to the relevant groups.

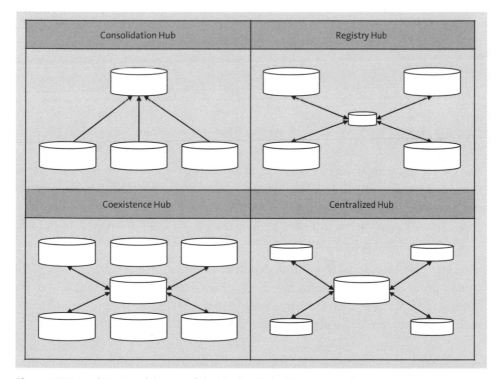

Figure 10.11 Architectural Approach to Master Data Management

To achieve this responsiveness, a master data management system must be included in the overall enterprise architecture, which may follow one of four commonly recognized architecture models, as shown in Figure 10.11 and summarized in Table 10.2.

	Consolidation Hub	Registry Hub	Coexistence Hub	Centralized Hub
Consolidation	Federation or physical consolidation	Federation and real-time change propagation	Federation, physical consolidation, and real-time change propagation	Physical consolidation and real-time change propagation
Synchronization Type	Batch or real time	Real time	Batch and real time	Batch and real time
Data Flow	Unidirectional	Bidirectional	Bidirectional	Bidirectional
Quality Controls	At repository	At the source	At the source and at the repository	At the repository

Table 10.2 Characteristics of Master Data Management Architecture Options

10.5   Summary

Master data is an important workstream in all Central Finance projects but should be separated from transactional data or configuration. The initial load process can be overwhelming, so an agile approach is preferred over a big bang implementation. To that end, SAP Application Interface Framework can be used during the initial load and for subsequent delta loads.

A master data management solution deployed in the landscape will help you in the overall process of extracting, harmonizing, rationalizing, disseminating, and maintaining the key master data domains. More than the data itself, the processes around maintaining master data will increase the value of the Central Finance project.

Assuming that Central Finance is now up and running, let's consider, in the next chapter, how else the platform can add value to your organization and explore the potential next steps for your new Central Finance environment.

PART III

Next Steps with Central Finance

Chapter 11
Mergers and Integrations

Of special consideration when considering Central Finance is its use for mergers and acquisitions (M&A) and integrations (post-merger integration), both from an enablement perspective but also from a collaboration perspective.

Today's business landscape includes many organizations that have joined forces. In this chapter, we'll focus on mergers and integrations, the process after a merger that involves handling legacy software in an IT landscape of a Central Finance implementation. We'll also discuss how you can, before a merger, leverage Central Finance as a mechanism for integrating third-party systems.

11.1 Integration Catalyst

In the context of mergers and integration, Central Finance is an integration catalyst. For both mergers and acquisitions (M&A) or post-merger integration (PMI), Central Finance provides integration and ingestion capabilities, as shown in Figure 11.1, that are nondisruptive, source system- and business model-agnostic, and available as a standard SAP solution, thus negating the need for custom build-out activities.

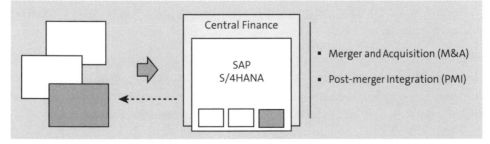

Figure 11.1 Central Finance for Mergers and Integration

Central Finance can act as an M&A hub to simulate or execute the onboarding of new entities and can be a platform and playbook for these activities repeatedly and efficiently.

11.1.1   Merger and Integration Platform

In the context of mergers and integration, Central Finance is an integration platform to onboard onto, as shown in Figure 11.2. Central Finance can onboard additional entities or systems by adding replication the SAP or non-SAP ERP source system.

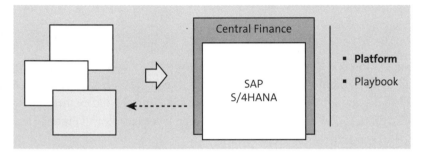

Figure 11.2 Merger Integration Platform

From a technical perspective, no limit on the number of additional source systems you can connect to exists. With SAP HANA as the underlying in-memory database, both reporting and process execution is scalable even for large datasets and complex requirements.

Central process execution can be adjusted by including new entities and datasets in the central process execution design, without the need for rewriting or redesigning processes. The same is valid for outbound interfaces: Rather than adding additional interfaces, new entities can just be integrated into and included into already existing outbound interfaces.

Where Central Finance is used as transformation platform (connecting to SAP Ariba for indirect procurement or to SAP Concur for travel, for example) or uses other central processes within the Central Finance system like treasury or real estate, the same holds true: New entities can be included rather than processes redesigned.

11.1.2   Merger and Integration Playbook

In the context of mergers and integration, Central Finance allows you to create an integration plan or to use an already existing integration plan as a foundation for a repeatable playbook for onboarding future entities or systems, as shown in Figure 11.3. This playbook includes both technical integration and validation as well as organizational change management.

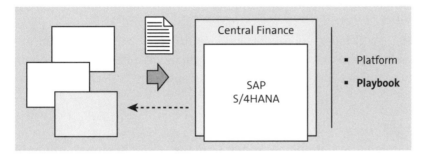

Figure 11.3 Merger Integration Playbook

Where source systems of the same ERP system type (Oracle, PeopleSoft, etc.) are onboarded, existing technical mappings can be reapplied, and with more and more systems onboarded, the probability increases that an entity using the same ERP source system type was already onboarded and previous experience can be leveraged.

With every additional iteration, the plan can be refined and increase in efficiency and effectiveness. With every additional iteration, your workforce will acquire additional, deeper skills, and the overall execution will be reduced in time and increase in quality.

Over time, external consulting support might not be needed anymore and can be executed or even be outsourced with only minimal internal support. Where automation capabilities are introduced, repeatable execution becomes even less time-consuming.

11.2   Mergers and Acquisitions

Traditional M&A systems are typically based on single-use spreadsheets, with each acquisition dealt with separately and highly disconnected within the different phases of an acquisition and between the different functions involved like finance, human resources, supply chain management, legal management, and executive management.

Data points and assumptions are often lost; numbers and values are interpreted without consistency, and proper governance and continuous improvement are substantially hindered. Few formal handoff capabilities may be in place in the corporate strategy, the existing resources may be heavily engaged with competitor monitoring, whitespace analysis, and other M&A activities (Section 11.2.2), and between M&A and post-merger integration activities, handoff mechanisms may be lacking.

M&A processes in traditional systems are neither efficient nor productive. In the following sections, we'll explore in detail how Central Finance is different by describing the use of Central Finance as an M&A platform, its architecture, and its capabilities.

11.2.1 Central Finance as an M&A Platform

Central Finance is an SAP S/4HANA-based platform that serves as a single source of truth for M&A process orchestration and execution, while providing consistent insights throughout the M&A lifecycle.

The same Central Finance system that can be used for central reporting and process execution can also be used to support the M&A process activities in your organization.

Central Finance brings together the following abilities in the M&A space:

- **Innovative technology with advanced capabilities**
  Central Finance is a single, integrated system that brings together a number of disruptive M&A technologies for process orchestration (SAP Shared Services Framework in SAP S/4HANA) and execution (SAP S/4HANA Finance). It also contains technologies for data modeling and data capture (SAP HANA); and visual and predictive reporting (SAP Digital Boardroom, SAP Analytics Cloud) without requiring custom applications or heavy data integration.

- **Finance/data model advancements**
  - Central Finance uses the Universal Journal as the foundation for a common information model when used as M&A platform.
  - Financial and nonfinancial data can be consumed securely by the different business partners across the enterprise based on the same single source of truth, which is used and shared across all lifecycle phases.

- **Internal/ERP data inclusion**
  - Central Finance allows to you to leverage existing ERP data—finance or otherwise—and whether the source system is an SAP or non-SAP ERP system.
  - M&A activities oriented towards creating cost synergies can directly access the company's critical financial information in the SAP and non-SAP ERP systems to be included in a combined evaluation. Where M&A activities are more revenue-adding, future overall revenue streams in the respective market units can be calculated. Of course, in both cases, you can include the anticipated acquisition costs as well.
- **External and manual data ingestion**
  - Central Finance allows the consumption of data from external service providers like S&P for enhanced financial and nonfinancial insight into public and private companies as well as manual data entry.
  - Data entry hubs can be enabled so that external organizations can enter unsolicited submissions directly in a standard format.

11.2.2 Building Blocks

Central Finance supports the M&A process through four major pillars, each of which we'll discuss in the following sections:

- A common information model
- Process orchestration and execution capabilities
- Assemble-able technology stack
- End-to-end M&A lifecycle coverage

Common Information Model

The M&A information model in Central Finance combines aspects of data recording, manipulation, and consumption in a manner consistent across the M&A lifecycle.

This conceptual data model, as shown in Figure 11.4, allows you to work with different data source types like internal data, external data, raw data, processed data, simulations, and plan data in a consistent way.

This model can be enhanced to include custom data dimensions and cover financial as well as nonfinancial (resources, people, locations, assets) perspectives.

Consumption
External
Planning/
Simulation
Actuals
Company / LOB / ...
Data
Type/Source
Time
Reference
Posting
details
Currencies
Values
Quantities
S&P, Bloomberg
Manual entry
File upload
SAP BPC
Excel Upload
Predictive
Manual Entry
SAP ERP and
non-SAP ERP
source systems

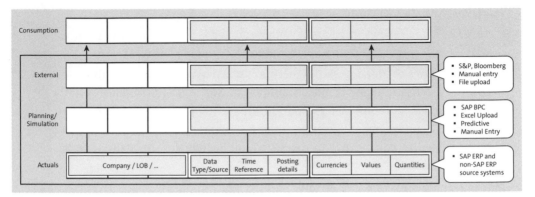

Figure 11.4 Conceptual Data Model

At the core of the conceptual data model is a common coding block, as shown in Figure 11.5, based on the Universal Journal (table ACDOCA).

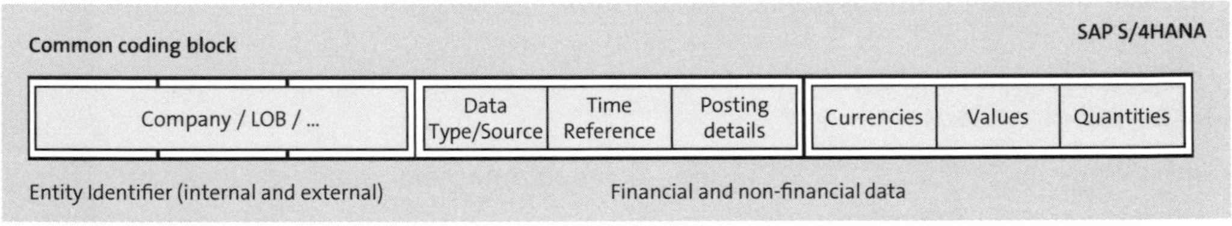

Common coding block
SAP S/4HANA
Company / LOB / ...
Data
Type/Source
Time
Reference
Posting
details
Currencies
Values
Quantities
Entity Identifier (internal and external)
Financial and non-financial data

Figure 11.5 Common Coding Block

Through the entity identification section of the common coding block, internal (including simulated data) and external data can be brought together and connected to each other.

Competitor data can be associated with a region you're already doing business in, or the revenue of a potential acquisition target can be added to your existing organization in certain market segment.

Existing classifications from internal ERP source systems (i.e., company code or profit center) can be applied, and new classifications can be established for external or manually entered data not yet classified.

The common information model is the foundation for consistent process orchestration and execution across all lifecycle phases, as listed in Table 11.1.

	Variance Reporting	Benchmark Evaluation	Forecast Outlook	Oppor-tunity Ideation	Scenarios M&A/ Divestitures	Synergies Post-Merger Integration
ACDOCA: Actuals	Yes	Yes	Yes			Yes
ACDOCP: Plan/ budget	Yes	Yes	Yes	Yes	Yes	Yes
ACDOCP: Forecast			Yes	Yes		
ACDOCEXT: External data		Yes	Yes	Yes	Yes	Yes
ACDOCP: Predictive			Yes			
ACDOCVIR: Virtual delivery	Excep-tions	Compari-sons	Trends	Options	Simulation	Execution

Table 11.1 Common Data Structure across the M&A Lifecycle.

The common information model provides a consistent data structure across the M&A lifecycle phases for data ingestion, processing and calculations, and reporting and analytics.

Process Orchestration and Execution Capabilities

At the core of every M&A activity is a clearly specified set of activities, procedures, deliverables, governance, and decision-making processes, as shown in Figure 11.6.

Organizations that rarely engage in or are engaging for the first time in a special type of M&A activity might adopt the methodology of a strategic advisor; others that engage in M&A processes more frequently might have their own methodologies.

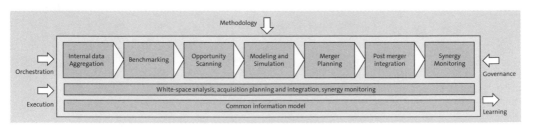

Figure 11.6 Integrated Orchestration, Governance, and Execution

Central Finance can connect to custom-built or commercial process orchestration, frameworks, and applications to exchange financial and nonfinancial information including activity status.

Alternatively, you can set activities and tasks up in the service orchestration layer of Central Finance directly, including guided procedures, process checklists, workflows, access rights and status management, and exception and compliance management.

Execution-related activities like reporting, analysis, planning, modeling, simulation, etc. can take place in Central Finance.

SAP Digital Boardroom as part of Central Finance allows for executive review of status, compliance, and financial and nonfinancial statistics and models as part of the process for ongoing M&A governance.

Assemble-able Technology Stack

Central Finance provides the technological foundation to support the M&A process throughout its lifecycle, as shown in Figure 11.7, without the need for extensive application integration or custom integration.

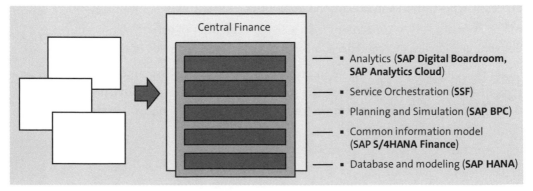

Figure 11.7 Central Finance as an Assemble-able M&A Hub

Data ingestion, processing capabilities, and reporting and analytics are all available in a single system via standard functions and features.

Moving between the different M&A phases and different processes is replication free because these phases and processes are always based on the common information model, and data is stored in the same SAP HANA database.

Post-merger integration can be realized in the same Central Finance system that is used to enable the M&A process before and during the deal.

Simulated/target data during the M&A process can become the plan and budget data for Day 1 and post-merger reporting and synergy tracking.

Entities acquired can continue to feed, on an aggregated level, into the model for statutory reporting. Over time, moving replication of actuals into Central Finance will not only allow for reporting in general but also enables central process execution and microsegment reporting.

End-to-End M&A Lifecycle Coverage

Central Finance provides a common information model and process orchestration and execution capabilities across the entire M&A lifecycle. Central Finance supports:

- Competitor analysis, by comparing financial and nonfinancial data with that of other competitors
- Whitespace analysis, by comparing financial and nonfinancial competencies and capabilities in the context of market and market growth information
- Acquisition planning, by modeling and simulating the addition of another entity into the organization, including merger cost and synergy modeling
- Deal execution, by tracking, monitoring, and safeguarding financial and nonfinancial information from scenario analysis, deal valuation, financial and risk analysis, due diligence, etc.)
- Post-merger integration, by enabling Day 1 and ongoing combined financial reporting
- Synergy tracking, by enabling actual costs to be tracked against original plans and budgets

Central Finance, across the entire lifecycle, uses the same, single database so that whatever information is used once, can be shared—across all phases, tasks, and individuals, without data transformations required in between.

11.2.3 Capabilities

With Central Finance as M&A hub, you'll get a solution that is:

- **Unified**
  A single platform for M&A shared by all business partners across the enterprise and across all lifecycle phases.

- **Flexible**
  Scalable solution that allows you to add additional data processing, calculation, and frontend consumption capabilities from the remaining SAP product portfolio as needed

- **Immediate**
  A nondisruptive adoption approach and ability to use internal or external, SAP or non-SAP ERP data that can accommodate your M&A methodology

Central Finance will increase confidence in the targeted outcomes with its enterprise-grade models, its use of internal and external real-time financial data, its end-to-end integration, and its scalability and reusability—all while being secure the whole time.

Central Finance prevents the pursuit of incorrect targets, unrealistic synergy expectations and integration cost, and poor handoffs during M&A The following contains details on the aspects of governance, synergies, cost reduction, and personnel retention:

- **Governance**
  Companies can screen for potential acquisition candidates based on preestablished risk profiles while also monitoring target company alerts and social media feeds, as shown in Figure 11.8.

- **Synergies**
  You can visualize additional synergy opportunities through rationalizing manufacturing, sales, distribution, and headcounts across any combination of entities, as shown in Figure 11.9.

- **Cost reduction tracker**
  You can use dashboards with drilldown, simulation, and prediction capabilities to provide visibility and accountability, as shown in Figure 11.10.

- **Personnel retention**
  In the acquisition integration phase, you can evaluate the time, costs, and resources required to successfully integrate into the new company structure, as shown in Figure 11.11.

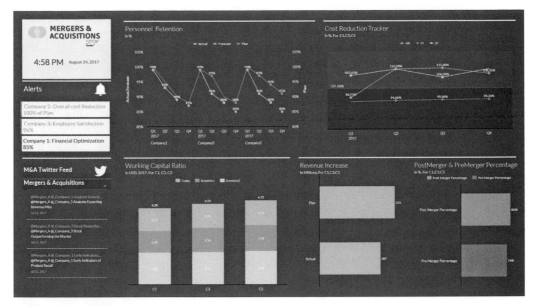

Figure 11.8 M&A Dashboard

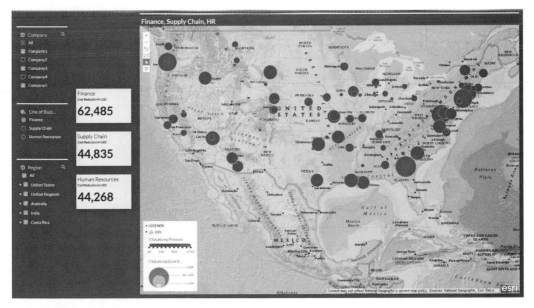

Figure 11.9 Synergy Tracking

11

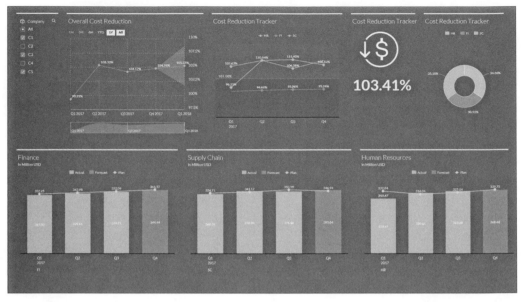

Figure 11.10 Cost Reduction Tracker

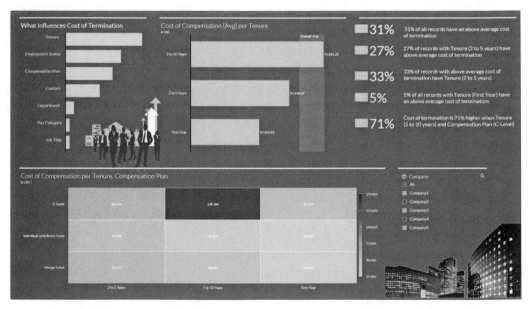

Figure 11.11 Personnel Retention

11.3 Post-Merger Integration

The vast majority of organizations today have multi-ERP system landscapes, largely as a result of previous, possibly incomplete M&A activities. Reasons vary, but generally, the high-pressure focus on integrating assets and people first and the technology limitations of legacy system technology can make the process of system integration difficult.

Integrating systems and processes is an important aspect of realizing target synergies, but these tasks often take place under time pressure and in parallel to running your business.

A quick realization of the benefits, paramount for maximizing the financial impact, however, is often adversely affected by skill, resource, and capability constraints. Compromises may be made to the speed, scope, and systems in question, often with decreasing focus and scrutiny on the post-merger integration phase and its execution over time.

The result is unaddressed system and process integration, resulting in and a higher complexity and total cost of ownership (TCO), on both the IT side as well as business side, as well as in suboptimal process execution.

With Central Finance, as shown in Figure 11.12, you can bring in and integrate inherited systems (complete post-merger integration) from a reporting and process execution perspective.

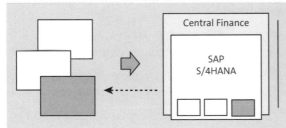

Figure 11.12 Central Finance as a Post-Merger Integration Platform

Note

For information about why you should choose Central Finance for your M&A activities, see Chapter 3.

When tackling post-merger integration from a process execution perspective, several business objectives can be supported. The following sections expand on centralization and shared services, the expansion of finance capabilities, and finance transformation aspects that can be addressed with Central Finance.

11.3.1   Process Execution Considerations

With post-merger integration, some of the most important considerations that you'll need to take into account include the following:

- **Centralization**
  Using Central Finance for post-merger integration allows you to execute reporting and finance transactions centrally from within the Central Finance system with replication of the source finance transactions from the SAP and non-SAP ERP source systems into Central Finance.

  Centralization allows you to apply economies of scale from an organizational setup perspective, eventually leading to the execution of processes via shared services or by adding new processes to an existing shared services center and introducing specialization to improve the overall service level and quality.

- **Capability transformation**
  Using Central Finance for post-merger integration allows you to extend native embedded process execution capabilities and digitally connected capabilities like central indirect procurement (via SAP Ariba) or travel expense management (via SAP Concur) to be extended to new entities.

  Capability transformation is enabled, and extended to the SAP and non-SAP ERP source systems, without any changes to those underlying systems.

- **Finance transformation**
  Using Central Finance for post-merger integration allows you to transform reporting and finance transactions to automated, exception-only, or zero-touch processes in the Central Finance system.

  Transformation is enabled by the many SAP S/4HANA-based technology innovations not otherwise available in traditional central legacy systems for finance.

11.3.2   Platform Considerations

Using Central Finance for post-merger integration allows you to consolidate transaction processing, reporting, planning, and consolidation capabilities into a single

Central Finance system. As such, you can also dramatically reduce the number of inbound and outbound interfaces connected to your remaining legacy systems.

Another possible result is that ERP systems can be decommissioned at large, and their logistics and finance processes can be brought into the SAP S/4HANA-based Central Finance system.

Consolidation is possible due to the embedded transaction processing, reporting, planning, and consolidation capabilities within SAP S/4HANA-based Central Finance and the fact that Central Finance—while often only initially used for finance—is a complete SAP S/4HANA system capable of running logistics as well.

Using Central Finance for post-merger integration also allows you to transform reporting and finance transactions, making them automated, exception-only, or zero-touch processes in the Central Finance system.

This transformation is enabled by the many SAP S/4HANA-based innovations not otherwise available in traditional central legacy systems for finance.

11.3.3   System Continuity

Central Finance allows you to integrate existing systems and processes into a common, central platform for finance. Initial requirements regarding consolidated reporting can be accommodated quickly, without changes to the ERP source systems and without disruptions to the business operations running on them.

As a result, you can keep existing systems and process in place, even if only initially, which reduces risk and complexity in post-merger integration. Smaller teams can focus on critical items due at specific times as part of M&A and post-merger integration, without the additional burden of parallel, secondary optimization tasks like process design or system and application consolidation.

Replacing and/or moving these systems later is possible, and you can use onboarding application capabilities like planning, reporting, or consolidation; introduce transformation initiatives like central indirect procurement or real estate management; or onboard entire (SAP or non-SAP ERP) source systems.

11.3.4   Interim versus End State

Post-merger integration is not a sprint—it's a marathon. Many organizations focus on the initial integration of assets and people and the provision of initial consolidated reporting, internal management, and external financial reporting. Post-merger integration can take years and may never be complete, most often due to lacking attention from management or a scarcity of resources being available due other internal projects.

Central Finance can bring together financial information from existing and new entities while supporting additional system and process integration and consolidation later. In the following sections, we'll look at the interim state of post-merger integration before moving on to discuss the end state.

Interim State

The interim state with Central Finance starts before Day 1 in organizations that already have a Central Finance system in place. If not, the interim state begins once a Central Finance system is put in place.

Often, organizations will introduce a Central Finance system within months to support them in the M&A/post-merger integration process. Central Finance supports pre-Day 1 activities, Day 1 activities, and post Day-1 activities, as follows:

- **Pre-Day 1 activities**
  Once the intent to acquire is communicated, data integration—its setup and replication—can be worked on by the relevant parties, as shown in Figure 11.13. These activities have no limitation besides the exchange of real values and numbers; integration can be technically set up, tested, and validated even before Day 1.

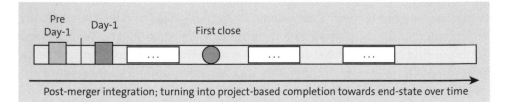

Figure 11.13 Post-Merger Integration (before, on, and after Day 1)

- **Day 1 activities**
  On Day 1, the setup can be completed, real master data can be loaded, historical data can be brought in, and real-time replication can be enabled.

  Unlike in traditional central systems for finance, with Central Finance, you'll be able to look at your consolidated numbers right after Day 1 and not only at Day 90/during the first close. With continuous insight during the first combined quarter, there will be no surprises about the numbers.

- **Post-Day 1 activities**

  The integration can be continued, with process execution added or business and finance transformation activities added to the initial cutover. How much can be done before the first close and how much/what will be enabled after first close is entirely up your organization to determine.

  Scope and business areas to be included are entirely selectable based on the business priorities, pain points, and resource availability (internal skills, experience, and capacity). Where corresponding finance processes are already in place and actively used, adding another entity typically does not result in major additional work.

End State

With Central Finance, the technical and functional foundation for post-merger integration completion and enterprise optimization can be put in place at the start of the post-merger integration activity. For organizations already running Central Finance, this foundation is already in place even before M&A activities happen.

With post-merger integration pressure, management focus, and attention diminishing over time, integration activities move from highly visible post-merger integration programs to just normal IT/finance projects. Projects can be executed in an agile manner, by smaller teams, iteratively by adding business and scope over time towards the envisioned end state, as shown in Figure 11.14. Central Finance does not require a big bang approach, so project teams can be smaller and value can be added before the entire project is brought live.

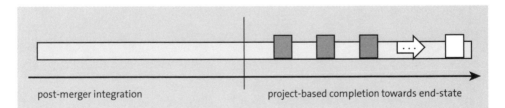

Figure 11.14 Project-Based Completion towards the End State

Innovations and improved capabilities are added to Central Finance on an ongoing basis, and every improvement can be leveraged for all entities already onboarded, as well as any new entities to be onboarded, in the same central system.

11.4   Summary

In this chapter, we provided information about merger and integration scenarios. We covered how Central Finance can be a playbook and platform for M&A, how Central Finance can help with both the M&A process itself as well as with post-merger integration activities where system and process integration from previous M&A activities has not been completed.

The next chapter will provide information about Central Finance as a stepping stone to SAP S/4HANA.

Chapter 12

Central Finance as a Stepping Stone to SAP S/4HANA

Central Finance is part of the SAP S/4HANA application and platform. The capabilities of SAP S/4HANA for logistics could also be available under certain scenarios that an organization may pursue as part of a simplification agenda for infrastructure and logistics processes harmonization across the enterprise.

Many roads lead to the same destination. The roads may be well trod, but the destination not be not known or clearly determined. One of these destinations is moving to a full instance of SAP S/4HANA with Central Finance acting as the foundational technology for this transformation. Using Central Finance as an onboarding platform for SAP and non-SAP ERP source systems is commonly referred to as using Central Finance as a stepping stone to SAP S/4HANA.

In this chapter, we'll discuss the options available to your organization for using Central Finance as a basis for moving to SAP S/4HANA with less disruption and risk. We'll also outline the available options, the current circumstances, and some recommendations based on the current technology.

Moving to SAP S/4HANA is all about balancing risk and transformation between the different options that may be available. Your starting position may be an older version of SAP software like SAP ERP 6.0, or your organization may not currently run an SAP instance. Regardless of your starting point, you'll find yourself facing a transformational agenda. This transformation should be the core of decision-making when adopting SAP S/4HANA. Figure 12.1 shows the possible options that balance the two principles, when the starting point is a legacy ERP platform (SAP ERP 6.0).

To move from SAP ERP 6.0 to SAP S/4HANA, only three options are possible: The first option would be to upgrade using the classic database and application migration process. The second option would be to start from scratch with a greenfield implementation. A third, new option is to use Central Finance as a brownfield or greenfield implementation to serve as a stepping stone to full SAP S/4HANA. Central Finance can leverage the configuration and data of legacy systems, both SAP and non-SAP, under a brownfield scenario, or you can use Central Finance as a greenfield implementation for configuration but as a brownfield implementation for master data and transactional data.

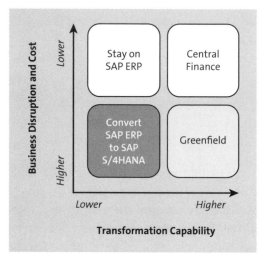

Figure 12.1 Options Matrix for Risk and Transformation

When starting your Central Finance journey, you'll need to consider a few options: First, charting your journey (Section 12.1) includes consideration of the initial steps—the what, how, when, and in which order questions—and an evaluation of potential future uses and build-outs beyond the use of Central Finance. The second step involves the planning of the transformation (Section 12.2) away from brownfield implementations and towards greenfield implementations and the potential use of SAP's cloud-based offerings. The final step in this chapter will be the planning of the journey itself (Section 12.3).

12.1   Charting Your Journey

Overall, the best way to bring existing SAP ERP source systems onto SAP S/4HANA with the lowest costs and the least effort is via a standard migration, shown in Figure 12.2.

Numerous accelerators exist for this technical migration approach, as well as a complete methodology to support the migration, and this method has been applied successfully many times.

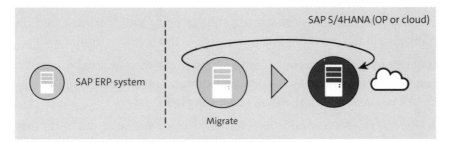

Figure 12.2 Standard Technical Migration Option

The migration of individual source ERP systems—although not suitable for central reporting and processing requirements—is important because, even with the use of Central Finance, your source systems will eventually have to be brought onto SAP S/4HANA. Individual migrations do not provide for central reporting and process execution capabilities in multi-ERP system landscapes, and thus, we won't elaborate on this topic further in this chapter.

For the eventual move to SAP S/4HANA, Central Finance can be a first step because, in the process, you'll implement a central SAP S/4HANA system for use as central system for finance (Section 12.1.1), followed (optionally) with the subsequent onboarding of additional functionalities onto this central SAP S/4HANA instance (Section 12.1.2).

12.1.1   First Step: Central Finance

A majority of Central Finance customers chose Central Finance as a stepping stone to SAP S/4HANA. Why would you use Central Finance in this way?

For some, in the initial investment rationale, as discussed in Chapter 3, Central Finance does not have to be evaluated as a stepping stone to SAP S/4HANA because the initial investment decisions for Central Finance by itself should be a positive ROI to begin with. For others, using Central Finance as a stepping stone is a logical conclusion: With investments in the SAP S/4HANA infrastructure and technology that Central Finance requires, subsequently leveraging these resources for the eventual full adoption of SAP S/4HANA and ERP system consolidation makes sense.

Central Finance helps a company get exposure to SAP S/4HANA and with it experience, knowledge, and some comfort with the new SAP S/4HANA technologies (SAP HANA, SAP Fiori, SAP Predictive Analytics, etc.) before existing SAP and non-SAP ERP source systems are moved onto SAP S/4HANA. Without any changes to the source systems, Central Finance can implemented, thus bringing SAP S/4HANA into the organization quickly and providing business value for finance right from the start.

Onboarding ERP source systems onto Central Finance can then be also be a smaller task than starting from scratch as the infrastructure and major technology components, like SAP HANA or SAP Fiori, will already be in place.

In cases where ERP system consolidation is targeted, Central Finance can be the platform onto which existing SAP and non-SAP ERP source systems are onboarded. You could choose to onboard all or just some of your existing source ERP systems.

With Central Finance in use as a system and for select company codes for finance processes, preexisting setup, master data, and transactional data needs to be considered when building out your onboarding project plan for the additional entities and logistics and for remaining finance functionalities to be moved.

With the introduction of Central Finance, you're automatically bringing SAP S/4HANA into your system landscape as Central Finance requires SAP S/4HANA as its foundation. The more capabilities are added, the larger the SAP S/4HANA footprint and SAP S/4HANA usage in your organization over time. Central Finance as a platform can be a key catalyst for full SAP S/4HANA adoption. In the following sections, we'll look at choosing Central Finance as a stepping stone to SAP S/4HANA from two perspectives: how it affects your organization's investment and how you can approach your journey.

Investment

Separating a general decision for Central Finance from the investment request itself is important. When putting forward the investment proposal, your focus should be on goals to achieve in the initial phase(s) of the rollout and the associated business benefits.

An assessment of long-term fit, including potentially the subsequent adoption of more SAP S/4HANA capabilities to use as stepping stones to SAP S/4HANA is very important. You'll validate whether the fundamental technical and process coverage of the solution is in line with the company's direction and objectives, but the initial investment decision does not have to cover the entire Central Finance journey.

When looking at an incremental investment later, keep in mind that Central Finance as a platform already supplies many of the technical components required to bring in additional capabilities later. You might have to increase the size of the database, even less of an issue in a cloud-based, highly scalable deployment option, but you won't need separate, additional infrastructure required as when deploying additional traditional applications or processes.

The investment in Central Finance can be leveraged again and again with only additional, marginal build-outs required to Central Finance, substantially reducing additional investment required, making subsequent SAP S/4HANA adoption effectively much cheaper.

Approach

After initial deployment, you can use SAP S/4HANA-based Central Finance subsequently as platform to onboard ERP and non-SAP ERP systems.

Existing logistics and (remaining) finance capabilities in ERP and non-SAP ERP source systems can be relocated onto the Central Finance instance, as shown in Figure 12.3. Data replication to move financial transactions from ERP sources to the Central Finance system is no longer required, and these ERP source systems can be decommissioned.

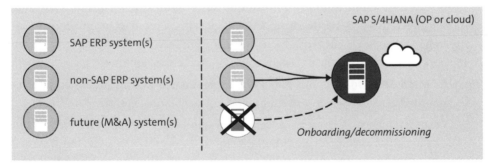

Figure 12.3 Central Finance as a Stepping Stone to SAP S/4HANA

Central Finance can be the onboarding platform for SAP ERP source systems (greenfield to greenfield or brownfield to greenfield migrations or even reimplementations) as much as for non-SAP ERP source systems—with the latter requiring reimplementations, of course.

Using Central Finance as an onboarding platform is possible since it is based on a standard SAP S/4HANA system. An SAP S/4HANA-based Central Finance system, built for finance, has the same functional capabilities, including logistics, as any other regular SAP S/4HANA system.

12.1.2   End State

Important in the context of using Central Finance as a stepping stone to SAP S/4HANA is also what happens (or could happen) in the end state. Various scenarios exist, with the most likely being that Central Finance will be a key component of the future/target landscape for most SAP customers. The scenarios are as follows:

- A central system for Finance:
  - SAP and non-SAP ERP source systems remain in place, eventually upgraded to SAP S/4HANA from SAP ERP or reimplemented as SAP S/4HANA, on-premise or cloud, in Central Finance.
  - In the multi-ERP system landscape, the ERP source systems continue to feed (replicate) financial data into Central Finance.
  - Central Finance is used as a central system for finance—with or without expected use as transformation platform.
- A central system for finance and as a stepping stone to SAP S/4HANA for the organization:
  - Selected SAP and non-SAP ERP source systems remain in place, eventually upgraded to SAP S/4HANA from SAP ERP or reimplemented, as on-premise SAP S/4HANA or SAP S/4HANA Cloud, in Central Finance. These source systems will continue to feed (replicate) financial data into Central Finance.
  - Selected SAP and non-SAP ERP source systems are decommissioned and onboarded onto the SAP S/4HANA-based Central Finance platform.
  - Central Finance is used as a central system for finance—with or without expected use as transformation platform.
  - Central Finance is also used for logistics processing for the onboarded systems and entities.
- Single-system stepping stone scenario:
  - Central Finance is used as a central system for finance—for and during the transition of a single-instance ERP system onto SAP S/4HANA.
  - With the decommissioning of the source system and onboarding onto the SAP S/4HANA-based Central Finance instance, replication is no longer required.

- Source systems consolidated in the Central Finance instance:
  - Central Finance is used as a central system for finance for and during the transition from a multi-ERP system landscape onto a single-instance ERP system onto SAP S/4HANA.
  - With the decommissioning of the ERP source systems and onboarding onto the SAP S/4HANA-based Central Finance instance, replication is no longer required.

Even if you plan to decommission source systems after onboarding, the value of Central Finance is available for potential future mergers and acquisitions (M&A) onboarding scenarios.

Otherwise, Central Finance can serve as a transition tool that, while in use, accelerates and realizes business value otherwise not possible without SAP S/4HANA in the existing system landscape.

12.2   Choosing Your Route

Using Central Finance as a stepping stone does not mandate the number of SAP or non-SAP ERP source systems are onboarded. Two options, as follows, are available:

- **Single instance**
  Sometimes, Central Finance is used to move a single-instance SAP or non-SAP ERP system onto SAP S/4HANA. While possible, this scenario is an exception than a norm—predominantly driven by decision criteria like risk averseness, lack of internal capability, or capacity to support an all-in large migration and transformation program or short-term organizational readiness to do so.

- **Multiple instances**
  Often, Central Finance is used to bring more than one ERP source system onto Central Finance, SAP or non-SAP. In this case, all ERP source systems can be brought in to arrive at a single SAP S/4HANA instance. Alternatively, you can bring in a select number of systems to consolidate and significantly reduce the overall number of ERP systems in your organization.

In the following sections, we'll look at two considerations for choosing your path to SAP S/4HANA: the choice between brownfield and greenfield implementations and an explanation of the SAP S/4HANA Cloud code line.

> **Note: Centralization**
>
> Central Finance as a stepping stone to SAP S/4HANA is not comparable to a technical migration as an alternative. Technical migrations are 1:1 efforts that do not address ERP system consolidation natively without modification and that change the nature of the migration to a larger business transformation program. Also, unlike in solely technical migrations, the Central Finance stepping stone scenario is also typically oriented towards greenfield implementations and not (preserving) brownfield implementation scenarios.
>
> These aspects are important to keep in mind—of course, SAP S/4HANA migrations can get you on the technical SAP S/4HANA platform, but your business may still need to be transformed and consolidated. Each option has its place and benefits, especially where migrations of unconsolidated ERP source systems are still required, but they are not the same.

12.2.1   Brownfield versus Greenfield

Central Finance deployments, in all but a few cases, are performed as a greenfield scenario but with brownfield reusability in mind. Often, the underlying issues of outdated and unaligned business models between different parts of the organizations are key reasons to deploy Central Finance to begin with.

If ERP source systems are in such a brownfield state (with old settings and overcustomizing), implementing Central Finance can be a greenfield project, without great need to change the source systems.

If ERP systems are new or have been changed to a greenfield state, new settings can be realized in Central Finance without further change.

For non-SAP ERP source systems, of course, a greenfield implementation is more of a reimplementation, but only for finance, and this approach is most likely based on the common Central Finance design and not a one-off additional reimplementation.

12.2.2   SAP S/4HANA Cloud Code Line

In the context of Central Finance as a stepping stone to SAP S/4HANA, keep in mind that Central Finance is—unlike your SAP or non-SAP ERP legacy systems—already based on the SAP S/4HANA Cloud code line. This fact holds true whether Central Finance runs as an on-premise system or on a private or hosted cloud.

SAP S/4HANA is based on the cloud-first principle, which means that new improvements and innovations are developed as part of the central SAP S/4HANA Cloud code line.

With SAP S/4HANA-based Central Finance, you've basically made that move from legacy system code line to the SAP S/4HANA Cloud code line. Planning a future reimplementation is not necessary, since the necessary code line has been inherited.

For some organizations, an important reason to invest in Central Finance is that it facilitates and accelerates future moves, for example, to a public cloud, when necessary.

Typically, the move is nondisruptive because the phasing of the move is based on the needs of the organization and the easier flow of budget resources when compared to a big bang approach in a classical migration or greenfield implementation. This approach is also lower risk because the baseline for a finance transformation is already in place with complete balance and transactional detail. Integrating logistics with finance is easier to manage and more in line with your organization's priorities. The move to full logistics can be performed in a two-phase approach, the most common approach due to its minimization of risk and disruption, or in one phase, depending on your organization's roadmap for deployment, the number of instances, and geographical presence.

Moving to full SAP S/4HANA represents two basic yet important and distinct end states. One meaning could be using full SAP S/4HANA on an instance where Central Finance is already active for a given company code(s). The second meaning could be using Central Finance as a low-risk and low-disruption tool to move to full SAP S/4HANA. This distinction is important architecturally.

Beyond the end state scenarios for Central Finance, some practicalities of moving the Central Finance instance to a full SAP S/4HANA instance should be considered. These practicalities are based on what is probably the single most important architectural decision: whether your organization wants to move to a single global instance or follow a multi-instance concept with or without a hybrid architecture. Under each scenario, the transition to a full SAP S/4HANA instance could be considered as a valid outcome for the organization.

12.3   Planning the Process

The question of adopting full SAP S/4HANA, with finance and logistics activated and used, comes up regularly in any thought process logically linked to architecture. In addition, the most common follow-up question is: How do you actually plan and execute this vision? The simplest way to answer this question is shown in Figure 12.4, an overview for any type of source system. The basic idea is to allow an organization to move in two phases. The first phase makes Central Finance fully live and working. The second phase would be to bring in logistics processes. The configuration of financials in SAP S/4HANA for Central Finance in the first phase would be leveraged when moving logistics into the same instance, as long as the relevant design thinking has been incorporated in the first phase.

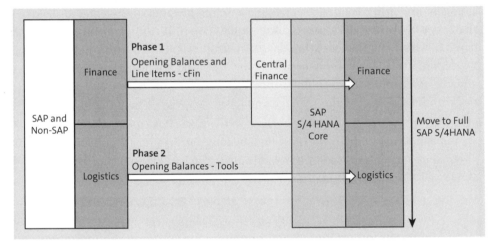

Figure 12.4 Overview of Moving to Full SAP S/4HANA with Central Finance

Before we talk about execution, let's consider what we mean by "moving to full SAP S/4HANA." This move requires careful thought about the target architecture, and the objectives of your organization will need to be incorporated into the planning for the move, as will the desired end state and the current setup of your existing landscape. We'll discuss each of these dimensions in the following sections.

12.3.1   Transition Planning

To move to full SAP S/4HANA, the transition needs to be scoped and planned as either a big bang implementation or in a phased approach. The big bang scope would include all logistics processes and their integration with finance and other logistics areas. Transition planning would depend on two core scenarios. Figure 12.5 shows three core scenarios in which Central Finance could be deployed and the movement from one core state to the next. An organization could move from a decisional scenario to an operational scenario and then to full SAP S/4HANA in a movement, shown in Figure 12.5 from left to right. In other words, you cannot move from full SAP S/4HANA to operational Central Finance as the full SAP S/4HANA scenario implies decisional and operational features.

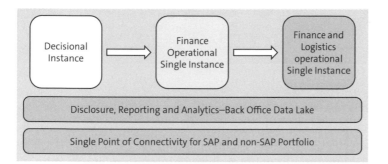

Figure 12.5 Core Scenarios for Central Finance as a Stepping Stone to Full SAP S/4HANA

You'll be either on the decisional phase of the project or on the operational phase for Central Finance, depending on the project plan and the end state architecture. Each offers a different scenario to implement full SAP S/4HANA.

First, moving Central Finance from a decisional (also called *reporting*) scenario to a transactional system for finance at a minimum. The Central Finance instance would become the system of record and potentially the system of record for final disclosure. Second, moving the logistics areas into the Central Finance instance should not be done independently of the first step, operational Central Finance, as you would miss the integration between finance and logistics. Therefore, doing the one of the following would make sense:

- **Move to full logistics in one step with operational Central Finance**
  Figure 12.6 shows one potential way to convert from a reporting scenario to an operational scenario prior to moving fully to SAP S/4HANA logistics. Financial operations would encompass receivables, payables, cash operations, payments, collections, disputes, and credit management. These operations need to be considered as part of the scope based on the current usage in the source systems and expected future usage of the SAP S/4HANA instance with logistics processes, such as order fulfillment.

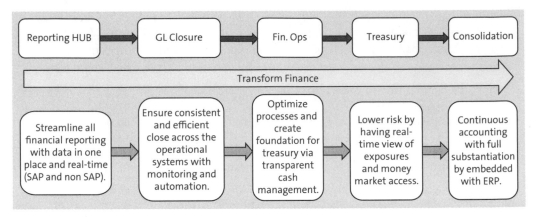

Figure 12.6 Moving to Operational Central Finance First

- **Move to full logistics in a two-step approach with operational finance as the first step**

  Figure 12.7 shows a method that you could use to move, not migrate, processes for logistics and integrate them with Central Finance. The exact sequence will depend on customer priorities and current processes in the source system along with whether the source systems, and their legacy applications, are SAP or not.

  For SAP-to-SAP moves, planning will be based on known configuration and potential changes. For non-SAP to SAP, you'll need to create a mapping of non-SAP objects to SAP objects and to carry out configuration changes. Planning will need to consider the current processes already managed in Central Finance that integrate with source systems logistics processes, for example, receivables management in Central Finance with order fulfillment in the source systems.

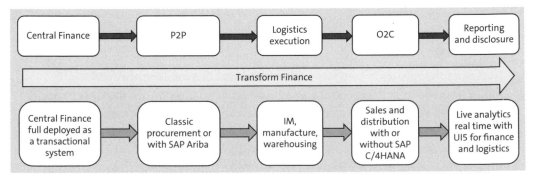

Figure 12.7 Moving to Full Logistics from Operational Central Finance

Whether you use a single step or follow a two-step approach depends on your own unique circumstances. In either approach, finance modules must be made operational. Whether you have chosen to phase in the logistics later rather than follow a big bang approach, the planning of the project must consider the following:

- Company codes must be linked to logistics processes.
- Master data must be shared between finance and logistics.
- Transactional data must be shared between finance and logistics.
- Development objects for logistics processes in scope for the phase must be moved without activation and then changed for table and working area references at a minimum.
- The cumulative and noncumulative impact of transactions for different processes must be determined.
- The move to new asset accounting for SAP S/4HANA, including any ledger integration for different local reporting requirements, must be considered.

Note: Lift and Shift Tools

Central Finance does not provide lift and shift tools to move to full SAP S/4HANA per se because this move is supported by carrying out a classical cutover with existing tools for SAP ERP 6.0 and SAP S/4HANA.

Figure 12.6 and Figure 12.7 show a customer that has gone through this process. The exact sequence to move to SAP S/4HANA will depend on the three factors: First, the industry sector of the customer will determine the nature and scale of processes that can be moved together or independently. Second, the integration between logistics modules that rely on data feeds from each other will influence the sequence, for example, availability control in order fulfillment with inventory management. Third, how much of the move is a brownfield vs. a greenfield implementation. The more a brownfield approach can be reused from source systems, the quicker the move to SAP S/4HANA logistics. Brownfield implementations include the ability to introduce new nomenclature and the ability to standardize processes to align with the SAP S/4HANA standard.

The salient points of planning the move to full SAP S/4HANA from Central Finance have been covered. Now, let's consider the potential patterns that can be used adopting SAP S/4HANA using Central Finance.

12.3.2   Adoption Patterns

At the most basic level, to say you'll "adopt SAP S/4HANA fully" means using logistics in the Central Finance instance alongside finance processes. Three possible outcomes exist:

- Central Finance will become the end state.
- Central Finance will be used as an interim state until logistics is activated in the same instance.
- Some business units will use Central Finance as the end state, and others will use it for logistics.

These three core patterns are shown in Figure 12.8.

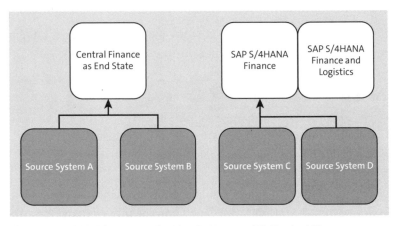

Figure 12.8 SAP S/4HANA Adoption Patterns with Central Finance

With Central Finance as the end state, the organization expects to retain at least one source system active for business reasons. Usually, multiple systems replicate data to Central Finance. Under this pattern, your organization may not want to deploy a single global instance of SAP S/4HANA or may intend to deploy both SAP and non-SAP systems that impact financial processes.

The hybrid scenario entails using a full SAP S/4HANA system for some company codes and Central Finance for others as a permanent feature of the system and process landscape. This pattern provides the flexibility to use the power of SAP S/4HANA for logistics as well as finance within the same instance while allowing the chief financial officer (CFO) to create a single instance of finance regardless of the origin of the logistics processes.

The full SAP S/4HANA scenario is the same as the hybrid scenario, but no source systems are linked to the finance processes of SAP S/4HANA using Central Finance. While this pattern is acceptable for some organizations, for others, mergers and acquisitions make this situation unwieldy. In this case, the full SAP S/4HANA system would remain active for Central Finance and is used only when a merger or an acquisition needs to be integrated into finance.

This end state is a very valid state for many organizations due to the size, the complexity, the use of multiple technologies, and other challenges to transitioning to a single instance. For others, the pursuit of a global single instance brings advantages with associated risks. Regardless of the choice made, moving to SAP S/4HANA is certain. This move can be from a single ERP instance of SAP or multiple ERPs.

12.3.3   Moving a Single ERP to SAP S/4HANA Using Central Finance

The traditional approach for moving to SAP S/4HANA from a single SAP ERP 6.0 system would be to carry out a classical migration. In this case, you need at least two phases to move the infrastructure to SAP S/4HANA, as shown in Figure 12.9: carrying out a database migration from a legacy database to an SAP HANA database and migrating applications and processes. The optimize phase is often given too little emphasis or becomes part of a post go-live activity.

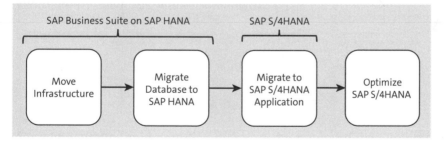

Figure 12.9 Classical Migration to SAP S/4HANA

Classical migration, while an option, has some drawbacks that either can't be fixed or require additional projects. For example, in a classical migration, if your organization requires changes to a currency, a chart of account, etc., you may require additional projects. Or, if your organization is using the classic general ledger (G/L), then a migration project to the SAP General Ledger (SAP G/L) should be performed as well. Now this classical migration project is no longer just a classical migration but has become multiple projects.

Under these circumstances, one option would be to move (not migrate) into SAP S/4HANA using Central Finance. In this way, your organization could change and standardize its financial and logistics processes in a two-step approach. The first step is to use Central Finance in SAP S/4HANA and logistics in SAP ERP 6.0. This change will accelerate finance to a fully transformed process in SAP S/4HANA (SAP G/L, changes to charts of accounts, etc.). The second step would be to move logistics into the same instance using a standard cutover, but in a brownfield scenario because finance is already live.

The full adoption of SAP S/4HANA using Central Finance would still require the same infrastructure as a classic migration, but the optimization phase for finance would occur during the project phase, and then logistics would be the second step, as shown in Figure 12.10. In addition, you could change design of the SAP S/4HANA system for both finance and logistics because a complete separation of the build in terms of configuration and transactions exists. Data loads can be validated with the new designs before go-live in a preproduction tier to prove out the new changes.

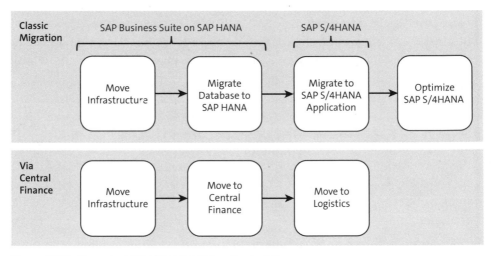

Figure 12.10 Move to SAP S/4HANA Using Central Finance

The basic distinctions between pursuing a classical migration or using Central Finance a stepping stone to SAP S/4HANA revolve around risk, disruption, and the ability for transformations during the move to SAP S/4HANA. In a nutshell, Central Finance could offer an alternative to classical migration where transformation of finance and logistics is just as important as other factors.

12.3.4 Moving Multiple ERP Systems to SAP S/4HANA Using Central Finance

Using Central Finance is a growing trend in the industry for adopting SAP S/4HANA to consolidate instances or to move to a single instance. Therefore, you should follow a clear and articulate pattern for the adoption of full SAP S/4HANA via Central Finance. First, you may have the simple strategic goal of moving to a single instance of SAP S/4HANA. Second, you may have the goal of simply creating a hybrid architecture of a single global instance for finance only while reducing the number of your ERP instances. Figure 12.11 shows the move from three source systems to a full SAP S/4HANA system.

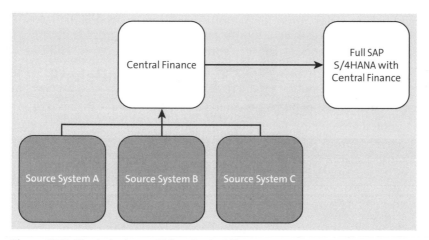

Figure 12.11 Single Instance Using Central Finance

The move to a single instance assumes the deactivation of the source systems without a need to carry out a classical migration. The source system simply becomes an archive or a read-only system subject to business and legal retention management processes. The source systems, if SAP systems, can remain connected for finance purposes as well as to provide a real-time drilldown capabilities into a read-only environment. As a result, you'll benefit from faster data provisioning without additional IT processes for keeping source systems connected.

If your organization doesn't want to adopt a single global instance, source systems could also be consolidated using the approach using the single ERP approach to SAP S/4HANA using Central Finance we described in Section 12.3.3. For example, let's say you have ten SAP ERP 6.0 source systems all are currently connected to Central Finance for a single instance of finance. Of the ten systems, four belong to strategic division A, and three each belong to strategic divisions B and C. One approach could be to move the first four systems in division A, as shown in Figure 12.11. Once this move is complete, the six remaining systems could be consolidated into two instances using the single ERP approach of moving to SAP S/4HANA using Central Finance. This step will reduce the number of instances from ten to three in the end state while allowing transformation, lessening disruption, and improving business flexibility on systems independently of the goal of a global instance for the CFO.

12.4   Summary

The move to a full SAP S/4HANA using Central Finance effectively means the system of record will move to the Central Finance instance in the first step. If full end-to-end finance processes also reside in the Central Finance instance, including group reporting (the forthcoming consolidation product), Central Finance may also become the book of record as well. Logistics processes could be used in the same instance of SAP S/4HANA as Central Finance by using normal tooling and cutover as a standard greenfield implementation. The timing difference between operationalizing Central Finance and full SAP S/4HANA would be determined as part of the project.

In the following chapter, we'll look at Central Finance as a trigger for a broader finance transformation for an organization.

Chapter 13
Finance Transformation

Central Finance projects generate a significant need for the transformation of processes, organizational structures, and responsibilities and can influence longer-term corporate objectives. A finance transformation requires the same amount of attention as when evaluating any other technical or functional solution.

Central Finance is a key enabler to transform the finance department and achieve the chief financial officer's (CFO) ideal vision of modern, innovative, efficient, and impactful corporate functions. Different aspects of transformation become critical for each Central Finance project, starting from the first ideation, through the implementation, and up to the realization of the expected business benefits in daily operations.

In this chapter, we'll guide you through some common topics in transformation management and provide insights into Central Finance-specific considerations and key topics in terms of strategy, value, risk, business processes, and organizational change.

The starting point is the definition and alignment of the business strategy and the strategic fit of Central Finance as a concept, followed by the creation of a solid value proposition including descriptions of each use case. Technical, organizational, and financial risks are assessed and continuously controlled via risk management as a project management activity.

Once Central Finance is implemented, use cases will impact business processes; starting with a light impact stage with reporting only up to fully integrated or shifted processes, different needs will arise in business process management. The specific architecture of Central Finance across systems requires different considerations than the usual global template approach.

Finally, Central Finance triggers a significant organizational change within the company—with again different change scenarios than a typical ERP implementation project. The expectations, interests, and concerns of all key stakeholders must be considered to ensure project success.

13.1 Strategy Management

Digital transformation has become imperative for all companies who want to take advantage of faster, more accurate, and more transparent availability of data, combined with a high degree of automation and the ability to learn from big data in multiple sources. In relation to finance processes, the company's own (historical) data often has great potential if this data can be made available in an easy, effective, and consumable way.

Knowing about new opportunities in technology, corporate vision, and the expectations of the CFO includes several aspects, which a modern finance department needs to provide to their corporation, as follows:

- **Automation of processes**
  Too often processes in finance still require multiple steps in different systems, the double entry of data, extraction for individual calculations or reconciliation, and the reentry of data back into the ERP system, when lacking integrated processes and automatic triggers of system-executed transactions or reports.

  Most of these problems could be solved even with previously available technology but still exist in the current landscape. The true automation of processes is expected to go beyond this issue-solving perspective, turning into truly automate processes that reduce the manual interactions of the user to specific decision points, while the system supports all other steps like data mining, proposing similar matches, or combining data for analytics. Additionally, the integration of data should allow seamless process chains that take dependencies into account and let the system execute (within defined borders and thresholds) transactions in sequence.

  The overall vision might be a kind of "lights out" finance process, where robotics and machine learning support any process execution and no human action or assessment is needed. Rules, consigned process flows, data integration, and the learning from previous user decisions allow the system to execute the (usually well-defined) day-to-day financial transactions or closing activities. Finance employ-ees can now focus on exceptions, management adjustments, business changes, and the support of business decisions. Usually our current ERP system has all the necessary data available, but the data is not used in this way yet because the technology is just now pushing further in this direction.

By creating a common financial language for the corporation as well as by bring-ing all (financial) data onto the SAP S/4HANA platform, Central Finance can be-come a key enabler for automation—utilizing the latest (and future) capabilities of automation and providing a platform of innovation for financial processes—inde-pendent to the release or version of the remaining source systems.

- **Data transparency**
  The identification, selection, and provisioning of the right data for the user's purpose has long been a challenge. Especially with its well-defined accounting processes and data model, finance is a viable candidate for data transparency efforts.

  In the past, two challenges often prevented a truly global or central view on profit-ability, balance sheet positions, or the tracking of cost or revenue from the origin to the final receiver. Larger corporations often have multiple ERP systems in their landscapes, perhaps due to acquisitions, segregation of markets/business seg-ments, or system limitations—in any case, the boundaries of system are equal to boundaries in transactional data. Granular data is rejoined in a business ware-house environment, but usually selected to specific reporting purposes. Even in the merging of data sources, true transparency can often be hindered by different posting procedures, controlling concepts, or unharmonized master data and orga-nizational structures. The financial consolidation tool is often the only system with comparable financial figures—but only on an aggregated level. The transpar-ency necessary to understand and analyze down to a single business event or transaction is usually not possible.

  The second challenge exists even in fully integrated and harmonized system land-scapes—e.g., when a single SAP ERP system connects with central planning and con-solidation tools. In SAP R/3 and SAP ERP, transactional finance data and attributes of individual line item were stored in multiple tables. Due to how postings have differ-ent granularities in general ledger (G/L) accounting, Controlling (CO), and nonrec-onciled postings in Profit Center Accounting or a special ledger, establishing a single source of truth with all details of the business event was not possible, especially when considering the chain of transactions from first cost occurrence to the final receiver.

The vision of the CFO for transparency should go beyond the technical restrictions of the past and insist on a single source of truth for all financial data, harmonized and with full line-item granularity. Only then can the CFO provide end-to-end insights to the business, supporting cause-effect analysis, which can help to evaluate the implications of decisions on financial realities, without strenuous efforts for reconciliation and data preparation. Negative effects can be tracked to their root causes—whether an unfortunate business decision, an erroneous entry, or potential fraudulent behavior.

The Universal Journal overcomes restrictions stemming from the lack of granularity, differences in data models, and multiple data storage systems—even within a single ERP system landscape. In combination with Central Finance, the goal of a harmonized, centralized, and granular financial data model for full transparency can be achieved.

- **Analytics and big data**

  Every year, each ERP system usually produces a huge amount of financial data. Thousands or millions of financial records are posted and used in monthly, year-to-date, or year-end reporting and of course serve the functioning of the day-to-day business processes and statutory reporting needs. Nevertheless, the sheer amount of data, its granularity, and cumbersome consumption make leveraging the true potential of big data difficult. Unless a user has a specific demand, knows what data to select, and knows how to aggregate and display, granular historical data is rarely used for business analysis. Often, single reports are built for specific business use cases and then used by only a small group of users and only to answer a distinct business question.

  The vision of the CFO regarding future analytics in finance requires a single source of truth for all financial data, harmonized and with full granularity. Depending on the specific need, this single source of truth can become even more powerful in combination with nonfinancial data—whether from the organization itself or from external sources.

  For users to benefit from a data source, consuming and understanding big data is essential. A single giant table (like the Universal Journal) is of no use unless the user can easily consume, understand, and select the right data, which requires a user interface prepared to slice and dice, apply, or merge massive amounts of data while providing tools to present the data. SAP S/4HANA's capabilities, including data consumption layers and available system intelligence, may support data selection by considering previous searches, illustrating correlations, and hiding unnecessary data.

- **Prediction and simulation**

  Often, the CFO and responsible system owner consider financial data as data to be protected and guarded from other parts of the organization or from user who have no operational need to access such data. Sharing financial data (granular or aggregated) outside the regular financial processes is not desirable, and of course, financial data can contain sensitive data on profitability, market strategies, or financial results not for publication, which require strict protection from outsiders. Therefore, the majority of financial data can be seen as reflection of historical transactions and can be used for statutory reporting or to steer internal control mechanisms.

  The CFO's vision should consider the use of this data beyond statutory reporting or internal control. By using technologies to apply historical data for prediction and simulation, financial data (possibly in combination with other sources) can unleash a new dimension of business value to gain insights for development.

  Simulations can be used to test different conditions on your actual data (e.g., product prices, internal costs, currency exchange rates, depreciation rates, allocation mechanisms). You can simulate financial effects on margins or balance sheet positions under different situations and conditions. Predictions can extrapolate trends from historical data into the future. By inputting a few parameters into a model, the system can apply correlations and create financial figures at a future state—e.g., to extrapolate the profit and loss (P&L) effect over the next 5 years of a buy or build decision. According to the parameter input (e.g., market prices, development costs, or exchange rates), different scenarios can be applied to support business decisions.

  Both simulation and prediction need data as input. While in the past the applied data, e.g., in a planning or consolidation tool, had been aggregated and limited, the potential is reaching now to Central Finance as a much larger data pool as source, which increases accuracy and improves the quality of results by extrapolating from multiple years of historical data, thus considering market cycles or trends undetected by a (rather static) typical plan simulation.

- **Integration**

  Integration among processes, systems, and departments is often a significant obstacle to achieve the desired objectives of the CFO. Reporting and processes may be conducted outside of the ERP system, and departments might operate on different software in different systems. The reasons might be numerous but often include a lack of consistent process, application strategy, and governance throughout the organization.

  Solving the lack of integration can be expensive and often does not provide the necessary business benefits, especially when the individual user group is happy with their current application.

  Shortcomings in integration are roadblocks to innovation, which often benefits from a central view on processes and data. Without a single source of truth on a granular level, any innovation can only operate within these limitations and may not leverage the full potential of automation, data transparency, analytics, and prediction/simulation.

  The CFO's expectations should not accept lack of integration as a roadblock, and technology should overcome such limitations. For this purpose, Central Finance is one way to establish a platform with a central and single source of truth with fully granular data and enables future innovation in processes, analytics, and prediction/simulation.

These general trends in a CFO vision might form the cornerstones of a strategy for finance transformation. But the company must develop its own strategy for finance that will fit with the general company's strategy. Especially when considering Central Finance as the technical vehicle for this finance transformation, confirming the strategic fit is of utmost importance.

Central Finance is often seen as a technical solution when in fact it comes with a number of implications in the areas of organization, processes, and application landscape and the strategic direction of all three areas.

The question for the CFO, the chief information officer (CIO), and to some extent the overall organization is whether a sufficient appetite exists for stronger centralization, with focus on finance functions, but including general master data governance, data analytics, and data governance (including access and security) as well as the company's ERP and application landscape. While the CFO and IT may be quite positive about using Central Finance to support these strategic objectives, additional stakeholders will be impacted as well.

Some organizations will find themselves already in a condition where embedding Central Finance in their landscape will be relatively easy. For example, when key finance objects like organizational structures, profit centers, charts of accounts, cost centers, and controlling already exist and already feed into financial consolidation under a central governance. Other organizations with a more business segment-driven governance—perhaps separated by system, ownership, or operation—will face significant challenges in organizational change management to introduce Central Finance. The degree of change required strongly depends on the use cases, how Central Finance will be used, and which expansion stages are planned. The good news is that (with the acceptance of some workarounds) Central Finance in a light usage for pure reporting purposes could be introduced with minimal effort.

To ensure a good strategic match, be sure to work carefully through the value propositions and assess the potential implications for other dependent strategies in the company, for example:

- Did the CIO already plan a system consolidation?
- Does sales or procurement have a conflicting application strategy?
- Are there already initiatives for new master data governance?
- Are there any plans to divest parts of the organization or transfer corporate functions to a shared service center?

Finally, using Central Finance for a finance transformation seldom works as a one-stop shop or in a big bang approach. Usually the chosen use cases are implemented in a sequence of two to three stages, which allows you to quickly realize immediate wins after the Central Finance system goes live. Other use cases like central payments, centralization of closing activities, central planning, consolidation, or tax reporting usually have additional prerequisites and would be activated in a second step. For the strategic fit decision, make sure you understand the full vision of finance transformation. We don't recommend starting small without having a mid-term or long-term strategy in mind, as this lack of vision might put Central Finance on a dead-end path in terms of future development or require significant effort for redefinition and reworking at a later stage.

13.2 Value Management

At the beginning of your finance transformation journey, you'll need to identify, assess, and confirm the most solid use cases. Usually, the finance and responsible IT departments already have a good understanding of pain points in their processes and in the application landscape, which they would like to resolve.

The opportunity to overcome pain points is a good starting point to identify a value proposition, but watching out for new opportunities created by technology, organizational readiness, or news trends should provide another, more innovative and forward-looking, perspective towards transformation objectives.

After a first draft of use cases that consider the capabilities of SAP S/4HANA, SAP Analytics Cloud, and Central Finance has been created, you must describe the expected scope and functionality as precisely as possible:

- Which business processes should be executed in Central Finance, and how should these processes be transformed and benefit from Central Finance?
- Does the scope of transformation relate to the entire process or only parts of it— e.g., for central payments only?
- Which reporting is expected in Central Finance—e.g., only parts of internal management reporting, a specific reporting scenario, or for all statutory and tax reporting requirements?
- Should Central Finance be used as platform for central planning processes and replace existing solution(s)?

Multiple questions need to be answered, but value management should concentrate on understanding the main scope and on determining what each use case intends to achieve. Questions about how to achieve these objectives are not independent but can be answered at a later stage.

A precise formulation of the scope, capabilities, and expected benefits allows you to assess whether expectations can be met by the SAP solution currently or in the future; its implications on the IT architecture, business procedures, and processes; and its strategic fit.

Table 13.1 shows an example of a business value network applied on Central Finance.

Technical Central Finance Capability	IT/Application Landscape	Business Processes	Benefit/Strategic Purpose
■ Real-time replication of financial transactions on full granularity ■ Mapping of master data/ organizational structures/ configuration ■ Transformation and extension of transactional data in CFIN ■ Audit track and reconciliation ■ Transition into the Universal Journal data model ■ Central Finance framework including error handling and interface features	■ Establishment of a new SAP S/4HANA system including a Central Finance interface to the source ■ SAP S/4HANA user interface and reporting capabilities ■ Additional SAP S/4HANA application ■ Central master data governance ■ Alignment of configuration and system maintenance ■ Centralized system security and access management ■ Integration of SAP Analytics Cloud or SAP Cloud Platform apps	■ Central process for financial planning and consolidation ■ Central payments and integration with treasury ■ Global analysis/ reporting of cost flows ■ Central closing steps ■ Reporting on-demand including root cause analysis ■ Central audit and tax reporting	■ Harmonized single source of truth ■ Higher degree of automation in month-end closing/reporting ■ Standardized processes to facilitate collaboration between business functions ■ High data standards and quality through global best practices ■ One financial language across the corporation ■ Faster absorption of acquisition in financial reporting ■ More impactful insights into financial data

Table 13.1 Example of a Central Finance-Based Business Value Network

Independent to the selected use cases and the size of finance transformation, you should conduct and document a fair assessment of the business case. Determining and calculating financial figures are often challenging. Prerequisites for accurate benefit calculations include a solid data source of process key performance indicators (KPIs), costs of operation, assigned full-time equivalents (FTEs), IT costs, and other related costs in the organization. Even more challenging are the quantification of improvements, cost savings, or benefits from new business opportunities and the support of better business decisions created by better insights. While typical benefits like those listed in the sample business value network in Table 13.1, could be used as starting point for discussion, you must derive the business benefits specific to your company's situation:

- Which capabilities and benefits will contribute to specific competitive advantages?
- Which will address specific pain points that could not be overcome in the past?
- How do the different stakeholders prioritize these benefits or improvements?
- Do the identified benefits support the strategic imperatives of the company?

Despite difficulties and uncertainty in data, the current state (including pain points, current costs, and missed opportunities as well as the expected benefits) should be documented, accompanied by the assumptions applied at the moment of assessment. Only if the value proposition is clearly defined (and updated) is the regular measurement of benefit realization or of changes in expectation possible.

Experience has shown two additional implications of the value proposition: It will help the implementation project team derive solution design principles to support the expected business outcome. Often design decisions are triggered by technical feasibility, without considering the (intended) business benefit, which may not be clearly described and documented. Second, the value proposition will help communicate the strategy of Central Finance within the organization and across multiple stakeholders. Due to the multiple groups and stakeholders in the organization, communicating who will be impacted and whose support is essential for the successful implementation of Central Finance.

13.3 Risk Management

Like any transformation, introducing Central Finance and accomplishing a finance transformation have specific risks during realization. Awareness of such risks is essential, and you should establish risk management as part of the project setup, which includes identifying risks at the beginning of project, assessing the impact and likelihood of risks, creating mitigation actions, regularly revising risk positions, and looking for new emerging risks. Usually this activity is anchored close to the program executive level for sufficient power for mitigation action enforcement.

The growing technical capabilities of Central Finance are accompanied by an increase in the functional scope of Central Finance projects, which creates a high number of potential risks. The typical risk profile of a global SAP template implementation project could serve as a base, but this standard risk profile cannot be applied without specific consideration of the nature of the Central Finance solution. The risk assessment must not be limited to a technical viability perspective but should include additional perspectives and parts of the organization—ideally anticipating a 360-degree view of the transformation's ecosystem. To focus on technical solution readiness seems most natural, especially as Central Finance is a software solution, which is maturing rapidly while implementation experience is still evolving. But other aspects must be included as well: Transformation projects usually fail because of nontechnical reasons than because of technical reasons.

The following sections describe a few Central Finance-specific risk factors, which may occur at the project start. With thorough investigation and assessment, some of these risks may turn into activities when the likelihood of risk is high. Potential risks can be categorized as technical risks, business changes, organizational risks, and financial risks factors.

13.3.1   Technical Risk Factors

To look for solution and technical risk factors, the most common starting point, you'll assess whether the current (or planned) software functionalities, as well as the individual IT architecture and application landscapes, contain any significant risks:

- **Technical novelty to the IT and business organization**
  While the concept behind or idea of Central Finance is not new, the SAP product and its Central Finance capabilities are relatively new to the market and are constantly being expanded by SAP's development team. Additionally, Central Finance is based on SAP S/4HANA, which not all SAP customer's organizations have yet implemented, and so some companies may lack hands-on experience with SAP solutions. Both (relatively new) software components require attention training and ways to gain experience to prepare the project team sufficiently. Otherwise, technical novelty might lead to uncertainty within the team and the choice of traditional, but unsuitable, project approaches.

- **Complexity in synchronizing a multisystem landscape**
  Central Finance is usually established as a new SAP S/4HANA system within the landscape, and configuration from multiple source systems is harmonized via

mapping into a single instance of Central Finance. While this view is static, you must consider the possibility of dynamic views during regular system usage as well, which includes (constant) changes to configuration, master data, and support packages as well as the implementation of SAP Notes and system downtimes. These activities are risks later in the lifecycle but should be assessed and addressed early in an implementation project.

- **Number of systems and configurations to be harmonized**
  By its nature, Central Finance's objective is to connect to multiple source systems and harmonize financial transactions into a single source of truth. However, widely diverse configurations and setups, as well as different SAP system releases or functional prerequisites in each source system, can become risks if not careful investigated. Additionally, different configurations and usage of attributes should be compared and analyzed as well. Differences in document splitting, ledger approach, usage of profitability analysis, and currency or tax setups can create the risk of technical roadblocks at a later implementation stage. Finally, specifics like applied naming conventions might deviate between systems and require a stronger harmonization effort than expected.

- **Certainty and stability of the business requirements and use cases**
  Often a change in scope can occur during the implementation of Central Finance because of gained experience, continuing discussions with business stakeholders, the adoption of an application strategy during the project phase, and the identification of technical restrictions. In any case, these changes case immanent risk during the implementation phase, which could—in case of a multistage implementation approach—last over a significant period. Good documentation and constant realignment with the business and IT project scope responsible are critical to mitigating these risks.

- **Harmonization and centralization of master data objects governance**
  One of the most underestimated risks of implementation is the need for harmonized master data in Central Finance. Of course, master data can be mapped from various source systems into a single source of truth in Central Finance, but you'll still need a set of globally targeted master data objects: Usually, Central Finance is based on a global chart of accounts, global customer and vendor master records (business partners), or global profit centers. If objects are currently governed decentrally (i.e., by division or system), you'll need harmonization towards a global structure and global governance at least within the Central Finance instance to leverage full benefits. Otherwise, the objective of a single financial language across the corporation will not be achieved. The need for harmonized master data

governance, on the other hand, may require a central master data tool. Central Finance integrates mapping with SAP Master Data Governance (SAP MDG), but regardless of the tool you select, the project must carefully assess the required implementation scope.

- **Adoption of custom-built solutions and the impact on replication to Central Finance**
  Usually the ERP systems connected to Central Finance contain several specific custom-built enhancements and processes, while the design of the Central Finance within a fresh SAP S/4HANA system often comes along with the need for SAP standard configuration. This situation creates a two-fold risk: On the one hand, the replication of financial transactions might require you to pick up data (elements) from sources and convert them into the standard data model in Central Finance. Of course, the Universal Journal field extension and the special ledger provide some flexibility, but depending on the custom solution, these components might not be sufficient, and additional enhancements could be required.

  Second, the replication of financial transactions from multiple sources into one Central Finance instance (which holds only one configuration unless configurations can be separated, for example, by company code) may bring an unexpected need for harmonization or for rebuilding custom enhancements. A careful analysis of enhancements with their impact on the reposting in Central Finance and related use cases for reporting or central processes is recommended to identify any roadblocks or additional implementation effort.

- **Potential impact on source system(s) and technical prerequisites**
  The installation of the required SAP Notes in the source system, which are needed to establish the replication, may be done without disruption on an existing configuration with little technical implications. However, the replication of financial documents has several restrictions and prerequisites, depending on the source system SAP release, applied business functions, configurations, or connected interfaces. Certain combinations of configurations are not supported as standard. The risk of additional workarounds or changes in the source system (e.g., upgrading business functions or release version) should be assessed and planned accordingly as part of the project activities.

13.3.2 Business Change and Organizational Risk Factors

Business and organizational changes create uncertainty and carry intrinsic risks. Program management should pay attention to the following immanent risks factors:

- **Senior management commitment to the Central Finance project and its approach**

  Engaging the executive level from both finance and IT departments into the implementation of Central Finance is critical. Other corporate functions, in sales, procurement, and manufacturing, should also be at least consulted. Due to the possible fast realization of Central Finance in a reporting scenario, the project sometimes starts with a loose commitment from the CFO and CIO—especially when major business processes are not impacted! This risk for problems is enormous, because often the Central Finance starts under a degree of uncertainty, use cases evolve, further prerequisites are detected, and/or scope is extended. If senior management is not involved and committed early, the (additional) impact on master data governance, organizational changes, or higher implementation costs become a high risk threatening the entire project's success.

- **Resource commitment by all involved business divisions and IT**

  The driving organization for Central Finance is often located at the company's headquarters, and project team staffing is conducted by global functions. This situation risks insufficient insights and knowledge of source system-specific processes, configurations, and (historical) data. Mapping or design decisions for Central Finance could be based on incorrect assumptions. Ideally, resourcing includes persons from all impacted systems, which will bring in knowledge as well as facilitate organizational change management into individual parts of organization.

- **Readiness of the organization to establish (extended) centralized processes and governance**

  The establishment of a central system with harmonized transactional and master data creates the need for certain centralized functions. These functions include the governance of key objects like charts of accounts, profit centers, payment terms, cost centers, customers, vendors, tax codes, etc. Depending on the mapping strategy, you may not need to centralize the full governance process of each object or configuration item, but at a minimum, a notification of a change between source and Central Finance system is needed to assess the implications on the respective systems and to keep the mapping in sync. Certain business processes during closing and reporting may need (new) processes for alignment between source and Central Finance systems. Finally, the SAP S/4HANA and Central Finance system requires ownership and maintenance itself—in some cases, ownership with a department needs to be established or prepared.

- **Changes to business processes and practices**
  In a loosely coupled multisystem landscape, the owners of and responsibilities for each system might be separated and have limited need for harmonization and governance of global procedures. The replication into a single Central Finance system increases the need for harmonization and centralized governance, especially the shift of processes from source systems into Central Finance, like central payments, central credit management, central planning, or certain closing activities, which will lead to changes in business processes and practices.

- **Redefining data access to a single source of truth for the entire company**
  The use case of a corporate-wide single source of truth for all financial data on a granular level creates the need to define a new concept of data access. By default, system-determined boundaries won't exist anymore, and copying existing authorization concepts by organizational objects and user groups may not consider the potential and desired analytical capabilities of Central Finance. At the same time, the replication of granular data into a central system could create a concern for current system/data owner: that data protection measures are softened too much and data is accessible to unauthorized persons. The risk of uncontrolled data access should be addressed at an early stage of the project, not only because the technical realization of access control will require effort but also because a conceptual agreement with data-owning business departments will need to be established.

- **Acceptance of Central Finance as the (new) single source of truth**
  One of the key use cases of Central Finance is the creation of a single source of truth for financial data—real time and on a harmonized, granular level. For a business user, this situation implies access to their relevant data from a new system, which often is not the system where the transaction is entered and processed. Document replication transforms objects like G/L accounts or profit centers during the mapping, or documents might be missing in reporting until an interface issue is resolved, which might not be evident for the business user.

  If business users are not convinced about the accuracy of the financial data in Central Finance and continue to rely rather on their (known) source systems, the value of Central Finance will be diluted significantly. As mitigation, two measures could be considered: At the handoff of the productive Central Finance system to the business user, data quality and replication mechanisms must be fully operational and transparent to the user. Second, business (key) users may be involved during project implementation as part of organizational change management to understand the potential and restrictions of the Central Finance architecture.

13

13.3.3   Financial Risk Factors

In Section 13.2, we mentioned the difficulties in creating a figure-based value proposition and the need for assumptions. Therefore, the costs of a Central Finance implementation project, as well as its related initiatives, are constant risk items for program management, as follows:

- **Degree of confidence into the financial business case and value delivery**
  Identifying and describing the use cases and expected value of Central Finance carefully is important under the existing constraints of uncertainty. During the project's duration, the realization of benefits and value will become more visible, and assumptions may need revision. Overly high expectations or overly low confidence in the value proposition can bring significant risks to the project, especially if uncertainties lead to a decrease in commitment on the executive level. The degree of confidence in the financial business case and the realization of value should be assessed as constant risk factors during the project's phases. New insights and lessons learned throughout the project implementation (both positive and negative) need to be incorporated into the value proposition to allow an up-to-date description of the project's potential contribution to the company's objectives.

- **Degree of confidence in all elements of project costs**
  Any cost estimate for Central Finance is based on multiple assumptions and conducted with uncertainty—especially the connection (and harmonization) of multiple source systems. Historical data and different configurations and processes create a large variety of influencing factors. To mitigate the risk of high deviation among cost estimates, the scope of use cases must be clearly described, and the need for harmonization (of data, processes, applications, or organizational structures) should be assessed as early as possible. Most SAP customers considering implementing Central Finance conduct a proof of concept at an early stage, which will support the identification of cost drivers. Additionally, we recommend conducting a (rather technical) data and configuration comparison of all impacted systems to estimate any needed adoptions.

- **Change of application strategy in (other) parts of the organization**
  As mentioned, a Central Finance implementation influences the corporate-wide application strategy and is usually not limited to the financial application landscape. Other initiatives like upgrading a (source) system to SAP S/4HANA, the conversion of multiple systems, or the implementation of a new module in one source system can influence the Central Finance project. Assessing the global

system landscape and architecture takes care of those dependencies, but it may require a new point of alignment if global application governance has not been established.

- **Dependencies of value realization on other projects**
  Central Finance and its related use cases often cannot be seen in isolation and instead depend on other initiatives within the company, which may include upgrading to certain ERP releases, retiring old applications, or introducing global master data governance (perhaps as planned). Again, a careful assessment of dependencies and their implied costs for the project is recommended—some dependencies might be on the critical path of implementation and could have a direct impact on the project's success.

- **Investment protection and sustainability of Central Finance application**
  If the Central Finance implementation is not sufficiently anchored into your company's application architecture, you run the risk that competing initiatives are conducted, which will devalue the use cases for Central Finance or make the system obsolete. The overall application strategy may partly use Central Finance, perhaps only as a bridging technology and for a limited period of time, but in this case, this strategy is a conscious decision and integrated into the value proposition and strategy.

This list of factors is a selection of potential risks during a Central Finance implementation project. We recommend conducting a careful risk assessment from various perspectives at the beginning of the project.

13.4   Business Process Management

While Central Finance usually is part of setting up a fresh, greenfield SAP S/4HANA system, the project and its design approach vary significantly from a traditional global template implementation. Global process reengineering and its related need for a common consensus within the company are not necessarily priorities during a Central Finance implementation. Especially because most customers chose a staged approach, the priority at the beginning is to keep the business processes intact as much as possible.

The most common use case for Central Finance is to establish a single source of truth containing all financial documents for global reporting purposes—the goal of the first stage. Harmonization and granularity on the line item level enables new capabilities for consuming, drilldown, or slicing and dicing the financial data. In the context of business process management, the reporting step usually occurs at the end of the process chain without interfering with the immediate transactional activities. Considering the data flow, the Central Finance system is in a listening position, receiving transactional data (in real time), but without generating any kind of business event or entering new transactional data. In other words, Central Finance is providing a transformed, harmonized, and central view of the financial data, without loss of business integrity in the process conducted without the Central Finance system.

Thus, as a result, Central Finance acts as a kind of side car implementation, with less risk exposure and little influence on the current business process steps executing in each of the source systems. Reporting in Central Finance can be an integral part of the end-to-end process—especially if Central Finance doesn't just serve internal management reporting needs but also covers certain regulatory requirements. However, in any case, the procedures of data entry and process execution steps are usually not impacted.

For most SAP customers, the reporting use case is often only a starting point, and their vision includes additional processes like central planning, source of financial consolidation (or integrated SAP S/4HANA consolidation), or central credit management—the goal of the second stage. These processes can ideally be operated with a degree of independence from the ERP system(s), and necessary applications can be deployed via interface connections to the source ERP. In essence, although substantially covering an end-to-end business process, in these examples, the receiver of data has a clear definition of handoff mechanisms, which facilitates these processes separate from the day-to-day business processes conducted in the source system. Once the transactional data has been replicated to Central Finance, the SAP S/4HANA landscape can leverage its power of integration with the latest SAP portfolio, which may include planning or prediction functionalities in SAP Analytics Cloud, acting as platform of central credit management or becoming the source of (integrated) financial consolidation.

In these examples, specific business processes are executed in Central Finance, but the usual data integrity of posting transactions from procure-to-pay or order-to-cash processes remains intact in each source system. These processes do not create any postings to actuals and therefore do not interfere with local statutory reporting, which remains leading (from a document entry perspective) in each source system.

Therefore, these satellite processes are good candidates for the second stage of extending Central Finance because the impact to day-to-day business processes as well as the impact to relevant user groups can be controlled somewhat.

In the third stage of expansion, the entry of actuals is conducted in Central Finance. As Central Finance is usually built on a one-directional replication of financial transactions from source to Central Finance, at this moment, the financial balance sheet will only be complete in Central Finance, which shifts statutory reporting requirements to the Central Finance system. Actuals are posted to Central Finance immediately; the use cases include typical accounting processes like procure-to-pay, order-to-cash, or month-end activities like foreign exchange evaluation or cost allocations.

Let's look at an example of a simple procure-to-pay process to illustrate the distinctive character of this scenario, when a regular end-to-end process including actual postings is split between source and Central Finance system. The process flow starts with a purchase order in one of the local source systems. The transaction of the purchase order is not replicated to Central Finance and therefore not available for any follow-on processes, as shown in Figure 13.1.

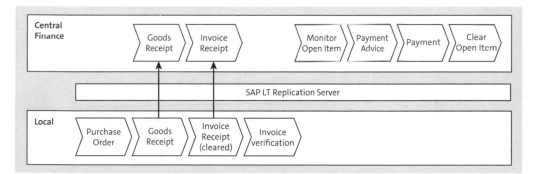

Figure 13.1 Example of a Process Split in Central Finance

Entering goods receipts and invoices and their verification occur in the source system as well, but if these activities trigger finance-relevant postings, the respective accounting (and controlling) documents are replicated to Central Finance. The subsequent handling of open items and liability management is executed in Central Finance, including the creation of payment advices, payments, and the clearing of open items. These postings are not transferred back to the source system, and therefore, the open item status as well as the financial statement in Central Finance becomes leading. At this point, the Central Finance system becomes the system of record for any financial reporting.

A second implication of the process split is that certain follow-on process steps are no longer available in the source system. This limitation could be relevant in the case of tariff calculations, cost variances (during payments), bank charges, or other adjustments, which may be used in product costing or profitability analysis. The shift of core accounting and controlling processes to Central Finance requires a careful assessment of all process steps and system of execution as well as an assessment of the consequences of a lack of information in dependent processes. The strongest dependencies have been experienced in processes related to material movements, stock valuations, and settlements as well as procure-to-pay, order-to-cash, and month-end closing.

Another character of centralization appears, when full processes (or modules) are shifted into Central Finance—the goal of the fourth stage. Examples can be found in financial asset accounting, joint venture accounting (especially in the oil and gas industry), or overhead cost management. Assessing any implications for dependent processes in the source system is mandatory as well, but you'll have greater opportunity to establish global processes in Central Finance, which may deviate from your various source systems.

In the fifth stage, you'll shift entire entities into Central Finance after a period in which financial documents are replicated. In this stage, process definition is performed just like in a single system, but with full integration except for the migration and load of potentially missing data or attributes. Processes are not specific to Central Finance anymore.

13.5   Organizational Change Management

When considering Central Finance, at first, the project may be met with high interest and enthusiasm. Technology to build a single source of truth, a single financial language used across the entire corporation, fast onboarding of new systems for acquisitions, the use of innovative processes and user interfaces—all with minimal impact on the existing business processes and application landscapes—may look like a dream come true. However, these discussions appear on the group level—that is, with the corporate CFO, the CIO, or the application and business process strategist. These persons are usually in favor of a strong(er) centralized approach, data harmonization, control of global governance, and data pooling for group-wide analytics.

Not all stakeholders relevant for a Central Finance strategy may share the same interests. For some groups, concerns outweigh benefits, and they are opponents of the approach.

Organizational change management (OCM) in a Central Finance project deals with the different interests within the company and is likely one of the most underestimated activities. The number of stakeholders impacted by Central Finance is usually much higher than with most other (SAP) implementation projects, as shown in Figure 13.2. To achieve the benefits of a group-wide single source of truth in finance, you'll need to connect all productive ERP systems and replicate their financial transactions—as well as change the distribution of master data objects and configure the mappings. Both finance and IT in the company will be involved to implement Central Finance. To spread the benefits of this organizational change process, effective change communication has proven effective in a Central Finance implementation. End users don't just face a system change; they are also confronted with a new agile business paradigm. The impact of this process-level change must be included in trainings and in communications, and the new possibilities must be made evident to all stakeholders.

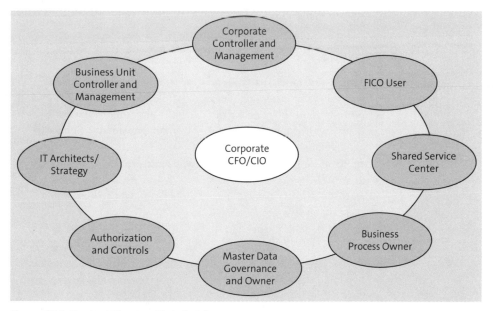

Figure 13.2 Central Finance Stakeholders

For project success and overall acceptance in the organization, you must understand each stakeholder's position, motivations, and interests as well as assess possible constraints with Central Finance. Table 13.2 provides a short analysis of the most typical and relevant stakeholders.

Stakeholder	Interest in Central Finance	Concern in Central Finance
Corporate CFO	<ul><li>Often the driver and executive sponsor of a centralized finance platform.</li><li>Positive to enable innovation, efficiency gains, better insight, and faster reporting.</li><li>Central financial platform—under the ownership of a corporate function to achieve higher transparency of the entire corporation and better steering of the individual business division's performance.</li><li>Opportunity to transform the organization and enforce the centralization of corporate functions.</li></ul>	<ul><li>Costs of Central Finance.</li><li>Burden to the organization and organizational readiness.</li><li>Speed of implementation.</li><li>Acceptance to use Central Finance by different business lines and controllers as sources for analysis.</li><li>Confidence in business that replicated data is the new source of truth—i.e., is all the data fully replicated and correctly transformed?</li></ul>
Corporate CIO	<ul><li>Similar motivation than the corporate CFO for increasing the centralization and bundling of IT services like application management, (master) data management, or system ownership.</li><li>Central Finance could serve as a platform to retire (older) ERP systems, bundle satellite applications, or delay the need to upgrade existing landscape.</li><li>Provide SAP S/4HANA application innovations and user experience to the finance department.</li><li>Flexible/staged implementation of use case.</li></ul>	<ul><li>Architecture to establish a finance platform versus keeping the integration of material management and finance in one system.</li><li>IT and process prerequisites (e.g., to establish a global master data governance).</li><li>Adding a (new) SAP S/4HANA system into the landscape.</li><li>Impact on total cost of ownership for the new system plus maintenance and governance processes.</li><li>Readiness of the absorbing IT organization.</li></ul>

Table 13.2 Stakeholders and Their Interests

Stakeholder	Interest in Central Finance	Concern in Central Finance
Corporate controller	- Data transparency and the possibility to use all financial data for analytics, root cause analysis, slice and dice by all attributes, trend analysis, and performance comparison on a granular level and with all possible attributes enables insights, which were impossible or hard to achieve, and opens up innovative ways to steer the company and support decisions. - Modern user interfaces and use of integrated tools instead of individual spreadsheet calculations.	- Full transparency will raise concerns of losing control over confidentiality. - Central Finance might become yet another source—next to source ERP, SAP Business Warehouse (SAP BW) or a data hub.
Finance user (operations)	- The SAP Fiori frontend in SAP S/4HANA provides new transactions for processes in the scope of Central Finance. - Ad-hoc reporting requests and related data collection will be significantly supported. - Reconciliation between modules of Profit Center Accounting, Overhead Management, Profitability Analysis (CO-PA), and the G/L as well as (potentially) the special ledger will be removed by design. - Learning to prepare for future innovations. - Operational processes may remain unchanged and could gradually move towards Central Finance, which gives some time for adoption.	- The operational processes might look more complicated due to the split across systems. - Some understanding of how Central Finance operates is required—e.g., to assist in error correction. - Especially at the beginning of Central Finance, confidence in the data replication will require thorough reconciliation with the source systems and related workload. This need could eventually be settled to a minimal check routine.

Table 13.2 Stakeholders and Their Interests (Cont.)

13

Stakeholder	Interest in Central Finance	Concern in Central Finance
Shared service center	<ul><li>Supports the possibility of central governance of processes.</li><li>Execution of e.g., chart of accounts maintenance, closing activities, master data maintenance, or reporting could be shifted towards the shared service center.</li><li>While the shared service center user previously needed to work on separate ERP systems, processes in Central Finance could operate with a global governance in one system.</li></ul>	<ul><li>The need for additional processes to run Central Finance may not have been planned and is pushed into the organization.</li><li>Transfer of processes will require a headcount shift, which usually needs agreements within the organization.</li></ul>
Business process owner	<ul><li>Depending on the anchor of this role, this group could be in favor of a stronger globalization or defend their divisional/regional independency.</li><li>Opportunity to change and innovate processes via Central Finance with relatively little disruption.</li><li>Critical for the definition of use cases and design of the Central Finance system—although it does not follow a classic global template approach.</li></ul>	<ul><li>Process adoption might be considered as a compromise—due to the replication approach of Central Finance, a fundamental reengineering of process is difficult—depending on the individual situation.</li></ul>

Table 13.2 Stakeholders and Their Interests (Cont.)

Stakeholder	Interest in Central Finance	Concern in Central Finance
Master data governance and data owner	■ Absolutely critical stakeholder, as Central Finance creates additional need to establish a (global) governance process and supporting system. ■ Opportunity to push harmonization of master data and configuration—e.g., a global chart of account, global profit centers/segments, a global cost center hierarchy, and global versions of financial statements—is essential for Central Finance. ■ The centralized and harmonized data becomes a key value-adding element for business analysis across the corporation.	■ The need for a global process and harmonized data triggered by Central Finance might come as a surprise to the master data governance group and interfere with existing timelines and strategies. ■ In case of decentralized data maintenance, the synchronization of Central Finance creates additional interfaces. ■ In a worst-case scenario, manual dual-entry might be needed for selected objects. ■ Issues in master data synchronization are the main reason for failed document replication at the start of Central Finance—this group will be a key player for a smooth implementation and go-live.
Authorization and control responsible person	■ Opportunity to support audit activities using a single source of truth. ■ Possibility to conduct better fraud detection as data is not separated by system borders. ■ General better control of central processes like the closing process (for steps executed in Central Finance).	■ Access control requires a new concept—without the system as borders, potentially new objects are needed to limit access rights. ■ Central Finance could act as source for subsequent receiving systems like SAP BW, consolidation, etc.—with respective aligned data control. ■ The global data source could conflict with country-specific legal aspects—e.g., in case of personal data.

Table 13.2 Stakeholders and Their Interests (Cont.)

Stakeholder	Interest in Central Finance	Concern in Central Finance
IT architects/ strategists	<ul><li>Central Finance opens up novel approaches to implement innovative applications and processes.</li><li>The IT architects are critical to ensuring Central Finance is embedded as an integrated part of the group IT strategy.</li><li>Central Finance is often the pioneer project to embark to the SAP S/4HANA journey.</li><li>Creates a significant learning curve in IT architecture regarding the capabilities and opportunities of SAP S/4HANA and related new tools.</li></ul>	<ul><li>The architecture of Central Finance carries the risk of an independent IT strategy path for finance—in isolation from other lines of business.</li><li>Central Finance radiates into the IT application landscape (e.g., master data), which creates the need to match the long-term IT strategy and align different interests.</li></ul>
Business unit controller	<ul><li>Availability of new analytic capabilities and user-friendly toolset.</li><li>Reporting needs—especially requested from corporate—could be created more automated and are easier to provide.</li></ul>	<ul><li>Could become a strong opponent of Central Finance, if transparency in the corporate headquarters is considered a threat.</li><li>What results may not be any improvement in the data source per se, as the individual data is likely already available and a global view is not the main concern.</li></ul>

Table 13.2 Stakeholders and Their Interests (Cont.)

The assessment of each potential stakeholder in Central Finance is critical for the success of the project and for the subsequent realization of benefits. Table 13.2 can help you identify symptoms and sources of resistance so you can address the different concerns of all key stakeholders.

Organizational change management offers different approaches to support finance transformation in your organization:

- **Involvement in strategic decision and value proposition**

  The first steps to building a value proposition are usually conducted by the corporate strategy group (IT and finance), but deciding on the strategic direction is strongly recommended in alignment with additional critical stakeholder groups. You'll need an analysis of impacted stakeholders and need to anticipate dependencies to other strategic initiatives. Often Central Finance is triggered by the strongest beneficiaries in corporate functions—with little consultation with divisional stakeholders, who might be running a conflicting IT or business strategy. Additionally, the involvement of key stakeholders could enhance the value proposition by identifying otherwise hidden pain points (or opportunities) and strengthen the commitment of impacted groups.

- **Organizational readiness assessment**

  Once the strategy and use cases have been defined, conducting an organizational readiness assessment is essential. You'll match the requirements of Central Finance (and its use cases) against existing business processes and organizational structures and determine whether you need new (or adopted) processes, governance structures, ownership, task execution, resource capacity, and skillsets.

  According the match between requirements and the current situation, the need for organizational changes is factored into the overall strategy of Central Finance, and its value proposition, and finally determines the activities of organizational change management. Is the company's organization (and the impacted stakeholders) ready for Central Finance, or are adoptions and changes in leadership structures, resource assignment, or governance necessary? Nontechnical changes can go along with the (technical) implementation project and should be considered with a focus similar to the technology readiness assessment and factored into any project implementation plan.

  For example, if your company applies individual charts of accounts in each of their ERP systems and no authority or governance to define a global chart of account exists, establishing governance within the finance department and defining a global chart of accounts are essential. In another example related to reporting strategies and data usage, let's say no corporate or global authority has decided a data access strategy in the Central Finance system. The authority to define a data access strategy resides on the executive level or at the data owner level. A third example might be global master data maintenance: Is the shared service center able to absorb or execute global master data changes in profit centers, cost centers, customers, or vendors? We should highlight once more that a Central Finance implementation is not at all "just" an IT project.

13

- **Executive sponsor buy-in and commitment**
  A new finance system expected to serve as central platform and single source of truth for all financial data can only be established successfully with the necessary sponsorship on the executive level and from the board. The commitment of top executives from the start is essential because their influence in reporting and data usage decisions extends throughout the entire organization.

  According to stakeholder descriptions, Central Finance as a concept is usually appealing to the corporate executive level as it opens up multiple capabilities that are otherwise difficult to achieve in a multi-ERP system landscape. Executive commitment becomes critical for overcoming obstacles to organizational change and to build the confidence in Central Finance as the new single source of truth. The corporate CFO (and other executives) may lead by example and show confidence, for example, by actively demanding that financial figures for group reporting are created from Central Finance instead of from individual source systems. (Only Central Finance will allow a harmonized group-wide view and while at the same time enabling instant drilldown for root cause analysis.) Of course, this step will require technically accurate replication and error-free processing in Central Finance as prerequisites.

- **Participation of key recipient and stakeholder groups in design and modeling**
  During the Central Finance design and modeling phase, the setup of the project team should consider the participation of the most impacted organizational unit and user groups from the start. Although financial processes are usually not reengineered as part of Central Finance, the implementation will require several decisions about organizational structures, reporting structures, mapping of configuration and master data objects, etc.

  Embedding representatives from each source system, for example, will serve multiple benefits: Their deep knowledge of processes and data structures, including historic data structures, is required to build the mapping and bridge the transactional data into Central Finance. Additionally, these project members could act as key users or ambassadors to the broader user community of the source system by sharing knowledge, progress, and benefits of the new Central Finance system.

  Finally, knowledge of Central Finance on SAP S/4HANA—and potentially further new applications like SAP Analytics Cloud, and its new features regarding the data model (e.g., Universal Journal), the user interfaces (e.g., SAP Fiori apps); or technical changes (e.g., core data services [CDS] views)—might not be widely spread. Thus, the project team will need upskilling on the latest SAP technologies to conduct the design and modeling phase. During and after the project, the team could act as knowledge multipliers in the organization.

- **Clear and transparent reporting and analytic strategy**
  Losing control of confidential financial data is one of the key concerns within a company, especially in decentralized organizations with strong divisional ownership. While existing business warehouse solutions and financial consolidation may already be collecting data from each source system, real-time replication and granularity on the line item level can raise privacy concerns: Confidentiality may not kept, and undesired insights are generated on corporate level.

  To address this concern, you'll need to create a clear reporting strategy that defines the rules for data usage, data protection, and access control (e.g., which user groups should be able to access which entity's data). The timing of this activity depends on the extent to which your company is accustomed to centralized data storage. A detailed user access rights concept might follow at a later stage, but establishing the responsible business data owner is critical as is ensuring all data provisioning is purpose-led and protected against confidentiality lapses.

- **Communication plan for extended stakeholder groups**
  A regular measure in organizational change management is the communication plan, which is an important instrument for the executive sponsor and the project manager to define and schedule different channels for communication. Which stakeholders need what information and how often? Business units without direct and active involvement could still be kept in loop by newsletters, global all-hands meetings, corporate videos, or articles on the company's intranet.

  Groups with a higher involvement or impact might be invited to project all-hands, to global or individual demo days, or to the project communication distribution list. Executives with high impact or active anticipation can become join the steering board, or topics can be addressed on an individual basis—e.g., for organizational changes in governance, in ownership, or in headcount. Distinct types of measures should be applied for different purposes—the communication plan defines and documents these activities and ensures execution by the project managers.

Finally, we should discuss a new trend in organizational change management: persona-based change models that fit well into the context of Central Finance with its various stakeholder groups in IT, finance, controlling, reporting, planning, and decentralized accounting functions.

The advantages of using a persona model are its impacts on structure and priority. In classic OCM cycles, the project team researches the needs of many user groups, collects all their requirements, and summarizes these needs in a long list without a clear indication of priorities. This approach results in designs that try to serve all users but in many cases end up serving no specific users particularly well.

In a persona approach, the OCM team identifies discrete sets of end users, which become primary and secondary user personas, i.e., fictional characters created to represent the different user types within a targeted demographic that might use the solution. This classification is more business-oriented than a technical SAP role, but less formal than an organizational chart. Examples of personas could be:

- Corporate finance manager
- Planner
- Shared services manager
- Plant controller
- Cost center manager
- IT partner for Central Finance

Personas are useful for considering the goals, desires, and limitations of your users to help guide decisions about features, interactions, and visual design. A persona represents the goals and behaviors of a real group of users, their experiences, specific change impacts, learning needs, and success criteria. These ideas help OCM team members share a common understanding of their users.

In summary, organizational change management helps you conduct the finance transformation based on a Central Finance approach. The analysis of stakeholders, their interests, and their concerns and the determination of relevant actions as well as organizational readiness are important factors to achieving the benefits put forth by the value proposition and to making Central Finance a successful driver of innovation.

13.6   Summary

In this chapter, we outlined several aspects beyond the technical solution itself and focused on some key components of a finance transformation. When considering Central Finance, any project should consider the technologic opportunities and assess the individual strategic fit for the customer's situation (strategy management). The identified business use cases, assumptions, and value propositions should be thoroughly documented along with the expected resolution of pain points and opportunities of improvement, which is key guidance for the later scope and design phase as well as for enabling clear cost-benefit tracking (value management). While dealing with assumptions and uncertainty, the implications and likelihood of failure can be significant in a Central Finance project, which makes risk management the mandatory third discipline.

As most Central Finance projects contain a vision beyond being a pure reporting scenario, the change of business processes is the fourth critical discipline. Especially the transition of processes towards Central Finance requires a thorough impact assessment and Central Finance-specific design considerations (business process management).

Finally, Central Finance should be considered a large finance transformation project with a wide range of impacted stakeholders due to the nature of centralized data collection, provisioning, and processing. Stakeholder management and communication management are mandatory elements of organizational change management.

In the next chapter, we'll provide even further insights into the technological aspects of transforming your IT landscape.

Chapter 14
Platform Transformation

Many organizations will use their new Central Finance implementation to kick off broader IT platform changes, like consolidating nonfinancial processes or third-party systems. In this chapter, we'll outline how Central Finance can be a first step toward a complete platform transformation.

Current digital transformation trends and newly available technologies such as in-memory and cloud-based computing enable large organizations to revisit their systems and their platform strategies. With SAP's emerging cloud technologies, including SAP S/4HANA Cloud, SAP Cloud Platform, and SAP Analytics Cloud, many ERP customers are rethinking their processes and landscapes and may decide to adopt an SAP platform strategy with Central Finance as its starting point. This stating point is crucial for customers who, for various reasons, cannot consolidate their ERP vendors and ERP instances. In a nondestructive approach, Central Finance allows you to consolidate financial ERP data without the need to immediately decommission your source ERP systems.

In this chapter, we'll unpack this strategy with a focus on corporate finance and show how SAP delivers an *intelligent core* within SAP S/4HANA and SAP Cloud Platform. This core vision requires an ERP dataset in SAP S/4HANA: Central Finance can achieve this requirement with lower risk and lower costs when compared to pursuing an upgrade/migration to SAP S/4HANA. We'll also highlight how Central Finance can orchestrate and streamline source data models and how customers can add value to the merged data in Finance (FI) and Controlling (CO).

14.1 Platform Transformation Strategy

The ongoing simplification of IT systems and applications has been a strategic goal for decades, but delivering on this goal has been elusive, partially due to constant increases in demand and requirements and partially due to a lack of connectivity between various enterprise functions. Another factor is the technical and functional limitations inherent in classic relational database systems. These trends forced IT departments to focus on vendor-optimized, vertical, horizontal, best in class, and various other textbook strategies to cope with a plethora of systems, interfaces, vendors, applications, and data storage methods. In recent years, the advent of new core platforms with higher levels of agility and service connectivity has changed the picture: Customers can now combine existing upstream business applications with new cross-product platforms and leverage state-of-the-art technology without the massive risk and disruption of past business transformation projects.

However, a shift from a product-centric to a platform-centric ERP model requires a powerful foundational technology stack leading the way. This stack fulfills the various integration needs across hardware, software, and services. In this context, a *platform* is distinct from a software suite or product family by its capability to meet a wide range of current and future business requirements in complex organizations, with impact on the application's availability, scale, and volume. Platforms also provide newly emerging technologies for organizations transforming rapidly, e.g., the Internet of Things (IoT), machine learning, user experience (UX), cloud services, mobility, and analytics as well as geospatial and social media data integration.

In addition to the latest technology, customers can expect additional business capabilities from a digital core platform. The corresponding elements of this new finance business paradigm are detailed in Chapter 1 and Chapter 3.

SAP offers a foundational target platform for the upcoming digital transformation. SAP now covers the full range from SAP HANA-powered systems up to modular and scalable cloud services that can be integrated with ERP data, as shown in Figure 14.1.

The SAP platform strategy has two major aspects: the cloud and SAP HANA's in-memory computing. You can combine these aspects, or SAP HANA functionality can be kept on-premise, either on physical resources or virtualized with tools such as VMware.

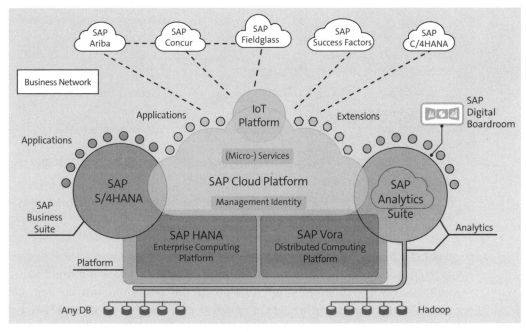

Figure 14.1 SAP HANA and SAP Cloud Platform

Virtualization

Virtualization means the creation of a nonphysical version of a server, storage, data, application, network, or operating system in which the provider (in the cloud or on-premise) splits resources into several execution environments per tenant, also known as *virtual machines*. A hypervisor, which can either be software or hardware with firmware, acts as a virtual machine monitor (VMM) to manage the required environments. The architecture can apply to on-premise as well as cloud-based scenarios, as follows:

- Physical, on-premise system (bare metal): The classic setup for best performance
- IT virtualization: An abstraction of IT resources (software-defined data centers)
- Private cloud: Provisioned for a single organization
- Public cloud: Provisioned for open use
- Hybrid cloud: Combination of distinct infrastructures

Most cloud providers offer various virtualization options. Evidence suggests that virtualization technology significantly increases infrastructure efficiency by providing a resource abstraction layer that divides available hardware and software resources and enables running multiple SAP HANA workloads on a single node or on scale-out certified SAP HANA systems. However, increased resource utilization comes at a cost: Additional overhead arises in system performance (depending on the technology and workload type, usually around 10%).

For optimal outcomes, each SAP HANA instance (virtual machine) needs to be sized according to SAP's sizing guidelines and corresponding vendor recommendations, especially to avoid CPU and memory overprovisioning. The maximum size of a virtual SAP HANA instance is limited (depending on the individual architecture). In any case, an SAP HANA-certified engineer must set up the SAP HANA system on certified hardware, and the system must be successfully verified with SAP's configuration check tool. On-premise, a system can be delivered preconfigured with virtualization software and SAP HANA, when installed by one of SAP's hardware partners (appliance option).

In addition to the SAP S/4HANA suite, SAP offers a wide range of cloud-based components to cover business needs in logistics, human resources, reporting, and finance. Figure 14.2 shows the financial perspective on the SAP Cloud Platform concept and the various opportunities to integrate, enrich, and harmonize upstream ERP data with new technologies such as SAP Leonardo Machine Learning.

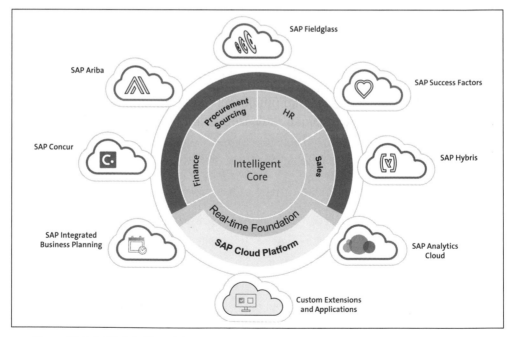

Figure 14.2 SAP's Intelligent Core

The intelligent core symbolizes SAP's new business suite on a relaunched data model with simplified code and flat table structures—the Universal Journal. It requires an SAP HANA in-memory foundation to unlock real-time features, such as calculating totals on the fly. The available cloud apps and services connect both ways to the core, and you can leverage additional machine learning and analytics services.

A truly platform-centric SAP transformation strategy requires a set of ERP data in an intelligent core, i.e., the SAP S/4HANA suite. A customer with a pre-SAP HANA ERP base can still use select components of the platform portfolio that do allow SAP ERP 6.0 integration (e.g., SAP Ariba, SAP Concur). However, the full benefits of all the components working together can only be leveraged with an SAP HANA-enabled finance core. As outlined in previous chapters, Central Finance enables this core data provision in an accelerated and simplified approach that distinguishes this deployment option from a classic upgrade to SAP S/4HANA. In the following sections, we'll focus on the value drivers in a platform strategy using Central Finance and outline the journey from isolated source ERP systems towards a fully integrated platform.

14.2 System and Application Consolidation

Simplifying ERP applications and systems has been a cumbersome exercise in the past due to limitations of merged functionality, data migration, and performance as well as sizing issues. Therefore, many customers run various applications and instances of the same ERP product for legitimate reasons:

- Different regions require different (sometimes conflicting) localization, maintenance windows, and languages.
- Different business units require different suites or functions that cannot easily be merged or implemented in a standard ERP (vertical strategy).
- Mergers and acquisitions have led to an exponential growth in the number of instances where, especially in times of low-cost storage and memory, the cost of consolidation does not match the potential benefits.
- Best in class strategies have led to finance data being produced in various upstream systems for HR, manufacturing, sales, trade, treasury etc., all of which are not part of the core ERP.

If your organization is complex, Central Finance allows you to consolidate finance application data, without the immediate need to decommission or retire source systems in the process. This light-touch, non-disruptive consolidation approach can be

useful for highly entrenched legacy environments with complex or vertical functionality profiles that prevent quick business transformations.

Numerous scenarios exist where Central Finance can add value to the total of incoming data in a multisource ERP business. The following sections outline the most popular use cases for a consolidated SAP platform strategy (see Chapter 3 and Chapter 12
for the full details of use cases for Central Finance). We'll touch upon Central Finance
as a stepping stone for SAP S/4HANA, but only briefly discuss mergers and acquisitions, which were covered in depth in Chapter 12 and Chapter 11, respectively. Once
we've looked at some of the most popular use cases, we'll continue with a discussion
of some use case-agnostic benefits.

14.2.1   Corporate SAP HANA Reporting Platform

In this scenario, the main pain point is delayed and overly aggregated group reporting. The legacy group close and/or reporting solution needs to be replaced with a
platform-enabled architecture that offers real-time, reliable, and instant drilldown
reporting into all aspects of group finance.

SAP HANA's analytics capabilities embedded in SAP Business Warehouse (SAP BW) in
SAP S/4HANA set it apart from classic date warehouse solutions that import external
ERP data from multiple sources in a complex staging process (real or virtual extraction). Central Finance—integrated with components such as SAP Master Data
Governance (SAP MDG); SAP Landscape Transformation Replication Server (SAP LT
Replication Server), including the SAP Application Integration Framework; and custom code enhancement spots—offers better checkpoints and toolsets to standardize
and harmonize incoming master and transactional data with a central set of operational system configuration. The fact that Central Finance posts fully validated
finance documents enables higher audit and governance levels and allows for higher
accounting accuracy.

Data can be consumed with hundreds of standard SAP Fiori apps, analytical web
pages, SAP BW queries, and core data services (CDS) views in a web browser, or with
SAP Analysis for Microsoft Office, you can create tailored reports for both your power
reporting and occasional reporting needs.

In addition, SAP's consolidation products can perform a simulated close (soft close)
or actual close (hard close) on an incoming FI-CO plan and/or on actual data in real
time and then send selected closing data back to operational systems. This new functionality can further expedite the close window and replace existing legacy group

closing mechanisms in classic standalone database systems such as previous SAP Business Planning and Consolidation (SAP BPC) versions or in third-party solutions such as IBM Cognos or Hyperion.

14.2.2 Corporate Finance Service Platform

SAP offers a wide array of central data transaction scenarios "on top" of replicated data from source ERP. Currently, as of SAP S/4HANA 1809, SAP offers these central transactional scenarios on Central Finance and is planning to continuously expand this list, for example, in the areas of tax and treasury. The current list of central transactional scenarios includes the following:

- **SAP Master Data Governance (SAP MDG)**
  Centralized and harmonized master data from customers, materials, etc. can be held in Central Finance and passed on to other systems (master data hub functionality).

- **Central payments (in/outbound)**
  This scenario allows you to reduce the number of external bank accounts and fees (e.g., for overdraft charges); bundles external payments (e.g., for costly cross border payments); allows shared services to centralize payment process; and supports using one SAP standard interface for uploading bank statements to a central platform.

- **Credit, collections, and dispute handling**
  These functions have been released in Central Finance for accounts receivables, as has the SAP Cash Application, an automatic, machine-learning based capability.

- **Cash management**
  Periodic liquidity and forecast reporting can be conducted in Central Finance across all financial positions in different ERP systems. Bank accounts can also be maintained in Central Finance system (either in SAP Fiori or via SAP MDG).

- **Planning, budgeting, and close**
  SAP planning and consolidation solutions are available with/for Central Finance, including real-time consolidation (simulation and posting) and disclosure management for stakeholder reports. The period-end closing cycle is further supported by the following SAP S/4HANA components:
  - Replication of trading partner and profit center information within replicated Central Finance postings (including the initial load) for automated central elimination in either SAP BPC or SAP's new group consolidation functionality for legal consolidations.

- The SAP Financial Closing cockpit for the periodic process roles, dependencies, and status monitoring,
- SAP Financial Shared Services Framework for the seamless integration of service processes.
- Intercompany reconciliation for an early intercompany data analysis in the closing process (on replicated open items) to match and clear affiliated invoices, avoid differences and the pressure of period-end deadlines and post clearings, posting corrections and supporting documentation into the general ledger (G/L) account as well as affiliated accounts payable and accounts receivable (AP/AR) accounts.

This approach requires you define a detailed landscape and usage type strategy by answering the following questions:

- Which system is purely transactional, and which is the system is of record (i.e., the endpoint of data flow)? This question is especially crucial for period-end closing: If your source systems remain the systems of record, they'll need to be updated with all transactions added in Central Finance (using additional custom interfaces, SAP standard functionality is partially available).

- What is the roadmap for these central processes going forward? If planning a complete transition of enterprise management away from the source ERP for the medium or long term, the migration and cutover strategy for the accumulated central data needs to be analyzed and verified (see the next scenario in Section 14.2.3).

14.2.3   Stepping Stone to Consolidated SAP S/4HANA Platform

As discussed in Chapter 12, you can start with deploying Central Finance and later migrate parts of an ERP environment or entire ERP environments into the same target SAP S/4HANA instance at to your own pace and according to your own priorities, while Central Finance ensures continuous dual operations until all legacy ERP processes are retired.

14.2.4   Corporate MA&D Platform

The ability of Central Finance to quickly include or retire parts of incoming data streams (e.g., plants, company codes, controlling areas, etc.) makes it highly suitable to serve as a data platform for an agile mergers, acquisitions, and divestitures (MA&D)

strategy, as discussed in Chapter 11. Instead of setting up lengthy integration or carve-out projects for upstream ERP modules, you can use Central Finance to accelerate ongoing changes in the enterprise by switching inbound interfaces on and off as needed and using SAP S/4HANA as an interim platform for short-term investments.

14.2.5   Orchestration of Source Systems of Record with Central Finance

As mentioned earlier, the downside of all the approaches we've described is data duplication in source ERP systems of record versus the new SAP S/4HANA Finance core. As a result, your finance department needs to clearly define the single point of truth, the system of record, and other go-to points for various reporting needs. In practice, this definition might involve the following sample criteria, which is based on a recent Central Finance implementation for a North American consumer products client (in a different customer context, the division of labor can differ):

- Central Finance is the single point of truth for the following:
  - Group reporting purposes, e.g., summarized financial statements, detailed profit and loss (P&L) statements for management reporting, etc.
  - Enterprise key performance indicators (KPIs) such as cash flow, earning per share (EPS), etc.
  - Group-wide accounts payable and accounts receivable analysis across legal entities and markets
- The source ERP systems are go-to point for the following:
  - Original document drilldown (possibly from Central Finance for SAP and non-SAP systems with a new SAP Fiori app in SAP S/4HANA 1709)
  - Country-level/local books (e.g., local GAAP), a full view on taxes and document/audit tracking (like scans, attachments, etc.),
  - Data views not yet implemented in central SAP S/4HANA, such as treasury, fixed assets, material pricing, etc.

In general, the disadvantages of copying ERP finance data can be minimized by smart mapping strategies that enrich, streamline, and harmonize incoming Central Finance data, leading to new insights and levels of comparability across various legacy datasets. In this case, Central Finance creates a whole greater than the sum of its ERP parts. Customer examples of how Central Finance can enrich business value include the following:

- Redesign convoluted organizational elements, such as company codes, cost centers, profit centers, segments, functional areas etc., in a central reporting tool that provides simplified, on-point finance data.

- Merge obsolete and/or split legacy company codes in an N:1 mapping strategy to make company codes line up with legal entities (e.g., by undoing past export scenarios).

- Optimization of the P&L structure across multiple source ERP systems via a system-specific mapping of source functional areas and accounts into centrally owned, unified hierarchies.

- Leveraging of SAP Best Practices fields instead of legacy solutions, e.g., mapping of special purpose ledger fields, such as business area or region, into standard SAP S/4HANA fields such as segment or ledger.

- Unified management reporting on profit centers mapping the segments, cost assignments, etc. from the source ERP to a centrally owned reporting hierarchy. In this context, legacy management units can be split into more meaningful central profit centers, and segments can use additional field heuristics, e.g., from sales order characteristics or material data such as product hierarchies.

- Data harmonization of business partners (e.g., consolidation of duplicates, numbering, shared master data fields) and the ability to use corporate open item reporting with aging analytics in embedded SAP BW and SAP Fiori.

- Best of Profitability Analysis (CO-PA) characteristics (i.e., collapsing various legacy fields into common denominator) in a central accounting-based CO-PA.

- Provision of non-GAAP pro forma reporting across the organization by mapping of pro forma postings to an SAP S/4HANA extension ledger that clearly distinguishes as-reported non-GAAP earnings for corporate stakeholders across data from multiple SAP and non-SAP instances.

- Calculation of working capital and other balance sheet KPIs provided in Central Finance using a custom document splitting mapping solution to copy P&L assignments into receivables, payables, cash, inventory, etc.

- Additional currency valuation of documents using SAP S/4HANA's extended currency block.

The reduction of the finance task footprint in non-SAP ERP source systems can be the driving force behind simplification. The integration of non-SAP source systems is not "prefabricated" because of the various vendors and products, but SAP provides a partner (or customer) layer for interface code (with a mass data staging area in SAP LT

Replication Server), which is suitable for fetching and normalizing source database information, before this data is passed to the SAP S/4HANA standard core, as shown in Figure 14.3. SAP delivers content for various objects such as the following:

- Source reference G/L data (including segments, profit centers, divisions, trading partners)
- Payable and receivable data (including discounts and payment information)
- Product and withholding tax
- Reversal information

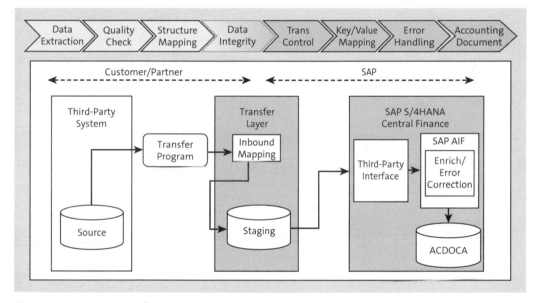

Figure 14.3 Integration of Non-SAP Source Systems into Central Finance

In addition to SAP's own content, a growing number of SAP Partner products for accelerating non-SAP connections to Central Finance have become available.

14.3   Digitization

The idea of digitizing business data and processes is not new: In the past two decades, many customers have invested heavily in ERP transformation, process outsourcing, shared services, and workflow automation. However, ERP transformation, before the current in-memory capabilities appeared, stalled at an inflection point of high investment risk (leading to change being avoided) and overburdening complexity, combined with outdated user experiences and disconnected data and process swim lanes. Nevertheless, these past digital initiatives constituted important precursors to today's digitization wave, which rightly builds upon this digital core and is geared towards inclusion and leveraging new and innovative sets of data and services, rather than turning an entire organization on its head, as was the case with past ERP implementations.

This lurking stagnation trap is now dissolving with new and incremental technologies offering rapid change with less transformation risk and cost, but how does the current digitization paradigm fit into a Central Finance platform strategy?

First, one aspect of the second digitization wave is the wide array of unstructured data that had not been directly accessible in corporate finance analytics. Some examples of this diverse data include the following:

- Free text content in finance documents, text fields, and header data
- Time stamps and user stamps
- Geospatial characteristics
- Patents, intellectual property, asset, and legal data
- Economic developments in the target markets
- Public media content (e.g., press reports, online news articles)
- Broker and investment reports
- Market share of competitors and their products
- Social media data

Using Central Finance immediately unlocks the analytics capabilities of the SAP HANA platform to combine structured and unstructured ERP data, internal data, with external data inputs, e.g., from the web or social media sites. Use cases for this new financial analytics approach are numerous, but here are a few recent case studies:

- Google-like enterprise search function for keywords (e.g., a customer or product name) across all ERP data, modules, and FICO data replicated into SAP S/4HANA.
- Correlation of P&L data with external influence factors, e.g., analysis of sales, profit, revenue etc. segments correlated with sentiment and favorability analysis in the respective market population.
- Integration of competitor market data time series into sales reporting.

- Service performance monitoring based on aggregated document details, e.g., days outstanding, records created with drilldown by team, by user, etc.

A second area of digital innovation is in machine learning and robotic process automation (RPA), supported by the performance that SAP HANA and a cloud infrastructure can add to complex processes. SAP launched its cloud-based SAP Leonardo engine with various new transactional and predictive applications that can address finance needs and that can operate on replicated Central Finance transaction data. Exemplary applications in this area include the following:

- The new *Payment Advice Extraction* application supports the processing of incoming customer payments on outbound invoices. The application extracts payment-related information from unstructured data like emails and checks (PDF or hard-copy) and automates the clearing process from end to end.

- On the record creation side of this process, *SAP Cash Application's* machine learning logic automates receivables matching (for items still unmatched after the legacy bank statement process) through its built-in training cycle: The application continuously improves itself to adapt its rule engine, including unstructured data that classic ERP-internal rules cannot consider, such as past manual actions. The application therefore captures more detail about customer- and country-specific behavior patterns, without the cost of manually defining detailed rules in a backend customization table. Proposed matches are either automatically cleared or suggested for review by accounts receivable. The accelerated and improved hit rate (i.e., eliminating the last 5% which cause 80% of the manual effort) reduces process delays and service costs as well as allows shared service models to grow at scale with increased volume.

- The newly introduced *Accounts Payable* application automates the handling of inbound invoices and extracts information to the G/L account (as part of the invoice-to-record process). An automated vendor matching process identifies the correct vendor ID and processes differences from previous purchase orders and goods receipts.

- The *SAP Business Integrity Screening* application uses predictive algorithms to reduce false fraud claims that convolute the process for legitimate transactions and false approvals that allow fraudulent documents to pass through. Due to the data flow, this application is purely forensic in a Central Finance scenario but can easily be implemented on SAP S/4HANA, instead of a fractured source ERP landscape, thus opening up new post-posting analytics functionality.

You can also develop your own machine learning apps with SAP's application programming interface (API) and deploy your own models in the cloud using SAP's Application Function Library (AFL).

Some of these applications interact directly with SAP S/4HANA and post additional transactions back into Finance, so the customer either defines Central Finance as the AP/AR system of record or must extend the Central Finance interface for records being passed back to the operational ERP (backposting) to keep all systems in line and reconciled. As of the current release 1709, a clearing interface back to the source AP/AR is possible but must be implemented as a custom solution: The standard Central Finance AP/AR setup applies a "technical clearing" process to the source system open items.

14.4   Readiness for Services Consumption in the Cloud

SAP Cloud Platform is an open platform as a service (PaaS) with in-memory capabilities for SAP and third-party apps and business services with collaborative and mobile-enabled user experiences, without needing to invest in or maintain on-premise systems. An overview of these connections is shown in Figure 14.4.

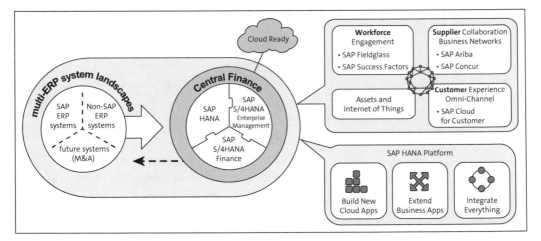

Figure 14.4 SAP Cloud Ecosystem

Besides the connection between source systems and Central Finance, numerous cloud applications can interact with the master and application data in Central Finance via SAP's standard cloud connections:

- Human resources solutions like SAP SuccessFactors and SAP Fieldglass can share master data for accounts, employees, etc. with Central Finance and can receive posting data.
- Travel and expense tools like SAP Concur can send payment runs and receive or send employee/supplier master data.
- Customer relationship and sales tools like SAP Cloud for Customer and other SAP C/4HANA tools can exchange customer master data and accounting data with Central Finance.

Many newly developed SAP services and applications run exclusively in the cloud and will therefore need a connection to an on-premise or cloud-based Central Finance instance. In other cases, a component in SAP S/4HANA itself may be able to solve the integration requirement, and the integration will be out of the box (especially the case with analytics). The right mix of SAP S/4HANA components and external cloud applications depends on your individual business and IT requirements and platform strategy. In any case, cloud apps and on-premise components can be seamlessly integrated once technical requirements are fulfilled.

In the area of technical readiness, a detailed analysis can help you prepare for a smooth transition, avoiding roadblocks and difficulties on the way. The process of connecting Central Finance to a cloud app is similar in most cases and generally proceeds according to the following path:

- Make sure you have a license and subscription to the SAP Cloud Platform Portal. In most cases, a limited-time trial license is available for you to connect to a nonproductive environment so you can assess the feasibility and value of a new app (see the box on consumption-based services).
- The trusted connection between the SAP S/4HANA instance and the SAP Cloud Connector software with user of type C (Communication) needs to be created, which includes technical settings such as HTTP ABAP connections, OpenSSL, and certificates. Checking for sensitive personal data (and their special handling requirements) is also part of this process.
- End users will need to be enabled to access the cloud application (via local security roles).
- Many apps allow or require customer-specific configuration for data that is not replicated on the fly, such as organizational structure, hierarchies, parameters, etc.

14

Consumption-Based Services

In February 2018, SAP announced a new consumption-based license model, switching to the flexible and metered use of selected SAP Cloud Platform services. The result is a simplified buying and consumption experience: Instead of including specific services, the new approach allows "access to everything" through an enterprise agreement.

This agreement includes a consumption-based offering, which complements the already available subscription pricing model. SAP expanded from a multiyear provision of specified capabilities, to an elastic, low-touch environment where customers can choose and consume cloud services as needed without a long-term timeline.

SAP also introduced Cloud Credits, which can be purchased and applied toward SAP Cloud Platform services. The customer acquires Cloud Credits via a prepay contract, which can then be used to activate data storage, bandwidth, user experiences, and services on demand via a self-service cockpit. In addition, SAP provides customers regular detailed reporting of their services consumed, as well as a customer's Cloud Credit balance.

While the relaunched, enhanced website is available globally, the new consumption-based commercial model is still currently being rolled out, starting with North America, Germany, the UK, and twenty-five additional countries in 2018.

Generally, Central Finance is ready to interact with any cloud app that uses financial data. Of course, many apps require logistics data (e.g., trade analytics). These apps cannot easily be installed without further data replication into SAP S/4HANA or additional external data flowing in. However, even with a purely financial dataset, hundreds of value-adding apps are already available online. In this chapter, we'll only highlight a small selection of apps due to their sheer volume.

Many apps address analytical requirements; some good examples include the Financial Statement Insight app and the SAP Digital Boardroom:

- *SAP Financial Statement Insights* is a comprehensive P&L tool that allows you to explore financial accounting data. You can compare the performance and efficiency of segments, products, profit centers, and company divisions in real time with a drag and drop interface and drilldown capabilities. You'll be able to identify time-series trends and growth drivers, for example, to analyze the impact of single customers on company performance, to find unusual patterns and irregularities within account groups, to visualize the impact of management initiatives on financial performance (simulation of alternate hierarchies and changes), and for nonaccountants to explore profits and losses.

- The *SAP Digital Boardroom* is a highly visual ad-hoc tool that provides decision-makers an interactive analytics experience accessible via large touchscreens in a presentation format. This app is aimed at C-Suite executives, supervisory board members with less in-depth interaction, and operations leaders at the director level.

Another group of apps addresses transactional needs useful in a process-specific context. As a starting point, be sure to check SAP Support to determine whether support extends to the app in combination with Central Finance. Since Central Finance is a normal SAP S/4HANA instance, limitations mostly extend to data backposting and subsequent postings, such as reversals, that are blocked for externally posted documents. Good examples in this app category include the following, some of which may be third-party offerings:

- Statutory or industry-specific reporting and adjustment tools, e.g., financial statement appendices, remittance documentation, and reconciliation tools
- Digital/AI assistants, e.g., for search simplification, tagging, media plug-ins
- Compliance, governance, and audit support apps for annotations and closings

14.5   Summary

Current digital transformation trends and newly available technologies, such as in-memory and cloud computing, allow large organizations to revisit their systems and platform strategy. Many ERP customers are rethinking their landscape and processes and could pursue an SAP platform strategy with Central Finance as its starting point. This chapter unpacked significant impacts of this strategy on the Corporate Finance vision and shows how SAP delivers an "intelligent core" within its SAP HANA and SAP Cloud Platform.

We demonstrated how Central Finance can unify, standardize, and harmonize source data models and add value to the merged replication data in FI and CO. Central Finance, with its full-fledged accounting dataset, is ready to interact with any SAP app related to financial data. On top of the replicated data, cloud and machine learning applications from SAP's platforms can also add process and analytics layers for robotic process automation (e.g., cash application or fraud detection), offer faster context searches, and yield predictive analytics with external or unstructured datasets included in the algorithms.

The next chapter will conclude our Central Finance journey with an examination of various business cases and value scenarios.

Chapter 15

Central Finance Business Case Development

Central Finance solves decades-old issues of system and data harmonization thus enhancing corporate functions while also accelerating value for all users, regardless of their function, across the broader business.

For many years, companies have tried to standardize their solution landscapes through a combination of strict governance, standardized templates, and centralized data management in a one-size-fits-all approach to enterprise solution deployments. This approach has mostly resulted in suboptimized underlying business unit processes and complexity when adapting to change or quickly integrating new businesses. Significant business value can be unleashed through Central Finance in heterogeneous landscapes, allowing existing business units to optimize operations with only minimal system or organizational impacts.

In this chapter, we'll address how to develop the business case for Central Finance. Relevant topics include the potential impact on people and roles; the potential impact to your IT organization; considerations for developing business value, cost, and relevant value drivers; challenges to anticipate; and how to achieve your desired return on investment.

15.1 Identifying Stakeholders

Possible Central Finance beneficiaries include not just all traditional finance-related roles, but also all consumers of enterprise information and insight. Naturally, decision-makers across the entire organization are measured, not only on financial performance, but also on the quality of their decisions. These leaders need good data and a deep understanding of the impact of those decisions. Central Finance can serve as the single source of truth and a platform for future innovation in an intelligent enterprise.

Your business use case begins and ends with a clear understanding of your users' needs and the effectiveness with which you can meet these needs. In the next two sections, we'll discuss the roles that typically benefit from a Central Finance deployment and the evolution of roles that must be considered.

15.1.1   Finance Organization and the Impact to Resources

The likely direct beneficiaries of a Central Finance deployment include the chief financial officer, the treasurer, the vice president of planning, the corporate controller, and others. A second group of beneficiaries includes other major consumers of enterprise-level information, such as the chief executive officer, the board of directors, enterprise risk officers, and senior leadership.

With Central Finance, the effort of extracting and manipulating data practically disappears; automation plays a much larger role, and workers' roles change from being data gatherers to data analysts. However, the truth is that some of these employees will never be analysts. Thus, companies must reevaluate whether existing workers can perform the higher-level analysis the solution enables. The reverse is also true for many finance departments that lack modern systems. For these companies, intelligent, qualified, and expensive resources are often underutilized because time is consumed with manual data gathering, leaving almost no time to focus on value-adding analysis.

With Central Finance, this paradigm changes, these workers will spend most of their time (and skills) analyzing the business, answering questions that were never before possible, and contributing in ways previously only imagined, resulting in a significantly more effective finance functions, greater job satisfaction, greater employee retention, and a more profitable enterprise overall. Employee roles will change, with new and greater emphasis on the following roles:

- Big data analysts
- Market observers and analysts
- New business modelers
- Simulation and prediction experts
- Business strategy experts
- Line of business experts/partners

Figure 15.1 shows how the skills required for the modern finance worker with Central Finance will change over time.

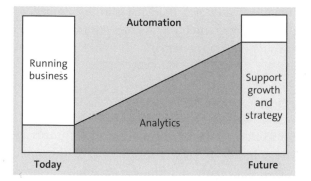

Figure 15.1 Finance Transformation: Supporting Growth and New Business Models

15.1.2   IT Organization

A revolution is underway for IT organizations, allowing them to focus on their core purposes: system performance and availability, development and delivery, and cost efficiency.

Early IT organizations were expected to deliver green-bar reports and static dashboards overnight. While this time constraint might have been acceptable in the past, today, information and analysis must be immediate and agile. The finance department's role is to deliver not just data, but also information and insight to the organization. This insight must be immediately consumable for the decision-maker and delivered within business contexts. With this shift, reliance on external, single-purpose reporting tools has decreased or been eliminated entirely as a modern and efficient digital core is deployed.

Central Finance is architected to capture and store data in the digital core (Universal Journal). This digital core stores data in its most granular form, at the document level. Advanced analytic applications then access detailed financial data, without the need to extract data from its native state. Data manipulation is performed on the fly, enabling filtering, sorting, and analysis based on any attribute of any posting in real time. This capability can have an immediate and profound impact on your enterprise's existing data warehousing, planning, consolidation, and dashboard strategies.

Deploying Central Finance also enables IT organizations to innovate while significantly accelerating development. Central Finance is a finance-focused deployment option for a full SAP S/4HANA solution, architected for simplification with the flexible

15

Universal Journal at its core, thus opening the door to machine learning, embedded analytics, open APIs, in-memory databases, predelivered cloud connectors, network extensions, predictive analytics, and a new user experience.

15.2   Evaluating the Status Quo

Most large companies have struggled for years to drive toward common processes, data, and analytics across sometimes rather diverse business areas within their enterprises. These efforts, in many cases, have proven futile and expensive because of system ownership battles, differentiating aspects of business areas, regulatory requirements, cultural bias, management preferences, and a general resistance to change. In some cases, the recognition that separate systems may have developed over the years for valid reasons may be lacking. Some systems may have been a product of convenience and timing (i.e., acquisitions, joint ventures, risk tolerance), but other systems may have been adopted out of real need to operate subsidiaries in a manner unique from the broader organization (i.e., validated environments in the pharmaceutical industry, sensitive programs in AD&D, or other highly restrictive environments).

Enterprises with diverse businesses often find that process harmonization efforts ultimately suboptimize the entire business by settling on only processes where agreement could be reached, the lowest common denominator. A proverbial sweet spot does exist where harmonized processes and data can also coexist with the need for differentiation and agility. Central Finance should be considered within your strategy to achieve the correct balance of control and agility while also being the first step toward future system consolidation. Central Finance is unique in the market and can provide with a compelling alternative to expensive, and often highly disruptive, system harmonization efforts.

The need for business unit diversity, agility, and market differentiation requires a critical review of your existing solutions to identify how Central Finance can add value to your company, as we'll discuss in the following sections.

15.2.1   Current Landscape

Large enterprises, and even many smaller enterprises, often find themselves with rather diverse technologies that have evolved over the years. Many of these technologies were deployed to meet specific departmental needs. Others evolved due to the lack of system governance and decentralized operations. In these situations, many companies find themselves asking, "How can we provide flexibility and agility to the organization to adapt to rapidly evolving business requirements while also enabling enterprise views and control given the diversity of applications?" Central Finance was created to answer this question.

Central Finance provides a single view into the organization without requiring changes to the underlying systems and processes. Central Finance brings together both SAP and non-SAP data into a single platform to post transactions in real time to a common ledger. Because documents are reposted into a central Universal Journal, which can and will be the system of record for an enterprise. Central Finance creates a complete set of financial records (a single version of truth) on a platform for continuous planning, thus creating a single view of cash and working capital and enterprise risk, which also serving as a platform enabling next-generation automation and shared services. With powerful analytics capabilities embedded in the Central Finance solution, you'll have complete flexibility to conduct analyses. With Central Finance, you can follow the data where it leads you instead of being handcuffed by outdated reporting strategies that predefined the format and presentation far in advance of its use, sometimes months in advance. Companies with the ability to analyze their business at an enterprise level have a clear advantage over companies that fall behind, as shown in Figure 15.2.

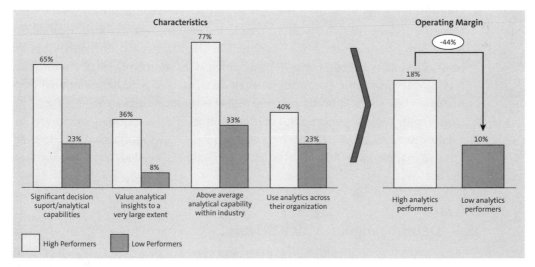

Figure 15.2 Analytics Gap Translates into a Real Profit and Loss (P&L) Gap for Those Who Fall Behind

15.2.2   Anticipated Challenges

Challenges do exist for deploying Central Finance. The first challenge is to manage innovation.

Because Central Finance provides so much opportunity for transformation, many teams find themselves bogged down by long process and data harmonization efforts. While the initial deployment of the solution is the optimal time to consider reimagining organizational structures, consolidation of systems, simplification, and automation, many companies can achieve value more quickly by viewing deployments as an evolution rather than a destination.

The second challenge is data quality and mapping transactions to the Central Finance solution. Let's discuss each of these issues separately:

- **Data quality**
  Most companies find that poor data quality exists across the organization. Poor data quality may be masked from senior leadership by an army of clerks and analysts painstakingly harmonizing and analyzing data for PowerPoint readouts to management. Bad data creates significant process inefficiencies that are often hidden by manual corrections across the enterprise. Executives relying on management reporting as the basis for significant decisions may find themselves shielded from these challenges. When inconsistent data is exposed in its most granular form, executives will make data quality a business priority.

- **Mapping**
  Mapping and reposting transaction-level detail enables organizations to avoid the limitations of using summarized information for analytics and opens the door for central transaction processing. This mapping does, however, require additional foresight to determine the target chart of accounts and whether additional non-financial data should also be mapped into the solution to aid analysis. For companies with diverse landscapes, additional effort will be required to convert an existing group chart of accounts into a more detailed operational chart of accounts, but this mapping will ultimately provide the flexibility needed to fully understand the business.

15.3   Determining Key Value Drivers

In a recent survey of 20 early adopters of Central Finance, speed and efficiency and transparency and accountability ranked equally as the most important drivers for a Central Finance implementation. These results illustrate how many companies need to create a single version of the truth to overcome challenges of system harmonization while creating an innovation platform enabling informed and timely decisions.

From a process perspective, these same companies stated their major goal for Central Finance was to act as a catalyst of finance/business transformation. Second to transformation is process standardization and using as a stepping stone to a full SAP S/4HANA roadmap. These companies have struggled for years with expensive harmonization efforts. Central Finance is the bridge for these companies, enabling both enterprise views and accelerating the step change to the latest available SAP technology platforms.

Additional processes targeted by these early adopters included a strong emphasis on reporting and embedded analytics using Central Finance as a first step, which allowed them to gain confidence and experience through enterprise-wide management reporting and analytics. These companies then naturally evolved, with the Central Finance becoming the trusted system of record for the enterprise. Next, Central Finance becomes the location for enterprise consolidations and centralizing accounts receivable (AR) and accounts payable (AP) and the source for dynamic planning, centralized cash management and treasury, intercompany reconciliations, and allocations, as well as ultimately enabling deep automation through machine learning. The most popular key processes targeted by customers in a Central Finance deployment include the following:

- Report/business analytics
- Intercompany reconciliation
- Management accounting (allocations/profitability)
- Accounts receivable/accounts payable
- Financial accounting/entity close
- Real-time consolidation/group close
- Planning and budgeting
- Cash position/liquidity forecast (Cash Management)

Central Finance's key value drivers are unique to the solution and manifest themselves in nine broad categories, each of which we'll discuss in the following sections.

15.3.1   Flexibility

Central Finance allows companies to quickly adapt to changing business environments by implementing growth strategies and changing the business model. Underlying source systems are only minimally impacted by any business model change, thereby accelerating the adoption of changes. Also, because Central Finance data is mapped into the Universal Journal at a granular level, maximum flexibility is enabled with summarization totals calculated on the fly, the ability to drill down to detailed documents and to source systems, and the ability to use any attribute of any posting as a filter.

15.3.2   Efficiency

Successful rollouts of Central Finance create a flexible and efficient information delivery approach with a single sign-on to all enterprise financial data. With embedded analytics, an MS Excel frontend, and a beautiful SAP Fiori user interface, users will be presented with intuitive screens, thereby reducing training and change management significantly. This user friendliness is particularly important for shared service scenarios that typically experience relatively high turnover rates. Fewer full-time employees (FTEs) are required, allowing for more user self-service and exception management. Remaining workloads dedicated to analysis are reduced because of the existence of harmonized and real-time data (maintained at the lowest available level of granularity), automation, and modern analysis tools and dashboards.

15.3.3   Service Level

Service levels will increase as more users are brought into a Central Finance environment, especially when self-service analytics start to take hold. Without the need to extract data to external reporting systems, to populate cubes in data warehouses, or to develop reports, analysts can perform their tasks using real-time data, resulting in the most timely and relevant information being delivered to decision-makers at the moment of decision.

15.3.4   Cost Reduction

Cost reduction is typically nominal in initial rollouts because of new business effort related to data cleansing and process standardization. The productivity of resources, however, will dramatically increase as the foundational benefits of Central Finance are realized and additional resources and processes are centralized. These benefits manifest themselves through better efficiency, transparency, and simplification.

15.3.5   Working Capital Improvement

Working capital is improved through proactive management of cash, collections, and receivables management as well as improvements in functionalities, including live credit checks and central credit blocks for sales processes. As customers evolve their Central Finance environment, free cash flow is accelerated, and the need for short-term financing is reduced. When SAP Treasury and Risk Management is deployed with Central Finance, data already residing in the Universal Journal increases accuracy in cash forecasting, predictive inflows and outflows directly from AR and AP, the optimization of discounts, the reduction of reserves, and the proactive management of financial risk.

15.3.6   Profit and Margin Management

Companies using Central Finance can achieve SKU-level profitability with the Universal Journal.

Consumer products companies, for example, can determine profitability at various levels, such as brand, channel, customer, ingredient, vendor attribute, and sales and volume information. Some attributes required for analysis may not typically flow into financial postings, but with Central Finance, these attributes can be mapped into the Universal Journal alongside finance postings to allow for deeper and more relevant analysis.

In other industries, some companies have achieved true end-to-end profitability visibility across multiple countries to isolate intercompany markups and enable profitability reporting for compliance purposes.

15.3.7   Simplification

Central Finance has benefited significantly from the complete modernization of SAP S/4HANA Finance. At the core of these improvements is the incredible performance of SAP HANA's in-memory database. With in-memory speed, the new Universal Journal can be maintained in its most granular form without the need for summarization. Users will have complete flexibility to create transactions, plan, and analyze data at the most granular level within the Universal Journal. Because business data is centralized, instead of in disparate finance systems and processes, this capability creates a common business language across the enterprise, a single source of truth, and can deliver continuous closing and consolidation processes and predictive results.

Better user experience for both light and heavy users is also enabled through SAP Fiori on Central Finance. For example, as shown in Figure 15.3, through the SAP Fiori workspace, you can measure business performance through live key performance indicators (KPIs) and embedded analytics.

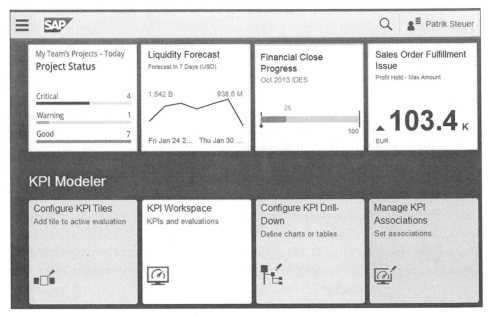

Figure 15.3 KPI Modeler: Standardize Live Measures

15.3.8   Business Continuity

Business continuity is maintained throughout the earlier phases of a Central Finance rollout, as existing source systems remain and are not affected or retired in the short term. Central Finance can serve as the bridge to optimization by allowing maximum flexibility at the enterprise level without risking major business disruption at the operational level.

15.3.9   Risk Mitigation

Companies can anticipate areas of enterprise risk, monitor and test risk scenarios, and proactively mitigate major issues. This capability is possible because all financial transactions, enterprise wide, are maintained in the Central Finance system. In addition, real-time reporting allows you to address issues as they occur, whereas before, issues might go unnoticed until month, quarter, or year end. Embedded process controls and tools to alert users of deviations from normal data patterns allow transactions to be audited completely, significantly reducing substantive financial misstatements.

15.4   Assessing the Cost

The cost of a Central Finance deployment is driven primarily by the following key factors:

- The complexity of existing IT environments
- The level of process and data harmonization in existing solutions
- The number and diversity of source systems
- The level of transformation anticipated during the Central Finance deployment.

Each factor should be considered carefully. System complexity in many cases is the very reason companies deploy Central Finance, but in other cases, companies with relatively few systems still see value in moving to Central Finance so they can quickly adopt next-generation technology.

Some companies also choose a Central Finance rollout as a catalyst for data standardization, business model change, or process optimization. In these cases, Central Finance projects can require longer timeframes.

Transformation itself is the major factor for most companies adopting Central Finance because of the minimal impact to underlying source systems, and the opportunity for this transformation to be a first step in a longer-term strategy to deploy SAP S/4HANA.

Many companies find the benefits of Central Finance so compelling that new opportunities are identified during their implementation that can significantly impact both timing and approach to achieving their end state vision. In the following sections, we'll discuss considerations for implementation and maintenance and touch on how this typically translates into an evolving vision of the desired end state.

15.4.1   Initial Implementation

Timeframes for initial implementation vary significantly due to the factors we've discussed in previous section, but the survey of early adopters revealed average timeframes generally in the range of 6 to 12 months for an initial rollout.

Implementations with good governance, highly standardized processes, a small number of source systems, and minimal transformation requirements will be on the low end of the range.

Implementations where significant data and process standardization efforts are introduced will require extended timeframes and be highly dependent on sponsorship and leadership within the company to remain agile.

15.4.2   Maintenance

Maintaining a Central Finance solution requires good governance over master data like general ledger (G/L) accounts, cost centers, profit centers, etc.; the maintenance of mapping; and proactive error correction to ensure all transactions reach the central environment.

Central Finance provides functionality to identify both posting errors and report discrepancies so maintaining the mapping is straightforward and manageable. Because Central Finance is a deployment option for a full SAP S/4HANA solution, but with a finance focus, normal operational maintenance proceeds like any other SAP solutions. To reduce maintenance costs, consider operating the system in a hosted cloud environment and to ensure continuous updates and improvements.

15.4.3   End State

A normal evolution exists within companies deploying a Central Finance solution. This evolution allows companies to change at their own pace, harmonizing data and optimizing processes while migrating functions and resources into the central environment. Finally, a tipping point is reached where legacy solutions are minimized to the point where decommissioning these systems with minimal impact is possible.

The optimal end state for a Central Finance rollout falls into two possible scenarios: Central Finance as an end state and Central Finance as a stepping stone to adopting SAP S/4HANA next.

In the first scenario, Central Finance operates in addition to other operational systems. In this scenario, maintaining a hybrid system environment brings the most value. Source systems will continue to be technically upgraded and maintained, but the Central Finance environment will be dedicated to enterprise finance functions. In this scenario, existing business areas will enjoy a degree of autonomy, thus allowing for customization to optimize specific processes and ultimately improve business area profitability.

In the second scenario, Central Finance serves a stepping stone to a full SAP S/4HANA implementation, and the company will have the flexibility to move functions and resources to the central environment opportunistically, with the end goal of having one common system being used for the entire enterprise. In this scenario, the natural evolution of the solution discussed previously begins with enabling enterprise visibility. Over time, transaction processing and people are moved to the Central Finance environment. As these functions are moved, additional opportunities exist to move other related functions, such as procurement, inventory management, projects and program management, and human resources as well as, ultimately, sales, manufacturing, and distribution. Over time, legacy source systems will be slowly diminished to a tipping point where shutting down systems is both possible and desirable, thus resulting in significantly lower total cost of ownership.

15.5   Return on Investment

The hard-dollar benefits of undertaking a Central Finance project can be classified as efficiency improvements and effectiveness opportunities.

Efficiency improvements include significant increases in process efficiency for finance departments and the business areas they support. The enablers of this efficiency include an intuitive user experience to drive higher user productivity, digital process automation, and continuous real-time accounting. Additional value is gained through simplification and transparency and by achieving both better accuracy and a single source of harmonized data, the Universal Journal, to act as the definitive source for all financial analysis.

Opportunity costs could also be impacted, and Central Finance's many benefits are already being realized by many companies. These same companies are widening the gap between themselves and the competition by quickly identifying efficiencies, integrating acquisitions, simulating new business models, predicting outcomes, and finding innovative opportunities for growth. The following is a list of value drivers to consider when building your business case for Central Finance:

- People
  - Organizational alignment between individuals and corporate goals through a single source of truth
  - Optimized resource allocation
  - Opportunity to redeploy labor to higher value-added activities

- **Processes**
  - Centralization and automation
  - Single platform for planning, consolidation, analysis, and transaction processing
  - Step change improvements in process efficiency; reduced cycle times/transaction costs
  - Reduction via manual processes, thus reducing process variability
  - Improved cash management, collections, and receivables
  - Fast integration of mergers and acquisitions (M&A)
  - New cross-entity market potential
  - Self-service analytics
  - Harmonized data and a common business language across the enterprise.
  - Efficiencies from economies of scale
- **Technology**
  - Platform for innovation, including open APIs, in-memory speed, cloud connectors, and extensions to business networks
  - Improved technical integration during M&A
  - Significant reduction in costs dedicated to interfaces
  - A modern user experience
  - Embedded analytics to reduce reliance on expensive and redundant reporting and analytics tools
  - Non-materials views into the data
  - Agility to adapt to changing business environments
  - Reduced development effort and cycle times
  - Next-generation technologies like machine learning, cognitive, blockchain, etc.
- **Financial metrics**
  - Increased G/L and financial closing productivity
  - Increased compliance and risk management productivity
  - Increased budgeting and forecasting productivity
  - Increased business and operations analysis and reporting productivity
  - Increased cost accounting and analysis productivity
  - Increased finance strategy and leadership productivity

- Improved invoice processing efficiency
- Increased accounts payable and expense productivity
- Increased accounts receivable productivity
- Increased productivity of payback or chargeback receivables processing
- Increased customer billing, credit and collections productivity
- Reduced days sales outstanding (one-time benefit)
- Increased travel management productivity
- Increased treasury and cash management productivity

15.6 Summary

Central Finance expands the finance department's ability to serve as true business partners through flexibility and innovation. As users realize "all the data is available in real time, at the lowest level of granularity, in one place, with world-class analytics," pent-up demand is unleashed. Planning and forecasting moves from annual and quarterly activities to dynamic and risk-adjusted processes. Batch processing goes away, and closing activities move to continuous processes. Profitability is available immediately. Predictive and machine learning is embedded into process, and enterprise risk is monitored and mitigated in real time. As Central Finance continues to evolve, users like you will increasingly create innovative use cases.

Central Finance is a unique solution in the marketplace and has been available since 2015. Since this time, SAP has seen broad acceptance of the solution across companies, large and small, who have proven Central Finance's value through proofs of concept, pilot projects, and full implementations. These same companies represent some of the largest and most complex companies in the world. They understand that change is inevitable and that survival doesn't depend on the size of a company but on its ability to adapt.

With Central Finance, organizations are realizing an improvement over competition. No longer are companies improving incrementally over the competition but instead, first mover advantage is creating an ever-increasing gap between leaders and followers.

Central Finance is *the* innovation platform enabling finance departments to lead companies to growth, to gain deep insights into profitability, and to simplify and automate processes to create a truly intelligent enterprise.

The Authors

Carsten Hilker is the global solution owner for Central Finance. He is the emcee and host of the annual SAP Financial Excellence Forum, an annual event for SAP customers to network and interact with domain experts and thought leaders in finance and management accounting. Carsten has been working in the field of financial and management accounting for more than 20 years in various roles including development, consulting, and product management. His past and current professional affiliations include ASUG, IMA, CAM-I, the Resource Consumption Accounting Institute (RCA-I), Society of Cost Management (SCM), and the International Controller Association (ICV).

Javaid Awan the global solution owner for Central Finance and is a qualified accountant with 25 years hands-on experience in software applications. He has held roles as a member of IT leadership teams, CIO, transformation director, DevOps director, chief architect, and head of shared services, and he has led large-scale delivery for major transformations globally. Javaid has worked in finance, treasury, sales, HR, procurement, supply chain, and analytics in the consumer goods, life sciences, oil and gas, telecoms, media, manufacturing, and public sector industries.

Julien Delvat is responsible for managing TruQua's SAP S/4HANA practice and solution portfolio while providing clients with industry guidance, roadmap strategies, implementation insights, and best practices for their financial transformation and optimization journeys with SAP S/4HANA, SAP S/4HANA Cloud, and Central Finance. Julien has more than 16 years of experience delivering innovative SAP solutions for organizations across the globe for industries such as consumer products, automotive, and high-tech.

Julien is well-known in the SAP world as an SAP Mentor, blogger, speaker, volunteer, and panelist at industry conferences. He has worked with a variety of companies guiding them through the enterprise digitization process, empowering knowledge workers, modernizing IT infrastructure, teaching the workforce how to utilize their data, and providing superior user experiences.

The Contributors

David Dixon is a partner at TruQua Enterprises. He has been a featured speaker worldwide at SAPinsider conferences. He co-authored the book Mastering the SAP Business Information Warehouse with Bill Inmon as well as white papers on business intelligence (BI) and enterprise performance management (EPM). David started his career in 1995 as a Financials and Controlling (FI/CO) consultant with SAP specializing in financial consolidations, product costing, and profitability analysis with particular expertise in ERP information systems and tools. David is not only an executive and practicing consultant, but also a hands-on developer. His skills span functional and technical domains. He has worked with SAP's development team in Walldorf and Palo Alto on numerous occasions in support of applications and initiatives in the SAP S/4HANA, EPM, and BI spaces. He has extensive project experience in implementing high-value global solutions for Fortune 100 companies.

Randy Garrison is the vice president for the finance global line of business and the head of value advisory at SAP. With more than 32 years of combined finance and IT experience, he has worked closely with senior executives across the Fortune 500 companies in the development of their transformation vision, value case development, and delivery. Randy has held positions in public accounting, treasury, finance operations, auditing, business intelligence, value management, IT strategy development and implementation, and program management. Randy is a Certified Public Accountant, Certified Management Accountant, Chartered Global Management Accountant, and a member of the AICPA and the Institute of Management Accountants.

Berker Kilinc started his career in 1995 as a Financials and Controlling (FI/CO) consultant. He has taken part in or managed many large SAP implementations with a focus on finance and reporting solutions. He has been involved with SAP S/4HANA Finance and Central Finance since their inception and has been a frequent presenter at SAP events. He is also an important contributor to SAP's Central Finance Thought Leadership group.

Bahram Maghsoudi is principal consultant for enterprise finance at Infosys Consulting with more than 18 years of experience in SAP and finance for both domestic and international customers. He focuses on accounting functions, reporting, and improvement for practitioners, users, and stakeholders across various industries (e.g., manufacturing, healthcare, public sector, and higher education). Recently, he completed the implementation of Central Finance and SAP Fiori at a major CPG organization in the U.S. and developed a mergers and acquisitions (M&A) playbook for a mining corporation. He also sustains partner relationships and conducts study papers and solution pilots (e.g., SAP). His focus areas include unlocking new finance capabilities, standardizing processes to reduce media breaks, enabling self- and shared services, and reducing IT and service costs. He is a Konstanz University, MPA graduate and also an avid social volunteer.

Tobias Nyholm joined SAP in 2011 and is a principal business consultant with the Business Transformation Services group. Based in Germany, he is engaged at SAP's largest customer globally and works with SAP and customer executives to ensure the strategic fit of SAP's finance solutions for implementation. Since SAP introduced SAP Simple Finance (now SAP S/4HANA Finance) and Central Finance, he has focused on supporting customers to develop their individual path towards a digital finance transformation using Central Finance as key enabling technology. He worked on several Central Finance lighthouse projects and consulted multiple customers during their Central Finance journeys.

Index

A

Account-based CO-PA 142
Accounting 61, 127
Accounts payable 119
Accounts Payable app 423
Accounts receivable 123
Activity types 333
Actuals entry 397
Advanced reporting 52
Advertising and promotion (A&P) 142
Amazon Web Services 150
Analytics 382
Analytics gap 433
Application Function Library (AFL) 424
Application Link Enabling (ALE) 156
Application programming interface
   (API) 182, 424
Application strategy 394
Atomic strategy 273
Attribute 107
Audit trail 69
Authorization 403
Automation 84

B

Background job 223
Background work process 223
Backposting 50, 427
BAdIs 336
Balances 295
Bank Account Management 132, 135
   master data 134
Banking 131
BC set 235–236, 240, 301
Benchmarking 85, 113
Big bang 203
Big data 382
Billing document 61
BlackLine 144
Brownfield implementation 362, 373
Business Add-In (BAdI) 65

Business

Business case 394
Business continuity 438
Business function 213
Business mapping 64
   actions 65
Business model
   changes 85
   evolution 84
Business object types 242
Business partner 329
Business process
   changes 393
   management 395
   owner 402
Business reconciliation 282
Business unit controller 404
Business value network 386

C

Capital expenditure (CapEx) 89, 141
Cash flows 131
Cash Management 136
Cash operations 136–137
Center of excellence 299
   key resources 300
Central collections 126
Central Finance
   approach 365
   architecture 179
   benefits 91, 388, 430, 433
   benefits timeline 81
   brownfield v. greenfield 368
   building blocks 41, 347
   business cases 429
   business value 419
   capabilities 59, 77
   central processes 35
   centralization 356
   challenges 434
   choosing your route 367
   code line 151, 369
   complexity 389

Central Finance (Cont.)

configuration 230
consolidation 415
cost assessment 439
cross-system reporting 77
data 419
data collection 61
deployment options 165
dual track landscape 185
efficiency 436
embedded SAP BW 159
end state 359, 366, 440
enterprise consolidation 435
evolution 32
finance organization 430
first step 363
flexibility 435
frontend tools 196
functional foundation 57
impact 169
initial implementation 439
innovation acceleration 78
innovation pressure 79
instance 211
integration plan 345
integration platform 344
investment 364
IT organization 431
key innovations 76
key landscape elements 183
landscape 182, 184, 209
landscape evaluation 432
local processes 34
M&A capabilities 346, 352
M&A platform 346
maintenance 440
master data 321
mixed landscape 186
motivation 73
multiple instances 367
onboarding platform 365
on-premise landscape 152
options matrix 362
orchestration 128
orchestration layer 350
process candidates 58

Central Finance (Cont.)

process execution 34
process groups 58
product vs. solution 177
project waves 308
restrictions 53
results 52
risks 389
ROI 441
sandbox 183
SAP S/4HANA core 33
SAP-only sources 185
scenarios 366
scope 308
sidecar 90, 396
silver bullet 74
simplification 437
single instance 367
single source of truth 393, 419
solution 178
stakeholders 399, 429
standard deployment 37
standard SAP solution 36
stepping stone 39, 307, 361, 371
sustainability 395
system consolidation 40
system onboarding 307
targeted processes 435
technical architecture 177
technical components 49
technical foundation 38
technical novelty 389
technology stack 350
terminology 150
without SAP BW 159
worker skills 430
Central payments 120, 122, 124, 218, 267, 269, 417
Central system 48
Centralization 83
Centralized finance 31
Change management 173
Charts of accounts 327
Chief financial officer (CFO) 379, 400
Chief information officer (CIO) 384, 400
Clearing document 304

Closing process 266
Cloud Credits 426
Cloud hosting 150
Cloud integration 50
Cloud transition 89
Cloud-based applications 414
Code list 248
Coding block 348
Collection factories 138
Collections on behalf of others (COBO) 139, 265
Company code 204, 270, 286, 309, 364
   alignments 110
   fields 282
Compliance 118
Conglomerate 51
Consistency checks 281
Consolidation 87–88, 357, 396
Consumer proxy 126
Consumption-based services 426
Controlling 139
Controlling postings 281
CO-PA segment 277
Core data services (CDS) 108, 416
Corporate close 130
Corporate controller 401
Cost center 332
Cost object 280
   creation 335
   mapping 278
Cost object replication framework 64
Cost object-dependent object 66
Cost reduction 436
Cost reduction tracker 352
Credit management 125–126
Cross-origin resource sharing (CORS) 201
Current landscape 432
Customer and vendor numbers 239
Customer hierarchy 273
Customer/vendor integration (CVI) ... 273, 338
Customer-defined field 66

D

Data access 393
Data bus 180

Data cleanup 294
Data consistency 300
Data digitization 66
Data duplication 113
Data exploration 94
Data extraction 289, 337
Data inclusion 347
Data integration 181
Data integration framework 230
Data load 62
   initial 68
   strategy 250
   test 255
Data logging 60, 62
Data management 261
Data Migration Server 152, 191, 217, 224, 227
Data provisioning 181
Data quality 434
Data reconciliation 69, 304
Data replication 45, 62, 181
   scenarios 63
   setup 251
Data steward 324
Data transparency 381
Data validation 238, 322
Datastores 158
Delta load 318
Dependent systems 207
Deployment 149
   cloud 161
Destination 225
Development environment 183
Dialog work process 223
Digital economy 33, 80
Digital transformation 380, 412
Digital twin 32
Digitization 421
Dimension 98, 106
Display Inbox app 147
Display My Account Statement app 145
Disputes 126
Dissemination 339
Divestitures 43, 86, 190, 312
Document relationship browser 218
Drilldow 130

Drilldown 69
Dynamic data 272

E

eBAM 134
Embedded analytics 438
Emergency corrections mode 68
Empty load 63
Enabling layer 38
End user 399
Enterprise optimization 85
Enterprise search 422
Entity close 129
Entity reporting 52
Error correction 47
Error correction and suspense accounting ... 68
Error handling 67, 256
Error message 257
Error monitoring 290
Executive commitment 406

F

Facet 97
Finance operations 59
Finance processes 115
Finance scope 206
Finance services 417
Finance transformation 53, 356, 379
Finance user 401
Financial accounting data 217
Financial close 127
Financial close governance 130
Financial disclosure 130
Financial information model 233
Financial postings 281
Financial transactions 79
Find Business Partner app 146

G

G/L account 328–329
General ledger 128
Global data types 247
Golden Record 272, 318
Goods receipts 397

Governance 352
GR/IR account 120
Greenfield implementation 362, 373
Group reporting 52

H

Harmonization 77, 272, 337
Harmonized data 381
Header staging table 254
Hierarchies 140
 flexible 333
History load 296
Hybrid landscape 171

I

Implementation 203
 end state 208
 first wave 207
 process selection 205
 project costs 394
 subsequent waves 207
 system setup 208
Inbound posting 66
Infrastructure as a service (IaaS) 150
Initial load 254, 259, 280, 315
 big bang v. agile 316
 CO postings 283
 complete 292
 configuration steps 317
 define groups 287
 delete data 292
 document type 316
 execution 289
 extract data 288
 financial accounting 286
 monitor 290
 objects 285
 prerequisites 281
 source system configuration 282
Input tax 265
Integration 384
Intelligent core 411, 415
Intercompany reconciliation 418
Interface Monitor 68, 241, 255, 285–286
 error handling 256

Intermediate document (IDoc) 192
Internal cloud 163
Internal order 277
Internet of Things (IoT) 412
Invoice 270
IT architects 404
Iterative rollout 203

J

jQuery 198

K

Key performance indicator (KPI) 100, 387, 438

L

Landscape Transformation Migration
  Cockpit 237
Liability management 397
Lift and shift tools 373
Line item 46, 295, 304
Line item access 94
Line Item Browser app 94
Liquidity forecast 137
Liquidity management 136
Logical system 219–220, 269
  check assignment 221
Logistics scope 206

M

Machine learning 84, 101
Magnitude SourceConnect
  Harmonization 157
Maintenance order 277
Manage Credit Reports app 146
Manage Investigation app 147
Manage Profit Centers app 331
Managed cloud 163, 167
Manual data ingestion 347
Many-to-one mapping 278
Mapping 46, 217, 229, 243, 246, 248, 276, 322, 387
  additional transactions 247

Mapping (Cont.)
  CO-PA 280
  cost objects 285
  entity 243
  external codes to internal 249
  individual maintenance 244
  mass maintenance 245
  master data objects 276
  rules for cost objects 279
  strategies 277
  tables 278
Mass transfer 226, 253
Master data 64, 68, 117, 230, 242, 270, 300, 305, 309, 334, 390, 403
  attributes 67
  change request 322
  change request execution 324
  configuration considerations 307
  configuration data 271
  governance 307, 334
  hierarchies 273
  maintenance 306, 339
  missing 303
  objects 325
  processes 320
  request approval 323
  segregated data types 270
  synchronization 325
  upload 236
Master data management 118, 320
  architecture options 340
Master record 238
Material number 331
Memory size 302
Mergers and acquisitions ... 44, 78, 86, 311, 343, 345, 367
  common information model 347
  data structure 349
  Day 1 .... 351, 358
  end-to-end lifecycle 351
  handoffs 346
  process orchestration 349
Message type 257
Microsegment profitability 104–105
Migration 238
Migration cockpit 238
Milestone-based rollout 205

Multitenant database containers
(MDCs) 156

O

Onboarding checklist 309
One Exposure from Operations hub 136
Online replication 260
Open item 121, 124, 295
OpenText Vendor Invoice Management
for SAP Solutions 122, 263
Operational expenses (OpEx) 89, 140
Operations 299
Opportunity costs 441
Order type mapping 278
Organizational change management
(OCM) 398, 408
Organizational readiness 392
Organizational readiness assessment 405
Organizational structure 117
Output tax 265

P

Partial load 303
Payables 121
Payables and receivables 119
Payables process 263–264
Payment Advice Extraction app 423
Payment factories 138
Payments on behalf of others
(POBO) 138, 264
Period-end close 303
Persona-based change model 407
Personnel retention 352
Pivate cloud 150
Platform 412
Platform as a service (PaaS) 150
Platform transformation 411
strategy 412
Post-merger integration 343, 351, 355
iterim v. end state 357
platform considerations 356
process execution 356
Predictive analytics 383
Predictive models 102

Pre-production tier 184
Private cloud 163
Process automation 380
Process boundaries 55
Process design 261
configuration 267
Process execution 85
Process onboarding 310
Process orchestration 115–116
project 116
Process order 277
Process Receivables app 100
Process transformation 82
Procurement 121, 263
Procure-to-pay process 397
Product cost collector 277
Product Profitability app 100
Production environment 184
Production order 276
Profit and loss (P&L) 102, 141
Profit and margin management 437
Profit center 66, 331
Profit Center Accounting 381
Profitability Analysis (CO-PA) 105, 142, 420
Program management 391
Project cloud 169
Project lead 299
Public cloud 150, 164

Q

Quality management order 277

R

Rationalization 83, 87, 338
Raw data 67
Real-time replication 45, 387
Receivables process 264–265
Reconciliation reports 70
Remote Function Call (RFC) 162, 216
assign destinations 219
define destinations 225
destination naming 219
Replication 301, 391
content 224

Replication (Cont.)
  error correction 303
  object 252, 254–255
  reconciliation 304
  transactions 302
Replication Cockpit 302
Reporting 45, 52, 84, 93, 130, 207, 217, 268,
  371, 407
  additional fields 104
  advanced 93
  business continuity 107
  consolidated 113
  cross-organizational functions 106
  dimensional 104
  embedded 99
  entity 108
  group 111
  harmonized 112
  line items 94
  local processes 109
  microsegment profitability 104
  Microsoft Excel 97
  multidimensional 97
  multientity 112
  predictive 101
  universal 95
Request Investigation app 147
Resource commitment 392
Reverse invoke proxy 171
Risk management 133, 388
  change management 391
  financial risk 394
  technical risks 389
Risk mitigation 438
Roadmap 206
Robotic process automation (RPA) 34,
  84, 423
Role 214–215, 217, 227
  new 216
Rollout 203
Root cause analysis 98
Runtime configuration group 222–223

S

SAP Activate 152, 227
  methodology 170, 310

SAP Analysis for Microsoft Office 98, 199
  benefits 199
SAP Analytics Cloud 99, 161, 166, 199–200,
  346, 386, 406
SAP Application Integration
  Framework 47, 68, 170, 191, 215,
  222–223, 240, 258, 267, 304, 416
  BC sets 194
  benefits 193
  configuration 194
  message processing 193
  monitoring 195
  users 241
SAP application management services 167
SAP Ariba 263, 344
SAP Best Practices 157, 170, 227, 420
SAP Business Client 201
SAP Business Integrity Screening 423
SAP Business Planning and Consolidation
  (SAP BPC) 88, 113, 130, 149, 160, 205, 417
SAP Business Warehouse (SAP BW) 61, 149,
  158, 416
SAP BW/4HANA 160
SAP Cash Application 144, 417, 423
SAP Cloud Connector 102, 171, 425
SAP Cloud for Customer 425
SAP Cloud Platform 92, 166, 171–172, 413,
  424, 426
SAP Cloud Platform Portal 425
SAP Cloud Platform, private edition 164
SAP Concur 344
SAP Credit Management 146
SAP Data Services 156, 158, 182, 188, 237
  predefined content 157
SAP Digital Boardroom 99, 346, 350, 427
SAP ERP 415
SAP Financial Closing cockpit 130, 132, 418
SAP Financial Shared Services
  Framework 418
SAP Financial Statement Insights 102, 426
SAP Fiori 92, 197–198, 332, 364, 438
SAP Fiori launchpad 101
SAP General Ledger (SAP G/L) 375
SAP GUI 197
SAP HANA 38, 49, 76, 158, 344, 364, 413–414
  database 179
  reporting 416

SAP HANA Enterprise Cloud 150–151, 163, 166–167, 188
SAP In-House Cash 205
SAP Leonardo Machine Learning 414
SAP Leonardo Machine Learning Foundation 144
SAP LT Replication Server 38, 63, 149, 153–154, 168, 181–182, 187–188, 195, 208, 218, 224, 226, 228, 250, 268, 281, 283, 301–302, 306, 316, 416
    benefits 181
    configuration 225
    deployment options 189
    initial load 217
    many-to-many deployment 190
    many-to-one deployment 190
    one-to-many deployment 190
SAP Master Data Governance (SAP MDG) 38, 149, 155, 195, 208, 229, 262, 301, 326, 391, 416–417
SAP Model Company 170, 230
SAP Predictive Analytics 364
SAP RealSpend 102, 172
SAP S/4HANA 38, 49, 165, 179, 193, 211, 364, 386
    adoption 90
    adoption patterns 374
    classic migration 375
    continued evolution 90
    core 179
    editions 227
    end state 369
    faster adoption 82
    full adoption 376
    implementation approach 373
    logistics 371
    migration 362
    multiple ERP 377
    paths 153
    planning 370
    releases 180
    SAP-to-SAP moves 372
    single ERP 375
    sizing 196
    stepping stone 418, 435, 441
    transition planning 370
    with Central Finance 374

SAP S/4HANA Cloud 78, 151, 166, 172, 174, 200, 211, 227
    benefits 173
    code line 368
SAP S/4HANA Cloud for credit integration 146
SAP S/4HANA Cloud for customer payments 145
SAP S/4HANA Cloud, single tenant edition 151, 174
SAP S/4HANA Finance 49, 76
SAP Screen Personas 197
SAP Shared Services Framework 346
SAP Solution Manager 154
Scalable process execution 77
Scope 386
Scoping 335
Secure Socket Layer (SSL) certificates 200
Security 95, 309
Security Assertion Markup Language (SAML) 200
Segment-level reporting 52
Service levels 436
Shared service center 402
Shares services model 36
Simulation 85, 239, 383
Single instance 377
Single-instance ERP 43
Software as a service (SaaS) 150
Source data
    non-SAP 247
    SAP 244
Source system 42, 117, 180, 204, 215, 250, 309
    non-SAP 78, 228, 253
    SAP 77, 227, 233, 252
Source type 203
SourceConnect accelerator 69, 182, 262
Staging table 228
Stamping strategy 273
Standardization 83
Static data 271
Statistical key figures (SKFs) 333
Storytelling 98
Strategy management 380
    dependent strategies 385
Subsidiary instances 78

Supervise Collections Worklist app 100
System and application consolidation 415
System architecture 177
System continuity 357
System landscape 74
   multi-ERP 42
System Landscape Directory 154, 156, 242
System of record 109, 261, 310, 397, 419
System setup 208
   activating business functions 212
   activating Web Dynpro 213
   security 214
   sequence 209

T

Table ACDOCA 275
Table logging 302
Tax optimization 111
Tax process 265
Tax reporting 267
   reports 268
   tables 268
Technical readiness 425
Technology transformation 87
Test run 293
Third-party interface 249
Three-way matching 122, 262
Total cost of ownership (TCO) 355
Traditional data warehouse 112
Transaction
   /AIF/CUST_FUNC 258
   /AIF/CUST_HINTS 258
   /AIF/ERR 195
   /AIF/IFMON 241, 255, 285
   /AIF/PERS_CGR 222
   /AIF/RECIPIENTS 241, 304
   CFIN_CPAY_CUST 269–270
   CFINIM 223
   CFINIMG 213, 219–221, 242, 336
   F-28 144
   FAGLF03 281
   FAGLGVTR 282
   FB03 217
   FEB_AUTO_REPRO 145
   FF_5 144
   FI12 134

Transaction (Cont.)
   FINS_CFIN_AIF_SETUP 241
   FINS_CFIN_DFV_FI_DOC 304
   FINS_CFIN_DFV_FI_NUM 304
   FINS_CFIN_DOC_DELETE 293
   FINS_CFIN_MAP_MANAGE 246
   GCAC 282
   KSB5 217
   LTMC 237
   LTRC 225, 255, 302
   MDG_ANALYSE_IDM 247
   MDG_KM_MAINTAIN 244
   MM03 258
   OY19 234
   PFCG 214–215
   S_ALR_87013611 282
   SARA 194
   SCC1 183
   SCMP 234
   SCPR20 .... 236, 241
   SCPR3 235–236
   SCUO 234
   SE16 .... 226, 295, 304
   SFW5 212
   SICF 213
   SM30 .... 261, 282
   SM37 288–289
   SM50 .... 168, 223
   SM51 .... 168, 223
   SM59 218
   SPRO 212, 231, 233
   STO3 168
   ST22 169
   SU01 217
Transaction settings 117
Transactional data 240, 309
Transactional posting 47
Transactional system 418
Treasury 131–132
Trial Balance app 95
Two-tier strategy 173, 313

U

Unicode 181
Unified Key Mapping Service (UKMS) 156

Universal Journal 96, 98, 346, 348, 382, 431, 433, 437

Unstructured data 422

User 207

User experience (UX) 197, 438

User interface (UI) 48, 387

Utility computing 150

V

Value drivers 434, 441

Value management 386

Value map 57

Value proposition 405

Vertex 265

Virtualization 413

VMware 412

W

Waves 206

Web Dynpro 197, 201, 213

Workflow templates 134

Working capital 437

X

XML 193

- Learn about the SAP S/4HANA Finance certification test structure and how to prepare

- Review the key topics covered in each portion of your exam

- Test your knowledge with practice questions and answers

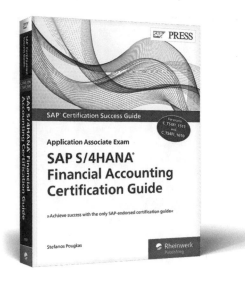

Stefanos Pougkas

SAP S/4HANA Financial Accounting Certification Guide

Application Associate Exam

Preparing for the SAP S/4HANA Finance 1511 or 1610 exam? Make the grade with this certification study guide. Explore test methodology and key concepts for each topic area, and practice questions and answers to solidify your knowledge. From the SAP General Ledger to financial close, this guide will review the key technical and functional knowledge you need to pass with flying colors. Your path to SAP S/4HANA Finance certification begins here!

447 pages, pub. 06/2017
E-Book: $69.99 | **Print:** $79.95 | **Bundle:** $89.99

www.sap-press.com/4414

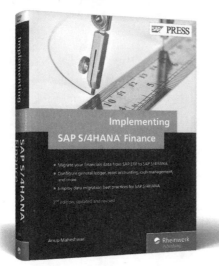

- Migrate your financials data from SAP ERP to SAP S/4HANA

- Configure the general ledger, asset accounting, cash management, and more

- Employ data migration best practices for SAP S/4HANA

Anup Maheshwari

Implementing SAP S/4HANA Finance

Ensure a smooth transition to SAP S/4HANA Finance with this on-premise implementation guide! Follow step-by-step instructions for data migration and functional configuration. From the general ledger to asset accounting and beyond, you'll align your new system with existing Finance requirements and go live. Get the nitty-gritty details and pro tips that will make your SAP S/4HANA project a success!

570 pages, 2nd edition, pub. 11/2017
E-Book: $69.99 | **Print:** $79.95 | **Bundle:** $89.99

www.sap-press.com/4525

- Master the profitability analysis functionality in SAP S/4HANA Finance

- Set up your value flows, reporting, and planning processes

- Learn how to migrate your profitability analysis data from SAP ERP to SAP S/4HANA

Kathrin Schmalzing

CO-PA in SAP S/4HANA Finance

Business Processes, Functionality, and Configuration

SAP S/4HANA Finance has transformed the CO-PA landscape! Learn about the updates and developments to profitability analysis in SAP S/4HANA Finance, and then configure your new system with step-by-step instructions and screenshots. Start with the basics: master data, actual value flow, and data enrichment. Then learn how to migrate your existing SAP ERP data into SAP S/4HANA Finance. The future of CO-PA with SAP is here!

337 pages, pub. 10/2017
E-Book: $79.99 | **Print:** $89.95 | **Bundle:** $99.99

www.sap-press.com/4383

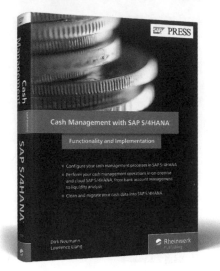

- Configure your cash management processes in SAP S/4HANA

- Perform your cash management operations in on-premise and cloud SAP S/4HANA, from bank account management to liquidity analysis

- Clean and migrate your cash data into SAP S/4HANA

Dirk Neumann, Lawrence Liang

Cash Management with SAP S/4HANA

Functionality and Implementation

Get greater insight into your cash operations with this comprehensive guide to cash management in SAP S/4HANA! Start by configuring bank account management (BAM), cash positioning, and liquidity management. Then perform your key processes: maintaining banks, processing cash transactions, forecast liquidity, and more. Choose your deployment model, dive into the new One Exposure from Operations data model, and see what it takes to migrate your cash data. Cash in on SAP S/4HANA!

477 pages, pub. 10/2017

E-Book: $79.99 | **Print:** $89.95 | **Bundle:** $99.99

www.sap-press.com/4479

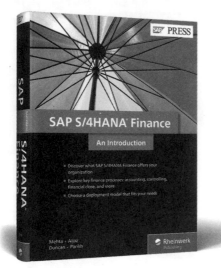

- Discover what SAP S/4HANA Finance offers your organization

- Explore key finance processes: accounting, controlling, financial close, and more

- Choose a deployment model that fits your needs

Mehta, Aijaz, Duncan, Parikh

SAP S/4HANA Finance

An Introduction

What will your financial transformation look like? This introduction to SAP S/4HANA Finance shows you next-generation finance in the new suite: financial accounting, management accounting, risk management, financial planning, and more. Consider how each process works in SAP S/4HANA, and explore the SAP Fiori apps that help you meet today's business user and reporting requirements. From previewing project planning to navigating deployment options, take your first steps toward financial transformation!

approx. 425 pp., avail. 01/2019
E-Book: $69.99 | **Print:** $79.95 | **Bundle:** $89.99

www.sap-press.com/4784